Organizing Entrepreneurship

Anna Grandori and
Laura Gaillard Giordani
with James Hayton

Routledge
Taylor & Francis Group

LONDON AND NEW YORK

First published 2011
by Routledge
2 Park Square, Milton Park, Abingdon, Oxon OX14 4RN

Simultaneously published in the USA and Canada
by Routledge
711 Third Avenue, New York, NY 10017

*Routledge is an imprint of the Taylor & Francis Group,
an informa business*

British Library Cataloguing in Publication Data
A catalogue record for this book is available from the British Library

Library of Congress Cataloguing in Publication Data
Grandori, Anna.
Organizing entrepreneurship / Anna Grandori and Laura Gaillard Giordani. -- 1st ed.
p. cm.
Includes bibliographical references and indexes.
1. Entrepreneurship. 2. Strategic planning. 3. Risk management. 4. Interorganizational relations. I.
Giordani, Laura Gillard. II. Title.
HB615.G725 2011
658.4'21--dc22
2010048528

ISBN: 978-0-415-57037-4 (hbk)
ISBN: 978-0-415-57038-1 (pbk)
ISBN: 978-0-203-81583-0 (ebk)

Typeset in by Times New Roman by Saxon Graphics Ltd, Derby

MIX
Paper from
responsible sources
FSC
www.fsc.org   FSC® C004839

Printed and bound in Great Britain by
TJ International Ltd, Padstow, Cornwall

Contents

List of Figures

List of Tables

List of Boxes

Acknowledgments

This book stresses that "entrepreneurship" and knowledge-intensive ventures are nurtured by networks. This is true also for "authorship". The virtual authorship network is especially important in the case of this book.

First, the book includes contributions specifically written for this book by other scholars, with long-standing relations of collaboration with the authors:

- James Hayton, University of New Castle, co-author of Chapter 5 on corporate entrepreneurship
- Carmine Garzia, Università della Svizzera Italiana, author of the end-Chapter 6 case on corporate entrepreneurship
- Santi Furnari, Cass Business School, author of the "Millennium Park" case

Second, the book includes contributions by entrepreneurs and professionals in the organization of entrepreneurship, who have devoted time and energy in interviews and discussions or have directly authored cases:

- Alexandra Albunia, CEO Nano Active Film and Researcher University of Salerno (Case Nano Active Film)
- Marco Brini, CEO Minteos-Enveve (Case Minteos)
- Roberto Crea, co-founder of Genetech and founder of CREAGRI (Case Taking off on olive water)
- Gianni Dell'Orto, former president Amrop International (Case "Promatem")
- Franco Fattorini, CEO Itaca Nova (Case Itaca Nova and Nano Active Film)
- Alberica Marzotto Caotorta, Project Manager EBAN (Case European Business Angel Network)

Third, the book includes cases based on theses conducted under the supervision of the authors at various levels (Bachelor, Master of Science, PhD) in the last five years, written and signed by these former best students and now young professionals:

- Michele Biancolin (Case JEME – Junior Enterprise)
- Andrew Briganti (Case Contract Farming in Australia)

- Alessandro Gava (Case Linux)
- Agnieszka Lesniewska (Case AX, Bio-medical sector, Poland)
- Milos Starovic (Case Minteos)

All contributions specifically written for this book are signed by the contributing authors, but the overall contribution of the authorship network to the development and articulation of the ideas and the organizational solutions for entrepreneurship presented in the book, goes surely beyond that.

As to the authorship of the entire book, the text is by Anna Grandori, with the exception of Chapter 5, coauthored with James Hayton; and Chapter 6, coauthored with Laura Gaillard Giordani. Most of the case studies, constituting a substantial part of the book, both quantitatively and qualitatively, have been written ad hoc, in specific connection with the argument in the text, by Laura Gaillard Giordani, as indicated in each of them.

Anna Grandori
November 2010

Introduction

Innovation is a core driver of the development of economies, and all the more so in modern, knowledge-based economies, and entrepreneurship is a core driver of economic innovation. In fact, in economic life and public policy initiatives, as well as in research and teaching, there has been a significant revival of entrepreneurship.

However, the way in which entrepreneurship is studied is characterized by pronounced fragmentation into different fields and the way in which it is taught is often not much ahead of practice. This book contributes to overcoming those limitations by integrating different perspectives in economics, organization and management, and in treating the subject in an accessible but theoretically informed way.

Focus

More than about entrepreneurs as people, this book is about entrepreneurship as an activity and about its organization. In that respect, the book is part of an emerging trend away from focusing on entrepreneurs as "special people" toward more structural features of entrepreneurship. In fact, for some time, entrepreneurship has been studied to a large extent as stemming from traits of personality or special personal qualities. This approach has not produced very consistent and useful results (Gartner 1989) as would be expected. Effective discovery processes, in science as in life, in fact, and fortunately, depend more on appropriate cognitive and organizational processes and structures than on exceptional individual attributes (Popper 1989). This book is about those analyzable structures and processes of entrepreneurship: cognitive and social processes for the effective discovery and crafting of opportunities; proper incentives for risk taking and risk sharing; systematic strategies for resource recombination; organization structures allowing knowledge sharing; ownership and governance structures capable of attracting the investments of human and financial capital. In other words, entrepreneurship will be considered as a set of analyzable, hence teachable and replicable, effective strategies for the discovery and exploitation of opportunities; sustainable by specific organizational arrangements, formal and informal. It will be analyzed in all the phases of its development, and both through the founding of new firms and through the infusion of entrepreneurial organizational practices in established firms.

Content-wise, in the course of reviewing and developing solutions to the problem of how to organize entrepreneurial activities, this book will offer some new theses on entrepreneurial organization and governance that enrich existing perspectives. In particular, those conceptual contributions will regard the central role played by *networked organization forms* in almost all the aspects and phases of entrepreneurial development, and a specification of those forms; and by *human capital investments*, specifying how the property right issues implied by knowledge asset investment give rise to peculiar "entrepreneurial governance" structures.

Various existing perspectives are used, integrated and enriched in order to cover the main problems to be addressed in organizing entrepreneurship, and to generate those conceptual messages, including:

- theories of entrepreneurship in economics (Casson 2003) and management (Bjerke 2007; Shane 2003);
- models of heuristic decision making applicable to entrepreneurial decision making, including not only the usually stressed ineffective and "biasing" heuristics to be avoided (Baron 1998; Vermeulen and Cur eu 2010), but also an emerging repertory of effective heuristics for the discovery of economic opportunities and actions (Sharasvathy 2001; McGrath 1999; Grandori 2010a);
- emerging strands in the theory of the firm applicable to understanding the nature of entrepreneurial firms (Rajan and Zingales 2000; Foss and Klein 2004; Langlois 2007; Alvarez and Barney 2007; Grandori 2010b);
- applications of social network analysis to explain and sustain the generation of new ides (Burt 2002; Singh 2000), the founding of new firms (Dubini and Aldrich 1991) and the growth and performance of new enterprises (Powell *et al.* 1996; Castilla *et al.* 2000);
- knowledge-based views of the firm and of internal organization (Grant 1996), of inter-firm networks (Grandori 1997; Siegel 2006; de Man 2008; Gilsing 2005; Graf 2006; Groen 2005) and of governance in general (Foss and Michailova 2009);
- agency theory, property right theory and transaction cost economics (Kaplan and Stromberg 2003; Sapienza and Gupta 1986; Clarysse *et al.* 2007; Alvarez and Barney 2007) in an "enriched" version (to include more knowledge factors and not only cost factors), so as to be applicable to the design of *new* and *innovative* firm boundaries and inter-firm networks;
- an integration between various (formerly rather unconnected) strands of studies contributing in defining which organizational practices may generate entrepreneurial behaviors in established firms, including "corporate entrepreneurship" studies (Burgelman 1984; Baden-Fuller and Stopford 1994), "corporate disaggregation" studies (Zenger and Hesterley 1997) and studies on "new organization forms" (Whittington *et al.* 1999; Lewin and Volberda 1999);

- the analyses of the "spatial" dimension of entrepreneurship, linking "international entrepreneurship" (Oviatt and McDougall 2007; Jones and Wadhwani 2007; Zahra *et al*. 2005; Zahra 2003) and "local systems of innovation" (Saxenian 1990; Shoonhoven and Romanelli 2001; Porter and Stern 2002) studies;
- a synthesis of the immense literature on public and institutional support to entrepreneurship and new firms creation (Powell *et al*. 2005; Link 2006; Etzkowitz 2008) reordered in an organizational typology oriented to the design of "organized environments" for innovation (either in the position of a policy maker, or of an entrepreneurial firm acting in those environments).

Many of the abovementioned studies have been published in scientific articles and monographs. This book, in addition to adding some contributions to those studies, organizes the knowledge produced in a unified format, also usable for teaching. The book can in fact be used for teaching, in spite of not being a standard textbook, and not covering all aspects of entrepreneurship (i.e. strategy, marketing, planning and control, etc.): as a core or supplementary reading in advanced/optional Bachelor and Master of Science courses in organization and entrepreneurship; and as a reading for PhD courses or theses on organizational and governance aspects of entrepreneurship. It can also be usefully read and used by learned entrepreneurs, investors and managers interested in the "practical value of good theory" that may put them ahead of common sense and common practice in organizing or investing in new firms, or in rejuvenating established firms.

In sum, the book offers a treatment of the *organization of entrepreneurship*, in its structural and process aspects, strong in its interdisciplinary conceptual foundations in economic and social sciences and rich in cases and empirical materials; especially applied to the modern knowledge-intensive and international contexts. The attention to the international dimension of entrepreneurship is sustained by cases from all over the world – and not only from the US and the EU – also considering that the fast-growing countries, such as China, India or Brasil, are a particularly favorable context for growth through new entrepreneurial firms.

All cases and experiences are presented so as to substantiate the core messages and are discussed in the text with respect to the core concepts. Each chapter is concluded by a wide and original case study, covering the main issues treated in the chapter, with the double function of supporting and illustrating the arguments, and to allow an exercise of problem recognition and problem solving on the case using the models and concepts outlined in the chapter. The cases are accompanied by questions that can guide analysis, explanation, and prescription in the format of mini-projects.

In the course of treating the various arguments, and of integrating various perspectives, each chapter offers enrichments of available models on entrepreneurship. These value-adding contributions are highlighted among the key points at the end of each chapter. They are proposed in the effort of giving more satisfactory responses to the core questions introduced in the next section of this introduction.

Framework

The term entrepreneurship derives from the Latin verb "imprehendére" meaning starting a new activity, taking initiative, exploring. In this sense, entrepreneurship is a core driver of the development of economies, and all the more so of modern, knowledge-based economies. However, exploration and initiative can take place in, and be supported by, a variety of institutions, even when only considering economic activities. In fact, classic definitions of entrepreneurship encompass all these phenomena and institutions.

Entrepreneurship is not only about taking initiative or having new ideas or discovering new products and processes. Researchers and "creative" people are most often engaged in producing new ideas, but are not entrepreneurs simply because of this. The concept of entrepreneurship has a fundamental organizational dimension.

Knight (1921) provided a founding definition of *the entrepreneur* as a figure *deciding* which project to pursue, under uncertainty about the project's prospects of success, *organizing* and paying the relevant inputs (capital, work, land, equipment) and being *rewarded out of the "residual"* result (e.g. for monetary costs and benefits, profit).

This classic economic definition corresponds to the legal definition of an entrepreneur – where it is given, as in some European legal systems – as a figure "professionally conducting an organized economic activity for the production or exchange of goods and services" (Galgano 1974). The definition is oriented to single out the "wealth creation" and value generation function (as opposed, for example, to mere financial trading) and the "organized" character (as opposed, for example, to the provision of professional services as an autonomous worker).

Let us analyze those starting definitions and link them to later developments, with a focus on understanding what they imply in economic practice and in what sense entrepreneurship is a specialized practice, differing from more general things that are often equated/confused with it, such as to "create a new firm", "invest one's own money", "offer a new product".

Entrepreneurs, capitalists and managers

Investing one's own money is not a defining feature of an entrepreneur – neither in economic theory nor in legal systems. As numerous cases of new enterprises testify, a person starting a new firm can in principle work entirely with money from external sources. On these grounds, an entrepreneur is distinguished from a "capitalist" (e.g. "venture capitalist" or other), who is in fact defined as an investor of money. The distinction is neither archaic nor just academic. As we shall see, it is important for understanding what an entrepreneurial firm is. Further on, it is rooted in a Nobel prized organizational economics approach (Williamson 1980; Baumol *et al.* 2007), in which it has been recently noticed that the incidence of "entrepreneurial firms" with respect to "capitalistic firms" (or the degree of blending among them) in an economy is a very important matter for the amount and type of growth that can be expected.

On the other side, an entrepreneur is also distinguished from a manager, who also professionally organizes economic activities. What is the difference if the entrepreneur does not invest his/her money? The crucial difference on this side is that a manager is "salaried" while the entrepreneur is entitled to the "residual rewards" (whatever they may be, not only money, but eventually patents or other property rights over results, or over tangible and intangible assets). Again this definitional issue is quite important in practice. For example, in assembling human resources, how the relationship with providers should be regulated. Through partnerships or through wage-based employment contracts?

What is an entrepreneur, then, if not necessarily an investor of financial capital, nor only a provider of work services? The response will hopefully become clear as the story of how resources can be attracted and retained in a new firm is told in the first part of the book. However, it can and should be priorly disclosed that something indeed is, and should be, invested to be an entrepreneur. This "something" has to do with the general definition of entrepreneurship given above: *the entrepreneur is a provider of "projects" with uncertain outcomes, and the organizer of inputs around them.* "Providing" projects involves the "provision" of intangible assets such as knowledge and ideas. These are the assets distinctively provided by entrepreneurs and, as we shall see, are the main basis for their entitlement to at least some property rights.

Ideas, knowledge and projects are rather special kinds of assets though. They are not like money or land. They need time, assistance, and complementary know-how to be developed. Property rights on them are difficult to define. These circumstances create a special tie between the persons providing them and the firm in which they are invested and through which they are realized. At the very least, the entrepreneur should work on project development, and do so for a sufficiently long period of time. This is why an entrepreneur can also been defined as a figure who *is both an "investor"* – the provider of at least a "project" – *and a "worker"* – the provider of at least some directive work.

Hence, a lower separation between "ownership and control", between who invests and who directs, has been considered one distinctive feature of "entrepreneurial governance" and the "entrepreneurial firm" (Williamson 1980; Alvarez and Barney 2007; Baumol *et al.* 2007). Specific organizational issues come along with entrepreneurial governance arrangements, especially if what they "govern" are highly innovative projects:

- How to craft projects with high return prospects and simultaneously reduce downside risk?
- How to govern the relations with co-investors of financial or technical assets so that everybody (including the entrepreneur) is motivated to invest?
- How to manage the investor-worker double identity, and to relate to other worker-workers (employees)?

- How to sustain the growth of knowledge and new possible projects/activities without increasing bureaucracy and the separation between ownership and control?

These kinds of questions are those that make *entrepreneurial governance and organization* a specialized field and a special activity.

This book is dedicated to those distinctively entrepreneurial governance and organizational problems. In other terms, the book will not address problems that (a) are not specific to entrepreneurial contexts or firms and could be addressed with the common, general economic, organization and management tools; and (b) are not organizational but pertain to specialized areas of management such as marketing or accounting.

Entrepreneurship and innovation

If "entrepreneurship" is to mean anything precise, it cannot be a synonym of "innovation". Innovation – and even more so the generation of new ideas behind it (i.e., "creativity") – is ubiquitous in the economy. Entrepreneurship includes conducting a new activity by means of a dedicated structure, governed in a specific mode. However, the activity might not be new in the sense of offering a product or service that was not offered before. In this respect, the classic distinction between "Kirznerian" and "Schumpeterian" entrepreneurship is clarifying. Some authors, Kirzner (1973) in particular, pointed out that new firms and new projects can first be started in response to existing market "*disequilibria*"; for example, to match increasing demand for a type of product that already exists, to reach some market segments/local areas that are not served, to connect demand and offers that are not connected. In this way entrepreneurship has been linked to market imperfections and disequilibria, and its *function identified* in the "*correction*" (and exploitation) of *market* "disfunctions" (or "failures"). Other authors, Schumpeter (1934) in particular, instead offered a more radical view of the *function of the entrepreneur* as an actor *imagining* "new ways" of utilizing resources, and *reorganizing resources* in new combinations to *generate innovation* in products or processes. New projects and new firms in this case "*create*" *market disequilibria*, rather than solve them, or *create markets* altogether.

Hence, entrepreneurial ventures can be more or less "innovative". Actually the "innovation" component may reduce in some cases to the pure establishment of a new entity, for conducting the very same activity formerly conducted within a larger firm (e.g. the externalization of the production of components by former employees becoming entrepreneurial suppliers), or conducted by many other firms (e.g. constituting a new firm in an industrial district). Not identifying entrepreneurship with innovation actually allows us to see the quite relevant problem of the many traditional small and medium enterprises that are "entrepreneurial firms", but are "not innovative", and to discuss how to make them so.

Entrepreneurship and new firms

Is "entrepreneurial governance and organization" the same thing as founding and organizing "new firms"? Actually not. Essential ingredients of entrepreneurial governance and organization are the dedication of resources to a project, the discretion and responsibility of the project provider in organizing them and developing the project, and his/her entitlement to at least a share of the results. These conditions can also be created by setting up dedicated units and projects within already existing firms. In other words, even within established firms, when innovation is a core concern, entrepreneurial governance creeps in through the constitution of autonomous units around projects, self-organized as quasi-firms entitled in varying degrees to returns on investments or even ownership of assets (e.g. Miles *et al.* 1997). Specialized sub-fields in organization and management – such as "corporate entrepreneurship" and "corporate disaggregation" – have flourished to support the maintenance or infusion of entrepreneurship in firms that were not born entrepreneurial and wish to become so, or were born entrepreneurial and do not wish to lose that characteristic.

Entrepreneurial decision making

It has thus far been stressed that entrepreneurship is not only about undertaking new activities but also about organizing them in a particular way. The fact that entrepreneurship has this structural component does not mean that the mindfulness, skillfulness and capacity of the entrepreneurs are not important. Actually, effective decision making is central to discovering opportunities, designing projects that best match competences, establishing useful relationships and much more. The challenge here, though, is to clarify, to analyze, to model the effective (versus ineffective) patterns of thought behind successful opportunity definition and project selection.

The trap, quite common in entrepreneur "mythology", is to think that if one succeeds in an activity, one must have some special attributes, at times not even well understood, such as "intuition", "risk-taking propensity", "proactiveness", etc. The "trap" (or the kind of biases involved in that reasoning)[1] may be simply illustrated with an analogy: it would be like teaching research methods to scientists by saying that scientists are more intelligent than others, or have more "intuition". Or trying to establish the correlation between the personality of scientists and their productivity. This would not be very useful for sustaining scientific innovation.

Therefore, the approach adopted in this book is to face the challenge to single out effective cognitive strategies, make them explicit, and therefore facilitate their adoption by anyone who may be interested. Important conceptual inputs and models are provided by the now-flourishing research on "entrepreneurial cognition" (e.g. Vermuelen and Curşeu 2010), which, however, emphasizes more the cognitive processes to be avoided (the "biases") than those to be followed. A distinctive effort will be made here to offer a repertory "heuristics for innovation" that can be justified as "effective", "robust" and even "rational" for conditions of high uncertainty.

In sum, the definitions of entrepreneurship provided in this introduction would lead to posing questions such as: Where do good new ideas come from? How can resources be effectively recombined? Is organizing an entrepreneurial firm any different from organizing a firm in general? In other words, this book is about the analyzable and replicable structures and processes of entrepreneurship: cognitive and social processes for the effective discovery and crafting of opportunities; proper incentives for risk taking and risk sharing; systematic strategies for resource recombination; organization structures allowing knowledge generation and sharing; ownership and governance structures attracting the investments of human and financial capital in new firms or in new projects within existing firms. The distinctive focus of the book can therefore be defined as the *"organization of entrepreneurship"*. The themes are organized roughly according to the phases, questions and solutions that may be encountered in constructing entrepreneurial actions starting from "zero", that is, from the very crafting of an "idea" or project – as represented in Table 0.1.

A scheme of analysis

- Is there any method in the discovery of entrepreneurial opportunities? Chapter 1 uses classic and recent theories of entrepreneurship for identifying three sources concurring in an effective exploration and exploitation of entrepreneurial opportunities: structural, relational and cognitive. On each, criteria and strategies for identifying opportunities effectively are provided.
- How to attract and retain resource investments in new projects and new firms? Chapter 2 examines which are the differences and structural implications of investing different types of capital – human, technical and financial assets – in new entities.
- What types of asset ownership patterns and organizational structures characterize effective entrepreneurial firms? Chapter 3 draws on classic and recent theory of the firm and entrepreneurial firm to define a set of effective governance and organizational practices that are distinctively entrepreneurial.
- When can projects, or parts of them, be organized under the umbrella of various types of contracts among different entities/firms? Chapter 4 addresses the problem of efficient firm boundaries and inter-firm contracting taking into account the specific challenges posed by new and knowledge-intensive activities.
- How can the features of entrepreneurial governance and organization be preserved as firms grow, and how can entrepreneurial projects be organized within existing firms rather than by starting new firms? Chapter 5 reviews a wide range of organizational and human resources (HR) practices that have been shown to be useful for the purpose, drawing and integrating elements

Table 0.1 A scheme of analysis

Key question	Where do good ideas come from?	How can resources be attracted and dedicated?	How to constitute and organize a new firm?	To grow or not to grow? Or how to grow?	How to organize grown-up firms in an entrepreneurial mode?	How can environments and external institutions help?
Themes	Opportunities - Sources and types: structural, relational and cognitive - Strategies for discovery	Resources - Types: human, technical and financial - Barriers and problems - Networked solutions	The governance and organization of ent'l firms - Legal forms and ownership structures - Internal organizational arrangements	Ent'l firm boundaries and external networks - Cost, knowledge and motivational factors in ent'l firms' boundary design - Networked birth - Networked growth	"Corporate entrepreneurship" - Structural organizational practices - Human resources and industrial relations practices	Organized environments for entrepreneurship - Spontaneous forms (industrial districts, clusters and communities) - Designed forms (parks, poles and regional systems of innovation)
Chapter	1	2	3	4	5	6

from various pertinent streams of study (corporate entrepreneurship, corporate disaggregation, new organization forms, new forms of employment, strategic HR).

- Finally, Chapter 6 examines the role of the wider organizational texture of the environment in which entrepreneurial ventures are embedded in sustaining entrepreneurship both in established and in new firms. It reviews the proliferating forms of clusters (from industrial districts to industrial communities) and of institutionally designed and publicly supported clusters (from industrial parks and incubators, to science parks and technological poles to regional systems of innovation) and provides a parsimonious organizational classification useful for understanding how to take advantage of them (from an entrepreneurial viewpoint) and how to design them (from a policy maker viewpoint).

Notes

1 Cf. Simon (1987), Popper (1989), Nisbett and Ross (1980), for the background methodological principles behind this criticism of the "cult of personality" and the "mystique of leadership" in entrepreneurial studies.

1 Sources of entrepreneurship

Opportunities

Chapter 1 contents[*]

1.1 Structural sources of opportunities: reducing and creating disequilibria

1.2 Relational sources of opportunities: social network management

1.3 Cognitive sources of opportunities: entrepreneurial decision making

---

Texts on entrepreneurship typically provide reviews of the main "alternative theories of entrepreneurship" that economic and management scientists have produced (Casson 2003; Shane 2003). Rather than being seen as alternative theories though, these contributions can be understood and used as indicating a variety of "sources" of entrepreneurship or "types of opportunities" that can be recognized by decision makers. Defining a reasoned repertory, if not a typology, of the kind of phenomena that constitute an entrepreneurial opportunity is important, if not necessary, for being able to "recognize", let alone "craft" them. We cannot recognize something if we do not have an idea or model of what it is. Unfortunately most treatments of opportunity recognition do not provide suggestions of what to look at for having a chance to recognize an opportunity, or of what to do for creating one. The typical treatment of the opportunity recognition problem is to provide a substantive list of things – trends and changes in demand, technology environments, culture, demography, etc. – that is practically too wide for guiding action (i.e. approximately amounts to saying that you can look to anything) and conceptually never exhaustive (so that the relevant thing for you may not always have been included). Therefore, we are rather going to treat and classify opportunities in an applied decision-making perspective, translating the main "theories" of entrepreneurship into categories of opportunities, so as to support their recognition and construction.

A second premise is useful. Entrepreneurial opportunities are often defined as "changes" – in technology, social customs, political conditions, legislation, demography, or "gaps" (e.g. between supply and demand) (e.g. Drucker 1985;

---

[*] Text by Anna Grandori, cases by the authors indicated in boxes.

Shane 2003). What is more helpful in these definitions of opportunities is not the substantive list of factors (i.e. social, psychological, technical, etc.) but the conceptualization of the sources of opportunities as "changes" and "gaps and disequilibria". If we focus on that part of the definition, rather than on the substantive list of factors, we are led to ask whether there cannot be other types of sources that are not "gaps" or "changes". And in fact there are, since new ideas that turn into opportunities may stem from "new ways of seeing" things (that perhaps have always been there), or from imagining things "as they might be" rather than as they are, or from connecting things that were not connected, with no need for external change.

We shall therefore define entrepreneurial opportunities as any possibility of new value-generating economic activity, and use a classification of opportunities that is both more conceptual and more "actionable", since it implies different types of entrepreneurial action. We shall use the term "sources" of opportunities in the same ways in which it is used in the social sciences for other complex concepts, such as "the sources of power" (Fisher 1983), with the aim of helping in understanding and building the entity in question. Actually, the just quoted classic paper on the sources of negotiating power is inspiring in this respect; and in fact the power to act, shape things and successfully negotiate with other actors is a capacity more related than is usually acknowledged with the capacity of exploiting opportunities. Negotiation theorists usefully indicated that negotiating power has structural sources (e.g. resources commanded), but also relational sources (the management of relationships) and cognitive sources (clever judgments and proper decision making). Analogously, entrepreneurial opportunities have structural bases in "gaps" and "changes" economic and technical reality, can leverage on networks of relationships, and require sound judgment and decision making for being discovered. The three sections of this chapter examine these three sources of good opportunity definition respectively.

1.1 Structural sources of opportunities: reducing and creating disequilibria

The entrepreneurship story summarized in Box 1.1, simple as it is, illustrates various structural sources of opportunities and ways to identify and exploit them, discussed next.

Box 1.1 Jack Brash (JB)

Jack Brash was born in 1912, from Polish immigrants in London. When Jack was still very young, his father abandoned his mother, who was forced to work making fashion garments. She worked from home, was paid piece-rate and Jack helped her with the outwork in the evenings after school.

Jack was quiet and withdrawn, and did not do well at school. Leaving school at the earliest opportunity, he became an errand boy and then a shop assistant. Finding that another steady job was hard to obtain, he resolved to go into business on his own.

It was a time of high unemployment, and many of the unemployed were so poor that they financed themselves by selling off family heirlooms. Jack noticed that if they were to sell locally their items would have "gone for a song". His experience with fashion garments had taught him that, while many people were poor, there were still those rich enough to afford expensive goods, if you knew where to find them. His idea was therefore to buy in bulk from the local neighborhood and sell to West End dealers at a much higher price. He soon learnt from experience what sort of things the West End dealers were looking for and actively tried to find them in his neighborhood, or even making some modifications (for example, changing frames to mirrors) so as to satisfy demand. He offered discounts to the dealers he knew for larger orders and for cash in advance. In this way, he collected enough cash to finance production activities, beyond the commercial activity.

The business took off, unit costs fell as batch size increased, and Jack accumulated some financial resources. He immediately began to look around for something to do with these. He knew that the mirrors sold because of the frame design and thought that the same sort of frame could be used for pictures, prints and photographs as well. So these products were added to his range.

Jack also gave thought to how to reduce costs and prices. He realized that he could cut out some of the dealers and sell direct to the public. Without the dealers' margin, he could sell more units at a lower price. He looked for premises in an attractive area where the market was bigger, beat competition on price, and eventually acquired the local dealer's stock and activity.

War broke out in 1939. Jack sold his business while it was still doing well and invested the proceeds in jewelry. He kept his savings throughout the war in this form. During the war, he nevertheless found a way of doing business by running the stores on an airfield. Times were tough, but he had the chance to come into contact with many people and to help them survive. After the war, Jack kept in touch with them, and some of them repaid the favor by investing in his business ventures or introduced Jack to useful contacts in his long entrepreneurial career thereafter.

Source: adapted from Casson (2003)

A first class of structural economic sources of entrepreneurship is constituted by *market disequilibria and "imperfections"*, which can be exploited by entrepreneurial action. They have been called "Kirznerian opportunities", after Kirzner's view of entrepreneurial action as "equilibrating" and supporting the functioning of markets. They include the following:

1   A classic way in which entrepreneurs can contribute to the efficient functioning of markets is through innovations bringing about "*cost reduction*" so that, through competition, "*price correction*" is obtained (Kirzner 1973). They include classic innovations in technologies, production processes or products themselves, reducing *production cost*. For example, the "modularization" of products is a broad innovation in product structure allowing the production of customized objects at a much lower cost.

In addition, innovations in organizational processes that reduce *transaction costs* are possible (Leibenstein 1968) and should be emphasized. In fact, in innovation practice (and theory) attention is predominantly paid to product and production process innovations. It is thus worth highlighting that it is possible to build entrepreneurial action on the reduction of "transaction costs"; that is, the invention of organizational solutions that reduce free riding, agency costs, control costs, negotiation and intermediation costs. A "high-tech" example would be how internet technology has sustained the flourishing of direct selling through the internet. But a pertinent example would also be the re-emergence of "old-tech" "street markets", or otherwise physical markets, selling natural food where farmers cut out dealers and sell directly to the public. In the JB case, the idea to reduce costs and prices by cutting out dealers and selling direct to the public was a case of price correction through the reduction of transaction costs.

2   Space for entrepreneurial action is generated by connecting offer to demand that is unlikely to be meet "spontaneously". Entrepreneurship can occur as an act of *intermediation* (Casson 1982). For example, Jack Brash connected two social groups with complementary preferences: a group of people interested in selling "old stuff" to which they assigned low value (while needing money) with another group interested in buying the old stuff as high-value "antiquities". This case is different from the former, as it is not based on cost reduction but rather on value increase. In fact, the price was "corrected upward" toward the higher value assigned to old furniture as "vintage" stuff.

Since these opportunities exploit "gaps" or "holes" in the webs of exchanges, the type of entrepreneurial action responding to them has been called "*gap filling*" (Casson 1982) or "*hole bridging*" (Burt 2002). As the economist Liebenstein identified earlier and clearly described (1978: 45; Casson 1982: 217), if we represent an economy as a set of nodes (producers and consumers) and ties or "pathways" of exchanges between nodes, then the "perfect competition model would be represented by a net that is complete: one that has pathways that are well-marked and well-defined, well-marked and well-defined nodes ... and each node deals with every other node". In reality however, markets are rarely "perfect" and "complete"; "*there are 'holes' and tears in the net* [italics added], obstructions (knots) along the pathways, and some nodes and pathways, where they exist, are poorly defined and poorly marked".

3   A more potent way of filling a gap in the market structure is that of creating an offer responding to an unmet demand, which entails more than the act of connection, since it implies the creation of a new product or service that was not previously offered. This is the case of "*missing markets*" and "*missing products*", which are also conceivable as particular types of "market failure" or disequilibria (Milgrom and Roberts 1992) and is the most obvious terrain in which entrepreneurship is both most needed and most likely to flourish. The search for, and detection of, *unfulfilled needs*, either perceived or not (yet) perceived by potential users, is the type of entrepreneurial action that can lead to the detection of missing markets. They may be constituted by problems for which people or firms have no current "buyable" solution.

One simple reason may be that no one has yet detected the need and provided the product or service. This may be the case for self-provided services and self-made products and are therefore good areas to consider. For example, the "travel accounting service", developed and successfully sold by some tour operators, was based on the observation that travel expenses were outside of the control of many firms and no service of this type was offered by the market.

A second reason is that unresolved "technical puzzles" prevented the construction of these products. In this case, the source of opportunities is a "*missing product*" problem instead of a missing market. Here, technical problem solving is required and not merely "alertedness" (see section 1.3 on cognitive sources).

A third reason is that the need is perceived in general and generic terms, but has not been operationalized – by the potential users or providers – into specific objects or services satisfying the need. For example, today people may have a generic need for more natural products, environmental safety and entertainment. Missing markets and missing products may be identified by asking with which existing or emerging new products and services those needs can be satisfied. However, these needs are broad enough to be responded to by an almost infinite array of products and services. The most promising responses can then be identified by matching those broadly defined "external" opportunities with the resources and response capabilities of a given actor.

Therefore, in generating hypotheses on which products or services may meet unfulfilled needs (a *market-driven* criterion) a *resource-based* criterion is also required. Among the many (actually infinite) possible new products or services, it would be more effective and efficient to think of something that may be better realized by starting with the entrepreneur's distinctive *resources and competences*. Actually, an analysis of resources may even suggest opportunities, thereby configuring a second type of structural economic source of entrepreneurial opportunities: *resource-based opportunities*. They are not rooted in exogenous changes or gaps but are creatively imagined as possible uses of existing resources. We can distinguish two ways of developing resource-based opportunities.

1   An important contribution to understanding the resource-based sources of entrepreneurship is the view of the firm offered by Edith Penrose (1959). She made the important observations that (a) resources typically come in bundles, especially when they are human capabilities embodied in people; (b) they are typically multi-functional; that is, they can generate a variety of services; and thus (c) they are typically acquired or accumulated in excess with respect to the particular use they are employed in. The definition of opportunities that can actually be exploited then involves an encounter between possible uses and users and the "resources" (in search of uses) of a would-be entrepreneur. Even when the resources are not sophisticated technologies with numerous possible applications, the logic of developing services from accumulated competences is common. In the JB case, for instance, pieces of knowledge as simple as experience in the home production of fashion garments and direct experience of the lifestyles and problems of low-income people can be identified as the initial resources enabling the development of the fashion mirror business.

2   The most far-reaching type of opportunity is the *"recombination of resources"*, capable of generating entirely new streams of products and services. These can be called *"Schumpeterian opportunities"* (Shane 2003) after Schumpeter's (1934) seminal contribution on entrepreneurship. Joining, and together employing, competences, technologies, relationships and information that had previously not been combined enable developing qualitatively different new action possibilities. Innovation case histories abound with accounts of this type of move. For example, Harrysson (2006) describes the case of a revolutionary packaging solution introduced by Combibloc, challenging the much larger competitor Tetrapack. This innovation was possible thanks to a combination of materials and technologies previously not used together for that purpose – carton and plastics – that allowed the creation of a new packaging solution. The case of the ultra-light assault rifle AR-10 as described in the next section (Box 1.2) also highlights how the design of a new aircraft was based on the recombination of competences in the use of plastics and aluminum in aircraft, military and engineering activities.

1.2 Relational sources of opportunities: social network management

The "imagination" of possible uses and users is greatly improved by contact with people who are active or experts in a field, who know what the unsolved problems and the latent needs are. Indeed, it is almost proverbial that "creative", even "genial" problem solving may not result in a successful innovation due to the absence of relevant connections with potential users (Singh and Robert 2000).

"Good" ideas do not come out of the blue and good entrepreneurial ideas even less so. For example, a recent account of the highly successful design firms concentrated in the Lombardy region of Italy (Verganti 2006: 2) illustrates how the strength of the research and development system is not to be found internally, nor even in specific inter-firm relations, but in the multiple competences and relationships present in "a free-floating community of architects, suppliers, photographers, critics, curators, publishers and craftsmen, among many other categories of professionals, as well as the expected artists and designers". Similarly, Saxenian (1990) described the strength of Silicon Valley in much the same terms, although the relevant actors are somewhat different since the industry is different. The key players of this "community" include R&D-intensive corporations and new technology-based firms, universities and research centers, financial angels and venture capitalists.

How can these webs of relations be analyzed, understood, managed and even designed? Attention should be paid to several questions and dimensions for responding.

In the first place, relations should be considered not as isolated ties between dyads (of people or organizations), but as belonging to a "network", defined as a set of multiple nodes and ties (Liebenstein 1978; Burt 1992). Thereafter, the nature of ties, the shape of the network and the position of each node can be analyzed responding to questions such as:

1   What is the content of a tie? Is it just "a contact" or are information and knowledge or materials, money and people transferred?
2   What is the direction of a tie? One-way or two-way?
3   Who is connected to whom? All to all? One to all? Are there subgroups?
4   What is the strength of a tie? Is it a frequent relation involving a broad set of issues, or the opposite? Is it long-lasting or the opposite?

Four dimensions of a network can correspondingly be identified, with particular relevance to entrepreneurial opportunities and action.

The first is the *intensity of ties*. A key distinction has been made between *"strong"* and *"weak"* ties (Granovetter 1983). The intensity of a tie can be conceived (and constructed) as composed by the following dimensions:

- *breadth* (number of matters and transactions);
- *depth* (depth of partner knowledge, importance of the matters involved);
- *frequency* (current frequency of contact, the history of past contacts and the prospects of future contacts).

Weak ties represent the polar situation (on an ideal continuum): they are narrow, thin and infrequent relations.

To think in terms of strong and weak ties is useful because people often underestimate "the strength of weak ties" (Granovetter 1983) and tend to over-rely on strong ties. This behavior can be particularly detrimental in entrepreneurship.

Both strong and weak ties are in fact important and complementary in sustaining entrepreneurial action. Strong ties can be *"exploited"* to start new ventures, at a stage in which uncertainty is far too high to gain collaborations by means of contracting with parties that are not directly or well known. However, the liability of strong ties is in "closure", in a clan-like fashion, and the limitation of numbers and varieties. Weak ties are valuable as new roads to be *"explored"*, coming in contact with different and fresh views, providing a pool of relations that may be transformed into strong ties as opportunities arise. The limitation of weak ties is their unverified reliability and potential value. Hence, actors holding a balanced "portfolio" of strong and weak ties are better positioned as potential entrepreneurs.[1]

The second issue is *brokerage*. Many opportunities come from "connecting the disconnected". Relationships are crucial in detecting these opportunities. More precisely, *having relationships in different groups that are not connected is crucial*. An actor in this position can be said to bridge the *"structural holes"* in a social and economic structure (Burt 1992).

A systematic way to deal with this issue is to visualize a picture of relevant nodes and the ties among them and to detect where there are groups of connected nodes and where there is a lack of connections among subgroups. These "holes" (lack of connections) provide opportunities for brokerage. Actors bridging "structural holes" are in the best position to become entrepreneurs and vice versa; those who wish to become entrepreneurs can be advised to think of bridging and brokering.

The third issue *is the diversity of nodes and ties.* The argument put forward in this respect is that if knowledge and information nodes that become connected are very similar, there would be little to gain in terms of knowledge sharing and information exchange (Nooteboom 1999). Ties among them would be "redundant" (Burt 1992). In addition, the "duplication of ties" may also be redundant if the content of the tie is very similar: if A gets some information or input from B, who includes inputs from C to B, then a further link of A to C can be said to be redundant (providing that the link between C and A is not diverse in content, in which case it could add value).

The fourth issue is the *centrality* of each single node/actor in the network. Although there are various measures, a node's centrality in a network can be broadly expressed as the number of links a node has with respect to all possible links. Actors with higher centrality have more relational power, especially if other nodes have lower centrality, and are more likely to gain further positions in the system; for example, they are more likely to be promoted within firms or to successfully start new firms (Burt 1992). In other words, actors occupying central positions in networks that are not fully connected are better able to "capitalize" on the relationships, to use them as "social capital" generating economically valuable yields.

Box 1.2 illustrates the importance of relational networks in generating opportunities, and the complementarity of strong and weak ties in the case of a "junior enterprise"; that is, an entrepreneurial initiative set up by university students, leveraging mostly on relational sources of opportunities.

Box 1.2 JEME (Junior Enterprise Milano Economia)
Michele Biancolin, 2010

Junior Enterprises: bridging university and business life
Junior Enterprises ("JEs") are non-profit organizations managed by students
whose aim is to carry out consultancy projects for companies, institutions
and small enterprises in order to bridge their university background with the
world of professionals. JEs are linked to universities
or graduate schools, and student status is the essential condition of being
a member.

Junior entrepreneurs are involved in two fundamental activities:
managing the JE and carrying out projects. Management of the JE concerns
the implementation of a business strategy together with the creation of an
effective organizational structure. On the other hand, projects are "the
Junior Enterprise's way to improve student know-how and to finance
activities" (according to the European Confederation of Junior Enterprises,
JADE Europe).

Their entrepreneurial success is well demonstrated by the proliferation of
the JE model in Europe, with over 300 JEs, as well as in the Americas and
Asia, which together count over 600 JEs.

Junior Enterprise Milano Economia (JEME) is the Junior Enterprise of
Bocconi University in Milan; it was the first JE to be founded in Italy by
four entrepreneurial-minded students in 1988. Similarly to other JEs around
Europe, the word "network" is a must for the economic life of JEME and
members are trained on the importance of relationships with external actors
from the start.

It is not by chance that many of the projects carried out by JEME come
from those contacts with which JEME has developed closer relationships.
This is a well-known fact within JEME, but a more detailed analysis of its
economic activities in the years 2005 and 2006 has allowed highlighting the
main opportunities and constraints of economic actions arising from the
network and to state the extent to which JEME was influenced by its
neighborhoods.

Network analysis of JEME
The starting point of a network analysis is the "Ego-network" of the JE,
defined as the structure of relationships that involves all nodes reached by
the focal node concerned (the "Ego"), its ties with those actors (the "alters")
and all ties occurring among the alters. The way this structure is considered
depends on the scope of the analysis and is influenced by the characterization
assigned to each node and tie.

The data used for this kind of analysis come from general information on each actor of the network, which can be people, firms, institutions or other kinds of organizations. Useful information concerns the industry in which they operate, the activities carried out, the size or the legal form of the organization, and whether the node is a new contact or has previously worked with JEME. As concerns people, it is important to know the kind of role each plays and which group each belongs to: JEME alumni or Junior Entrepreneurs, students or professionals; furthermore, some people have different social roles within groups – for example, the members of a board of directors, or simple interns. In this way, nodes are "dressed" and it is easier to make some assumptions or to describe their behaviors.

Relationships among nodes are organized in a matrix form, which describes the presence or the value of ties between nodes: these data reflect standard relationships such as "node A and B have worked together" or "A is a member of the board of B".

One of the most informative aspects of a network analysis is that once nodes and ties have been defined according to the desired aim, it is possible to plot them into a graph called a sociogram, which represents the map of the entire network. The sociogram in Figure 1.1 represents the Ego-network of JEME for the year 2006. The position and grouping of nodes helps to highlight the distinct groups of nodes that are mainly interrelated.

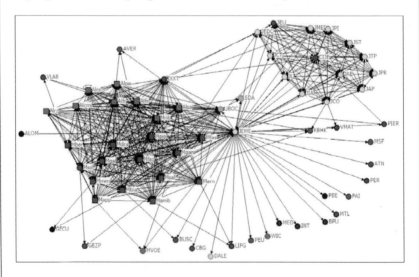

Figure 1.1 JEME's network
Note: ○ Junior Enterprises   ● Firms   ■ Individuals

JEME's network encompasses a wide range of actors, who can either belong to specific groups or be isolated nodes in the whole picture. Alumni and members of JEME represent almost 36 percent of the relevant contacts in negotiations and economic activities, followed by other Junior Enterprises, which represent another relevant group with 24.3 percent and 19 percent of contacts in the two years. The drop is determined by two factors: the higher number of negotiations with JE in 2005 and the increased number of contact groups in 2006, which brought higher heterogeneity to the network. Consultancy firms contributed to 11.4 percent and 9.5 percent of JEME's network in 2005 and 2006 respectively, while banks and firms operating in the field of finance represent 5 percent of the contacts. Other actors are present in lower percentages.

Once a snapshot has been taken, the first approach in JEME's network analysis is based on the qualitative difference between those ties that are fundamental for the entrepreneurial actions of the JE (JEME's strong ties) and those contacts with a less important and more explorative contribution (the weak ties). Over the years, some of the weakly tied nodes increased their collaboration with JEME and became strategically relevant, so that new, strong ties were created. The distinction between strong and weak ties provides some key information on how the entrepreneurial activity is sustained by strong ties – but also somehow limited by them – and how weak ties can provide a valuable complement.

Strong ties and exploitation
JEME's strong ties have common traits, such as the high degree of social coordination in the negotiation phase and delivery of the project, which are based on trust between the two nodes.

This occurs because strong ties have been linked to JEME for a long time, and have therefore been reciprocally involved in their growth path and strategic changes; this feature allows a strong tie to remain strong without the need to reinforce or recall the relationship continuously. In this sense, the importance of these ties cannot be indexed or translated into a number since they are on a different level with respect to the other nodes.

The community of alumni represents the first group of strong ties: they have always been a fundamental source of projects, contacts and training for JEME. Indeed, having worked together in the past means that there is deeper knowledge between some people and this is helpful to select partners for new projects; in fact, some alumni work in important companies operating in different industries, while some others have chosen to create their own firms. Within this structure of relationships, as long as JEME keeps on being reliable, each tie reinforces itself and makes it possible for an alumnus to share his/her contacts with JEME, introducing JE to new firms or people that can foster its growth. Choosing partners this way is economically efficient, as transaction costs are lower – and JE's prices are certainly lower when compared to a consultancy firm. Alumni also offer JEME support with training, which is also useful when they ask JEME to carry out projects for them, or when they address a contact, with the awareness that a specific competence is present within the JE. Furthermore, as working in a JE implies sharing particular values, these act as mechanisms of social coordination among alumni and among the association. JEME keeps its connections with the entire alumni network by organizing social events and meetings where many ideas for collaboration usually emerge: a feature of this social network is that most of these nodes do not need much effort to be "woken up" when they have not been active for a while – it has been observed within JE that when a project coming from the alumni network is proposed to JEME, negotiations are much smoother than those with external customers.

In 2005, the alumni community brought JEME six negotiations and four of them became projects. One of these is a consultancy firm created by two ex-members of JEME, which assigned three projects to JEME in 2005 and 2006. The other connections brought by the alumni network involved a bank, a small ICT company, a cultural foundation, a multinational soft drinks company and another marketing firm. In 2006, seven negotiations came from these ties, involving three business consultancies, a cultural foundation, a service company and two firms operating in the electronics industry. The first five negotiations became projects. Of an average 11 projects per year, this network in the years 2005 and 2006 accounted respectively for 36 percent and 45 percent of the total amount of projects accepted by JEME.

As the presence of Junior Enterprises is extended across many countries of the world, they are often grouped into confederations: in Europe, there are 11 national confederations and a Central European Confederation, JADE Europe, which was founded in 1992. JADE fosters the development of JEs and acts as a framework for cross-border cooperation between JEs. JADE arranges international meetings to facilitate the exchange of knowledge and experiences. In 2006, JADE Europe counted 225 JEs coming from 13 countries for over 20,000 Junior Entrepreneurs.

Within the JEME network, other JEs provide several negotiations every year: what makes JEs bind with each other is of course that they share values and targets, they have the same legal form and they are all managed by students. A key difference with respect to the alumni community is that the coordination mechanisms among JEs are much more formalized, and everything is developed through contracts or, when there is the presence of a central confederation, through a voting mechanism. More in depth, the role of the central confederations is to connect JEs in the development of projects and to attract opportunities within this network.

Two nodes within JEME's Ego-network deserve some individual considerations. The first is the consultancy company mentioned above, which is also connected to the JEs' confederations of Italy and Europe. As its owners are ex-Junior Entrepreneurs, they have always been close to the world of JEs and have chosen to establish partnerships with these two confederations: these partnerships involve collaborations in several projects and training sessions. Advantages of these partnership for JEs are also in the opportunity to meet managers and professionals, to learn from them and share knowledge. On the other hand, the company as a partner has the opportunity to count on, and observe, an entire network of future professionals who are willing to learn and are open to many activities.

Another dominant node of the network is one of the four students who founded JEME in 1988, who is now a strategy professor of the SDA Bocconi graduate school. His many connections with the academic and consulting world have always brought JEME many contacts and projects: the particular role of this node is also crucial in its brokerage activities. What is relevant here is that the most significant nodes in JEME's Ego-network have two important features: they are almost totally socially coordinated and they come from the past success of the association, so that they all know each other and they have never left JEME without support. Thus, a social network is in this case the primary source of strong ties.

Weak ties and exploration
The principal role of a weak tie is to provide projects, even if small in size and scope, allowing JEME to expand the scope of entrepreneurship beyond the borders of the strong tie network. The coordination of weak ties is fully formalized, as it is often the case that partners do not know each other well enough to use other means.

The "weak ties" allowed for spotting the drawbacks of embeddedness and dependence on the strong tie network. The main examples encompass situations in which the strong ties, leveraging on their privileges, outsource some projects to JEME whose tasks are mostly labor-intensive. In these cases, it is natural to think of JEME as a partner for several reasons: first of all, a JE can do the job at a reasonable price, and second, as highlighted before, these kinds of projects are useful to JEME as they contribute to developing best practices, implementing a learning-by-doing culture on all organizational levels and supporting the economic sustainability of the JE.

Despite these premises, in normal conditions JEME looks mainly for skill-intensive projects, in order to pursue the core objective of training its members; in this sense, it would not be optimal to carry out too many labor-intensive projects and therefore strong ties are not always the optimal answer to the JE's needs. Through weak ties, JEME creates a valid alternative to escape the constraints of partner and project selection and enhances its entrepreneurial skills in terms of promotion and marketing.

In addition, it has been remarked that strong ties are not necessarily active in a continuous and repeated way; there can be periods in which they are "dormant", so that weak ties buffer the risks of periods of inactivity or fill the open slots in JEME's schedule.

Another advantage of weak ties is that sometimes they require activities that are initially outside of the scope of the JE's background: it is often the case that JEME invests in training (or asks for training from some strongly tied nodes) or to learn the mechanisms of a new industry, bringing more and more variety into its Ego-network, as occurred between 2005 and 2006.

Implications

Exploiting its strong ties, JEME has the opportunity to establish best practices and continuous economic activities; strongly tied nodes do not need to request projects for themselves – in fact, they can also act as brokers with contacts that would otherwise be hard to reach. On the other hand, weak ties create new opportunities for projects that are often innovative in their content. The quantitative network analysis has helped to understand precisely and concretely what was only perceived as a tendency of JEME, systematically unveiling where strong and weak ties lie. From this analysis, it has been possible to determine in which direction JEME has its main expansion potential.

Notes and sources

The case was constructed based on M. Biancolin's (2007) "Social networks and network governance. The case of a Junior Enterprise" (Bachelor thesis in International Economics and Management, Bocconi University, Milan).

The software used to carry out the network analysis, freely downloadable from the internet (Borgatti, S.P., Everett, M.G. and Freeman, L.C. 2002) is Ucinet for Windows: Software for Social Network Analysis. Harvard, MA: Analytic Technologies. Version 6 and NetDraw graphic software.

JEME Bocconi Studenti's website: http://www.jeme.it/

Box 1.3 helps in expanding the analysis by considering a variety of "brokerage" strategies usable for creating opportunities, discussed next.

Box 1.3 Cases of economic brokerage

- Eugene Stoner, father of the M-16 rifle, was an acclaimed genius in the world of small-arms experts. Stoner's own explanation of his insight, however, makes clear how his creativity was an act of brokerage, moving knowledge familiar in one group to a second group in which the knowledge was a breakthrough idea. Stoner was an engineer with the Fairchild Engine and Airplane Company when he entered the company's start-up prototype-gun division, ArmaLite. Before joining Fairchild, Stoner served in the Marines as an ordnance technician. Stoner's familiarity with ordnance and the use of plastics and aluminum in aircraft gave him an advantage in designing a radically new, ultra-light assault rifle, the AR-10. As Stoner explained in an interview, "I think my aircraft background and experience allowed me to get into some of these light-weight materials, for instance forged aluminum receivers, which were rather unknown at the time in weapons. But it was nothing particularly new to what I'd been doing all along in aircraft equipment, in fiberglass and all that."
- In the arts, Paul Sachs acted as a broker in establishing the Museum of Modern Art in New York. He succeeded in this great enterprise because he had strong ties to sectors and players that had previously been only weakly connected – museums, universities and finance – and that were critical to the art world of that time.
- Some research institutes in Germany circulated and diffused among rival German companies information and knowledge in basic R&D (on adhesive technology) to everybody's advantage. The institutes informed each competing producer about the "state of the art" of adhesive technology.
- *IDEO* uses brainstorming to create product designs. The firm's employees work for clients in diverse industries. In the brainstorming sessions, technological solutions from one industry are used to solve client issues in other industries where the solutions are rare or unknown. In other words, the firm profits from employee bridge relations, through which they broker technology flow between industries. A similar process in Hewlett-Packard has been reported: their policy was to move engineers between projects rather than having each project hire and fire individually. The result was that HP technologies were constantly mixed into new combinations.
- A higher probability of innovation for semiconductor and biotech firms that establish alliances with firms outside their own technological area has been reported. Companies with a heterogeneous mix of alliance partners tended to enjoy faster revenue growth and a significant advantage in obtaining patents.

Source: adapted excerpts from Burt (2002)

These cases highlight, first of all, that an important component of superior idea-generating capacity is the distinctive access to previously unconnected information and resources. A case where the diffusion of information is the primary function of the network is that of research institutes pooling and diffusing information among rival German companies.

But there is more to networks than information transfer and pooling. Most of the other cases illustrate that the ties in the network convey and sustain the exchange and sharing of knowledge and competences. In fact, uncertainty about possible good projects requires information exchange and knowledge sharing (de Man 2008). However, governing knowledge transfer and sharing is generally difficult (Foss and Michailova 2009). Contracts typically fall short of providing complete coverage of possible hazards. Property rights on intellectual and knowledge assets are also typically weak. Hence, without reliable relationships with potential partners to leverage on, new hazardous ventures may never be undertaken. Thus, for both cognitive and motivational reasons, new ventures need to make use of networks of reliable relations that therefore can be qualified as "*social capital*" invested in the venture (Burt 2002).

Finally, in some of the cases – such as IDEO and Hewlett Packard – ties are constituted by transfers or sharing resources, in particular people, bringing their otherwise untransferable expertise with them.

Hence, the cases can be used to define different types of brokerage strategies, all useful in generating entrepreneurial opportunities, as summarized in Table 1.1:

- *one-way transferring* of information and resources versus two-way or all-way *pooling and sharing* of resources;
- transferring or pooling *information/knowledge resources* versus also transferring or pooling *human and technical resources* (people, materials, equipment);
- connecting nodes through a hub (giving form to a *star-like network* structure) versus putting all nodes into contact (giving form to a *fully connected network* structure).

Table 1.1 Brokerage strategies sustaining entrepreneurship

Tie content	Tie direction/shape	
	Transferring	Pooling
Information	• Diffusing information across unconnected nodes	• Putting unconnected nodes into contact
Technology/knowledge	• Transferring K&T into new fields	• Pooling K&T from diversified sources
People	• Transferring people across projects/organizations	• Pooling people into new projects/ organizations

1.3 Cognitive sources of opportunities: entrepreneurial decision making

The review of the nature and type of structural sources of entrepreneurial opportunities offered in the previous sections should sustain the capacity of recognizing them. However, the cognitive processes and strategies that may lead to their definition and to the choice of one particular course of action constitute a fundamental complementary support.

First of all, there are no opportunities without "*alertedness*" (Kirzner 1979) that is, without some actor paying attention to them. Gaps, changes, resources and potential uses without cognition would simply remain structural phenomena, sources of no river. Cognition and decision making is therefore an essential ingredient for defining entrepreneurial opportunities.

Entrepreneurial decision making, as with any decision making, involves the definition of a problem, the generation and evaluation of alternatives, the selection of a course of action, and the implementation and evaluation of results (learning) (Gustafsson 2006).

In a decision-making perspective, good entrepreneurial decision making, as with any good decision making, does not necessarily stem from exceptional personality traits or from unanalyzable "illumination" processes. Effective decision making in complex problems, even if apparently "intuitive", can actually be analyzed, understood and therefore, at least in part, reproduced (Simon 1987). Hence, under the aspect of innovative decision making, entrepreneurship can be analyzed, understood, systematized, predicted and taught as a matter of "*disciplined innovation*" (Drucker 1985). The challenging question is which decision-making strategies can sustain such processes of "disciplined" innovation. Any "discipline" is a set of rules and procedures, some about behaviors that are "correct" and should be adopted and some about behaviors that are "incorrect" and should be avoided.

The available treatment of entrepreneurial decision making is largely based on "behavioral" and "cognitive" models of decision making, which in turn largely privilege the analysis of common and commonly biased decision making, and of the behaviors to be avoided (Baron 2004; Vermeulen and Curseu 2010). For example, Baron and Shane (2005) give an extensive account of behaviors biasing those behaviors, which are also summarized and extended in the last part of this section. What is typically missing, both in the literature on decision making in general and on entrepreneurial decision making in particular, is an analysis of the "positive" and "strong" heuristics for innovative problem solving, of the logic of economic discovery. This section also offers a repertory of such heuristics for innovation, built on recent research.

Unstructured problems and heuristic decision making

A first relevant distinction of which decision procedure is applicable and superior in a matter is between structured and unstructured problems (Simon 1955). A problem is structured if the sets of relevant alternatives are given, and their consequences, under a set of relevant states of the world, can be evaluated against a utility or performance function. Structured economic problems can be solved by standard expected utility maximizing strategies; that is, by calculating which course of action is (expected to be) superior. The problem of "finding" an opportunity is typically not of this type though, and therefore cannot be typically addressed in this way (Shane 2003). Problems to be solved are not "given" to start with, let alone the possible alternatives. They have to be found. In addition, alternatives that are relevant to conceiving new projects can only be partially searched "in nature". In some entrepreneurial sub-problems – such as "finding a good team member" – they can and should be found. However, for the core problem of finding "a good business idea" they must be searched in imagination rather than in nature. In these conditions, decision makers have to use "heuristics", namely methods for discovering effective action, rather than just procedures for choosing among them (Simon 1955). Entrepreneurial decision making is thus, first and foremost, *heuristic decision making*.

In the following section, an overview of the variety of "*effective heuristics*" that may sustain entrepreneurial discovery is provided. Next, the "dangerous" or "*ineffective heuristics*" that are likely to bias the decision process are examined.

Opportunities as problems

In classic literature on heuristic decision making, problems are defined as "performance gaps" (Simon 1955). In fact, in ongoing, established business activities, problems tend to be defined as "things that do not work", or at least do not perform according to aspirations and expectations.

In entrepreneurial decision making, while some types of opportunities do take the form of "performance gaps", many cannot be reduced to this. As illustrated in section 1.1, opportunities can be separated into two groups. Opportunities of price correction, cost reduction, and missing products and markets – in brief "Kirznerian opportunities" – can be formulated as "performance gap" problems; and in fact the entrepreneurial strategies oriented to capturing them have been called "gap-filling" strategies. By contrast, all "resource-based opportunities" – such as Schumpeterian and Penrosian opportunities – define problems in terms of what the potential uses of resources might be, hence one should think more of "performance potentials" (what else might be done) rather than "performance gaps" (what does not work) (Grandori 2010a). In innovative parts of the economy, opportunities derive more from exploratory and even "uncertainty-seeking" and "trouble-seeking" cognitive processes, rather than from "uncertainty-avoiding" and "trouble-avoiding" processes. In other words, innovation, once seen as stemming from "dissatisfaction" with the current state of things (Cyert and March 1963), can also, and more importantly, stem from the imagination of the world as it might be (Simon 1969; Shackle 1979).

"Problem definition" heuristics differ in the two cases.

- Kirznerian opportunities "wait" to be "recognized". "*Opportunity recognition*" is in fact a frequently used term in entrepreneurial literature, but only recently has it been noted that it applies only to a subtype of opportunity, where the "gaps" to be filled "are there", and the problem is merely to see them (Sarasvathy *et al.* 2003; Vaghely and Julien 2010). The cognitive operation behind opportunity recognition is, as the very word indicates, "pattern recognition" (Simon 1977). Pattern recognition is a mental operation matching observed data with a repertory of models that may represent the observed situation. If it is observed, say, that visits to ethnic restaurants are increasing with respect to international restaurants, a "growing demand" pattern for ethnic food may be recognized as an opportunity. Or, if a problem of curing a new form of flu is given, the search for a suitable drug can be guided by scanning possible formulae and recognizing combinations of elements with higher rather than lower potential of solving the problem – i.e. of filling a gap in therapeutic performance.
- Schumpeterian and Penrosian opportunities are not "there" to be "recognized"; they have to be "generated" through conjectures and tested on the field. Hence, this type of "*opportunity generation*" process rests on a logic of discovery and invention (Shane 2003; Felin and Zenger 2009; Grandori 2010a). The cognitive operations behind effective opportunity generation of this sort are less well understood and analyzed, but knowledge of them is increasing. Some interesting "heuristics for innovation" can be identified by analyzing the "Cases in economic discovery" described in Box 1.4 and are discussed next.

Heuristics for innovation

Box 1.4 Cases in economic discovery

Edison's business plan
Zander (2007) notices how "the inventive genius of Thomas A. Edison coincided with meticulous market analysis in the process of substituting incandescent light with gas illumination in New York City". From the archives it is reported that, in 1878, Edison noted: "I started my usual course of collecting every kind of data about gas; bought all the transactions of the gas engineering societies, etc.; all the back volumes of gas journals. Having obtained all the data and investigated gas-jet distribution in New York by actual observation, I made up my mind that the problem of the subdivision of electric current could be solved and made commercial. Additional efforts included canvassing the district to obtain information on the number of gas

jets burning each hour up to three in the morning, a house-to-house survey provided complete data on exactly how many jets were in each building, the average hours of burning, and the cost of this light to the consumer. Edison collected some 24 books containing gas-light bills of consumers in the district. Eventually, Edison was able to calculate the variable and overhead cost component of gas, which sold for $2.25 per 1000 cubic feet, and was confident that he could get one-half of the lighting business in the district by setting the price of electric-light equivalent to gas at $1.50."

Source: Zander, I. (2007) "Do you see what I mean? An entrepreneurship perspective on the nature and boundaries of the firm"
Journal of Management Studies 44/7

Start-ups as hypotheses: from olive oil to olive water
"I am a chemist by training. I founded five firms in 25 years. I am also fond of natural food and environmentally friendly agriculture. My last firm was actually born thanks also to the cultivation of this side-interest. I was thinking of buying a piece of land in Tuscany to spend some holiday time at, cultivate olive trees and produce extra-virgin high quality oil. In reading and studying about oil production I first discovered that in olden times (even back to the Greeks and Romans), oil was not produced by pressing the entire olive, as is nowadays mostly done, but by pressing only its pulp. Being a chemist, I first gathered evidence that indeed, not only is the juice from pulp sweeter, but that there are harmful components coming from seeds that increase the acidity of oil (which in fact is then treated and sweetened with additional substances). Visiting some farms to see if any had kept some equipment for pressing olives separately from seeds, I made a second discovery. In the process of olive pressing (with or without seeds), the liquid produced is stored to let oil separate from water, and the water is thrown away. My economic and environmentalist mind made me think: What a waste! My scientific and chemist mind made me pose the question: 'Do you know what you are throwing away? Have you ever analyzed this water?' No, they hadn't. The hypothesis coming to my mind was that 'waste water' (actually a costly and problematic disposal problem for the industry) could contain precious chemical components. After all, some of the beneficial substances present in olive oil may well be present in olive water. I had the water analyzed. The answer was yes, olive water was very rich in highly beneficial poliphenol, with tremendous anti-oxidant capacity, found mainly in olives, responsible for most extra-virgin olive oil health benefits, and contained 300–500 times more in olive water. The possibilities of uses were to be defined, but with that anti-oxidant capacity, they couldn't be few. I patented the process and constituted the firm, which extracts the poliphenol, through a proprietary process and technology, and provides it

to pharmaceutical, healthcare, agriculture and food industries and still other application sectors. We also directly produce some dietary products employing the substance."

Source: Grandori, A. (2010) "A rational heuristic model of economic decision making" *Rationality and Society* 22/4: 1–28

"Rational drug discovery" in the pharmaceutical industry

In earlier phases (1950s–1990s), the prevailing approach was "random screening": "natural and chemically derived compounds are randomly screened in test tube experiments and laboratory animals for potential therapeutic activity. Pharmaceutical companies maintaining enormous 'libraries' of chemical compounds added to their collections by searching for new compounds in places such as swamps, streams and soil samples. Thousands, if not tens of thousands, of compounds might be subjected to multiple screenings before researchers honed in on a promising substance" (p. 272).

The more traditional path of starting with a problem and searching for a solution was also common, especially in commissioned research, e.g. "Find me something that will lower blood pressure".

The shift from the "traditional synthetic chemical world" to biotechnology changed effective search strategies, "since it calls for firms to develop a deep understanding of the role of particular proteins in *causing* disease". Two new strategies defined as "rational guided search" or "rational drug design" emerged in response: the first explores the therapeutic properties of a known protein, a "protein in search of a use"; the second "attempts to find a protein that might have a therapeutic effect" for a specified disease.

The authors argue that the adoption of these "rational drug discovery" strategies was one of the main sources of competitive advantage for pharmaceutical firms.

Source: Henderson, R., Orsenigo, L. and Pisano, G.P. (1999) "The pharmaceutical industry and the revolution in molecular biology: Interaction among scientific, institutional, and organizational change" in D.C. Mowery and R.R. Nelson (eds) *Sources of Industrial Leadership*. Cambridge: Cambridge University Press

The design of JAVA

"In 1990, Patrick Naughton, a top programmer at Sun Microsystems told Sun's chief Scott McNealy that he was quitting to join NeXT Computer where he could work on more interesting projects. Convinced by Naughton's contention that Sun was becoming insufficiently innovative, McNealy told Naughton he could have a million dollar budget to put together a small team of outstanding programmers and engineers that would work without corporate interference from Sun. With carte blanche to pursue new projects, Naughton recruited Gosling and a few other top people, and in a hot tub in Lake Tahoe in 1991, they decided to build a prototype of a small device that could control everyday consumer appliances. To control this device, they originally decided to program the device in C++, a popular computer language ... However, for use in consumer appliances, the program needed to be more reliable and simpler than was possible with C++, so Gosling decided to develop a new computer language. The result was initially called "Oak" ... it was a simplified, more reliable adaptation of C++, but its major innovation was in the way it could be used by different kinds of computers ... By August 1992, Naughton, Gosling and their seven-person team had produced a prototype personal digit assistant with a small, touch-operated screen that could control TVs and VCRs, but attempts to sell the device for use in interactive television and computer games failed. Then, in June 1993, the first Mosaic browser was released and the world wide web began to take off. Bill Joy, Sun Microsystems' co-founder realized that Oak could naturally be adapted for use on the internet. By 1995, Gosling had produced a web-suitable version of Oak, now renamed Java, and Naughton had written HotJava, an interpreter for Web browsers. Since then, many thousands of Java applications have been produced and are available on the world wide web."

Source: Thagard, P. and Croft, D. (1999) "Scientific discovery and technological innovation: Ulcers, dinosaurs extinction, and the programming language Java" in L. Magnani, N.J. Nersessian and P. Thagard (eds) *Model-based Reasoning in Scientific Discovery*. Dordrecht: Kluwer Academic Publishers

Various effective heuristics suitable for innovative entrepreneurial decision making, identified in research on innovative problem solving and scientific discovery, are recognizable in the examples in Box 1.4, summarized in Table 1.2.

Table 1.2 Effective heuristics for innovative decision making

1	Systematic 'search' and 'research'
2	'Modeling' and 'theory testing'
3	'Robust action' and 'opportunistic multipurposeness'
4	'Effectuation'
5	'Real option' reasoning

1 Many cases illustrate that in order to construct a good model of the problem at hand, an important basic heuristic is *systematic data gathering and data analysis* (Fiet 2002). The Edison "business plan" case illustrates that systematic research is important in understanding whether a new product idea can become a business. Writing a good business plan is not an accounting exercise. Its fundamental role is the production of evidence that a product or service can be economically sustainable. This is a research question and should be responded to as such, through appropriate enquiring methods – surveys, experiments, documental analyses. Superior observation tools and superior access to information are likely to help in the task (Simon 1977). These may consist of superior technologies for data analysis, such as the software employed to detect the properties of proteins in the "rational drug discovery" case. But they can also be "simple" contacts and access to the private or otherwise not easily observable aspects of people lives as in the Jack Brash case (section 1.1). In this case, the emerging taste for the new among some population segments, and for the "sophisticated old" among others – and therefore the possibility of brokering the trade as an entrepreneurial idea – was possible thanks to the particular web of social ties developed by an entrepreneur of humble origins.

  A further "technique" for generating "ideas" from systematic data analysis is emphasized in product design literature. Systematic sources of opportunities for innovative product development are "contradictions" between two or more elements, such as: "If we want more acceleration, we need a larger engine; but that will increase the cost of the car"; that is, more of something desirable also brings more of something less desirable, or less of something else that is also desirable (Altshuller 1973, 1984).[2] Detecting those contradictions and trying to solve those technical puzzles is an effective heuristic for designing "born useful" missing products.

2 A most recommendable process in new settings, where direct and vicarious experience is not available and would be too slow and costly to accumulate, is *"modeling"* (Bandura 1986) and *"theory testing"* (Grandori 1984; Magnani *et al.* 1999). This "theory-driven" process has been contrasted with experience-based learning, as it would generate alternatives that are less imitative, more innovative and more likely to be valid in the specific and eventually new situation at hand (Felin and Zenger 2009). Modeling refers to the construction of causal models of the situation and the generation of alternatives as possible "causes" of the sought effects, or possible effects of available "causes". A "good heuristic" is thus *"questioning"*: in all research processes, formulating the right questions is of core importance, as much as finding the right answers (Magnani *et al.* 1999). Consider the "olive water" (OW) case. The entrepreneur asked how a hitherto unused (actually junked) material could become a resource usable for some productive activity. The systematic analysis of the material corroborated the hypothesis that olive water was not a waste material but a precious resource (a mine of poliphenoles) usable for pharmaceutical, dietary and cosmetic products.

The OW case also involves a heuristic called *"reframing"*: the "reinterpretation" of the "data" and "observations themselves". In this case an object formerly classified as "waste material" was reinterpreted as a potentially useful resource.

One may wonder, however, where "correct" rather than wrong new "frames", and correct rather than wrong new hypotheses, come from. If they were generated at random, the chances of being right would be very small and the decision process would be very long. The way out is to use available "theory" and construct ad hoc "causal models", eventually with the use of *"analogical reasoning"* (Gavetti and Levinthal 2005). In the OW case, the causal hypothesis that olive water could contain useful substances was not randomly generated. It rested on a logical analogy between oil and water coming from the same source (olives), and constructing a causal model of the possible uses/consequences/applications of the resource (poliphenol).

3   No matter how well grounded and systematically constructed, any hypothesis can always turn out to be wrong. Hence, it is interesting to have the possibility to "modify" and "correct" them, especially if they have entailed some investment.

A first observation is that, in case of difficulty in finding appropriate alternatives – that is, suitable products or processes – it is possible and advisable to *modify either or both the kinds of causes or consequences considered.* This is especially justified if what is under test is not so much the value of consequences, because it would certainly be high, as the way of obtaining them, or if alternatives can be *designed,* rather than "found" in an "environment". A template example of the first case could be that of health care-like problems: in searching for remedies to cancer or AIDS (or to a business crisis or public administration deficit), even if it is difficult to find solutions, it is not rational to lower aspiration levels, it is rational to generate and test a series of other alternatives that differ in kind. In the second case, if the decision maker can design alternatives, they can be designed to produce the desired output, thereby significantly simplifying the task. For example, in the entrepreneurial choice of which product to launch, or which new project to invest in, research can be applied to develop solutions whose stream of consequences can be judged to be superior to other courses of action, and whose worst possible outcomes are compatible with resource constraints (and better than in other options), "no matter what" the state of the world is.

The Java case helps illustrate how to formulate business hypotheses so that they can be more easily modified, thereby reducing the risk of failure. Both the *multifunctionality of resources*, that is, their capacity to generate multiple streams of actions and services, and the *multifunctionality of services and products* themselves can be exploited to this end. The language designed by the Sun engineers was a case of a multifunctional object. The same trait can be identified in the risk prevention device of the Minteos case at the end of this chapter. Hence, multifunctionality can be pursued in the design of products, as a strategy for risk reduction and opportunity enlargement.

Multifunctionality is all the more pronounced at the level of resources, as in the case of the competence of engineers. The multifunctionality of resources and objects can be systematically exploited to devise "robust action"': actions that are likely to generate positive consequences from the perspective of different actors (users, clients) (Padgett and Ansell 1993) and under a broad range of circumstances (different environmental states, different uses) (Padgett and MacLean 2006; Grandori 2010a).

In sum, two further heuristics for innovation may be defined as:

- *"robustness"* heuristic – the search for a robust course of action, which may have positive consequences under a very broad range of situations;
- *"multipurposeness"* heuristic – the willingness to actually change either or both the kinds of causes or consequences considered; that is, either the purpose and destination of products or the kind of product and service to satisfy a particular purpose; the awareness that trying to solve one problem may actually lead to solving a different problem (Campbell 1960).

4   The logic of robust action and multipurposeness implies defining problems in terms of *"resources in search use"* and *"means in search of ends",* in addition to the more traditional decision logic of finding means to a pre-defined end, or of finding resources for a specified use. This logic has been studied, modelized and applied to entrepreneurship as a logic of search for possible effects (*"effectuation"*) rather than of search for possible causes ("causation") (Sarasvasthy 2001).[3] The evolution of innovation strategies in the pharmaceutical industry illustrates how the new approach called "rational drug discovery", based on logics such as "proteins in search of a use" or "compounds in search of a therapeutic effect", is more flexible, more efficient in discovery and offers more protection from downside risk. Of course, this approach is not meant to substitute problem solving whenever there are specific problems to be solved. Entrepreneurship can come about as a response to well-defined problems. The point is that this is not the whole story. The imagination of new opportunities can be nurtured by logics that differ, and are somewhat reversed, from that of solving a given problem.

5   *Real option reasoning* is another way of proceeding and testing the validity of projects under uncertainty (McGrath 1999). This approach was developed in analogy with the notion of financial options, that is, the acquisition of a right (to buy, to invest further), after seeing what the conditions turn out to be, rather than investing directly by trying to foresee the future. The logic, transferred to the realm of non-financial or "real" investments, becomes an incremental logic of sequential investments, in which further investment or withdrawal decisions are taken based on success/failure information. As examples of this strategy are not present in the preceding boxes, consider the following case in Box 1.5 that describes how the logic can be applied to new project selection. This case refers to decisions on which projects to invest in within a firm, but could be applied to the decision on which projects in the sense of new firms to invest in. That investment process is in fact highly

"staged" and "sequential". Typically, investments occur in "rounds" or phases: "seed" investment, "first-round financing", "second-round financing", etc. This practice arguably embodies real option reasoning since initial investments are relatively small, but grants the "option" to further invest if the project is demonstrated as successful.

Box 1.5 Project selection in a real option approach

ALFA is a large microelectronics firm. Its approach to investments in new ventures is inspired by a real option approach. ALFA continuously holds a portfolio of projects, all staged in the following way:

1   If an opportunity is diagnosed, one or two people are asked to investigate the new idea.
2   If results are positive, a team is assembled, a unit is dedicated to it and pilot studies and market tests are run.
3   If results are positive, the technology is verified and eventually partners are sought.
4   If results are positive, financial and non-financial commitments are made to actually start the venture.

On a standing portfolio of around 40 projects passing from stage 1 to stage 2, around one-third do not enter stage 3, and another third do not enter stage 4. As a result, the firm selects its actual portfolio of new ventures through contingent option reasoning.

Source: summary of a case described in Keil, T., McGrath, R.G. and Tukiainen, T. (2005) "Real option reasoning and the management of uncertain ventures: an exploratory analysis" Working paper, Helsinki University

---

In sum, it may be worthwhile noting that the definition of entrepreneurial ventures typically implies more than the classically highlighted "*adaptation*" to market and technological trends and changes. Whatever the trend, there are many possible responses, and for any response, new functions may turn out to fit with other, or new, environmental features. This type of "creative adaptation" also occurs at the natural level (i.e. it can occur even without intention and cognition) and was termed "*exaptation*" as contrasted with adaptation. A classic example is that of bird plumage, initially "adapted" to the need for warmth but thereafter "discovered" (through natural selection) to have the even more interesting function of allowing flight. Innovation can, and typically does, leverage on "exaptation" and is not bound to "adaptation" (Villani *et al.* 2008). Therefore, in *entrepreneurship the possibility of exaptation rather than the need for adaptation should always be kept in mind.* The JAVA case (Box 1.4) illustrates how exaptation has worked to allow the new language, initially developed to adapt to the consumer appliance niche, to take off as adapted to the internet. Another more complex case of exaptation sustaining the development of an innovative project is described in Box 1.6: the development of the famous "Millennium Park" in Chicago.

Box 1.6 The "Millennium Park"
Santi Furnari, 2010

Millennium Park is a multi-awarded, $475 million total, innovative urban park completed in 2004 in Chicago. The interesting organizational aspect of Millennium Park is the process through which the innovative design of this park emerged, totally unexpected, from a much more traditional design envisioned in the earlier stages of the design process. The park design was initially conceived as a classic *beaux-arts* garden in continuity with Chicago's local aesthetic repertoires, but in the end it turned into the outdoor art museum of today, emphasizing global avant-garde architecture, interactive monumental sculpture, and contemporary landscape designs.

A longitudinal case study of the design process of this project has shown that this radical design change was triggered by *aesthetic exaptation events*: instances in which the aesthetic features previously envisioned for a design function had been re-functionalized for a new design function. In the context of the case, an aesthetic feature is represented by the aesthetic repertoires and design styles used by an architect or artist. For example, the aesthetic repertoires defined by architect Frank Gehry (aesthetic feature) were initially selected for the design of a sculpture on a music band-shell to be located in the park (design function at origin) and later used for the design of a larger and more complex performing arts pavilion (new design function).

The case study shows that exaptation events can be produced by the combination of two basic types of cognitive processes. The first is a process of establishing relations among different sub-problem domains. In the context of the case, the sub-problem domains are represented by the different "topics" into which the project team divided the larger task of developing the design of the park (e.g. the "problem" of the project). Specifically, the team identified three sub-problems or topics: (1) selecting garden landscape designs; (2) selecting artworks; (3) finding the private funds to support the selected designs. Although each of these sub-problems was assigned to a different specialized committee, crucial brokers between these committees envisioned and made new connections among them. For example, they engaged in analyzing the artworks selected in one committee, in the context of the garden landscapes selected in another committee, and discussing these different topics together. In turn, this process of establishing new connections among formerly disconnected sub-problems gave rise to new interdependencies among the aesthetic features selected for the park design. These unexpected interdependencies constitute an important antecedent to the exaptation of these features.

The second set of cognitive processes leading to exaptation consists in the reinterpretation of the relationships connecting the parts that had been combined together. This reinterpretation is described as a process of *re-framing* or *changing the perspective* – for example, the representation of the overall problem itself – from which the relations among the parts are perceived and evaluated. The project team of Millennium Park interpreted the interactions among the aesthetic features via visual maps and models projecting the overall design of the park. In these maps and models, each aesthetic feature was applied to different geographical areas of the park, bounded and separated among them by walking paths. These walking paths were used by members of the project team as *visual interfaces* to interpret the relations and interactions among the aesthetic features. Specifically, by visually manipulating the maps and by experimenting with the existing paths, the team was able to imagine and draw *new lines* connecting the areas of the park. Through this process, the team perceived and started discussing new connections among aesthetic features and design functions, thereby discovering new functions for aesthetic features that had been previously selected for different purposes.

Overall, the case study shows that in design, like in biology, innovation-by-exaptation can be usefully contrasted to innovation-by-adaptation. Adaptation assumes that features of products, services and other artifacts (including organizational artifacts) are selected according to which perform better in a given function. In contrast, exaptation involves the selection of features on the basis of their performance in *new* functions, different from the function for which the feature was originally designed or selected.

> Source: Furnari, S. (2009) "Mechanisms of aesthetic exaptation in architecture: how a beaux-arts garden evolved into an avant-garde art park", paper presented at the XXV EGOS Colloquium, July 2–4, Barcelona, Spain
> (winner of the EGOS 2009 Best Dissertation Paper Award)

Heuristics for innovative interdependent decisions

If relations are such an important source of opportunities, then being able to manage them matters. Entrepreneurial decision making is almost never a one-actor exercise and nor should it be. But decision making with others entails its own distinctive difficulties, especially if it is to be "innovative". "Others" are likely to hold other "views" and, more often than not, also other "interests".

As already observed, *different views* are more an asset than a liability. Actually, they are fundamental in providing new frames, generating creative hypotheses and reducing the likelihood of mistakes. To make this happen, the "others" should not only be "convinced" but should also be listened to. It is well known that a key way of sustaining the quality and innovativeness of solutions in uncertain and unstructured problems is to connect multiple information inputs, to discuss and criticize hypotheses, and to use multiple frames and perspectives. Although counter-intuitive for many, and somehow in contrast with the mystique of the entrepreneur as a visionary leader, a very well-established organizational law asserts that the more complex and unstructured the problem is, the more joint decision making pays off. In fact, in these situations it is less likely that all the relevant knowledge for solving it is concentrated in one person, no matter how "visionary" he/she is. This organizational and cognitive law suggests that the notion of the entrepreneur as a "leader", in the sense of knowing where to go and convincing others to "follow", should be greatly de-emphasized. As no lesser than Sir Karl Popper (1989) took pains to illustrate, the logic of discovery is the same everywhere, in business and in science, and no one can purport to know any truth or "right way to go" without experiments, criticisms and discussions. *Consultation*, up to *joint decision making*, among free participants with differentiated complementary competences is therefore a valuable social and cognitive heuristic.

One may wonder, though, whether there are not dark sides to this "decentralized" and "open" approach. In fact there are. With particular reference to entre-preneurship, some of the classic liabilities of group decision making are weaker while others are stronger.

The *risk of "groupthink"* is pronounced, especially between the entrepreneur and his/her close collaborators: collective enthusiasm, group pressure, strong leadership and excessively homogeneous views can lead to undertaking dangerous actions without sufficient scrutiny. The antidotes are known: encourage the expression of different opinions and judgments, avoid forming highly homogeneous teams, understand that leadership in complex tasks should be more oriented to designing a proper information and decision structure than to instructing on what to do.

The risk of "free-riding", in the sense of letting others contribute while reducing one's own effort, is likely to be lower in innovative tasks. The core reason can be expressed in a simple way by stating that if one does not participate, one does not learn. In other words, "effort" (activity, participation) is the very source of the learning benefit rather than a cost. Motivational factors are likely to reinforce this effect. In fact, the motivation to join entrepreneurial ventures is often intrinsic (people love the project/task or the profession or the co-workers/the team) (Baron and Kreps 1999). Thus, free riding in the classic sense of people trying to reduce effort may not be substantial. On the other side, free riding in the sense of a *risk of knowledge expropriation* is a paramount problem. Even among partners of an entrepreneurial team, there may be a risk of subtraction of know-how and contacts, let alone in relations between entrepreneurs and external partners. Some self-correcting mechanisms for the first problem are based on games of reciprocity:

everybody exposes themselves by sharing knowledge; have incentives to do so (if they do not contribute, they do not learn); and the shared resources act as pledges (everybody is a hostage of everybody else). This equilibrium may be fragile though. It should thus be acknowledged that entrepreneurial decision making does not typically involve only "problem solving" and "joint decision making" among parties with different ideas (as is frequently stressed) but also, and frequently, involves "conflict solving" and joint decision making among parties with different interests; that is, negotiating.

The "art and science" of negotiation (Raiffa 1982), as much as of group problem solving, is not very different for entrepreneurs than for any other actor. Therefore, let us mention some basic concepts and tools of particular relevance to entrepreneurial interactive decisions and which are necessary to understand and solve the entrepreneurial problems of attracting resources and forming alliances in later chapters. In order to introduce the issue and to highlight the main shift in decision-making procedures that interdependent decisions should bring about, consider the basic entrepreneurial problems of whether or not to enter a new market or to launch a new product as described in Box 1.7.

Box 1.7 To start or not to start? – that is the question

Suppose that you are considering entering a new market with a new product, but that you have also identified some potential competitors (e.g. firms already present in the market, or likely to respond by developing competing products). Suppose that the situation can be stylized as follows:

- If you do not enter, you remain with your status quo (you neither gain nor lose, i.e. the worth is zero).
- If you enter and there is a permissive competitive response, you estimate your net gain to be $10K in the coming year ($20K income minus $10K investment); but if you enter and there is a strong competitive response, the costs of investment would not be recovered and you end up losing your investment plus the time and cost of the operation, say $12K. What would you do? Entering may seem unattractive.

However, the problem is not well framed. Essential information is missing. Suppose that for your competitor (assuming there is only one for simplicity) the decision looks like this:

- If you do not enter, he gains his regular $20K per year.

- If you enter and he does not respond or responds permissively, he loses $10K due to lost sales; if he responds – with a price war or a product differentiation race – he can reduce his losses to half, but sustains costs of action for a further $6K.

What would you do now? Your decision may be reversed, as, in fact, your competitor has no incentive to compete.

First, the fundamental information that was not considered in the first analysis (wrongly) was *the problem as seen by the counterparties.* To analyze decision problems from the point of view of other interdependent parties is a sort of first commandment in interactive decision making. Hence, in any situation with two or more parties and potential conflict, a useful starting exercise is to fill out a *negotiation grid or portfolio* (Bazerman and Lewicki 1983):

- What are the relevant matters for each party?
- What are the gains or losses of each party if they get more or less of a certain item?

The core process in negotiations is in fact about finding exchanges of matters among the parties that increase everybody's utility. For example, if you as an entrepreneur greatly value the rights to decide in the firm more than, say, the rights to dividends, while a financial investor has the opposite preferences, it would be more efficient for you to retain the CEO position and the right to choose collaborators, and for the investor to acquire more protected shares, rather than the other way around.

Second, as much as decision making in well-defined problems is different from decision making in innovative problems, *negotiation oriented to creating value (expanding the pie) is different from negotiation oriented to dividing given resources (dividing the pie).* At the outset, the surplus from collaboration (the "pie") is entirely to be constructed. Hence, negotiation on whether and how to pool resources with which partner, and which project to pursue, should be framed in a highly integrative (win–win) way. In other words, given that at the beginning all routes are open – that is, it is possible to change partners, products and types of agreements – the focus should be to find solutions from which all can benefit. The time for (more) distributive games will come later on when the shaping of organizational structures and inter-firm contracts is on the table: who owns what and how much, what share of the surplus created will go to whom, who shall have the last word on unforeseeable issues that unfold. But even at this time and in these matters, as we shall see, the effective contractual and proprietary structures diffused in the governance of entrepreneurial ventures are most often constructed on the allocation of various resources and rights to those who value them most, rather than their mere division.

Biasing heuristics

While the notion of heuristics as "methods for discovery" thus far employed focuses on logically sound, even "rational" processes, there is another class of heuristics, much more analyzed in cognitive psychology (Kahneman *et al.* 1982) and thereafter in management and entrepreneurship (Shane 2003; Baron and Shane 2005). These heuristics are predominantly oriented to saving cognitive effort and reducing the costs of search, rather than to properly investing in research. Due to their "search shortcuts" characteristic, these heuristics may lead to dangerous "biases", especially in innovative decision making under uncertainty, that is a core field for entrepreneurship. These patterns of behavior can therefore be considered as mainly negative in the context of entrepreneurship and prospective entrepreneurs are better advised to avoid them (Baron and Shane 2005). Heuristics that are particularly relevant and dangerous in entrepreneurial decision making and negotiation are the following (some of them can be detected in the end-chapter case "The Body Shop").

"Satisficing" and the "sour grapes" bias

"Satisficing" (Simon 1955) is a widely applied decision-making procedure employed to solve problems that are too vast to be completely mapped in order to select an optimal solution. The templates of these problems are "finding a good move in the game of chess" or "finding a good needle in a haystack". The decision procedure consists in setting an "aspiration level" that defines what an "acceptable" rather than an "optimal" solution would be – for example, a needle "sharp enough to sew with".

Although this heuristic may be suited to the haystack-like and chess game-like problems, actually it is dangerous in entrepreneurial decision making, for which more effective and ambitious heuristics are available, as has been shown in the former paragraph.

The "satisficing heuristics" is inadequate for innovative decision making for various reasons. First, it implies that what is sought is known to the point that a precise "aspiration level" for expected payoffs for evaluating alternative moves is set, which is not realistic in entrepreneurial and innovative decisions. Second, it implies that if alternatives are "difficult to find", then the aspiration level is lowered. This is a particularly ineffective heuristic in innovative problem solving. The implied fallacy or "bias" is called a "sour grapes fallacy" (Elster 1985):[4] inferring that what was sought was not desirable from the difficulty in finding it. By contrast, effective innovators are typically "persistent" in trying to achieve results deemed desirable (e.g. inventing an electric engine for automobiles, or finding a cure for a new disease), in spite of the difficulties in finding solutions (Simon 1977). If they had concluded too quickly that electric cars were not attainable/desirable (lowering the aspiration level), we would still only have petrol cars.

The dangers of satisficing in negotiation are even more obvious. To accept a counterparty's proposals just because they are superior to our acceptability threshold is a strategy that no one would recommend. Rather, it is recommended to go to a negotiation having set ambitious goals, actually with hypotheses on the "maximum" one thinks could be achieved, in addition to the minimum one is willing to accept (Thompson 2008).

Availability and the "local search" bias

People tend to consider easily available information rather than relevant information. Most available information tends to consist, for a number of reasons (see Tversky and Kahneman 1974; Bazerman 1986), of anecdotal and case-based information rather than structural and systematic data. Using an availability heuristic in entrepreneurial decision making, for example, would mean becoming enthusiastic about a project based on having observed a few cases of similar projects that succeeded. The neglect of basic structural trends (e.g. demographic trend, societal and cultural transformations, technological advances) is the other face of the coin, which may lead to betting on a product or service – say fast food – where and when the industry is actually saturated and much better opportunities may lie in "slow food".

"Local search" biases are strictly linked to the use of availability heuristics, trapping people in search of alternative products or structures that are too similar to formerly employed solutions and in imitative "benchmarking" with comparable actors, or in search of partners who are too close and similar.

The "escalation of commitment" and opportunity costs

Once a course of action has been initiated, people easily fall into sunk cost errors and do not revise the course of action in which they initially invested in the face of new information on the unsatisfactory results of the action. This is a rather significant danger, not only as applied to technical and economic investments and project selection (escalation in investment in a product or "business plan" in spite of negative signals), but also as applied to relational investments and partner selection (escalation in collaboration with a particular partner, just because the relationship has begun, thereby neglecting potentially better partners). Behind the escalation of commitment, there is not only a sunk cost fallacy, but also a perceived need to be "right" and an unwillingness to accept mistakes. Thus, the intensity of this bias does not only depend on individual cognition but also on the system in which entrepreneurs operate. The commitment trap is reinforced if partners, banks and financial institutions, and business culture and institutions punish any "error" as a sign of weakness rather than admitting that no error means no trial and accepting a certain failure rate.

"Self-confirmation" and "over-confidence"

People tend to be too certain that things will go in certain ways, especially if they have taken some steps along the way, overconfident in their judgments and even more so in projects that they have conceived in person. Among the roots of this phenomenon, beyond plain wishful thinking, and self-serving biasies, there are well-known inference mistakes (Nisbett and Ross 1980). In particular, decision makers tend to look at and search for confirmatory evidence that their ideas and theories are correct, rather than trying to find objections, things that may go wrong and to design proper experiments and tests. As a result, they tend to over-estimate the probability of being right. Entrepreneurs are no exception. Actually, they are likely to be particularly prone to be overconfident in their ideas. This "optimism" may be quite self-deceptive and lead to "excessive entry" and/or escalation in projects and investments which are not worthwhile (Baron and Shane 2005; Camerer and Lovallo 1999). At times this tendency toward "optimism" has been praised as a source of risk-taking capacity and a factor that facilitates the start-up of a new business and agreements with business partners (if a person is "sure" of succeeding they require fewer guarantees). However, it is hardly justifiable on rational grounds to recommend "wishful thinking" and overconfidence to prospective entrepreneurs. Entrepreneurial overconfidence stems from "optical illusions" such as the "illusion of control" (people think they have an influence over events, and can "cause" successes and escape failures far beyond what is statistically justifiable) (Nisbett and Ross 1980). Hence, for an entrepreneur it would be more recommendable to be "robust" and "multipurposed" so as to increase the actual chances of success, rather than to be "optimistic", that is, to see prospects of success where there are not many. In addition, if entrepreneurs have to convince others, particularly financial capital providers, to invest in their projects, reliable estimates and well-calibrated probability assessments are more likely to be persuasive than sheer enthusiasm.

The "fixed pie" myopia

A common bias in the perception of negotiations is that what one party wins the other must lose. As widely stressed in the negotiation field (Thompson 2008), this is actually a particular type of negotiation called "distributive negotiation" and typically involves one type of resource only, in fixed total amount, to be divided. The template situation is a buyer–seller negotiation over price. However, most negotiations can be defined so that they are not strictly distributive; hence to see them all as distributive is called a "fixed pie" myopia. Even in a buyer–seller relation, if other matters are introduced, such as services and assistance, delivery time, quality requirement, etc., space is created to improve the transacted package so that each party gets what it most values ("integrative negotiation"). Given the abundance of unstructured problems in entrepreneurial decision making, it is important to see negotiations not only as a problem of division and distribution of given resources, but mostly as a problem of finding technical and economic solutions, and of resource exchanges that "enlarge the pie", especially in the early stages.

Key points

Content-wise, the sources of entrepreneurial opportunities can reside in any aspect of reality – new technologies, customers' preferences, demographic changes, competitors' moves and so on. Hence, rather than listing possible contents (as is mostly done), opportunities and their sources are here classified and analyzed in ways that make a difference as to how recognize or build them.

A first partition is between *"Kirznerian" opportunities* on one side and *"Schumpeterian" (and "Penrosian") opportunities* on the other. Opportunities of the first type reside in *"gaps" that can be filled* and *"disequilibria" that can be "corrected"* by entrepreneurial action. Opportunities of the second type are generated by the "imagination of the world as it might be": hypotheses on new services and uses that may derive from resources, as they are or in new combinations. Entrepreneurial action capturing and exploiting this second type of opportunities *"creates disequilibria"* rather than correcting them. The structural features of markets and resources are therefore important in determining to what extent an environment or industry is rich in opportunities – for example, highly competitive and close to perfect markets versus markets and industries rich in "holes" and "gaps"; highly specialized versus more generalist resources. Therefore we refer to those sources of opportunities as "structural sources" (section 1.1).

Looking at resources and markets only would, however, miss a second important source of opportunities, namely *"relationships"*. Being "networked" is always an important asset, but in entrepreneurship and innovation it is indispensable and, in addition, can be justified in terms of innovation capacity (rather than mere power), as a fundamental enabler for both the definition and the exploitation of opportunities. The distinctive contributions to entrepreneurship of different types of ties (e.g. strong and weak ties), and different brokerage strategies are discussed.

Finally, acts of cognition are necessary for transforming any "gap" or "potential" in an opportunity. *Opportunities need to be "recognized", "discovered" or "created".* A variety of decision heuristics are reviewed and assessed in terms of their effectiveness in sustaining those processes. In addition to the (commonly stressed) *"biasing" heuristics* to be avoided, the analysis offers a repertory of *"effective heuristics for innovation"*, built on recent research on innovative and entrepreneurial decision processes.

Analysis questions

On in-chapter cases

- The successful entrepreneurial initiatives of JB leveraged on various economic sources of opportunities (analyzed in the text). What were the relational sources exploited?
- The cases on entrepreneurial discovery in Box 1.4 are discussed in the text in terms of cognitive processes for opportunity discovery. What structural sources of opportunity did they discover?

On end-chapter case

- Anita Roddick constructed her entrepreneurial adventure on meager resources. Where did opportunities come from? From which sources?
- How do the strengths and weaknesses of relational and cognitive strategies contribute to understanding the lights and shadows of the experience?
- Which future problems can be anticipated considering how the relationship with internal collaborators and the negotiations with external partners (franchisees) have been "managed"?

End-chapter case: "The Body Shop"

Laura Gaillard, 2010

Body Shop International PLC, known as "The Body Shop", is a global manufacturer and retailer of natural and ethical cosmetics products. Founded in the UK in 1976, The Body Shop (TBS) now has over 5,900 employees. With 2,400 stores in 61 countries, it is one of the largest cosmetics franchises in the world.[5] It also sells its products online and via The Body Shop at Home. L'Oréal has owned TBS since 2006. Dame Anita Roddick (1942–2007), founder of TBS, was a human rights activist and an entrepreneur; she is known for having said about entrepreneurship that "The new entrepreneur is a social-change agent more than a businessperson: making a difference is more important than making a fortune."[6]

Background

In the early 1970s, the interest in environmental issues was gradually taking on a political character and the first Green parties began to pop up around the world. The Green movement incorporated many of the values of the counterculture and the new social movements of the 1960s (ecologist, feminist, advancement of civil rights, anti-war movements, gay liberation), including the hippie culture that transcended national boundaries and gave rise to an alternative global awareness. Since the mid-1960s, London was the centre for worldwide youth culture where new cultural trends emerged. In the 1970s, a generation of outsiders was searching for "the next big thing". It is in these fluctuant times, with a mindset of these emerging values, that Anita Roddick started The Body Shop in 1976.

Anita Lucia Perilli was the child of an Italian immigrant couple living in a small English town. She says she was a natural *outsider*, and was drawn to other outsiders and rebels. Her first political and moral instincts were awakened as a teenager: "What I felt then was a deep, emotional aversion to suffering, death, aggression."[7] When she was young, she worked in Paris and in Geneva – where for a period she joined the Women's Rights Dept. of the International Labor Organization (ILO), based at the UN – and traveled throughout the South Pacific and Africa.[8] Politically active, she demonstrated against the bomb, campaigned for nuclear disarmament and was expelled from South Africa for being in a black club. On returning home during the 1960s, Anita met Gordon Roddick in her mother's bar, El Cubana. He shared her love for travel. Soon Anita and Gordon were a couple and after the birth of their first daughter, Justine, they took the "hippie trail"; they got married in Reno in 1970. With the birth of their second daughter, Samantha, in 1971, they felt they had to settle down. When they returned to Littlehampton, they opened first a restaurant, then an eight-room bed and breakfast. In their restaurant, the political slogans of the day were posted on a blackboard. Gordon and Anita were interested in politics although they did not support any major political parties. They soon felt overworked and needed a change of direction: "Nobody works as hard as somebody running a restaurant … I have never been so tired in my life!"[9] Anita's husband wanted to fulfill a lifelong dream of riding a horse from Buenos Aires to New York. With his wife's approval, Gordon went off and Anita was left to support herself and her two children.

"A series of brilliant accidents"[10]

It was simply out of the necessity to create a livelihood for herself and her two daughters that she decided to open a little shop. She wanted to escape the pressure of the restaurant and she wanted "a nice, easy, controllable nine-to-five, pick-up-the-kids-from-school existence".[11] The original concept of The Body Shop came from her experiences with women of other cultures matured during her travels and also from the dissatisfaction of not being able to find the products she wanted in normal cosmetics stores "that dissatisfaction gave me the energy to set it up".[12]

She found a shop in a pedestrian precinct in Brighton, West Sussex, which was richer and trendier than Littlehampton. To open her shop she needed £4,000, not easy to obtain from a Barclay's bank manager: "probably because I was dressed way too casually for him, while my two kids were destroying his office". Anita says she kept repeating: "I got this great idea and it's going to be called *The Body Shop* and I have all these knowledgeable ingredients from wise women around the world."[13] She used the B&B as collateral, eventually got the £4,000 and opened up her little shop in Brighton in March 1976. It was named after a small botanical personal care product shop she had noticed while visiting friends in California.[14] Europe was going "green" and green was "the only color that we could find to cover the damp, moldy walls" of the first Body Shop. "On the first day I was in trouble, because my shop was between two funeral parlors and they didn't like … the words *"The Body Shop"* … then I did something very smart." Anita had the idea of calling the local newspapers to tell a somewhat inflated story of her life. Newspapers took the bait and published the story, which resulted in free and very effective publicity.

> The original Body Shop was a series of brilliant accidents. It had a great smell, it had a funky name. It was incredibly sensuous. It was 1976, the year of the heat wave, so there was a lot of flesh around. We recycled everything, not because we were environmentally friendly, but because we didn't have enough bottles. It was a good idea. What was unique about it, with no intent

at all, no marketing, was that it translated across cultures, across geographical barriers and social structures.[15]

"Business as unusual"[16]

When she started The Body Shop (TBS) in Brighton, Roddick had no training or experience: "Nobody talks of entrepreneurship as survival, but that's exactly what it is and what nurtures creative thinking."[17] She had an obsession: getting £300 per week to live. Some weeks the figure fell short of the required £300, so she opened on Sundays. She was the sole employee and did everything from formulating products to running the store. Roddick concocted cosmetics from "every little ingredient with a story" (jojoba oil, rhassoul mud, etc.) and the stories were handed to the customers (on recycled paper) together with leaflets about social causes. Roddick did everything to draw attention to her business: in the evenings, she went to talk to institutions; the windows of the TBS store featured posters for charity and community events; she even sprayed pleasant fruit scents in the street to lead customers to her door. Her products and new approach to business appealed to a new generation of consumers; she subsequently developed a loyal clientele and the store proved successful. She took on a helper on Saturdays, her friend Aidre. Six months after the opening of the first shop, Roddick wanted to open another one in Chichester. But the bank rejected a second loan of £4,000. Aidre's boyfriend, Ian McGlinn, was a garage owner and had some spare cash, and Anita knew him from the restaurant business. He lent her the money to open the second shop in return for a half share of TBS.[18] At that time TBS products were homemade and the packaging was minimal (cheap urine-sample bottles!). Roddick turned to a small manufacturer: Mark Constantine[19] was 22, and was, he says, "a bit of a hippy with some herbal products that had been rejected as honest but uncommercial wherever I went".[20] Eager to expand, Anita drew up a list of 25 products using ingredients that were readily available and Mark became her main supplier. At the beginning "The Henna Cream Shampoo looked and smelled like horse s**t."[21] They then improved, working as a small team to select better ingredients and doing tests on staff volunteers. Later she wrote: "my journey was constantly experimental. I made mistakes constantly."[22]

"Growing without knowing"

On her husband's return in 1977, he joined the business and took charge of the administrative and financial aspects. They wanted to expand further but they had no spare money and the banks were not interested in lending it to them. They were approached by a friend's (Max Bygraves) daughter, Chris, who said she was interested in opening her own Body Shop in Hove. This was agreed on the understanding that it would still be called "The Body Shop" and Anita and Gordon would supply all the products. Though there was no formal contract or fees, this was the first TBS franchise. Gordon called it *"Self Financing"* but he could see this was the way they could expand. Aidre married Ian McGlinn and they opened another TBS store. When the two franchises in nearby towns both succeeded, the Roddicks began receiving calls from other people interested in TBS and the first series of franchises began operating: "We didn't even know the word 'franchising' existed and my friends were saying: you can't do this, I can do this … we just had friends, and sold [our products] to them, we had this alliance of friends." Anita and Gordon accumulated sufficient funds to open a further shop for themselves in Reading. The first franchises were given to friends with no contract, no start-up charges, and no royalty fees: "and then we got a bit more professional". The franchisee paid "a pittance" (legal fees, a basic amount for stocks and they were granted a free period without royalties) to open a store and afterwards "made out famously". "Other people wanted to have a shop like ours, and we wanted to sell our product in them."[23] That was it. By 1978, a kiosk in Brussels became the first overseas franchise. The next, in 1979, was for the whole of Canada: Margot Fransen paid nothing in 1979 for the franchise rights (then her boyfriend joined her, they operated nine stores and ten years later had sold sub-franchise rights for 52 franchise stores in Canada). Once TBS opened in London's Covent Garden, the media started to take notice. From then on Anita described herself as becoming "Ms MegaMouth" and enjoyed promoting the business via chat shows on television and radio – all free advertising. She became an inspiration to women striving to set up and grow their own stores.

"Profit with principles"

TBS was not only a product-oriented company: "we had great products … otherwise we would have soon closed down, but our thing was about campaigning human rights". From inception, TBS did far more than sell environmentally friendly products: they also acted as "billboards"[24] to create awareness of societal injustices in the world. Anita Roddick was known for her charisma, she was a central character and her inputs were a core strength for the company. She campaigned for green issues many years before it became fashionable to do so: "I'd rather promote human rights, environmental concerns … than promote bubble bath." Roddick wanted TBS to be a company that changed the way business was carried out. Today, TBS's Mission Statement still opens with the commitment, "To dedicate our business to the pursuit of social and environmental change. We use our stores and our products to help communicate human rights and environmental issues." TBS was from its inception committed to being an environmentally responsible retailer, and this is still applied through TBS's business activities. For instance, the principle of minimizing waste and resource use through minimal packaging and use of recycled materials applies to all business units owned by TBS (2006). The company was one of the first firms in the world to campaign against animal testing for its cosmetic products. From the earliest years, TBS promoted self-esteem as one of its values, challenging "unrealistic beauty". Defending human rights was another core value of the company and still is.[25]

The key area where business and Anita's personal interests combined was through TBS community trade initiatives:

> It all started in 1989 when I attended the gathering at Altamira of Amazonian Indian tribes protesting against a hydro-electric project which would have flooded thousands of acres of rainforest, submerging native lands. There had to be something practical I could do to help these people preserve their environment and culture. Nuts? Specifically brazil nuts, which the Indians gathered sustainably from the forest and which when crushed produce a brilliant oil for moisturizing and conditioning.

After this first trading relationship with forest people, Anita traveled every year to a number of TBS projects and met long-term partners in southern India, in Nepal, the Chepang indigenous people, sesame seed oil farmers in Nicaragua, etc.

John Sauven, the executive director of Greenpeace who worked with Anita on many campaigns, said, "she was an amazing inspiration to those around her … She was so ahead of the time when it came to issues of how business could be done in different ways … She was a true pioneer."[26] Roddick was also a pioneer when she formed alliances with major international NGOs: in 1985 she helped create awareness of the charity Greenpeace and the following year raised awareness of the Greenpeace project "Save the Whale". Since then Anita's company has supported other causes such as Amnesty International, Friends of the Earth, Shelter and CND. In 1990, she also created the charity Children on the Edge, which helps children in Eastern Europe and Asia.

"A Revolution in Kindness"[27]

Anita Roddick used to say, "If you think you're too small to have an impact, try going to bed with a mosquito in the room." Roddick made cosmetics fun, sexy and affordable, and there was always a message. Instead of "Buy this mascara, it will change your life", her message was, "Buy this mascara, it could change someone else's life".[28] She never advertised her stores, and she never relied on a marketing department. The flagship stores represented the company's major communication tool. From its inception, TBS relied on store activity and window displays rather than advertising. Roddick used to regularly visit the regional head franchisees and the stores. She kept tight control of the "packaging" of the stores (window displays, sales style, layout, literature) and she had a PR staff, writers and graphic designers. She also maintained informal relationships with employees and encouraged suggestions, ideas and "eccentricity". She understood from the beginning that the media were instrumental in the success of TBS; she recognized the importance of publicity but made a point of getting it free. TBS has traditionally relied upon its campaign activities to generate publicity and generate commitment from its employees and franchisees. Roddick constantly worked at communication outside and within the company. Anita's daughter Justine says: "Our family home had a never-ending revolving door through which came people from all walks of life, people who Mum encountered and connected with." In fact, she helped build the business ecosystem which incubated not just her own business but a bunch of other ventures. In 1989, Gordon and Anita created the TBS Film Company to finance the production of a ten-part television series to be broadcast in 1991 (*Millennium: Tribal wisdom and the modern world*). They owned 80 percent of Jacaranda Production Ltd for the production of videos. They also had an in-house video production company, which produced a monthly video magazine, training tapes and documentaries: "we do whatever we must to preserve that sense of being different. Otherwise, the time will come when everyone who works for us will say TBS is just like every other company."[29]

Notes

1 The arguments of two leading organizational sociologists are combined here: the point that innovation benefits from blending exploitation and exploration strategies (March 1991) and the more structural observation that weak ties are good for opening new roads, while strong ties are good due to their supportive capacity (Granovetter 1983, 1985).
2 This is known as the TRIZ methodology. It was developed by Genrich Altshuller, a Soviet engineer and researcher, in 1946 and is used by many companies around the world, such as BAE Systems, CSC, Procter & Gamble, Ford Motor Company, Boeing, Philips Semiconductors, Samsung, LG Electronics.
3 The implications of this strategy should not be overstated though, as is often the case. "Effectuation" does not increase "control" over exogenous factors, and should not be contrasted with "causation" in the sense that it provides exemption from causal judgments. It just involves "reading" causal relations forward rather than backward.
4 After Aesop's tale of the "the fox and the grapes": a fox sees an attractive grape in a vineyard. He jumps, but does not reach it. He jumps again and again. Having found it difficult to get to the grape, the fox not only renounces his meal but concludes that the grape was sour.
5 Second after Brazil's O'Boticario.
6 Anita Roddick (2000) *Business as Unusual: The Triumph of Anita Roddick*, London: Thorsons.
7 www.anitaroddick.com.
8 www.thebodyshop.com/en/ww/services/aboutus_history.aspx.
9 www.anitaroddick.com.
10 *Third Way* magazine, interview of Anita Roddick, 1993.
11 "Reflections on Success, Part I", posted on September 9, 2003 by Anita, www.anitaroddick.com/readmore.php?sid=154.
12 Ibid.
13 Anita Roddick (1991) *Body and Soul: Profits with Principles*, New York: Crown.
14 Body Time, the original Body Shop, opened in 1970 by sisters-in-law Peggy Short and Jane Saunders. In 1987, they sold their name, The Body Shop, to the English company (www.bodytime.com/body-time-history.html).
15 *Third Way* magazine, interview of Anita Roddick, 1993.
16 Anita Roddick, *Business As Unusual*.
17 Idem.
18 When the company was floated on the stock market in 1984, Ian Bentham McGlinn was worth some £4 million. He was and has always been a sleeping partner of TBS. McGlinn's 22 percent stake in The Body Shop was worth £137m when it was taken

over by the French giant L'Oréal in 2006. The Scot was also an investor in the Hotel du Vin chain, which was sold in 2004 for £66m.

19   Mark Constantine is the co-founder and managing director of cosmetics group Lush. He was a long-time business associate of Anita Roddick and one of TBS's largest suppliers, until TBS bought out the rights of his products in 1995.
20   "Anita Roddick inspired a generation recalls Mark Constantine Lush founder" *Telegraph*, September 12, 2007.
21   Idem.
22   "Further Thoughts on Stepping Down", posted on February 18, 2002 by Anita, www.anitaroddick.com/readmore.php?sid = 34.
23   www.anitaroddick.com.
24   A large outdoor advertising structure.
25   The Body Shop, Values&Campaigns, 2010.
26   Anita Roddick orbituary, *Guardian*, September 10, 2007.
27   Anita Roddick (ed.) (2003) *A Revolution In Kindness*, Anita Roddick Books.
28   "Anita Roddick. The Queen of Green" *Time*, September 11, 2007.
29   www.anitaroddick.com.

2 Entrepreneurial resources

Access problems and networked solutions

There are no real options on opportunities without resources.

As argued in Chapter 1, opportunities cannot even be seen without competences – a fundamental human resource – let alone be exploited. In addition, opportunities are infinite, and the selection of an opportunity that is suitable for one particular actor stems largely from matching possible opportunities with the actor's resources. Social ties and connections are also an important type of resource to a large extent of a human kind (constructed and owned by persons) which enables seeing and exploiting opportunities.

Hence, the first types of resources that are central to entrepreneurship are *human resources*. They are often referred to as the *human and social "capital"* contributed to new ventures, in addition to the more classical forms of capital, namely technical assets and financial resources in search of productive uses. The first section reviews the fundamental problems involved in attracting and retaining the investments of these three types of resources in a new venture. The nature of these "problems" to a large extent explains why networks are so central in granting access to relevant resources and why property rights are central in attracting and retaining resource investments. Hence, understanding these problems enables the proper governing of the processes of resource attraction and resource assembling.

---

[*] Text by Anna Grandori, cases by the authors indicated in boxes.

2.1 Entrepreneurial resource attraction: barriers and problems

Human capital and the "inalienability" problem

A resource is any stock of tangible or intangible, natural or artificial objects capable of generating services and activities (Penrose 1959). A forest or a piece of land are not resources when only considered as a landscape; they are resources if used for producing wood or wheat. Hence, a resource is such if it has some use. As is known though, the "use value" is not the same as the economic or "exchange value" of something. Air is a very useful resource, but it has very little economic value. The economic value of a resource depends on the possibility of accumulation, exchange and investment, and dedication to productive uses that generate economic value. If those processes are possible, then a resource may be defined as an "asset" or a form of "capital". Money per se is not capital, although it is always a resource. It becomes capital if it can be dedicated and invested in activities with economic value, which in turn accrue to the initial investment.

Human resources are considered a form of capital because they can be accumulated and dedicated to economically valuable uses (Becker 1964). According to Becker, who in turn revisits and makes use of earlier classic economists, human capital is distinguished by the particular types of resources compounding it. The argument is that, while the traditional focus in economics has been on material assets, such as machinery and natural resources, the growth prospects of modern economies derive predominantly from the growth in human assets. These assets have various components: personal attributes (including physical energy and health); competence and abilities; and knowledge (Becker 2002).

In entrepreneurship-related literature, human capital (HC thereof) has received special attention. It is in fact generally acknowledged that the HC endowment of the entrepreneur is: (1) the type of asset he/she distinctively provides to a new venture; and (2) it is empirically correlated to the growth or profitability of the entrepreneurial firm built on them (Colombo and Grilli 2005; Davidsson and Honing 2003; Hsu 2007; Shane and Stuart 2002).

Studies on HC have also singled out different components in it, entailing different modes of application, different degrees of "transferability" and therefore different roles in the birth and growth of entrepreneurial ventures. They include:

- *formal education* – measurable as the titles achieved – as distinct from *"expertise"* – the body of competences acquired on the field, through learning by doing, and through observation of other actors' experiences;
- *explicit knowledge* – notions, ideas, methods and know-how that can be communicated to others – as distinct from *"tacit knowledge"* – what one knows beyond what can be communicated;
- *personal capabilities*, with *physical and psychic* (energy, health) capabilities distinct from *"intellectual capital"* – for example, cognitive and relational skills and intellectual resources;

- the *networks of relationships*, or *"social capital"* of people from their individual attributes.

It has been generally observed that in entrepreneurial settings, and in particular in knowledge-intensive and innovative ventures: (1) the *"intellectual" components* of HC are particularly important (Petty and Guthrie 2000); (2) important *components* of human and social capital are likely to be "specific" to the venture and the firm eventually constituted (i.e. they have higher value in that use than in possible alternative uses) (Lepak and Snell 1999); and (3) important *components* of H&SC are likely to be *"tacit" and non-separable from people* (Teece 1982; Nahapiet and Ghoshal 1998).

Building on the basic tenets available in organizational economics on those issues, the core implication of those analyses has been that the tacitness and venture specificity of HC are major reasons for establishing strong and long-lasting links between people holding that type of HC and the entity in which it is deployed (e.g. the new firm constituted).

We can observe that those analyses all together provide some *basic reasons why entrepreneurial firms exist* – if the entrepreneurial firm is defined (see Chapter 1) as a firm characterized by high involvement of human capital providers in ownership and direction.

On the other side, those analyses of HC also created a "puzzle" for understanding the nature of entrepreneurial firms, to the extent that human and social capital are conceived as assets that are not only "made of" human resources, but are also "non separable" from the person. In the economic analyses of the issue, this view has become even a definitional feature of HC: human capital has the special property of being "inalienable", non-saleable, non-contractible. HC can be accumulated and dedicated to productive uses, but it necessarily remains the "property" of a physical person. And persons cannot be "invested" in an economic activity. They can always leave.

This view creates quite a puzzle for understanding entrepreneurship. If not separable from people, human capital would not be really "investible" in any firm or venture. The problem then arises of how a firm can "lock-in" human capital, if it cannot own it (Hart and Moore 1990, 1994) and how entrepreneurial firms, largely relying on human assets, can be governed or can exist at all (Rajan and Zingales 2000). As these last authors have observed, if HC is "firm-specific", incentives to leave would be low. However, this is a very particular situation: some entrepreneurs contribute knowledge and competence which often is, or "becomes" after some time, usefully turned to other opportunities (Gimeno *et al.* 1997; Kaplan and Strömberg 2003). In other terms, entrepreneurs, intended as people, do often leave.

The problem behind this problem is the equation between people and human capital. People are inalienable, and they are not capital: they are physical and juridical persons, entitled to own various types of resources, among which are their energy, knowledge and ideas. Not all these human resources, not all the components of HC listed above, are equally inseparable from the person: *physical energy, personal skills and tacit know-how are not separable from the person; but ideas, explicit knowledge and know-how, contacts and information are separable* (Grandori 2010b). Actually, they are so separable to be often exposed to expropriation risks and to create intellectual property rights protection issues, on which a wide literature is in fact flourishing. Significant parts of knowledge assets are different from human capital that is strictly embodied in the physical person. Knowledge, ideas, contacts and know-how can be transferred and therefore can also be "invested". Actually, a "pure" entrepreneur, investing only human capital (knowledge, an idea or project) in a firm, whereas other actors invest money, would demand and in exchange would typically obtain ownership shares in the firm. In conclusion, *investments of human capital into new firms* – as distinct entities with respect to the person of the entrepreneur – *are possible*[1] and this very fact contributes to fully answer the question of why entrepreneurial firms exist and how they can be governed – the topic of Chapter 3.

Technical assets and the "appropriability" problem

Property rights over *technical assets* are not easily definable in innovative settings either. In times and sectors where technical assets are physical goods, equipment and plants for which a market exists, they can simply be bought, and the issue is reduced to gaining access to financial resources. However, technical assets that are relevant for entrepreneurship and innovation are increasingly intangible, immaterial, intellectual and composed of knowledge rather than of things. The definition and protection of property on knowledge assets is notoriously difficult though. In fact, in this domain, property is considered a matter of "degree" rather than a clear-cut provision: technology can be more or less "appropriable" (Ouchi and Bolton 1988).

Aspects that influence the degree of *appropriability* of a technology are:

- the extent to which it is composed of *patentable* equipment or know-how, or of non-patentable knowledge;
- the extent to which the knowledge involved has the feature of a *"public good"* (cannot be protected from outsider access);
- the extent to which the knowledge to be used involves highly specialized and sophisticated research so that it can be more effectively found or produced in *organizations specialized in research* – that is, universities and research centers;
- the extent to which the technology requires complementary human know-how that is embodied in people – in which case technology has limited appropriability because of its *links with inalienable human capital*;
- the extent to which the success of products based on the technology depends on the availability of *complementary resources* stemming from other sources (e.g. particular raw materials or equipment; particular distribution structures; technological infrastructures).

Hence, the construction of a pool of "dedicated" assets is problematic not only for human but also for technical assets in innovative ventures.

Uncertainty and financial investment evaluation problems

There are fundamental judgmental problems in the evaluation of investments in new ventures. The prospective entrepreneur faces the problem of finding and selecting holders of complementary human resources and attracting investments of complementary financial or technical assets. Conversely, these co-investors face the problem of how to evaluate and choose entrepreneurial projects and entrepreneurial teams – against each other and against alternative allocations of their resources.

These judgments and choices, in the case of new initiatives, entail two fundamental problems.

The first problem is *uncertainty on project results*. New ventures are always hypotheses and always involve a test, albeit varying in uncertainty. The more ideas are new – new products and services, new technologies, new markets – the less their success can be predicted. Myriad contingencies that cannot be foreseen at the outset may intervene. Even the precise features of the final product, let alone the research and production activities to be conducted, can only be hypothesized ex-ante, but it is almost certain that technical and commercial problem solving will change them. In other words, the assessment of projects or plans is very difficult.

A possible response to this difficulty is a shift from "*betting on projects*" to "*betting on resources*". In fact, in practice, a hot debate and dilemma among financial investors is whether to "bet on the jockey or the horse"; that is, on the team or on the plan (Kaplan and Strömberg 2009). In theory, judging resources rather than future activities that may stem from them does have advantages (cf. Chapter 1, robustness and effectuation heuristics). In fact, as has already been observed in respect of selection in entrepreneurial contexts, knowledge of people – their potentiality and reliability – is more important and somehow easier to achieve than knowledge of activities (Knight 1921). It is like saying, "With such excellent resources something good will certainly turn out, although we do not know exactly what."

However, knowledge of people is not easy either. Although proficiency, degrees and experience are good signals, in uncertain situations a second class of problems of *asymmetric information and moral hazard on resource quality* emerges. People (usually, though not always) know their own qualities better than external evaluators, and if they are interested in attracting investments on them they have an incentive to overstate their value. The value itself is difficult to assess; actually the more people possess unique and rare resources (an attractive feature), the less their value can be measured (because they cannot be compared with others).

Assessing the quality and potential of technical assets may also be difficult if they include new technologies and inventions. How many technical problems may emerge in its application? Will potential users accept it? Will negative unexpected effects emerge?

Is there a way out of this dilemma? Actually, there are various ways.

First, there is no need to choose between jockeys and horses. Both are relevant, and, actually, not only these. Staying with the horsemanship analogy, the "race-track" is also relevant. Empirical evidence, both qualitative and survey-based, both in Europe and the US, indicates that investors in new ventures in fact systematically consider four key factors: *team, market, technology/product and finance* (Clarysse *et al.* 2007; Kaplan *et al.* 2009), although the relative weight may vary according to sectors and type of investor.

Second, "people" are different from "human resources". As highlighted previously, people may leave (sometimes considered a reason for not betting on them). However, the human and social capital they invested in a new firm, the competences and know-how they have transferred and that have become embodied in the organization (rather than in them) are bound to remain, both *de facto* and *de jure*. Hence, a second solution is *betting on competences and resources, especially of the investible kind, rather than on "people"*, *tout court* (Grandori 2010b).

Third, "projects" are different from "sectors, technologies or business areas". Any evaluation grid employed by associations or public entities to evaluate business plans include as key factors not only the quality of prospective products/services, and the quality of human resources, but also the attractiveness/expansion of the market and the promise of technologies and sectors. Hence, *betting on a field* – actually on *"resources in a field" capable of generating a stream of projects* – *is better than betting on a specific project*.

Fourth, entrepreneurship is not the only case where the quality of agents, techniques and products/services is difficult to evaluate. For example, difficulty in evaluation is common in professional services – doctors, lawyers, consultants, etc. The issue has already been considered in general terms (e.g. Karpik 1989) and the organization of entrepreneurship can learn from the solutions found. That standard markets do not work well where there are information asymmetries and evaluation difficulties is well known. This is often the case in labor markets and in knowledge markets. The classic solution to these external market failures has been to use "internal markets", exploiting fuller information on the quality of human and technical assets (Williamson 1975). Internal labor markets – that is, selecting, promoting, staffing projects or otherwise moving human resources "within" an organization – and internal capital markets, that is, allocating technical and financial assets to projects or divisions within firms – are supposed to overcome the basic evaluation difficulties and information asymmetries.

The internal market option, however, has at least two significant drawbacks in entrepreneurial settings. First, it is at odds with innovation capacity in that it restricts the recombination of resources to those already available in the firm. Second, and even more significantly, the internal option is just not available in the case of new firms. There is no internal market to use because there is no firm yet.

What could the *solutions* be when "neither markets nor hierarchies" work? The nature of all solutions can be captured by one word (Karpik 1989; Powell 1990; Jones *et al.* 1997): *networks* work.

2.2 Networked human resources

Human resources (HR) are critical in entrepreneurship, but "access" to them is by no means easy. Information on their location and quality is quite difficult to obtain.

A standard response to these problems in labor markets is to integrate them with "brokers" and intermediaries who link labor supply and demand.

Research results in fact consistently indicate that the formation of partnerships and access to core human resources in new firms are largely governed by professional and personal networks, rather than by open markets or even by standard intermediaries (head hunters, staff agencies) (Bagdadli *et al.* 2003). In the cited research (on the top teams of Italian firms listed in the New Market, 164 people), for example, in a question proposing a list of eight possible channels of access, 56.9 percent of subjects ticked the single channel represented by all types of professional and personal networks. Data from this and other studies indicate that different contexts may differ in the type of network used, but networks are always important. For example, in situations, activities or regions that are wealthier in common associations, circles, educational institutions, technological poles and parks, etc., the ties formed in institutionalized networks are more important.

The main explanation of these patterns is that past professional collaborators, former co-workers and study mates, or even personal friends, *know* a lot about the true level of competence and reliability. That is the main reason why, in early stages of venture development, *access to human resources is effectively governed by social and professional networks, rather than by standard labor market and human capital market institutions and intermediaries.*

If these are the reasons and advantages of networked HR, there are also *dark sides* and disadvantages in the use of networks. The main problem, especially as far as innovation is concerned, is the *restriction of access.* Personal contacts are not generated by a systematic search but are dependent on personal history. Relying on them can generate opportunity costs for the prospected entrepreneur (the best partners may be outside of the network) and can generate unequal opportunities for outsiders (who are not networked enough). In addition, networks may be misused: rather than leveraging on them to evaluate competences, they may be used to privilege the incompetent, simply because they are a friend or family member.

Some antidotes are available to limit these possible pathologies of networked HR. First, *professional networks* are more likely to be based on competence and less prone to working as "clans" based on favors with respect to merely *social networks* (Grandori 2001a). Second, *professional network brokers* may facilitate the formation of collaborations in more systematic, competence-based and open ways. Players of this sort include associations and dedicated entities (agencies, firms):

- Institutional, publicly supported associations and foundations – such as incubators, poles and parks – support the development of new entrepreneurial firms by facilitating contacts and contracts among the providers of the different key resources (knowledge, financial investments, management expertise, relations with markets, etc.) (cf. Chapter 6, Section 6.3).

- Professional associations of early stage investors provide screening services of business plans for new ventures, and organize sessions of presentations of projects and teams to investors, thereby facilitating the value-adding matching process (cf. Box 2.8 on the European Business Angel Network).
- Firms and entities specialized in technological brokerage have emerged. Their very "business idea" is the brokerage among different types of knowledge (scientific, productive, managerial) and "intelligent money" providers specific to a sector. The Itaca Nova case (Box 2.1) illustrates this emerging type of brokerage activity.

Box 2.1 Itaca Nova
Franco Fattorini, CEO Itaca Nova

Successful companies in the coatings field rely mostly on their research in development capabilities, focused on new product launch leveraging both on internal know-how and on technology of their suppliers, and occasionally involving selected research centers and partnering entities in new technologies scouting.

An effective approach to new technologies is a critical issue for all such companies, and to establish good relationships with the academic world is fundamental. However, both firms and research institutions are experiencing how difficult it is to establish communication channels and working teams between the "manufacturing" community and the "research" community, in both directions; namely, for the company it is difficult to assess the potential of new technological opportunities, and for the research community it is difficult to deploy their potential through an understanding of the needs of the company; that is, to deliver practical solutions.

Since the 2000s, coatings companies were also facing new technological challenges, such as the emerging opportunities coming from "green chemistry" materials, nanotechnology-based formulations, and advanced performances polymers.

How to effectively face those challenges and capture those opportunities?

The key issue was to establish an operational bridge between the firms' technical community (e.g. their development laboratories) and the external technological community (e.g. universities and research centers), in order to attract key people, either scientists or technologists, to work together; to bring together financial skills and research competences to handle critical research projects; to build multi-competence teams, being most of the cases based on very extended clusters of different resources and capabilities – technological, administrative, financial and behavioral.

This was the "humus" on which grew up the idea of a new entity, filling the "space" between the company world and the scientific and technological communities, to bring together the required resources. The new entity was a firm in itself – "Itaca Nova" – devoted to that type of brokerage and consultancy service.

Itaca Nova srl (limited liability company) was founded in 2006. Its shareholders include a business angel and a technologist (a top industrial consultant and a professor in a leading Italian university). The "company concept" proved to be very effective, and despite the difficult environment, Itaca Nova progressively grew, to become today an established "brand" in the field of "green chemistry" materials, nanotechnology-based formulations, and advanced performances polymers; moreover, it is a leading company in the field of technological ventures. Today, it offers a broad portfolio of services, including research project management, laboratory analysis, management tools and "venturing" assistance.

Its most significant contribution to entrepreneurship is the capability to bring together very different resources, and to find out feasible and effective "formula" to start up business from innovative technology. In other words, its distinctive contribution is to help inventors walk the last mile to become an entrepreneur, finding out practical solutions to critical issues such as project financing (e.g. to design the right mix of the different available financial tools – seed capital and venture capital, equity and loans, etc.), and identifying proper approaches to intangible assets (e.g. Intellectual Property Rights). In this context, a specific venture could require or could attract a direct involvement, even a direct investment, by Itaca Nova, in the "coached" start-up. A good example of a technology-based start-up supported by Itaca Nova is "Nano Active Film" (Box 2.4).

Entrepreneurial teams

There is another way in which human resources for entrepreneurship are networked. They often "come in teams". Where human resources are complex and difficult to evaluate in terms of competence or reliability, networking *among them* also has a reassurance function toward third parties – in particular toward clients (Karpik 1989) and toward financial resource providers (Varian 1990). In other words, the fact that people, who know each other well, are willing to bet on each other and to jointly put their human capital at risk is a signal to other actors that the commitment is credible and worthy. The discovery of this mechanism can be ascribed to a professor-entrepreneur, who, thanks to this, has been able to develop entrepreneurship in the most difficult situations where, in addition to all the informational problems highlighted, poverty and the lack of any collateral or guarantee was blocking economic development. The Grameen Bank experience of Bangladesh is briefly described in Box 2.2.

Box 2.2 Grameen Bank
Laura Gaillard and Anna Grandori, 2010

The Grameen Bank (Bengali: গ্রামীণ ব্যাংক) is a microfinance organization and community development bank founded in Bangladesh by Muhammad Yunus that makes small loans (known as microcredit or "grameencredit") to the impoverished without requiring collateral.

Yunus was born in 1940 to a successful Muslim jeweler family in Chittagong, then a part of colonial India. While teaching at a local college in the early 1960s, he noticed the need for a packaging plant in eastern Pakistan and established one with the help of his father and a loan from the state. In 1965, Yunus left to study at the University of Colorado and Vanderbilt University under a Fulbright Scholarship. While teaching at Middle Tennessee State University in 1971, the War of Liberation broke out in eastern Pakistan, and Yunus lobbied for the Bengali cause in Washington, DC.

Yunus returned home to the newly formed country of Bangladesh in 1972. Soon he was heading the economics department at Chittagong University. While there, the plight of the poor in the nearby village of Jobra distressed Yunus greatly as famine enveloped the country. With the help of his students, he surveyed the economic situation of the villagers and organized a project to plant higher yielding varieties of rice. Such agrarian reforms required some financial and political finesse and stirred up considerable controversy. Yunus developed a distrust of governmental and non-governmental aid programs whose funds, usually due to greed or infighting somewhere along the line, simply did not reach the society's very poorest members.

These people, Yunus found, existed in a cycle of debt, at the mercy of moneylenders charging 10 percent interest a week and usurious traders. A person would borrow money for raw materials, work all day, and then sell their handiwork back to the trader for a profit of only 2 cents. In 1976, Yunus had one of his students tally a list of villagers trapped in such situations. She came up with 42 names, who together needed less than US$27.00 to break out of the cycle and set up in business for themselves. Yunus loaned them the money himself.

The professor's attempts to get traditional banks to lend to poor people who had no collateral met with solid resistance. However, he was able to arrange for such a loan from the Janata Bank after months of wrangling and signing himself as guarantor. With this money, the Grameen Project (literally, "of the village") was launched in January 1977. The "project" became the Grameen Bank in 1983.

Yunus then set out to develop a lending methodology that would work for clients with little collateral. Rather than have a large lump sum payment at the end of the loan period, he structured the loans with minuscule daily payments in order to detect problems early and to increase borrowers' confidence. This was soon changed to weekly payments to reduce the accounting load. The loan term was set at one year.

The most important and unique feature was the "group-based" credit. Individual entrepreneurs would cluster in groups of five, in line for similar credit. The concession of loans to the members of the group was made contingent on the repayment capacity of others. More precisely, two members could apply first, if they repaid the next two got financed, then the fifth (Varian 1990). In this way, all the members would be collectively responsible for each individual's loan. The "group" acted as collateral. Besides peer pressure, the groups were also a source of mutual financial support in case of difficulty.

The result has been astonishing. Grameen was able to grant 475,000 loans per month in the late 1980s with a repayment rate in excess of 97 percent. Five percent of each loan went into a group fund that served as a kind of insurance. Without a legal instrument between Grameen Bank and its borrowers, the system is based entirely on this mutual guarantee mechanism.

Grameen Bank currently lends more than $500 million a year; its Group Savings Funds have assets of $186 million, operating 1,100 branches in half of Bangladesh's nearly 80,000 villages. The program has been successfully replicated in dozens of developing countries. It has also been applied in inner cities and rural poverty areas in rich nations in North America and Europe.

Yunus served as managing director, but the bank is owned by the borrowers. Of the total equity of the bank, the borrowers own 94 percent, and the government of Bangladesh owns the remaining 6 percent. The bank grew significantly between 2003 and 2007. As of October 2007, the total borrowers of the bank number 7.34 million (and 97 percent of those are women) and the bank has a staff of over 24,703 employees and 2,468 branches covering 80,257 villages.

Nowadays, the Grameen Foundation supports microfinance institutions in the following regions: Asia-Pacific – Bangladesh, China, East Timor, Indonesia, India, Pakistan, Philippines, Saudi Arabia; Americas – Bolivia, Dominican Republic, El Salvador, Haiti, Honduras, Mexico, Peru, US; Africa – Cameroon, Egypt, Ethiopia, Ghana, Lebanon, Morocco, Nigeria, Rwanda, Tunisia, Uganda, Yemen.

In 2006, Muhammad Yunus received the Nobel Peace Prize for the invention of microcredit.

The *guarantee function* illustrated above is one of the reasons why *entrepreneurs tend to come in teams*. This function is particularly important when uncertainty on the prospects of activities and the likelihood of repayment is high. This may be due to scarcity of resources and/or established effective industrial norms, as in the case of microcredit in developing countries. Project uncertainty and the difficulty of judging competence can also be very high in highly developed contexts though, and actually in the more advanced sectors it is all the more so. It is in fact in the knowledge-intensive economy that the one-man-show entrepreneur of traditional small firms has tended to disappear. Research has shown that entrepreneurs able to assemble a team (Baron and Shane 2005), and to do so by using their own network of relationships (Hsu 2007), are more likely to attract financial investments.

There are other important reasons, beyond the highlighted mutual guarantee and competence evaluation function, why it is effective to form an entrepreneurial team, especially in knowledge-intensive ventures.

First, it is unlikely that a single person can master all the *complementary competences* relevant for conducting a new activity, especially if the new activity stems from the combinations of resources in new ways, that is, in the case of capturing Schumpeterian opportunities. If competencies are critical, that is, the activity cannot be realized without them, the providers of these resources have coalition power and should demand some rights over the output. On the other hand, it is also in the interest of the other parties – that is, the focal entrepreneur or the investors of financial capital – to secure and lock-in those critical competencies in the new venture. Hence, a partnership among entrepreneurs is likely to emerge.

Second, *teamwork* is a well-known organizational requirement for high-quality, creative problem solving, provided that the requisite variety of inputs is present (cf. Section 1.3; Katznbach and Smith 1993). As a corollary, a desirable feature of an entrepreneurial team is that it be composed by *diverse complementary profiles, rather than by homogeneous people*. One should then take care to contrast the well-known psychological tendency of clustering with the similar (Baron and Shane 2005). A typical case in start-ups would be that of people who shared the same studies, even the same schools, or the same previous working experience, grouping together to start a new venture. Although there are advantages in cohesion and understanding, this team composition is likely to fall short of the requisite adaptation and problem-solving capacity. Hence, in team formation, an "*innovation paradox*" is faced (Wilkins and Ouchi 1983): the features of a team that favor decision efficiency, social control and trustworthiness are at odds with creativity, innovation and decision quality. Which should be favored? Or how can the dilemma otherwise be solved?

A solution is to treat the issue as a trade-off and find an optimal intermediate point; for example, not too much similarity nor too much diversity, an "optimal cognitive distance" (Nooteboom 1999). One may further refine this reasoning by considering that the "optimal" degree of diversity should be larger in innovative settings than in known and stable situations, as in the former case the benefits of multiple inputs are larger.

A better solution, though, is conceivable. It consists of avoiding the trade-off by devising "hybrid" or "ambidextrous" arrangements that achieve both things simultaneously; that is, both homogeneity and diversity in the same group. The history of the birth and development of Virgin (Box 2.3) is suggestive of how this can be realized.

Box 2.3 The Virgin team
Laura Gaillard, 2010

Richard Branson was born in 1950; he started from scratch when he was 15 years old and with only a high-school education built himself an international business empire.

Virgin has created over 300 branded companies worldwide, employing approximately 50,000 people in 29 countries. Global branded revenues in 2009 exceeded £11.5 billion (approx. US$18 billion). The Virgin Group has expanded into leisure, travel, tourism, mobile, broadband, TV, radio, music festivals, finance and health. Some of the businesses Branson has collected include: Virgin Atlantic, the international airline which is now the biggest company of the group; Virgin Megastores; Virgin Books; Virgin Credit Card; Virgin Direct and Virgin Direct Personal Finance; Virgin Holidays; Virgin Trains; V2 Music, the largest UK-based independent record label; Virgin Active, a chain of fitness clubs; Virgin Galactic, the flight to space venture; Ulusaba, a luxury game reserve located in South Africa; Necker Island, Branson's own private island. Through the Virgin Green Fund, Virgin is investing in renewable energy and resource efficiency. Virgin Unite is the Virgin not-for-profit entrepreneurial foundation that focuses on entrepreneurial approaches to social and environmental issues.

From a crypt to a manor
Richard (Ricky) Branson was an entrepreneur from a young age: he was 11 and "he wanted to help his family"; with his best friend Nik Powell they tried to grow pine trees for Christmas (unfortunately eaten by rabbits); then to breed and sell parrots, not a success. He was 15 and in high school when he set up *Student* magazine with Johnathan "Jonny" Holland Gems, a school mate. In 1970 "Virgin" was born out of a community of 20 young people – "a mixture of incredible characters"[2] – living in a basement in London (they called it "the crypt"; it was actually under a church in Bayswater), working on the *Student* magazine and a Student Advisory Center (later HELP!): "We were very poor, remembers Branson, but a really strong team. We loved working together."[3] They each got £20 per week. When Jonny was forced to return to school, Branson brought in his childhood friend Nik. Nik did not study as an accountant but he was an excellent manager, keen on savings. While Richard was bringing Virgin forward with "grandiose visions and energy", Nik made sure the operations ran smoothly. Soon Branson understood that it is the combination of talent that makes things work: "Throughout my life, I've always needed somebody as a counterbalance, to compensate for my weaknesses and to work off my strengths"(Branson 1998). Finding partners has become the theme of all Virgin ventures; it has indeed turned into an integral part of its new-venture formation process.

Virgin started as the Virgin Mail Order Record Company. Branson and Nik shared respectively 60 percent and 40 percent of the new venture. When a postal strike crushed the activity, they responded by opening a small discount record shop in Oxford Street, London. Branson brought in his cousin Simon Draper. Simon was "music obsessed ... he spent his nights in jazz clubs in South Africa ... he knew about music more than anybody else" (Branson 1998). Richard admitted he was too busy dealing with sponsors and printers to have time to learn anything about music. Simon's musical tastes soon became the keystone for the development of Virgin Records. In 1972, Virgin opened 14 stores in England; they were a new brand of discount record shops inspired by the atmosphere of "the crypt". In 1973, relatives and friends contributed the start-up capital to buy "The Manor" and built a recording studio in Oxfordshire. The first Virgin artist, Mike Oldfield, recorded *Tubular Bells* there; it stayed in the UK music charts for 247 weeks. In 1977, Virgin signed the Sex Pistols, then went on to sign many household names from Culture Club to the Rolling Stones, helping to make Virgin Music one of the top six record companies in the world.

In 1977, Virgin had a PBT of £500,000. From the outside, the company looked like a heterogeneous set of different activities. For each, Branson relied heavily on a core group of close friends: Simon Draper and Ken Berry, who performed as an intricate and effective team (until in 1992 Virgin Music was sold to Thorn EMI for £510 million), and Nik who managed the record shop chain until 1980. "We can trust each other," Branson says. "They know I won't let them down, and vice versa. It's almost like a marriage." And Virgin Vision's manager Robert Devereux, who joined the company in 1981, was married to one of Branson's sisters: "Virgin is a family business, not a classic one ... it is a 'vertical' one, I have always worked with family members." It was also by relying on friends that Virgin started developing internationally: Ken in New York, Patrick (Zelnick, founder of Virgin France) and Udo in Germany. But the financial situation was very fragile; in 1980, Virgin lost £900,000, and Nik left the company: "There's something about teams," said Branson, "they don't last for ever ... like a cast in a theatrical play" (Branson 2009).

Managing as unusual

Branson was restless and continued to seek new opportunities; after some failures, he understood the absolute necessity of separating the different activities of Virgin. In the meantime, thanks to the success of Culture Club, Virgin sales reached £94 million in 1983, with a PBT of £11 million. Then more than ever, Branson wanted to use the Virgin brand to diversify his activities. In 1984, Branson was receptive when a young lawyer named Randolph Fields called him to ask for help in financing a start-up that was miles away from Virgin's core business. Fields wanted to open an international airline. In June 1984, Virgin Atlantic took off, flying to all sorts of glamorous locations. Not space though. That came later.

Virgin is an unusual group of companies and Branson has an unusual management style. He says he realized simply that he had to promote the airline and applied himself to the effort as he would to any other project. This is why since 1985 he has been getting his adrenaline rushes through boat and hot air balloon world-record-breaking attempts. Several distance and speed records have been attempted and achieved. Branson makes each record attempt a media event with his Virgin logo prominently displayed during every launch, which has been an excellent source of free advertising and brand placement for the Virgin Group.

The public thinks of Virgin and sees one man. Behind the scenes, the reality is different: "It is never a one-man job" (Branson 2009).

Branson the showman symbolizes Virgin's high profile. But Branson the manager keeps it lean and responsive through delegation of power. Virgin companies are part of a network rather than a hierarchy. They are empowered to run their own affairs, yet the companies help one another, and solutions to problems come from all kinds of sources. Hence, Virgin companies are independent but are also a community with shared ideas, values, interests and goals. Virgin relies on an unrivalled network of friends, contacts and partners.[4] The approach is to hire bright people, and give them a stake in the ventures so that they are motivated to be even more successful. Branson focuses his time more on the end-user experience, doing publicity and promoting his products, while his staff often take care of the daily operations of a company. According to Branson, you must have the ability to know when to back away from a task: "As much as you need a strong personality to build a business from scratch, you must also understand the art of delegation," he says. "I have to be good at helping people run the individual businesses, and I have to be willing to step back. The company must be set up so it can continue without me." Clearly, this means Branson has to pick people who can handle the responsibility: "His ability to hire the right people to take him to the next stage of development has been nothing short of extraordinary," says Peter Hilliar, analyst in London.

New ventures are often steered by people seconded from other parts of Virgin, who bring with them the trademark management style, skills and experience. Virgin Bride, Britain's largest bridal emporium, is a persuasive illustration. A first-line employee buttonholed the chairman and got permission to start this new business. Virgin companies are of two kinds: a wholly owned subsidiary or one in which Virgin is a partner. Into the first category fall the airline and megastores, into the second the insurance and drinks businesses.

Expanding without growing

"When a company gets to a certain size, instead of letting it grow bigger and bigger and bigger and putting it into bigger and bigger offices, I will take, say, the assistant marketing manager, the assistant managing director, the assistant sales manager, and I'll say, 'Right, you're now the marketing manager, the managing director, the sales manager of a new company'." Typically, Branson will be heavily involved in the idea for a new venture. Once the new business has been launched, usually in a blaze of publicity with Branson at its heart, he will leave it to a handpicked deputy. The only one of his operations where he has maintained a close executive role is the one dearest to his heart, the airline.

"The public perceive it as a company but more and more we act like branded venture capitalists." Even the businesses Virgin does not wholly own are managed by trusted Branson lieutenants. Just because Branson is not the majority shareholder does not mean he will allow the operation to be run by someone he does not personally know, and has vetted and appointed. Originally the team working with Branson was his childhood friend Nik Powell, then Robert Devereux, Branson's brother-in-law, Simon Draper, his cousin and first business partner, Don Cruickshank, who took Virgin public, and Trevor Abbott, Virgin's first financial controller, they have now gone or, in the case of Devereux, their influence has diminished. Hired originally as Branson's press spokesman, Will Whitehorn's role has evolved over the years; he is now effectively the number two at Virgin, and no major decision is taken without his involvement. Branson hired Brad Rosser in 1994 as Virgin's corporate development head. Effectively the group's new business manager, Rosser is charged with maintaining Virgin's relentless quest for new ventures. Rosser is one of the handful of senior executives capable of taking an overview of the whole Virgin Group. He defines his role as "identifying new opportunities and when selected, to implement them". By "implement", he says he means, "source funds and possible partners, find a management team and take a non-executive directorship". Rosser sits on the boards of several Virgin subsidiaries, ranging from fashion to bridal wear to helicopters to the London Broncos, the Rugby League team owned by Branson. All this and yet Rosser is still only 34. Another partner is McCarthy: a mixture of business partner, best friend and soul mate for Branson.

Branson is often criticized for his management style – or lack thereof. He holds no regular board meetings, has no business headquarters, and has no idea how to operate a computer. He keeps in touch with the doings of the company largely through informal meetings and phone calls. But directly below Branson is a raft of high-caliber executives who supply the ballast to Branson's casual air: "Branson constantly expanding his eclectic empire is neither random nor reckless. Each successive venture demonstrates

Branson's skill in picking the right market and the right opportunity."

Sources: Branson, R. (1998) *Losing My Virginity*, Virgin Publishing Ltd;
Branson, R. (2009) *Business Stripped Bare*, Virgin Books; www.virgin.
com/about-us/; www.virgin.com/richard-branson/

This case illustrates that, at the outset, similarity among group members prevailed in terms of background and basic values and dreams; however, diversity was also present and growing over time: competences and passions ranged from communication to media, music, organization, accountancy, law, etc. In general, a good way of thinking of the composition of an entrepreneurial team is that of *similarity in basic values and languages, but difference in terms of competences and relationships* (that is, in human and relational capital provided).

The case also illustrates other important points about decision teams – and entrepreneurial teams in particular. First, there is no team among unequals. *Decision power* should be distributed, or delegated, in a balanced, parity-based fashion, so that everyone is able to fully express their contribution. The more centralized decision making is, the more the "team" reduces to one actor thereby losing the distinctive benefits of teaming as a creativity generator. Second, *group size* disrupts team decision making. Hence, Virgin provides an example of an ingenious process of regenerating "smallness" while growing by splitting down and spinning off so that the large structure continues to be formed by "molecular" entrepreneurial units, based on teamwork. Third, *powerful entrepreneurial incentives* for performance and innovation (centered on property rights over results) are not at odds with *team* production and teamwork (as is often thought). They are the rule rather than the exception in entrepreneurial firms. These two human resource management practices are also often applied in combination to reproduce entrepreneurship within and around a firm once established (cf. Chapters 3 and 5). Fourth, *teaming* for innovation should not be thought of as a "stable marriage" but as a "dance" (Powell 2001; Meyerson *et al.* 1996; Grabher 2002). The important thing is not to set up and maintain "the" team (actually it may be detrimental for innovation in the long run), but to always have "a" good team, like always dancing with good partners but not necessarily the same ones.

2.3 Networked access to technology

"Open innovation" is gaining importance as a technology strategy (Chesbrough and Vanhaverbeke 2006; Kogut and Metiu 2001). It broadly refers to all strategies of innovation that are not self-contained and based on internally conducted research and development, but are based on collaborations with others (Andretsch and Litan 2009). As argued in the opening section, networked strategies and structures are a fundamental response to the failures of both purely external market procurement of resources for innovation and to mere internal development.

In this section we present some important network strategies in gaining access to/invest in technological resources, in connection to the "problems" they can overcome: (1) different sources of inappropriability – namely, knowledge distribution, knowledge as a public good and complementary assets; and (2) the establishment of compatible technical standards, another important factor affecting the prospects of technology investments.

Outsourcing and licensing

Appropriability problems can stem from *the distribution of relevant knowledge among different actors. If those other actors are small in number and identifiable, then technology can be "outsourced" through agreements with them.*

Among these agreements, *licenses* are of particular importance. These agreements typically involve much more than a market exchange of technology. Direct information exchange and assistance is often involved, especially if the licensed technology is complex. Data on technology licensing relations consistently indicate that license agreements are typically preceded by prior informal links among firms, and that formal contractual mechanisms are most often accompanied by control systems, informal relations, and dedicated coordination roles (Siegel 2006). In addition, appropriate incentives for these additional assistance and know-how transfers should be provided. Hence, if the licensed technology is of a "basic science", "early stage" and complex type, the licensing agreement will include not only fixed fees and royalties contingent on the development and success of applications, but also equity stakes that secure the further collaboration of the licensor (Jensen and Thursby 2001).

If some components of the relevant knowledge are of a kind that are produced and "owned" by research institutions (and/or researchers), it is efficient that those actors are assigned some property rights in new firms based on the technology they produced.

In fact, a dramatic increase in the presence of university and research institutes, or individual members of those institutions, on the boards and in the equity of new technology-based firms has been consistently reported in all developed economic areas (Siegel 2006). Research data show that there has been a dramatic increase in university equity holding in new firms (Feldman *et al.* 2002) and that around 25 percent of university–new firm technology licensing agreements include equity assignments to the university (Jensen and Thursby 2001).

The Nano Active Film case (Box 2.4) illustrates the sharing of property rights among the co-investors of different types of assets in a new technology-based firm, as well as some different options in solving the intellectual property right allocation problem.

Box 2.4 Nano Active Film
Franco Fattorini (CEO of Itaca Nova srl) and Alexandra Albunia (CEO of Nano Active Film srl and Researcher at the Universita' di Salerno)

Nano Active Film srl (limited liability company) is a *spin-off* of Universita' di Salerno.

The spin-off idea was developed by its founders through a very original path that took many years to be deployed and completed.

The technological root of such an idea refers to the research activity of a well-known Italian top scientist, Professor Gaetano Guerra, and its research team. Professor Guerra is one of the most prominent Fellows of the Italian "polymer school" founded by Nobel Prize winner Giulio Natta, the "father" of polypropylene (key industrial plastic materials). His team studied the structure configurations of syndiotactic polystyrene and patented a nanoporous structure that allows huge selective absorption of specific molecules.

Over the years, and thanks to the participation on the same scientific and technological community, Professor Guerra and one of his researchers, Alexandra Albunia, developed a particularly strong relationship with the founders of Itaca Nova (Box 2.1). The potential of syndiotactic polystyrene became one of the topics in their discussions. One evening, in a nice restaurant in Trastevere, Rome, on the occasion of a conference on macromolecules, they had the idea to apply this material to one of the most critical topics in the food industry: the shelf life of fruit and vegetables. The idea was very simple: to avoid the fast degradation process of fruit and vegetables, it is essential to remove from the environment a specific molecule, named "ethylene". They decided to try to use syndiotactic polystyrene for a selective absorption of this molecule.

A research team at the University of Salerno, with the help of Riccardo Bianchi, a well-known specialist in the packaging field, and an Itaca Nova team, led by Maurizio Galimberti, a top industrial consultant in the field of "active" and "intelligent" coatings, started to study new packaging materials based on the idea, looking for dramatic improvement of shelf-life performances.

The first technical results were excellent, and the news of such smart new material started to circulate in the technological community.

Understanding the potential of the material, the team decided to assess its market potential; a good chance was offered by the Italian "innovation prizes" process that gives a participant the opportunity to expose their project to a qualified panel of senior experts coming from very different fields (including venture capital, corporate finance representatives, business angels, etc.). The result was impressive: two national prizes and a special prize from the Italian Republic President in six months!

On that basis, the team decided to move forward to the launch of a company: a spin-off of the Universita' di Salerno in partnership with Itaca Nova srl. The Itaca Nova team led the business plan development process and within a few months, in August 2010, Nano Active Film srl was founded. Professor Gaetano Guerra was appointed company chairman, Alexandra Albunia took the CEO helm, Maurizio Galimberti became company chief technology officer and Riccardo Bianchi marketing and sales director.

As a technology-based company, linking academic resources and business resources, intellectual property rights issues represented a major topic of discussion. A possible approach examined has been that of a shareholder community where every single scientist contributing to the innovative know-how would have been directly involved, and consequently directly rewarded for such a contribution. Other possible approaches considered included technology licensing, and agreements with the academic institution rather than with the single scientists. A good solution to such problems is crucial in technology-based new ventures, as it could drive the success or failure of an entire technology transfer process. In Nano Active Film, the selected formula was a mix of such different approaches, in order to establish a strong and flexible technological "platform" sustaining fast upgrading and evolution, and at the same time to secure a motivated involvement of the key people.

Open sourcing

When appropriability problems stem from knowledge dissemination among too many actors to be identified, and/or are of a "public good" kind, "open sourcing" can be a solution.

The case may be exemplified by, but should not be reduced to, the famous software open sourcing communities, such as Linux, described in Box 2.5. In these situations, a wide game of reciprocity in knowledge production and acquisition is sustainable: each player contributes a tiny fraction of knowledge and can access a huge knowledge base in return (in addition to other benefits, such as visibility, reputation and relationships) (Frank and Jungwirth 2003). Hence, rather than a "property right" securing approach, a "property left" approach can be sustainable (De Laat 1999).

Box 2.5 The Linux open source community
Alessandro Gava, 2004

Linux is an IBM compatible operative system originally developed by Linus Torvalds in 1991 as a hobby. The first version was developed for running on IBM compatible servers; later a PC version was distributed and today we can find the system embedded in microchips, making it possible to buy Linux-based computers. How could it happen that a young man's hobbistic project could compete with systems developed by big companies such as Microsoft, Sun Microsystems and IBM?

Linux has the same potential as, for example, Windows but at the same time is more flexible (easy to adapt to the user and to the purpose), has a number of compatible applications and is cheaper. Actually, to have Linux on your personal computer you do not have to buy any license; it is free and you simply download it. While installing an operative system provided by Microsoft, Sun or IBM costs around $40,000 per server processor, Linux costs only $1,500 per server processor. It can be this cheap because it is not developed by a real company but by a community of thousands of programmers that freely cooperate, participating and posting new lines of the code in one of the Linux communities on the internet. Without any monetary reward anybody can download the software free of charge, use it and modify it. The question is: how can this happen? Why are so many brilliant programmers working for free to develop a product that is distributed for free? What are the incentives for them to keep on upgrading Linux? How are they organized? Who coordinates the community? What are the rules?

The basic difference between Windows and Linux is that while the former is a proprietary code the latter is an open sourced software. The code that creates Windows is protected by a copyright owned by Microsoft and nobody can copy it, modify it or create applications without Microsoft's permission and the payment of a license fee; to the contrary, the Linux code is public, anybody can get it from the net and use it for free; people can also study the code, modify it and release their own version of Linux.

At the beginning of the computer industry, when computers where used only by universities and research centers, no packaged software existed and so every programmer had to modify the software for their purposes. This process was difficult and time consuming because of the writing and debugging process that every programmer had to undertake. This is why programmers started to freely exchange discs containing code lines so that the programmer that received the discs could improve the software and fix some bugs. Thanks to this collective effort, it was possible to develop the first operative systems and the first computer applications. So, at the beginning of the computer industry, the open sourced software was the general rule and the programmers had already created a community of free exchanges. In the 1980s, MIT decided to sell a software package to a private company and restricted the code, also excluding the developers of the software from modifying it. In response, Richard Stallman, a talented programmer at the Artificial Intelligence Department of MIT, founded the Free Software Foundation to develop a legal mechanism to maintain free access for all to the software developed by software hackers. The General Public License was promoted for this project. Software developed under this "copy-left" condition has a public source code, and anybody who possesses a copy of the software can use it at no cost and also distribute modified and unmodified copies of the software at no cost. With the diffusion of the internet it became easier and easier for programmers to exchange software and it was these technical improvements and the hacker culture that permitted the development and diffusion of systems such as Linux.

Even if there are no monetary rewards (at least not directly) for collaborating in the development of an open sourced software, there must be some incentives to participate. We can distinguish between personal incentives and business incentives. Personal incentives are created by the personal learning prospects and the reputation that a programmer can achieve. Software developers highly value the possibility to learn, because it is only by programming that they can learn to program, and the possibility to find better solutions to their problems. In addition, there are some ownership aspects, at least in a socially recognized, if not in a legal sense. This aspect is enforced by a rule that is present in all online communities of software developers: the project initiators become the project maintainers and they are responsible for project management. When new lines of code are posted on the website of a community, if they are considered interesting by the maintainers, they are added to the official code; thanks to this function maintainers act as gatekeepers of the project. In the Linux case, Linus Torvalds has played the important role of leader since the beginning of the project; it was he who set the objectives of the community and the first rules for exchanging information, such as, the channel used (the website) and the general rules. From another point of view, we can also see that an active participant in a development community is a valuable resource for a company that is interested in adopting the system developed by that community. For example, if a company decides to implement a Linux system there would be no better choice then to hire a member of the community who participated in its development and knows the system.

The business incentives for collaborating come from the different sources of benefits within a community instead of a big company. While a company such as Microsoft benefits from selling the innovation, a member of a community such as Linux benefits from the use of the innovation and typically from modifying the software for their particular purposes. Not only can the single programmer benefit from collaborating, but a company can also benefit from investing resources in the development of Linux. For example, by paying programmers to collaborate in the development of Linux, IBM does not get any direct benefit, but could push the development of a better operative system that increases the performance of its own computers.

There are also network-level reasons for sharing information within a community: network externalities first and foremost. Network externalities occur when the utility of consuming a good or a service increases with the number of users. In the case of open sourced software, the number of participants increases the importance of the project and the probability of success. The greater the number of developers, the more the system is adopted, driving the diffusion (market share), and the quicker the system is developed thanks to the greater number of efforts.

Another important aspect to consider in order to understand the dynamics of a community of developers is the interaction among members. Taking part in a project creates a game of reciprocity. Everybody shares because they think the others will do the same and sharing is necessary to obtain the expected results. Being considered a good member in terms of quality of programming and sharing permits interaction with the best programmers and access to much more information. On the other side, the contribution costs are relatively low in software production (as well as in other sectors of the new economy). Actually to post lines of code on the internet entails only the cost of the contributor's effort.

However, the question may be posed as to how such a system is not destroyed by free riding. In fact, there is a high rate of free riders that visit the web pages of the communities and download the software freely without putting anything in. Nevertheless, this does not reduce the innovative capacity of the communities, and the active members of the communities do not set up any system or explicit reward to cooperate or to preclude access to free riders. Indeed, the presence of free riders does not reduce active members' incentives to participate. Not all the benefits previously described are obtained by free riders. Rewards for those who contribute will always be higher than for those who do not contribute. The free rider does not obtain personal benefits (learning, personal contacts, reputation) or business benefits (customized software).

Second, free riders are considered assets rather than liabilities by the community: they increase market share and the diffusion of the software, thereby making it all the more attractive to adopt.

Source: Gava, A. (2004) "Management by communities"
Bachelor thesis in International Economics and Management,
Bocconi University

Alliances

When appropriability problems come from other firms and entities owning complementary assets, the new venture should start out with a portfolio of cooperation agreements that ensures the availability of these resources.

In fact, in dynamic sectors, where opportunities are often of the Schumpeterian resource recombination variety, such as biotech and semiconductors, new firms starting out with a wide array of alliances in diverse technology areas have a higher probability of survival, higher earnings and growth rate, and a higher number of patents and new products (Podonly *et al.* 1996; Colombo *et al.* 2006).

The more the technical assets involved are complex, the more their value is difficult to evaluate, and the more the output is uncertain, the more effective alliance agreements are likely to include "proprietary" right sharing (Grandori 1997; Grandori and Furlotti 2006). The following case of an alliance in biotechnology (Box 2.6) illustrates how these inter-firm collaboration contracts are – albeit to varying degrees – partnership contracts that associate and dedicate assets to a common venture, and establish a common organization, always through shared decision rights and often also through shared property rights over outputs.

Box 2.6 Lucent Technologies and Broadband Technologies (BBT)

The alliance links a researching party (BBT) offering specialist expertise to a commissioning party (LT) that lacks it and is in need of it. The contract is a Master Agreement, regulating a stream of future projects, each of which requires specific Project Letters for actual implementation.

The specific task to be carried out by the research partner is described in very general terms. The agreement rather establishes a procedure for determining task content and envisages a process of progressive discovery and specification:

> As soon as practicable … the Parties shall agree on a preliminary list of possible Projects, and associated fees … The Parties recognize that the list of potential Projects on such a list is subject to additions and deletions, by mutual agreement, and shall not bind either Party until an appropriate Project Letter for any given Project is executed by both Parties.

Despite the fact that at the time of drafting the agreement the tasks can be specified only in very general terms, the parties already commit to each other rather significantly. Overall, the agreement is configured as Lucent "hiring" the development firm, for a still-vague technical purpose, based on a prior assessment that BBT will be able to deliver what Lucent will detail in due time. For instance, the agreement establishes an obligation for Lucent to pay BBT a certain amount, which cannot be waived even in the case that Lucent deems it appropriate to purchase the agreed deliverables from alternative sources. Additionally, the agreement states that Lucent can refuse delivery of a deliverable that meets specifications only if the delivery delay exceeds six months. This is indeed not a trivial period in view of the fact that the collaboration is expected to last about three years, and is an implicit acknowledgment of the uncertainty of the tasks.

In addition, the contract specifies with which mechanisms the alliance is to be governed. These consist essentially of team-like governance, complemented by the assignment of some authority to one of the parties. Various clauses establish that decisions at the strategic as well as the organizational and operational levels of the alliance will be taken "by mutual agreement". Paragraphs 2.02 and 2.03 provide that each Project Letter shall specify "the name [one per party] … of Lucent's and BBT's representatives assigned to administer the Project" and assign the representatives action rights, decision rights on operational matters, and reporting duties, thereby configuring them as liaison roles.

The agreement also includes clauses that establish bilateral governance devices to ease disengagement from the relationship upon a change of circumstances, thus acknowledging that at times the expected benefits may not justify continuing cooperation.

Source: adapted from Grandori and Furlotti (2006)

Technical standards formation

A further important issue that makes investments in new technology puzzling is technical standard setting. *The establishment of new technical standards is also largely a matter of networking (and even lobbying).* In fact, the game of standard diffusion is such that the higher the number of adopters, the higher the convenience of adopting. However, from the point of view of new technology-based firms, the problem is that they typically leverage on first mover advantages and early adoption, at a time when a technology is not yet diffused. Hence, they face a problem of certification and legitimation of the new technology, as well as a problem of convincing others to adopt their technology. In addition, from the general economic point of view, the free interaction of players in the technology adoption game is highly prone to "band-wagon effects" (there are benefits in doing what others do) (Rohlfs 2001) and in some cases to the emergence of "wrong standards" (David 2005). Therefore, the establishment of technological standards is a terrain of intense public and regulatory intervention; and the role of regulatory bodies and standard committees may be critical in favoring one technology or the other. In a domain where committees and deliberate decision making counts – rather than just "spontaneous" market adjustment – alliances and coalitions also matter. From the point of view of new firms, *alliances with established firms, established institutional players in the industry, and universities and knowledge certification institutions are likely to be crucial in providing legitimacy as well as in opening versus closing the possibility to follow technological trajectories.*

The end-chapter case on the birth of BlackBerry illustrates – along with many of the issues on networker resource attraction and assembling – the problems faced by RIM with respect to technological standard formation.

2.4 Networked finance

In new ventures, *standard capital markets and intermediaries tend to fail in effectively providing access to key financial resources*, as much as standard labor and technology markets tend to fail in effectively accessing and pooling key human and technical resources. Bank loans are possible, but are typically guaranteed by personal patrimony and collateral – whereby they are standard loans, not specialized methods for financing new ventures. There are exceptions; that is, banks are sometimes involved in financing entrepreneurial ventures. For example, as illustrated in the Graamen Bank case, microcredit leveraging on guarantee networks among entrepreneurs is possible and effective. Less extreme examples, from high-tech sectors, involve the participation of banks supported by players competent in the industry (e.g. a technological broker) and regulated by contingent agreements (e.g. a conditional investment upon availability of information on the project's worth). Both provisions are likely to reduce the riskiness of the investment for the bank and therefore to mitigate information asymmetry problems. If looked at closely, therefore, these cases are not standard bank loans, but networked and brokered finance.

Analogously to what has been observed for internal labor markets, *the "internal capital market" solution is by definition lacking for a new enterprise* (although it is an option for financing new business ventures within existing firms).

The nightmare of financing in the early stages is illustrated in the Waterproof MP3 case (Box 2.7) along with some possible alternative sources of capital, and a creative way around the problem.

Box 2.7 The waterproof player
Laura Gaillard, 2010

Stephan Bird, an electrical engineer and product design wiz who last served as CEO of an apparel company, got the idea for a submersible MP3 player while watching surfers near his home in Del Mar. Then, in late 2003, a friend dropped an iPod into a cooler full of water and ice, rendering the device useless. Bird got to work designing his waterproof player. By August 2004, a prototype was ready. It was lightweight (40 grams), with a 40-hour battery and 512MB flash memory, capable of holding about 80 songs. The headphones wrap tightly around a swimmer's ears, and all of it is waterproofed using a proprietary technology. Bird had spent months slaving over his invention designed specifically for athletes who want to rock out while surfing, swimming, water-skiing or snowboarding. The idea was now technically feasible.

In classic bootstrap fashion, Bird invested his personal savings and somehow convinced half a dozen friends to work for him for free. He enticed his friend Mike to join the firm; Mike had worked at plenty of sporting goods companies as CFO. He had good experience of management and finance, Bird gave him 40 percent of the equity. Enter Greg, a friend of Bird's who had worked as a sales strategist for a number of large sporting goods companies. He showed the player to some of his contacts in the big-box retail world. "I've never had such a quick and positive response on any consumer electronics," he says. The question was how to capitalize on that interest. For Bird this was amazing news. Several major retailers wanted to put the gadget on their shelves alongside popular players. A deal with just a single big chain, Bird knew, could instantly push sales over $1 million.

Bird quickly convened a meeting at Jimmy O's, a local ocean-view hangout. Greg presented the good news to Mike. "Mass distribution gets your name out fast and gives you an instant hit," Greg said. "Your vendors really start to take you seriously." That was not the only advantage. With mainstream retailers on board, it would be easier to attract investors. That appealed to Bird: his first source of capital was a "loan from himself" and credit cards. There were simple advantages here: pure control and ownership. But he was growing tired of depleting his own bank account and depending on his family.

At first, Bird was elated. But the more Bird thought about it, the more nervous he became. Pursuing mass retailers had never been part of the San Diego start-up's plan. Instead, the idea had always been to start small, selling through specialty shops. Pursuing a big-box strategy meant crafting an entirely new business plan – one that would involve mass production and potentially huge investments. What is more, the retailers wanted the players in time for the holiday shopping season, which was just four months away.

Mike was wary. In his previous experience in sporting goods companies, he had always succeeded by starting small, becoming a hit with an influential niche group, and going for bigger distribution deals only after the groundwork had been laid. How, he wondered, would Freestyle get its key customer groups – surfers and snowboarders – into big, decidedly unhip retail outlets? Meanwhile, ramping up production would require significant capital investment. How could Freestyle find that kind of money? Would the company's manufacturing partners be able to maintain quality if orders suddenly spiked?

Mike said that, roughly speaking, capital investment could come in two forms: debt and equity. They had the option of borrowing money from a lender, and paying interest on that investment, meaning they would be compelled to repay the money with interest over time. The other option was to take on an equity investment – in which they had to sell a portion of the company to an investor in return for cash or something else of value. Each source had advantages and disadvantages. Bird, Greg and Mike knew they had to consider each option well before making choices, for finance decisions are hard to undo. It is not enough to find lenders and investors, you have to pick the right ones: investors who bring more than cash to the table, supporters who can help you with financial advice, technical assistance, or who can connect you with key customers.

Mike called investor Andrew Anderson, a shareholder and active supporter of a company he had worked for in the past. When Andrew seemed receptive to the Freestyle MP3 concept, Mike paid him a visit with a plan: "We figured out that we would need about $500,000 in the next months to hire engineers and pay new manufacturers and materials." Andrew said great, he was ready to put up about half the money they needed to meet the quantities and the delivery required by the retailers, on the following terms: Freestyle will have to hire an experienced CEO whom Andrew knew and approved, and he required a 40 percent share of the equity.

Time was running out. The three-day action sports retail trade show – where independent retailers go to test and order new gear to sell in their surf, dive, skate and snowboard shops – was just weeks away. Making a big splash at the show had always been part of Freestyle's plan. If Bird signed on for a big-box deal, that plan would have to change.

Greg suggested that they should accept the partnership with Andrew; it was the best alternative if they did not want to find themselves shut out of the retailers' deal. When a partnership's synergy clicks, Greg said, the resulting growth can often yield far greater capital options later on. Stephan and Mike were not willing to give away such a high percentage of stock in return for capital investment. Greg argued: "Who cares how much stock you give away going into the deal as long as you maintain control? If you can get a good chunk of it back based upon your performance results, that's what matters." But Bird and Mike would not change their attitude.

Bird asked Greg to call his contacts at the big boxes and respectfully decline their offer. They were not easy calls to make. "I told them, 'We have to pull back from this wonderful opportunity. We're not ready'," Greg says. Instead, the Freestyle team focused on preparing for its big trade-show debut, creating a display that seemed certain to turn heads: the players would sit at the bottom of fish tanks, with the headphones dangling out so anyone could come by and have a listen. "We were swamped," says Bird, who estimates that some 1,800 visitors stopped at the booth. About 40 small and mid-size retail shops pre-booked orders for the spring of 2005. *Surfer* magazine put the waterproof MP3 player at the top of its Christmas wish list.

In addition to retail buyers, marketing and licensing executives from some of the surf world's biggest brands visited the booth. After sampling the player, the executives sought to explore co-branding opportunities – a source of revenue that Bird and his partners had not even considered.

The strategy of selling through specialty retailers and co-branding with bigger, better-known brands made more sense than pursuing mass retailers, Bird and Mike said. Sitting on the shelf at a big box, Freestyle's gadget could get lost among other MP3 players. But in surf shops, "we're the only game in town," Bird said, which would build credibility with consumers. Even Greg, who negotiated with the big boxes and was hoping for a smash hit, agreed. Greg estimated that Freestyle could have grossed $20 million in 2004. "But it's a huge expenditure to get that production moving," he said.

As for the 2004 holiday season, Freestyle opted to avoid retailers altogether and to sell the MP3 players directly through its website. They raised $140,000 through family and friends to meet production, website development and sales administration. The devices – sold for $180 each – proved so popular that the company ran out of them on December 23. Even with the small-store strategy, Bird expected 2005 sales to hit $10 million. "With 4.9 million surfers, 3 million wake boarders, 8 million snowboarders, and 10 million water rafters and kayakers," he said, "we're looking at a lot of demand."

Source: adapted from Lora Kodonly, Inc. Magazine, April 1, 2005

As this case and many others illustrates, at founding, new venture financing is characterized by heavy if not exclusive commitment of personal savings and investments by "strongly tied" partners (*the "three Fs": friends, family and "fools"*). The good news is that many new ventures require small initial investments. Baron and Shane (2005) report that more than half of all new ventures in the US require less than $5,000 in initial capital. However, this option is clearly not sufficient and not efficient to sustain growth.

Financing by debt is not a particularly well-suited alternative. In fact, *banks* would demand high premiums and guarantees for risky ventures. This should not be seen as "nasty" behavior; rather, it should be observed that investment in new ventures is not well suited to most banks either, since the risk profile of the investment is not aligned with that typically preferred by deposit holders.

Investment banks do not have that limitation, since they are specialized in investment, but can typically intervene in later stages of development, before or as an alternative to initial public offerings (IPOs) (Baron and Shane 2005; Clarysse *et al.* 2007); when the entrepreneurial idea has been tested, risk is lower, and firm-specific insider information is less crucial.

Financing through *equity investment by other firms*, typically corporations, is another possibility, but is not generally well suited. In corporate financing, the economic terms may by particularly favorable, but the investment would typically be made in exchange for decision and control rights that are more extensive than the entrepreneur would be willing to release at an early stage. In other words, there may well be no "zone of agreement" in the negotiation on the terms of investment between those two parties.

If the typical ways and the institutions financing regular activities have limited capacity to finance new ventures, specialized financial operators have emerged to respond to this particular opportunity. They are *"financial angels"* and *"venture capitalists"*.

The first round of professional financing of new ventures can typically count on "financial angels": former entrepreneurs in the same field, or otherwise people knowledgable enough about the field and the entrepreneurial team to be willing to risk their wealth; while typically asking and being asked for high-decision involvement and competence contributions.

Second-round financing can be based on the observed sustainability of the firm and can attract investment of financial institutions specialized in risky investment but not in the substantive area of the entrepreneurial projects – namely, venture capital (VC) and private equity funds. Those financial firms pool funds from other financial institutions – pension funds, insurance companies, etc. – with the purpose of investing the funds in high-return activities. VC firms typically ask, and are also asked, for some managerial involvement and some provision of managerial competences in the new firms financed (Sapienza and Gupta 1986; Robert 1991). However, the involvement (and the relevant competence) in sector-specific problems is much weaker and the objective structure is also more distant from those of the entrepreneur. VCs are diversified investors playing with other actors' money. Hence, they are more profit-oriented and risk-neutral players than an entrepreneur (or a financial angel).

The salient differences among the average profile of these two types of investors can be summarized as in Table 2.1.

Table 2.1 Financial angels and venture capitalists – key differences

Key dimensions	Financial angels	Venture capitalists
Personal characteristics	Entrepreneurs	Financial managers
Invested funds	Own money	Fund investors' money
Investees	High-potential start-ups and early stages	Growing companies, second-round financing
Due diligence	Experience based Lower cost	More formal Expensive
Geographical proximity	Important	Less important
Form of contract	Simpler deal based on common intent	Complex and demanding
Post-investment monitoring	Operational	Strategic
Involvement in management	Important	Less important
Exit route	Less important	Very important
Return on investment	Important, but less central	Very important

Source: Starovic (2007)

Both financial angel and venture capital "financing" involves much more than financial transactions. They are highly organizational relationships involving thick knowledge transfers. That is the very reason why they are effective in knowledge-intensive and uncertain investments, as discussed. Both networking with entrepreneurs – before and after the investment (Robert 1991) – and networking among investors (Castilla 2003; Steier and Greenwood 2000) helps in reducing uncertainty and risk.

Box 2.8 illustrates the role played by financial angels and by professional investors' associations in sustaining the delicate matching phase of the entrepreneur/investor relation. Box 2.9 introduces the complex content of the relationship between early stage financial investors and entrepreneurs (discussed below).

Box 2.8 The European Business Angel Network
Alberica Marzotto Caotorta, EBAN Project Manager

The European trade association for business angels, seed funds, and other early stage market players, EBAN, is the pan-European trade association for business angel networks and federations of networks, early stage venture capital funds (investing less than three million euros per transaction and interested in co-investment opportunities with business angels) and other early stage investors.

EBAN was established in 1999 by a group of pioneer angel networks in Europe, with the mission to represent the business angel market in Europe. EBAN's mission has broadened to represent early stage investors in Europe as well as a result of a widening equity gap for companies.

The role of early stage investors
Business angels (BA) are private individuals who invest part of their personal assets in one or more start-ups (becoming shareholders of the company) and also share their personal business management, expertise and network of contacts with the entrepreneur. Business angels invest very early, at the seed and start-up phase, and the average amount of investment per deal is around €200,000 at the moment (involving two to three angel investors).

BAs usually invest in high-growth innovative companies with scalable businesses which can guarantee a significant return on investment in about six to ten years. They do not have any sector of preference, although ICT, medtech and cleantech are the most frequent sectors of investments according to recent EBAN analysis on the angel market.

What do business angels look for in a business proposition? The vast majority of BAs think that, for investing their own money into young and promising businesses, the quality of the management team is the single most important criterion. Also, BAs usually look for high-growth businesses with scalable market potential, intellectual property protection, knowledge of the market and clarity of selling proposition. The exit strategy for the business has recently assumed a growing importance (a typical assessment tool kit can be downloaded at www.eban.org/resource-center/publications/eban-publications).

By providing capital but also advice to high-growth innovative companies in their start-up phase, BAs are generally referred to as those actors filling in the "equity gap": BAs invest between the maximum invested by Family Friends and Founders (FFF) which is around €25,000 and the minimum invested by venture capital investors (VCs) around €3 million. Often BAs are the first provider of equity finance to companies for which it would not be possible to raise funding otherwise, lacking collateral needed for debt funding or not being attractive enough to venture capital funds. BAs also act as ambassadors for the business since their investments offer a guarantee for other financiers to invest.

The recent economic crisis is making life harder for all actors seeking finance and especially for innovative small and medium enterprises (SMEs), which have seen banks tightening conditions to grant credits and venture capital funds moving to later stage investments (from €5 million onward). Recent EBAN analysis of statistics data on the market shows, however, that, despite the crisis and its negative effect on SMEs, angels have continued to invest and, although some countries such as the UK were more affected by the crisis, other countries did experience a rise in terms of money invested by angels. This phenomenon is explained by the fact that an increasing number of SMEs turned to BAs to raise money for their business after having faced an extremely hard time to raise money from more traditional sources of finance. The coaching and experience delivered by the experienced angels has also proven extremely important in times of crisis.

It is well recognized that high-growth technology firms are fundamental for economy recovery and job creation. Due to their attitude toward risky investments, BAs have been among the only financers of innovative businesses in the market in time of crisis. This explains the key role played by BAs and early stage investors in the context of the social and economic recovery. BAs and serial entrepreneurs are the drivers for innovation. As the voice for early stage investors in Europe, EBAN aims to support the professionalization of these actors and to establish them as a class of professional players in Europe.

The role of EBAN
As the number of business angel networks in Europe grew exponentially over the last ten years, so did EBAN, passing from a small member organization in 1999 to an over 100-member organization in 2010. Through

direct and indirect membership, EBAN reaches out to 300 angel groups, 20,000 angels and 40,000 entrepreneurs across Europe, today.

This transformation has been made possible by different factors, including the development of the market and the hard work of the EBAN secretariat. If today EBAN is a stronger organization able to offer quality and unique services to its members, most of the merit goes to members of the EBAN community itself, starting from the EBAN bodies – the members of the executive committee and board of directors – which believed in the work carried out by the association, and recruited a growing number of members, sponsors and collaborators into it.

In a few words, EBAN has been able to exploit the power of the network by building and leveraging on the cumulated expertise and best practices among its members to share knowledge, experience, tools, start cross-border collaboration, etc.

In particular, the organization of EBAN events, the EBAN Congress and EBAN Whiter University, on a biannual basis allows members of the community to have a live debate on some of the hottest topics on the market and discuss trends in the industry, while interacting among each other, sharing best practice and looking for common solutions to daily challenges.

Challenges range from how to efficiently run a BAN, to how to set up a co-investment fund, an early stage fund, how to collaborate with other actors in the financial supply chain such as VCs and banks, how to dialogue with public authorities to raise public funds, etc.

After the crisis, most common challenges are how to exploit the good deal flow received by the network with scarce resources to efficiently run the network, how to keep angels active in the network, how to collaborate with governmental institutions and set up private–public partnerships, protecting and commercializing IPRs, and much more.

EBAN events attract the participation of several actors in the industry such as mangers of angel networks, early stage venture capital fund managers, federations of networks, business angels, venture capitalists, policy makers, academia and other intermediary organizations.

A good example of a winning interaction at the occasion of an EBAN event is the encounter between representatives of the Portuguese angel community with representatives of the Dutch angel community during the EBAN Congress in Estoril, Portugal in 2007. The Portuguese delegation recognized the Dutch governmental model to support BAs' initiatives in the country through co-investment funds as one of the best developed in Europe, and decided to implement a similar one in Portugal.

Two years later, the Portuguese government was approving a €43 million business angels co-investment fund modeled on the example of the Dutch co-investment technopartner program in the Netherlands.[5]

In several circumstances, sharing of good practices and networking in EBAN European events proved to be successful.

More challenges ahead

Despite a number of improvements on the angel scene, challenges remain ahead, some of which are due to the changing scenario of today's economies in Europe and worldwide.

Some of the most important common challenges to be overcome for BAs in Europe at the moment are:

- The professionalization of the angel market.
- Lack of understanding by policy makers of the importance of business angel activity and therefore missed opportunities for public–private partnerships.
- The financial self-suitability of many angel networks and co-investment funds, mostly due to the withdrawal or reduction of public financing to these structures.
- Follow-on round for early stage investments and exit routes for early stage investments.
- Structural obstacles in collaborating across borders.

As a consequence, EBAN decided to set its top priorities for the next three years in the following five main areas of activities:

- Creation of professional standards and accreditation's system.
- Lobbying and policy influencing.
- Awareness and capacity building.
- Collection of data and converting it into useful information for key players of the ecosystem.
- Cross-border syndication and co-investment support.

EBAN perspectives regarding the key challenges for business angels and early stage venture funds in the twenty-first century are constantly updated in a freely downloadable periodical document called the "EBAN White Paper".

Box 2.9 illustrates some of the intricacies of the subsequent negotiation phases of the financial investors/entrepreneurs relationship, in the highly entrepreneurial and high-tech context of Silicon Valley's start-ups. The possible solutions are discussed below.

Box 2.9 The negotiated co-investment of human and financial capital: interviews in Silicon Valley

It's a highly negotiated relation and contract. The main issue is how much is the human capital versus the financial capital worth.

(Entrepreneur 1)

We provide seed ground financing. We are now financing a start-up developing applications of a face recognition technology to security. The basic tech has been developed by and acquired from a university, and could actually be applied in a host of directions. The entrepreneurial team is a mix of a Russian team with expertise in the field and two researchers hired from CERN. An important issue is how to link them to the company: they have salaries, bonuses, stock options (vested in four years), and a percentage on patents. Formally the company was based in the US, which we estimate being the biggest market (in fact the US government itself). We are testing and focusing on other potential customers: banks, airports, etc. The potential users contacted are providing valuable information as to specific requirements, adjustments of products and services, pricing. It's like proceeding in the fog with a compass: we can see only as we proceed.

(Financial investor 1)

I admit the financial investors are taking a bigger risk at the outset: they invest, but the idea is unproven initially. Therefore, there are some conflicting interests between investors and entrepreneurs/founders. We must be very careful about the quality of people we are bringing in. We have to negotiate with them all along. And both sides have to protect themselves. For example, we have, as entrepreneurs, severance packages and can be "fired" only for just causes. However, these events are very unusual. We are de facto irreplaceable: without our work and competence, the company is worthless. If I had to renegotiate my agreement, though, I would have paid more attention to the liquidation preference: too often preferred shares take it all, before anything is distributed to common shares.

(Entrepreneur 2)

Sometimes the founder feels he has little bargaining power vis-à-vis the VC. I would never start with only one investor, at least two … after all, it is also good for them, since they can share the risk and balance evaluations.

(Entrepreneur 3)

The financing structure in our case was supported by a trilateral agreement. A big company was interested in acquiring our R&D services and to sell the ensuing products. The partner corporation asked and got seats on the board and a non-exclusive right to commercialize products. But I asked and obtained the right of hiring engineers, complete property rights on technology and patents; and the right to choose a VC financer.

(Entrepreneur 4)

We are investing much more than money. We provide visibility, PR, valuable contacts and managerial experience. The entrepreneurial team provides mainly technical competence and business ideas. The negotiation of the contract between the two involves an estimate of the value of the firm before the investment: this is the value of the entrepreneurial investment. Thus, according to how much we invest, we arrive at the division of shares. In our case, we entered with 33 percent in preferred shares. We were more interested in liquidation preferences than in board control: our board turned out to be composed of two entrepreneurial representatives, two VC representatives and two independents.

(Financial investor 2)

In the initial period after our investment we held one meeting per month and we were updated on everything. In addition, we had intense and frequent informal contacts. The intensity of coordination gradually decreases over time.

(Financial investor 3)

The approach to insert everything in the contract is obsolete. What is essential is a "letter of intent" between entrepreneurs and investors, so that they understand why they are negotiating and joining. When we come to the contract, there are many matters to specify – from sought outputs, to milestones, to warranties and indemnities, to decision and control rights, to exit procedures – but one issue is particularly important and completely specified: who owns what.

(Law firm)

Interviews conducted by Anna Grandori, 2005

The recurrent effective solutions to those starting up investor/entrepreneur negotiations are sensitive to various factors. They can be grouped into three main variables affecting the likely proportion of ownership shares and decision positions (board seats, chief offices) that can be obtained by the different types of investors.

- *Life stages*. In early stages, the entrepreneurial share is, and should be, dominant, and in any case larger than in later stages. In fact, the relative importance of the infusions of knowledge and know-how on behalf of who has generated the business idea is generally essential. Over time, the relative importance of ongoing infusion of know-how becomes less crucial. Competence becomes diffused and learned by others, and codified in organizational procedures. In addition, if the firm is successful and grows it will need further financing, and new financial partners may enter. As a result, the share of the entrepreneur, as well as of the initial financial investors, is typically "diluted". Another important negotiation and contractual matter, in fact, are *"antidilution clauses"*: early investors may predefine the minimum share of ownership that should be preserved in case of capital increases.
- *Incidence of tacit and inalienable human assets.* In spite of the fact that the codifiable or patentable aspects of the idea have become the property of the firm, many tacit knowledge-complementary aspects and many relevant relationships and contacts remain with the entrepreneur. He/she has some intrinsic incentive to contribute them to the firm through continuous association if the firm is to succeed. However, he/she will demand a relatively large portion of decision rights to be able to direct the firm – the CEO position and extensive representation on the board – and a relatively large portion of shares or stock to be able to realize the value of his/her investment. The financial investors, on their side, will demand that the shares held by human capital providers are not immediately available for sale, but are subject to a "vesting" period. This provision guarantees that the entrepreneurs (and eventually scientists) will provide the human resources that are a necessary complement to the invested human capital for the period in which this is essential and will not leave too early. In fact, there is evidence that the share vesting period is significantly associated with the complexity of entrepreneurial projects (Kaplan and Strömberg 2004). (The average vesting period, in recent years, in high-tech sectors, has been four years.) In addition, financial investors would demand, and are typically assigned, preferred stock – having preferential treatment in case of failure of the entrepreneurial idea and liquidation. These rights are typically more extended the higher the market risk (possible competitors, market expansion rate, volatility of demand, etc.) (Kaplan and Strömberg 2004).
- The relative *criticality and scarcity* of financial capital versus human capital also affects the division of property rights between the providers of human and financial capital. Some factors of relative scarcity are external, such as the expansion/contraction state of the economy (Aoki 2004). For example, in the market bubble period in around 2000, entrepreneurs were able to obtain much larger shares of ownership than in more recent years when the financial market went through a contraction, linked to the general condition of the economy, as well as with respect to the previous period. Data from personally conducted interviews with both entrepreneurs and venture capitalists in the Silicon Valley in 2005 indicate that the average entrepreneurial share was

around 30 percent at the time, and higher before that. Interviewee entrepreneurs also admitted that there is an asymmetry in investments: "the delivery of the VC is certain: money now. Our investment is uncertain: will the idea work?" In case of VC investment, it is thus likely that a majority of shares will be demanded in any case. For example, a study on US firms going through IPOs in 2004 (Kaplan *et al.* 2009) reports that in the pre-IPO stage the founders' proprietary share was around 15 percent, while the VC share was 53 percent. These same firms had, however on average, at the business plan stage (on average three years earlier) 35–38 percent ownership in the hands of founders. This same study also reports that while at the business plan stage 42 percent of firms can count on proprietary knowledge such as patents, the percentage increased to 60 percent at the time of the IPO, an indicator of the increasing importance of technical assets and decreasing criticality of human capital as the firm evolves.

While the relative scarcity or abundance of financial capital is heavily affected by the availability of other types of investment and by the general state of the economy, the criticality of human capital largely resides in the rarity and unreplaceability of knowledge and competence provided. And the more human capital is critical, the higher the share of property rights that should go to the entrepreneur (Hart and Moore 1990). As previously mentioned, this is the case in the early stages of development of new firms, but the technical complexity of the project is also a basis of entrepreneurial power. In fact, it has been found that the more complex the project, the higher the entrepreneurial share of ownership and of positions on boards (Kaplan and Strömberg 2004).

In sum, financial investors should obtain larger shares of ownership and of positions on boards, as well as more preferred stocks, and stronger redemption rights[6] for projects in more uncertain markets and in periods of contraction of capital markets; while entrepreneurs should obtain larger shares in the early stages, during economic expansion periods, and in technically complex projects.

Key points

The view of ventures and enterprises as gathering on the market the three basic "inputs" of land, capital and labor is particularly off the mark in entrepreneurial innovative ventures. The most important resources in that case are three forms of capital all difficult to gather through market mechanisms: knowledge-intensive human and social capital, "intelligent money" and new technologies. The first section illustrates the core barrier or problem characterizing the attraction and investment of each of them: *the inalienability of human capital; the appropriability of technology; project uncertainty and information asymmetries in financial investments.* The subsequent sections discuss the solutions, which turn out to be all based on "*networks*" among resource providers: the reasons for *entrepreneurial teams,* and their selection through *social and professional networks; access to technology* through *licensing, open sourcing and alliances; networked finance* by specialized investors as *financial angels and venture capitalists*. The possible negative sides and costs of networked resource attraction – that is, various forms of "closeness" – and the possible ways to sustain "openness" and reduce opportunity costs are also discussed.

For each type of key resource, the problem of "retention" is also examined: to what extent and through which mechanisms can resource investments be "locked-in" and dedicated to a new venture for a sufficient period of time? The solutions introduce to the property right pooling and sharing issues that are central in the constitution of a new firm (treated next in Chapter 3). The analysis includes the following innovative key points:

a) some knowledge-based components of human and social capital can be separated from people and are investible in a new entity;
b) this contributes in solving the *"betting on the jockey or on the horse"* investors' dilemma; and
c) the *efficient and fair division of property rights on new ventures' assets* among investors is a *negotiation problem*, and can be understood and designed with negotiation analysis tools.

Analysis questions

On in-chapter cases

- Why do entrepreneurs tend to "come in teams", especially in uncertain settings? Which function of teaming is highlighted by the Grameen Bank case? What are other advantages and disadvantages of entrepreneurial teams?
- Why do FAs and VCs tend to "come in networks"? What is the role of early stage investors' associations (e.g. EBAN case)?
- Consider the Itaca Nova and Nano Active Film cases. Which types of barriers and problems in the attraction and combination of financial, technical and human resources can brokers contribute to solve? By which mechanisms and organizational arrangements? Why was the collaboration among partners, in the Nano Active case, regulated by constituting a jointly owned firm (rather than by other kinds of agreements)?
- How can open-sourcing phenomena such as Linux be explained? When can technology open-sourcing be an option?

On end-chapter case

- Describe how and explain why the BlackBerry and RIM development has leveraged on networks of all kinds in attracting and maintaining the core human, technical and financial assets; and in securing complementary technical and commercial assets.

End-chapter case: RIM and the BlackBerry

Laura Gaillard, 2010

Research In Motion (RIM) is the designer and manufacturer of the award-winning BlackBerry® smart phone, used by millions of people around the world, including 85 percent of the Fortune 500 companies and President Obama who said, "In just the first few weeks, I've had to engage in some of the toughest diplomacy of my life. And that was just to keep my BlackBerry."

Birth and take-off

Research In Motion (RIM) began life in Waterloo, Ontario as a two-person tech start-up in a one-room office. The company was founded by 23-year-old Mike Lazaridis and his childhood friend Douglas Fregin, while they were still engineering students. The company was set up as an electronics and computer science consulting business. When he was able to obtain a $15,000 Government of Ontario New Ventures loan, Mike's parents matched the amount of money. So in February 1985, Mike Lazaridis and Douglas Fregin launched Research In Motion (RIM), Inc. The company's first big contract came from General Motors of Canada Ltd for industrial automation.

In the late 1980s, RIM's wireless venture took off. RIM received a contract from Rogers Cantel Mobile Communications, Inc., a paging and cellular telephone operator. Rogers and Sweden's LM Ericsson started to build miniature radios and modems to let PCs send data and messages over mobile networks. RIM was soon manufacturing tiny wireless radio modems. RIM boosted their staffing to over ten employees, adding engineers Herb Little and Gary Mousseau, a network expert. Besides Mike, the pair turned out to be RIM's most prolific patent producers. To protect its advantages, RIM followed a very careful and consistent policy of securing as much patent protection for its products as possible.

Lazaridis chose Waterloo for his company – he said "because we wanted to build the factory next to the gold mine" – the William G. Davis Computer Research Centre at the University of Waterloo, one of the most respected computer-science schools in North America.

Wireless technologies

By 1991, RIM was developing software to support a complete wireless email system. The company was part of a three-way partnership with Ericsson GE Mobile Data Inc. and Anterior Technology that was formed to develop the system. In January 1992, Ericsson introduced its first portable radio modem, which was designed for Hewlett-Packard's palmtop computer. Anterior Technology was to provide a gateway to major email systems, and RIM provided the application-programming interface (API). At that time, RIM had acquired a high level of knowledge and experience in wireless technologies. The company became the first wireless data technology developer in North America and the first company outside Scandinavia to develop connectivity products for Mobitex wireless packet-switched data communications networks.

Meanwhile, Lazaridis and Fregin realized that they were better at engineering than corporate finance. James Balsillie was invited to join the company in 1992. Balsillie was a chartered accountant with an MBA from Harvard University. He was experienced and had a talented business mind. He mortgaged his house to buy RIM shares. He put $250,000 of his own money into the company and became co-CEO with Lazaridis, while Fregin was vice-president of operations. Shortly after Balsillie became CEO, he made the decision to focus on just one key area, which was wireless, and the convergence of mobility and digital data, with a mandate to build the patent portfolio and sell directly to clients.

Inter@ctive pagers

The company had been focusing on working with pagers, but the focus shifted to two-way wireless communication when the research staff found a way to not only receive a message on a pager, but to send messages back as well. Lazaridis was determined to turn this into a way of sending email over wireless networks. In 1996, when manufacturers were beginning to focus on developing smart pagers that would utilize packet-based networks to provide wireless internet access, RIM was ready. In September 1996, RIM came up with the Inter@ctive Pager 900, the world's first pocket-sized, two-way pager. It featured a QWERTY keyboard and a small, text-only display screen. It was developed jointly with Intel Corporation. Released commercially in 1997, the Inter@ctive pager quickly became RIM's best-known product. By early 1998, the company had signed a contract to supply IBM with Inter@ctive pagers for use by its field service representatives across North America.

Lazaridis and his team worked tirelessly in those days to optimize the network performance of the early RIM 900. But it was still a large and cumbersome "brick" by today's standards. He was determined to produce a cheaper, friendlier and even smaller device that could be the basis of what Ericsson, Rogers and BellSouth wanted – a true two-way "Star Trek-type" communicator for business and consumers. In summer 1998, RIM launched the next-generation pager, the RIM 950; they also made a marketing agreement with the American Mobile Satellite Corporation (AMSC). The 950 could send and receive emails, pages and peer-to-peer messages as well as send faxes and text-to-voice messages. At the PCS 1998 trade show in Orlando, RIM and BellSouth Wireless Data announced they were working together with Sybase to develop a mobile enterprise solution that extended critical business applications to a two-way pager. The solution included the RIM Inter@ctive Pager 950 and Sybase's UltraLite, a smaller version of its Adaptive Server Anywhere mobile database. The solution enabled corporate users to download and upload data on demand from their pagers.

RIM built everything themselves (except the wireless network itself) and they fine-tuned every piece to make it work in the best way. However, RIM lacked an important ingredient for success in any part of the wireless communication industry: the "bandwidth" on large computer networks that handled wireless communication traffic. To solve this bandwidth problem, RIM's leaders began developing a network to help achieve their telecommunications goals, cultivating relationships with other wireless companies. In developing and commercializing the Inter@active pagers, RIM established relationships with BellSouth and Intel; they contracted with BellSouth to purchase bandwidth in exchange for licensing agreements.

From its inception, RIM has not sought to compete with wireless carriers; rather, RIM opted to sell its products through wireless carriers. There were benefits for both parties: the carriers are able to market a popular device that causes people to use more airtime, and RIM has enjoyed success in markets it never could have entered on its own.

RIM's financial resources

RIM got off the ground with a combination of personal investments from its founders as well as significant funding from the federal government. In 1994, the company received a $100,000 contribution from the federal Industrial Research Assistance Program, facilitated by Lazaridis' University of Waterloo connections. The Business Development Bank of Canada and the Innovations Ontario Program lent the company nearly $300,000. Both Lazaridis and Balsillie negotiated private funding from companies – Lazaridis secured a $300,000 investment from Ericsson and Balsillie attracted almost $2 million in financing from COM DEV, a local technology company based in Waterloo. RIM went public in 1996 and raised $36 million in a special warrant – which is similar to an initial public offering (IPO), but occurs privately – the largest technology special warrant at the time. The company raised an additional $115 million the following year when it was listed on the Toronto Stock Exchange in 1997. In 1998, RIM received $5.7 million from Industry Canada's Technology Partnerships Canada. This money was lent to help further the government's agenda to establish Canada as a global technology center, and to assist RIM in developing the next generation of mobile email handhelds. The loan was repayable out of future profits.

In 1998, RIM reported revenues of US$21 million and a net income of US$400,000. The company was in good financial shape. It had C$100 million-worth of backlogged orders and C$109 million of cash and short-term investments. It planned to use about half of its cash on new equipment, sales and marketing, research and development, and as working capital. The company planned to use 10 to 15 percent of its sales revenue toward research and development.

1999: the birth of the BlackBerry

Sensing that the time was right for corporate email appliances, RIM introduced the BlackBerry mobile email solution in February 1999. Later Mike Lazaridis declared: "You have to understand, the BlackBerry didn't happen overnight; it

happened over a decade. It's not like one day we woke up and said, 'Eureka!'"
Despite the user-friendly nature of the device, the technology inside was complex.
RIM was able to develop the technology – hardware and software – create an
attractive product for executives, associate it with a brand name and even license
the software to important mobile phone manufacturers. The name "BlackBerry"
was the result of the collaboration with Lexicon Branding, a Sausalito, California
marketing firm.

As a result of its past product development and its efforts to develop the
BlackBerry, RIM was ahead of its nearest rivals by almost two years. Furthermore,
its early and extensive experience with its products and early-adopter customers
allowed RIM to correct many shortcomings of the technology and the product. All
employees of RIM carried BlackBerrys and used them; and in the small
organization, without formal barriers, communication, cooperation and ideas
flowed freely. The result was a product that was easy to use, and simple but
powerful enough to also satisfy corporate users.

The BlackBerry included a wearable wireless handheld device with service
initially provided by BellSouth's wireless network in the United States. A unique
aspect of the BlackBerry was that it featured a push system for email delivery,
whereby email messages were relayed from the user's personal computer or
corporate server to the BlackBerry without having to dial in. Push technology
allows emails to automatically show up on the device without the lag time of
having to refresh a web browser to view new emails. The BlackBerry was the first
wireless device that synchronized with company mail systems, so that users did
not need a different email address when traveling. It included an address book,
calendar, task list and alarm clock features. The RIM service gave users a "one-
mailbox" solution, combining their proprietary BlackBerry devices, middleware
software (BlackBerry Enterprise Server or BES) and a network operations center
(NOC) that retrieved email using triple DES encryption and "pushed" it to the
device in the user's pocket. RIM's first NOC was a server located under software
engineer Matthias Wandel's desk.

According to Jim Balsillie, RIM's original entry strategy into the marketplace
was to build great handheld devices, and offer them to alliance partners, such as
BellSouth, to integrate into their own operations. The company signed agreements
with several companies including BellSouth Wireless, IBM and Rogers Cantel to
provide wireless service.

Technology standards

In late 1998, the three networks for wireless data communication were Mobitex,
operated by BellSouth in the United States and Rogers Cantel in Canada; the
DataTAC Network operated by AMSC in the United States, and Bell Mobility in
Canada. These networks were designed exclusively for data and were not capable
of handling voice calls. Wireless voice communication, such as the mobile phone,
was made possible on three technology standards – GSM, CDMA and TDMA.
Both GSM and CDMA were working on developing new standards. Once the

standards were upgraded to support data communication, they should converge into a single worldwide standard. RIM's engineers thought that future generations of networks would support and encourage the development of multifunctional devices that would combine email, voice and internet connectivity, as well as allow for multimedia functions.

Industry standard committees essentially directed the development of technology standards; such committees consisted of industry leaders and significant network providers. In 1999, although RIM's technology was perceived as one of the few practical wireless solutions, the company was too small to participate in the standards committees. BellSouth, Rogers Cantel and AMSC were among the organizations that did participate in these committees. For RIM, waiting for standards to emerge would reduce the risk of wasting resources on dead-end technologies, but continuous product development in anticipation of new network deployment would mean that RIM could enter the market ahead of the competition.

Challenges and frontiers after the turn of the century

The company was at a turning point and had to face various challenges. Until then it had pushed forward its products under license agreements with big names while remaining "in the shadows". As a consequence, potential users would not readily allow a small company to become an important element of their communication infrastructures unless they knew it, and knew it could deliver on its promises and would be in business for a very long time. Meanwhile, most IT departments resisted new products such as the BlackBerry as complicating an already complex environment, particularly when the technology was not proven. To complicate matters further, because BlackBerry was so novel, no ideal distribution channel existed for the product. RIM had no sales force nor could it acquire one easily. Of course, complementary products such as specialized applications would aid its adoption, but RIM lacked the resources to produce a wide variety of complementary goods.

In 1999, RIM had only 270 employees, but it was significantly ahead of its nearest competitors and was ranked as one of Canada's fastest-growing technology companies. Its revenues had more than doubled from the year before and it was able to raise C$250 million to further develop the BlackBerry technology. RIM introduced the BlackBerry 850 Wireless Handheld, putting together email, wireless data networks and a traditional – if tiny – QWERTY keyboard so successfully in a handheld device that demand for it exploded. At that point, some consumers were so addicted that they referred to the device as the "Crackberry".

But was this enough to ensure the firm's survival and success? What capabilities and resources led RIM's success and might be of value in the future? Should RIM delay product development and wait for standards to emerge, or should it move aggressively into the market? Should RIM allow its network partners to private label its products? The dynamics of the IT industry posed a unique challenge for RIM and it was only a matter of time before large competitors would turn their attention to RIM's market.

New competitors and technical upgrades: the 2000s

In January 2000, RIM and Canadian telecommunications giant Nortel entered into a joint marketing and product development agreement, which included a $25 million investment in RIM by Nortel. It was expected that the joint agreement would lead to making RIM's Inter@ctive pagers and BlackBerry service available in Europe. RIM also signed another agreement with Compaq Computer, which agreed to distribute RIM's BlackBerry service to its corporate clients. By mid-2000 RIM's BlackBerry service was hosted by numerous ISPs.[7] The company had just signed a partnership agreement with America Online (AOL) to provide AOL Mail and AOL Instant Messenger service through RIM handheld devices. While Palm, Inc.'s line of PDAs held the largest market share, RIM was doing well serving the niche market of professionals who required mobile access to business-related email. RIM had about 200,000 BlackBerry units in use, with about 50,000 of them at corporations.

In 2001 BlackBerry wireless email service became more widely available in Europe. In April the British wireless service, BT Cellnet, committed to purchasing 175,000 wireless handheld devices and related software from RIM. Other agreements were signed in Ireland and in The Netherlands to offer BlackBerry service. RIM also expanded in the United States through agreements with companies such as IBM, which agreed to issue about 6,500 BlackBerry devices to its field-support staff and market the service to its customers. RIM also took steps to target the US military market. It reached an agreement with Kasten Chase to develop secure wireless access to the US government's Defense Messaging System, which had 300,000 users globally.

Throughout 2001 RIM added enhancements to its products. In January it introduced the BlackBerry Enterprise Edition server for Lotus Notes and Domino. Previously, the BlackBerry system worked only with Microsoft Exchange servers. In March RIM introduced the BlackBerry Enterprise Server 2.1 at the CTIA Wireless 2001 trade show in Las Vegas. The new version enabled web access for BlackBerrys for the first time and also allowed users to send updated calendar information to and from their central system. At the same time the company announced an alliance with GoAmerica Communications Corp. that allowed wireless downloads. In North America, RIM added many channel partners for BlackBerry: Aether Systems Inc., Bell Mobility, Cingular, Compaq Computer Corporation, GoAmerica, Communications Corp., Motient, SkyTel Communications, Inc., Rogers AT&T, Vaultus Inc. and IBM all began selling BlackBerry as part of their product offerings. These enhancements moved RIM's BlackBerry service significantly beyond wireless email.

Expanding options and reducing costs: 2002–3

At the beginning of 2002 RIM announced that it was developing a wireless device capable of handling both voice and data communications. The new BlackBerry device was being developed in association with Nextel Communications Inc. and

Motorola. RIM also teamed with AT&T Wireless to offer AT&T Wireless's corporate customers a BlackBerry that could place telephone calls over AT&T Wireless's GSM/GPRS network. RIM's new BlackBerry with phone service and always-on email connectivity was introduced in March 2002.

RIM's expansion into European markets proceeded in 2002. In April the UK mobile operator Vodafone agreed to market BlackBerry wireless devices that operated over its GPRS network in the United Kingdom. In mid-2002 BlackBerry service was launched to corporate customers in Germany through an agreement with Deutsche Telekom. Around this time BlackBerry service was also launched in France through an agreement with Vivendi Universal's mobile subsidiary SFR, which operated a GPRS network, and in Italy through Telecom Italia Mobile.

In addition, RIM announced relationships with a number of other carriers in Europe and North America, and an agreement with Hutchison Telecom to bring BlackBerry to Asia for the first time.

RIM continued to add new product features, introducing new models, and partnering with technology providers throughout 2002 and 2003. New BlackBerry models included the 6710 and the 6720, which were Java based and included an integrated speaker/microphone and delivered email, phone, SMS, browser and organizer applications. The BlackBerry 6510, which functioned as a walkie-talkie, was introduced by Nextel at the end of 2002, and Nokia announced it was developing a BlackBerry 6800 that functioned as a mobile phone.

However, 2002 was a difficult year: RIM reported a revenue of US$294.1 million, a 33 percent increase over the previous year, but its second consecutive operating loss, which increased from $4.7 million (in 2001) to $58.7 million. Overall, RIM's net loss was $28.3 million. Lazaridis and Balsillie had gone ahead of the market and bet everything on the Java-based 5800 series. Prior to these devices, RIM sold direct. This let them pocket a greater percentage of the revenue. Once they switched to Java-based devices with cell phones, they had to sell through carriers. The complexities of next-generation network rollouts proved to be significant. Several carriers were forced to delay the commercialization of these networks and consequently their GSM/GPRS BlackBerry deployments. For RIM costs spiraled almost out of control. In November 2002 the company announced it would lay off about 10 percent of its workforce and they concentrated on developing even better devices and helping carriers learn how to sell the devices. RIM's CEO Jim Balsillie foresaw rising demand for wireless devices, and the company continued to announce new and enhanced wireless devices and services.

Technology: developing applications and fighting for appropriation

In 2004 RIM celebrated its twentieth anniversary as the BlackBerry surpassed one million subscribers worldwide. The BlackBerry was evolving from a device focused largely on enterprise email and designed to be a secure and easy-to-use tool toward a multimedia handheld. Deployed by tens of thousands of organizations around the world, BlackBerry has evolved into a global wireless data platform that supports a wide range of applications on a variety of proprietary and third-party devices.

BlackBerry smartphone stays true to the original spirit of security, simplicity and value, but they now connected both enterprise customers and consumers to a much wider world of communications, information and entertainment.

In 2005, the BlackBerry Connect and BlackBerry Built-In licensing programs made excellent progress. A number of BlackBerry-enabled devices have been launched including the Sony Ericsson P910, the Nokia 6820 and the Windows Mobile-based MDA II and XDA II. In addition, the Siemens SK-65 with BlackBerry Built-In was brought to market.

On March 3, 2006 RIM and NTP finally announced a settlement of their long-running patent dispute started in November 2001. Virginia-based NTP Inc. claimed to hold patents that RIM infringed to create its mobile email platform. They filed a patent infringement suit against RIM. The issue was threatening: it could have been an injunction that shut down BlackBerry service in the US. US Patent and Trademark Office has issued final rulings rejecting most of NTP's patents. Nevertheless, the threat of a shutdown sent the BlackBerry users into a panic and RIM agreed to pay NTP $612.5 million to settle all claims and allow RIM and its partners to continue selling BlackBerry products and services completely free from any future claims by NTP. RIM's settlement was a way for the company to return to business as usual without the distraction of a looming court battle and possible blackout.

From the start of August 2006, RIM outperformed its competitors Palm, Nokia and Motorola, launching the consumer-oriented BlackBerry Pearl, a GSM cellular smartphone, the first Blackberry device with a camera and multimedia features. It used a modified QWERTY layout on a four-row five-column keypad. Typing on a Pearl was different from the use of other BlackBerry devices. It supported the full range of BlackBerry enterprise functionality, and it included a music player and other multimedia features. At the same time, to monetize its investment in the development of the Pearl, RIM introduced a mixed-use, "prosumer"[8] product, the 8800, that can please both corporate and retail customers. RIM had the first symmetric keyboard and the first real successful use of the track wheel. "Other companies have tried using track wheels and they gave up", said Mike Lazaridis. The founder of RIM explained that RIM had very sophisticated labs "with high-speed cameras, electronic scanning microscopes and infrared fast frame rate transform scanners that we invested in a long time ago". This is how they discovered and invented a suspension for their track wheels: "A very big breakthrough for the industry, but we patented the technology."

On February 21, 2007, RIM chairman and co-CEO Balsillie presented at the 2007 RBC Capital Markets Communications, Media & Technology Conference. He predicted that the BlackBerry would soon become the music player of choice for consumers. RIM's BlackBerry subscriber list has passed the 10 million mark. In October, Alcatel-Lucent announced an agreement to distribute BlackBerry smartphones in China. The news sent RIM shares up 8 percent, making RIM the most valuable company in Canada, based on market capitalization.

2010 frontiers

In February 2010 RIM introduced BlackBerry Enterprise Server Express – free new server software that wirelessly and securely synchronizes BlackBerry smartphones with Microsoft Exchange or Microsoft Windows Small Business Server. "It is an exciting new offering that further expands the market opportunity for the BlackBerry platform," said Mike Lazaridis. "In a marketplace where smartphones are becoming ubiquitous, BlackBerry Enterprise Server Express significantly raises the bar by providing a cost-effective solution that allows companies of all sizes to support enterprise-grade mobile connectivity for all employees without compromising security or manageability."[9]

Revenue for the third quarter of fiscal 2010 was $3.92 billion, up 11 percent from $3.53 billion in the previous quarter and up 41 percent from $2.78 billion in the same quarter of last year. The revenue breakdown for the quarter was approximately 82 percent for devices, 14 percent for service, 2 percent for software and 2 percent for other revenue. During the quarter, RIM shipped approximately 10.1 million devices, including its 75 millionth BlackBerry smartphone.

The next step for RIM is *digital music*: BlackBerry is expanding into digital music and hopes to attract consumers who have gravitated to Apple's iPhone or Nokia with Music mobile phone. In February 2010, RIM was a main sponsor of the Cannes music conference, with co-CEO Jim Balsillie demonstrating the company's products and promoting its open platform for digital music applications. "We're rocking, we're totally rocking," Balsillie said in an interview. "The company is forecasting 20 percent to 25 percent growth for this quarter and expects to exceed that target. We are already very music centric, what we are talking about now is our platform." The company is cementing partnerships with a variety of application developers. RIM has relied on a strong developer community for many years. If users are paying for the application, the developer will receive 80 percent of the revenue back and 20 percent will be kept to help maintain and pay for the system. So it is an 80:20 revenue share split with the developer. RIM plans to open an online applications store for BlackBerry users, showcasing content deals with Slacker, an Internet radio device, and Shazam, a music recognition service.

Sources: American National Standard, Telecom Glossary, 2007
Carayannopoulos, S. (2005) *Research In Motion, A Small Firm Commercializing a New Technology*, E.T. &P
Sweeny, A. (2009) *BlackBerry Planet. The Story of Research in Motion and the Little Device that Took the World by Storm*, Wiley & Sons
www.rim.com/index.shtml
www.blackberry.net/
http://valuewiki.wikia.com/wiki/RIMM
http://press.rim.com/release.jsp?id = 3546
www.rim.com/investors/documents/pdf/AIF/AIF_Fiscal_2010.pdf

Notes

1 The observation may also contribute in clarifying the admittedly obscure notion of "organizational" human and social capital (Davidsson and Honig 2003; Adler and Kwon 2002), referring to that part of knowledge and relationships that are "embodied" in the organization rather than in individuals and cannot be "withdrawn" from the organization in which they have been infused.
2 Richard Branson (2009) *Business Stripped Bare*, Virgin Books.
3 Richard Branson (1998) *Losing My Virginity*, Virgin Publishing Ltd.
4 www.virgin.com.
5 TechnoPartner is the joint initiative of the Ministry of Economic Affairs and the Ministry of Education, Culture and Science in The Netherlands (www.technopartner. nl).
6 Redemption rights are rights to demand that the firm repay the VC at a predefined liquidation value and time after the investment.
7 Internet service provider (ISP), also sometimes referred to as an internet access provider (IAP), is a company that offers its customers access to the internet.
8 Professional+consumer.
9 http://press.rim.com/release.jsp?id = 3546.

3 Entrepreneurial firms

Chapter 3 contents*

3.1 Governance, ownership, and legal forms

3.2 The internal organization of entrepreneurial firms

Resources for innovation are difficult to evaluate, distributed across different actors, uncertain in service delivery potential, and subject to appropriability problems. As argued in Chapter 2, the structural solutions to these problems are all networked, in one way or another. As the uncertainty of projects and the complexity of the resources invested grow, property rights issues emerge in order to provide incentives to invest under uncertainty. In addition, wider governance and organization issues on the distribution of various types of property rights among different investors and participants should be solved. Surprisingly, studies and models specialized in entrepreneurial governance structures and the internal organization of entrepreneurial firms do not abound. Those issues are treated in the literature on small and medium enterprises, which is not specific to entrepreneurship and usually not linked to the theory of the firm and of the entrepreneurial firm.

A distinctive contribution of this chapter is to define some salient and distinctive governance and organizational configurations for entrepreneurial firms.

First, the legal and governance structure is considered. A variety of considerations matter for its choice, including the variety of juridical systems and fiscal regimes and set-up costs around the world. We cannot enter into these matters here, and in any case legal assistance specialized by country and sector would always be needed. However, the implications of different legal forms of enterprise, defined under different names in the legal systems of most developed countries, can be indicated and are briefly discussed in connection with recent developments in the theory of the firm and of the entrepreneurial firm in particular (Blair 2004; Hansman *et al.* 2006; Alvarez and Barney 2007; Grandori 2010b).

---

* Text by Anna Grandori, cases by the authors indicated in boxes.

Rather than listing a series of legal forms with some pros and cons, as manuals tend to do (Baron and Shane 2005), the mentioned recent contributions in the theory of the firm are used for identifying two quite different forms of enterprise: *people-based forms* and *asset-based forms*. The partition between these two classes of legal forms is fundamental in terms of the nature of the firm constituted, since societies of people do not have juridical personality (as they are not distinguished from the physical persons constituting the society) while asset-based societies do, protecting the firm from the liabilities and mobility of people, in addition to protecting the person from the liabilities of the firm. This distinction is formally present in Civil Law countries, in which "societies of people" ("societè de personnes", "società di persone") are distinguished and regulated differently from "societies of capital" ("società di capital", "societè des capitaux").

The distinction – and the choice among the two broad types of companies or societies – is particularly relevant for entrepreneurial firms. In fact, on one side the specific identity of people typically matters (whereby they would/should be societies of people); but on the other side, "capital" of both the human and financial kind is invested and there is a need for "locking" it in (whereby they would/should be societies of capital, entitled to own assets, including knowledge assets, as separated from the people who conferred them). Hence, a further contribution of this chapter is to identify "*hybrid forms*" between societies of people and of capital that are particularly interesting for entrepreneurial firms.

In addition, the chapter enriches the usual treatment of the governance structures of entrepreneurial firms by considering *collective forms*, usually neglected in the entrepreneurship literature but quite important in practice in many sectors, such as agribusiness, professional services, and services to the person.

3.1 Governance, ownership, and legal forms

People-based forms

Individual entrepreneurial firms – A centralized decision and ownership structure can still be observed and be effective in the particular case of entrepreneurial firms that are not based on innovation in products or technologies, but are just new firms conducting traditional and known activities – say a new restaurant, or a new shoemaker, or a new farm – or where the relevant knowledge can be, and actually is, concentrated in the single person of the entrepreneur – say an engineer or other professional (Baron and Kreps 1999). The legal form typically used and suitable for this situation is that of the individual firm (Galgano 1974; Baron and Shane 2005).

By contrast, this configuration is not particularly suited for innovative and high-tech sectors. In fact, whereas innovation is important and uncertainty relevant, it is unlikely that all relevant knowledge can be concentrated in one single actor (Grandori 2009). In addition, the concentration of ownership and control in a single actor is inefficient in risk-bearing respects (Jensen and Mekling 1976) as it is likely to generate high-risk aversion and under-investment. In fact, it is commonly observed that "traditional" entrepreneurial firms in which a single person invests money, provides competence and ideas, and centralizes direction, often suffer a limited capacity to grow and innovate.

Partnerships – If two or more persons wish to start an activity together, they can form a "partnership" or "society of people". This form may be chosen by work-intensive firms in mature industries where, however, the relevant competencies are distributed in a team, as occurs in craftsmanship-based entrepreneurial firms, but also by professional firms.

People partnerships are, however, unsuited to conducting risky activity due to exposure to full rather than limited liability, and unsuitable for the firm and third contracting parties, since the defection of people would jeopardize the continuity of the firm (Blair 2004).

On the other side, these companies are easy to set up and enjoy several other advantages. In particular, two benefits are usually stressed for entrepreneurial firms: the flexibility of internal arrangements, since partners can divide rents and allocate decision rights and responsibilities, respond better to the contribution and knowledge of members; and the avoidance of double taxation of both the firm's and the members' incomes, since only members are individually subject to taxation (Baron and Shane 2005).

Hybrids: between people and assets

Some "hybrid" legal forms preserve some features of partnerships while introducing some distinctive features of asset-based forms, such as limited liability.

One form is the *Limited Partnership* (called "società in accomandita" or "societè en commandite", etc. in Civil Law countries). It is characterized by two classes of partners: a group of general partners – fully liable but entitled to manage and decide – and a group of limited partners – providing financial capital and liable for only the invested capital but excluded from management. In Civil Law countries (which distinguish societies of people from societies of capital), there are in fact two versions: a "simple" form (classified as a society of people) and a share-based form (classified as a society of capital). In both versions, the form is interesting for entrepreneurial firms since it formalizes a situation in which "labor hires capital" (or human capital hires financial capital) and all decision rights are explicitly reserved to the partners providing managerial work.

Another form is the *Limited Liability Company (LLC)* or *Limited Company (LC)*. In this form, the hybrid between a society of people and a society of capital is not achieved by having two types of partners but by mixing the features of the two forms: all partners have limited liability and can freely transfer ownership, but the income goes directly to members rather than remaining with the company (with possible tax benefits). The internal management and organization is more flexible as it is not subject to the predefined structure prescribed to full societies of capital as corporations. In addition, "members" can be either persons or firms and other entities.

Asset-based forms

Limited Liability Partnerships (LLP) are very similar to LLCs in terms of liabilities and taxation. The distinctive feature and interest of this form, especially for entrepreneurship, becomes clear only when considering the distinction between people-based and asset-based societies. In fact, in this case a separate legal entity is created, having a juridical personality distinct from that of partners. While the protection of partners in terms of limited liability is the same as in an LLC, here the assets invested in the firm by partners are also protected by other uses or claims on them from the partners or the partners' creditors. However, being a partnership, the identity of the partners remains important and the partners must be individuals (in some legal systems, e.g. the US, in fact the use of this form is restricted to professional firms).

These features make the LLP extremely interesting for entrepreneurial firms formed by pooling predominantly human capital as it allows dedicating and protecting human capital investments in the firm, and at the same time maintaining a formal connection between them and the specific persons who provided them.

The corporate form

Entrepreneurial firms can assume the legal form defined "Corporation" in Anglo-Saxon countries, and "share/anonymous society" in most European and East European countries (Società per Azioni, Sociètè Anonyme, Sociedad por Acciones).

The main advantage of the corporate form is the full separation between the firm as a set of dedicated assets and the particular investor who conferred the assets. It involves the constitution of a separate legal entity, under which not only the investors are fully protected through limited liability, but also the invested assets are fully "partitioned" from the investors and their identity, and "shielded" from claims that pertain to the investors (Blair 2004; Hansman *et al.* 2006). Shares can thereby be freely bought and sold, and risk can be shared and growth sustained through capital increases and initial public offerings (IPOs) on the open stock market. Therefore, the corporate form is better suited to risky and growing activities.

In particular, in the case of entrepreneurial firms, the corporate form allows full separation between the entrepreneur as a physical person and the human capital invested in the firm: entrepreneurs can exit as persons by selling shares, but cannot withdraw the knowledge and relational assets invested in the firm. In addition, share-based ownership greatly facilitates property right sharing and variation in ownership shares among different actors, which is highly valuable in the evolution of new firms.

Finally, in entrepreneurial firms based on new technologies, not only is human capital important but also relevant investments in technical assets should be attracted. The corporate form provides the incentives to invest to financial capital providers as it tightly links decision rights to the amount of capital invested and, as stated, better "locks-in" complementary human capital investments.

As a result, in the ownership and governance structure of an entrepreneurial firm using a corporate form, the investors of various types of assets are typically proportionally represented: the entrepreneur (or entrepreneurial team) investing human capital; the financial investors (venture capital or financial angel), and eventually research institutes or universities where these organizations provide new technology. The main property rights divided among investors are in fact the proportion of stock and the rights attached to them (e.g. preferred versus common shares), and the proportion of board positions (decision and control rights).

Collective and non-profit forms

The legal forms of enterprises so far examined "allow" the "pursuit" of any "objective", including profit. In fact, they allow the distribution of residual income to partners (or even envisage that the partners, rather than the firm, are directly entitled to it), and constitutionally guarantee decision rights only to the providers of the resources constituting the firm. There are other forms of enterprise, that have both people-based and capital-based variants, which are more "fixed" in the activities that they may undertake and in the internal governance structure. They are "collective" and "non-profit" forms, formally requiring that the firm is devoted to a substantively defined mission or purpose – that is, health, environment, technological improvement, etc. (not just to cover their costs and eventually generate surplus) – and the internal governance structures are statutorily limited to democratic arrangements.

Albeit not often recognized, these forms may be quite interesting in an entrepreneurial perspective for more than one reason. In the first place, in entrepreneurial firms motivations and objectives that differ from profit may be more important and even prevail more often than not. For example, the actual dedication to a substantively specified mission and purpose (rather than to economic residual income or profit) – such as The Body Shop's "making a difference" and "pursuing environmental change" or Grameen Bank's "poverty reduction and economic development" or "technological innovation and scientist motivation" in the JAVA case – is not that remote a possibility. Hence, why not seize the fiscal and regulatory advantages that may come from formalizing this commitment? In fact, enterprises adopting these forms, accepting commitment to well-being development functions, enjoy facilitations and institutional support – especially in the EU – that are not provided to other kinds of firms and can be quite valuable in the early life stages of a firm.

In addition, "democratic governance" may be the most effective form of internal organization in the case of innovative, knowledge-based new firms (Rajan and Zingales 2000), professional firms (Greenwood *et al.* 1990) and highly labor-intensive firms (Pencavel 2001). The statutory formalization of diffused decision rights would provide a solution to the weaknesses and instability of decentralization realized through mere "delegation" by a set of "owners" restricted to financial capital providers (a problem of possible "opportunism of the principal" who might renege on the commitment to decentralize; cf. Foss *et al.* 2006).

Cooperative firms are an important legal form in this class. A cooperative – as per the Statute of the European Cooperative Society – is a "society" having a legal personality that can be formed either by people or by firms "for satisfying any economic, social or cultural aspirations of members" and constitutionally characterized by "collective ownership" and "democratic governance".

"Worker cooperatives" have always been diffused as an effective way of organizing entrepreneurship in labor-intensive activities such as agriculture, manual construction work, art work, medical and other personal service provision (Pencavel 2001), but are also suitable for professional firms. Entrepreneurs in a worker coop are all workers and are entitled to residual decision and reward rights: all decide according to the one-man one-vote principle; and all share the net returns equally.

In addition, a cooperative can be formed not only by individuals but also by firms and other entities. In this way, it provides a very interesting and indeed much-used form of association among entrepreneurs in a higher order entity that in turn has the status and prerogatives of a firm, without being a corporation (see also Chapter 4 on inter-firm organization).

On the minus side, the cooperative form of enterprise, in particular the worker coop, is considered unsuited to risky or even only unstable activities. Being oriented to the improvement of members' well-being, it may generate under-investment because of the excessive exposure of members to risk and could entail little incentive to grow (rather, owners–workers may have incentives to restrict production and access of new members in the face of increasing demand and prices).

Another form of interest for entrepreneurship, with the advantage of being less oriented to the advantage of members, is the "*foundation*". Foundations are legal entities (with juridical personality in Civil Law systems, although not in Common Law systems), endowed with owned assets and devoted to a statutory mission. Foundations can "make" but not "distribute" residual economic results; they have to reinvest them in the foundation's activities – a rather adequate feature from an entrepreneurial perspective.[1] Foundations make particular sense in the now expanding field called "social entrepreneurship". The term "social entrepreneurship", in fact, indicates ventures that are explicitly oriented to solving social problems and explicitly exclude the appropriation of residual rewards (profit) as an ingredient of the venture. Although in some sense all entrepreneurs may be "social" (Schramm 2010)[2] – that is, contribute to the solution of some problems/opportunities thereby bringing about societal and economic improvements – a "social entrepreneur" is one willing to commit and bound his end to the purpose, and choose an institutional form that excludes the appropriation of net income and signals that to the public.

As the above discussion should have made clear, although there is no one-to-one correspondence between the ownership and legal form of the enterprise on one side, and its organizational structure on the other, there are important interactions. Therefore, it would be in principle advisable to co-design them

(Grandori 2004). The AX and Egon Zehnder cases, included in the following section, provide material for such an exercise.

3.2 The internal organization of entrepreneurial firms

The internal organization structure of entrepreneurial firms can and should vary according to various "contingencies", as any firm structure. This statement may sound to some extent divergent from the common view that a "team-like", "organic" and "networked" structure is "the best way of organizing" an entrepreneurial firm. The diversity stems, to a large extent, from the fact that, in entrepreneurship literature, scholars tend to think only of innovative entrepreneurial firms. However, sectoral uncertainty and venture innovativeness vary in degree also for entrepreneurial firms; and their value should always be taken into account in firm organization design. In practice, in fact, the organizational solutions that are viable in "traditional" entrepreneurial firms, operating with known technology in mature industries, can be expected to differ substantially from those necessary in "innovative" entrepreneurial firms. For the sake of completeness and clarity, let us distinguish the two cases, although dealing with the innovative enterprise in much more depth.

Organization in "traditional" entrepreneurial firms

As long as knowledge is concentrated in the entrepreneur as a single person, the internal organization can be, and often is, a "*simple hierarchy*": the entrepreneur runs a "one-man show", and centralizes most decisions, directing the actions of collaborators out of an authority relation. Therefore, this organizational structure is typically complementary with the proprietary structure of an individual firm, assigning all property rights – ownership, decision, profit – to the single figure of the entrepreneur.

This structure is prone to problems either as the firm grows in size, or if it is or becomes subject to uncertain environments. In both cases, the star-like configuration of a simple hierarchy is notoriously insufficient due to a lack of information-processing capacity. Sticking to the one-man ownership and one-man governance is in fact the core problem behind the growth limitations of many traditional entrepreneurial firms.

Entrepreneurial firms in traditional industries, however, may also be organized differently. Whereas in such industries competencies are based on craftsmanship, are diffused among various, or even all, firm members, and activities are relatively stable, the organization of firms may be closer to that of a "*simple community*" rather than a simple hierarchy. For example, consider the production of craft-based artifacts, such as glass-blower objects, or leather or wood handmade objects – as described in Box 3.1.

Box 3.1 Craftsmanship entrepreneurship

Over more than 60 years, Pipa Castello has become known for being the only producer who directly performs all the phases in the construction of the pipe, including research, work on the briarwood and the construction of the mouthpiece.

Every pipe is carefully handmade from one single piece, thanks to the characteristics of the raw material (briarwood).

Among smokers, the Castello Pipe is a true cult object, which is often purchased for the simple pleasure of owning one or for a collection. The founder's son-in-law, who also owns it, manages the firm.

However, the organization of work is entirely team based. Each worker is an artisan, who in turn feels a bit like an artist and wants to work on his own. Each worker is responsible for one detail, not the entire piece, as this is good for maximizing the quality of each and every component. However, the seven artisans who compose the team that makes one pipe need to be able to carry out each step of the process: they are perfectly interchangeable and actually often rotate. This allows them to check each other's work. The team ensures the best quality: 14 eyes are better than two.

In truth, it is the group that controls the entire production process of the pipe. Each morning the group decides who does what. In addition, it is always the group who regulates the behavior of its members. The group even decides on new employees to hire. Quality is "the" objective, but as the entrepreneur-owner says, "I cannot interfere and control the work of my artisans. I can only check the final results. But this in turn is very subjective. The pipe must be weighed in the hand, touched, felt in the mouth, to see what emotion it sparks in you." Hence, quality control becomes a collective ritual: the team tests every pipe before it is sold.

More than controlled, quality is almost certainly infused by the traditional techniques mastered by the craftsmen.

Source: adapted from the case "Castello Pipes"
by L. Golzio, in Grandori (2001b)

In these firms, activities can be conducted out of "routinized know-how" and established shared work practices; each member of the team knows his position and expected contribution, can count on other members' cooperation, and share the same industrial culture.

These features highly simplify governance. Actually, the described firm, if it were not for the international market of its products, would easily be governed, with little need for managerial roles, as a team-based worker cooperative. On the other side, craftsmanship, routines and cohesive cultures are likely to exacerbate the problem of innovation and growth. In more complex and dynamic activities, in fact, these traditional entrepreneurial firm profiles are put under strain.

Organization in "innovative" entrepreneurial firms

Whereas innovation is important and is systematically pursued, the internal organization structure of the firm, whether small or large, needs to be organized in a more sophisticated way than following the templates of a "hierarchy" or a "community".

Consider the internal structure of the new firm in the Polish medical sector described in Box 3.2.

Box 3.2   AX: structuring an entrepreneurial firm in the Polish pharma industry[3]

AX produces and markets pharmaceuticals and medical devices. AX is a Polish small and medium enterprise (SME) based in Bydgoszcz – capital city of Kujawsko-Pomorskie – one of the main cities in northern Poland.

AX's founder studied medicine and specialized in ENT (Ear, Nose and Throat). He started his activity as an entrepreneur in 1998, licensing a product – let's call it P1 – from Sweden, and introducing it to the Polish market. The subsequent development step came from a merger with two little firms selling a wider range of licensed laryngological products. They failed in 2004 due to public funding cuts. The sales of an innovative product – say P2, a simple way of balancing the pressure in the middle ear – brought the first profits to the firm. Today it sells the initial laryngological products and other products added later to enrich the offer. AX is constantly doing research to offer new ENT medical devices. AX's strategy is to address the market through niche products.

Central-northern Poland is known for its good medical care and education. Accession of Poland to the EU influenced regional help for SME development especially in the pharmaceutical and medical sectors. From 2004, Poland got the green light for regional funding to boost activity and the establishment of SMEs. The Regional Entrepreneurship Incubator (REI) in Solec Kujawski,[4] Kujawsko-Pomorskie Voivodship, was built with the assistance of regional and EU funds. REI allowed developing production that otherwise would never have taken off.

Legal issues and ownership
AX had to face a series of legal constraints: the pharmaceutical and medical market is rather heavily regulated in Poland. This necessitated the presence of legal specialists: to manage the relationships and contracts with wholesalers on one side, and the licenses and patents on the other. Mr. ML

– the founder of AX – was a medical doctor, and the Polish law set various restrictions for the business activities of doctors. Consequently, the legal form of the company – a limited liability company – was the answer to both liability and proprietary issues for Mr. ML and his two partners.

Mr. ML's two partners provided funds and Mr. ML – who had an operational role from the beginning – had the majority of shares and the CEO position. The two partners initially contributed to the activities of the company but quite soon settled into hands-off positions and Mr. ML started thinking about buying back the shares to become the sole owner. Mr. ML is in fact, in practice working alone toward its growth and development. He says he would like to claim full ownership of his company unless the other members contribute more actively.

Division of labor
In the beginning, AX's[5] human resources base included:

* the three founding members, two of whom were only initially involved in activities;
* two employees working "on the field" (sales people);
* a part-time accountant (book-keeping for the LLC was complicated and none of the founders had any accounting background, while at that point it was risky to have the accountancy externalized);
* a legal consultant, who worked on an occasional job contract with hourly rate remuneration. For Mr. ML "a business always needs a legal consultant, because you [the CEO] cannot follow it yourself".

As of today, a total of 20 people are working for AX in the positions described below (Figure 3.1):

* CEO: general supervision, close cooperation with the area manager, legal advisor, head of office, accountant, R&D pharmacist;
* area manager: pricing policy, market research, HR, sales people;
* head of office: overlooks production workers, office administration, client relations, billing, discount negotiations, import activities, production planning, stock;
* accountant: invoicing, accountancy; cooperation and occasional task interchangeability with head of office (on billing);
* legal advisor: related legal issues;
* driver and warehouse worker: delivery and warehouse checks;
* wholesaling director: legally required position, paperwork;
* R&D pharmacist: working in Warsaw, definition of chemical formulae, their registration, regulatory affairs, work on innovations with the CEO.

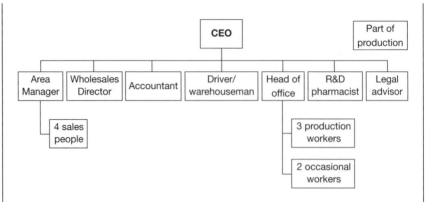

Figure 3.1 The organization structure of AX in 2010

Coordination

The office and sales people are coordinated directly by the CEO, while production people do not have much to do with the CEO, unless occasionally. The R&D pharmacist works in a laboratory in Warsaw, so he is not physically very integrated in the firm. However, there has been no need for this so far – claims Mr. ML – because online communications as well as constant phone calls stand for these needs. On occasion, the CEO travels to Warsaw to consult on R&D ideas, new discoveries or to solve regulatory issues.

The office workers meet on a daily basis, while the sales people (working out in the field) have one monthly meeting with the CEO. The production department is highly automatized; hence, not much ad hoc coordination is needed. Ad hoc meetings are organized when there are marketing strategies to be discussed and when there is a need for temporary or regular employees. This kind of situation/need usually results from a discussion started through the "SharePoint".

In fact, a core coordination mechanism at AX is the intranet "SharePoint', where all the workers (even the production employees were trained to be able to use it!) cooperate and consult. In particular, official documents – for example, accounting related, financial issues, legal novelties, or details about the developed projects – are posted here. The system is perceived to be quite efficient. For example, when they needed to work quickly on a document that was to be submitted to the EU to apply for additional funding they stated: "We finished the paper in an hour as we all gathered online in an instant while it would have taken a single person several days." However, when there is a server failure, the work is paralyzed. So *heavy dependence on the IT system*[6] facilitates communication but also carries risks.

With evolution and expansion, all work procedures were written down, based on internal experience, which in turn stimulated the internal need to codify the processes. These *extended codification of business practices* responded to the need for precision and common interpretation. The rules were also developed to meet the GMP (Good Manufacturing Practice) system requirements.

Employment and HR

The recruitment process is deemed as critical, supervised by the area manager but also influenced by Mr. ML directly. Interest in the job and willingness to commit are basic entry requirements. Mr. ML claims that the attitudes and skills of the potential employee should also "fit" the task. At AX, there is also a belief in team building and a preference for reduced turnover.

The recruitment process starts with an official call announcement[7] of the requirement. Candidate CVs are collected and screened. Around 20 potential candidates are involved in a two-day meeting. Activities performed during this time serve the partners to get to know and assess the potential candidates. Thereafter the final decision is taken and the person selected. This kind of process strongly favors the search for employees on the basis of "fit" with the firm as a whole, although professional and technical job qualifications are also important.

Once employees are selected, the employment contract is rather standard since in Poland there are standard full-time employment contracts, and they are obligatory. Some freedom is given to the company to integrate the standard contract with some clauses, which in the case of AX is done for three subgroups: sales people, production workers and office workers. The differentiation is not pronounced, contributing to the unity of the firm.

Fixed rewards are prevalent, with the exception of some performance-related payments for the sales people (for sales beyond forecasts, which, however, in this company and market are very reliable). Work schedules are very flexible. The positions are by now defined; nevertheless, they are continuously developed, adapted and updated as needs arise.

All in all, the team is stable, and has been with the firm more or less from the start. There have been only two recruitment calls so far – one of the specialists, after having worked for a substantial time at AX, resigned when offered a better job. The overall policy is to keep the number of employees low, but to retain them for a long time.

Most of the full-time employees are in managerial positions. They are fully responsible for the accomplishment of their tasks before the CEO.

When asked about who takes decisions, Mr. ML immediately said that he tries to make every decision a balanced one together with specialists in the participating field. He eagerly reaffirmed the importance of each worker's knowledge on particular issues, details he would never be able to learn. Thus collecting opinions from the parties involved is considered key to good decisions and responsibility is spread.

> However, some problems arise at the managerial level. For example, the CEO reported that a quarrel broke out with the accountant. In his view, the accountant was trying to bargain her working conditions beyond market prices. The quarrel ended up in the termination of the accountant's employment contract.
>
> Source: adapted excerpts from Leśniewska, A. (2010)
> "The internal organization of an entrepreneurial firm",
> Bachelor thesis in International Economics and Management,
> Bocconi University

The structural solution described roughly corresponds to the organizational model generally found to be effective in innovative sectors, namely a *"differentiated and integrated" structure* (Lawrence and Lorsch 1967).

Work and responsibility is divided according to technically different disciplines and competences. Coordination across units/jobs is achieved through a set of mechanisms among which hierarchy and rules are not key, but mutual adjustment devices prevail: coordination technologies, lateral communication, platforms for knowledge sharing, meetings.

Some particular traits can be identified that are different from what would generally be expected for a SME, and can be considered specific to differentiated and integrated structures in knowledge-intensive and entrepreneurial new firms.

- *The degree of differentiation of competences and diffusion of responsibilities is particularly high.* The hierarchy of responsibilities is very flat: on its very first level, the number of directive positions is about half the number of people in the firm (and almost equal to it when considering full-time employees only). This feature and organization design principle fits the general organizational law that the more complex and uncertain the activities, the more differentiated and decentralized organizational structure should be (Garicano 2000; Grandori 2009).
- *The degree of formalization is much higher than in traditional firms of comparable size.* Documents, electronic knowledge-storing devices, codification systems and procedures for knowledge exchange are all formal supports that increase the capacity of processing complex information. This feature also fits with information-processing theory tenets (Galbraith 1974).

A second organizational model useful for entrepreneurial innovative firms is the *"networked structure"*. In this form, not only are units highly differentiated, but they are also fully and horizontally connected. More precisely, in a fully connected network-like structure, people and teams with different competences are entitled and helped to communicate all to all, are free to identify opportunities and join and collaborate around self-selected projects, and are endowed with high discretion and responsibility. Fundamental integration devices in these structures are *projects*, namely team-based, multi-competence internal temporary units for complex knowledge exchange, creative problem solving and new product and service design (e.g. Aoki 2004).

Box 3.3 gives an example of an organization that was born as a "simple hierarchy" around a single entrepreneur, but has been successfully transformed into a full-fledged and democratic partnership. As the described situation illustrates, and as has been pointed out for network structures in other types of firm (Bartlett and Ghoshal 1989), *network structures "go beyond structure"*. In other words, *organizational practices and systems* are more important than structure (which in fact may not even be defined in a stable way).

Box 3.3 Egon Zehnder International
Laura Gaillard, 2010

Egon Zehnder International (EZI) is one of the top five executive search firms in the world. The firm, founded in 1964 by Egon Zehnder, now operates in 37 countries with 63 offices. In 2010, the firm has 1200 employees, including 375 consultants. EZI offers services and expertise in the field of assessment and recruitment of top-level management resources through executive search, board consulting and leadership strategy services. The firm, which operated from inception as a single profit center, claims to have a distinctive structure and a unique vision.

Birth and growth
The idea of executive search – seeking managers for companies – originated in the United States. At the end of the 1950s, European companies also looked ripe for this innovative service. And so it was that one of the leading US executive search firms (Spencer Stuart) dispatched Egon Zehnder, a Swiss national, back to his homeland to set up offices for them first in Zurich, then in London, Frankfurt and Paris. Zehnder, a Harvard Business School graduate (1956) and former successful top manager in the advertising industry, soon discovered how unusual the idea of executive search seemed to European companies. Zehnder became convinced that the only way to overcome the resistance he encountered everywhere in Europe was to adopt an entirely new professional approach marked by absolute discretion: "I knew if I behaved discreetly and professionally, search would eventually be accepted in Europe" (E. Zehnder).[8] It was a realization that led him to found his own firm in 1964. The corporate goal was not high-speed head hunting, but a professional, systematic search for the best candidate in the long term for the needs of each individual client.

The beginnings were modest. In the first years of its existence, Egon Zehnder operated out of the Zurich office, which was staffed by a handful of consultants and a few employees. Profits were plowed back into the firm to enable new consultants to be recruited. The firm's geographic expansion was driven by client demand for a rapid response and competent local contacts. Over the years, the firm's expansion became a reliable mirror of market developments around the world. The opening of EZI's Tokyo office in 1971, the first outside Europe, reflected the opening of the Japanese market to the West. The inauguration of new offices in São Paulo (1975), Mexico City (1982) and Buenos Aires (1984) paralleled the advent of market economies in a large number of South American countries.[9] With the onset of globalization, executive search took on worldwide scope.

Continuous expansion has been a hallmark of the firm's history, but EZI members were very protective about maintaining the culture of the firm as the firm evolved. To this day, the firm's golden rules state that new offices must be financed without recourse to external funds; markets must not be accessed through acquisitions; and an experienced partner from the outset must manage each new office.

A distinctive vision and culture
Zehnder created and developed his firm with a distinctive vision, embodied in keywords and "mottoes", but also in the firm structure. He intuitively recognized that placing client interests ahead of personal interests was central to EZI's identity. To this day, *"Clients First"* remains the uppermost value that has shaped and guided the work of EZI since day one. Part of this philosophy is that every commission is handled in line with the same professional approach and standards on the basis of a *fixed fee* and conflict avoidance. Another important precept of the firm is its *"One Firm"* approach. Achieving the best possible professional results is in each case perceived as the joint responsibility of the entire firm. Egon Zehnder International sees itself not as a collection of disparate profit centers, but as a single entity – One Firm: "The most fundamental expression of our vision resides in our structure." All the consultants are organized around a single-profit center partnership, eliminating de facto competitive barriers between offices: "The three immovable pillars on which the long-term success of Egon Zehnder International was founded, in the opinion of the firm's founder, were an absolute focus on its clients, a commitment to quality, and, crucially, the principle of a partnership of equals."[10]

Governance and organization of the partnership
Egon Zehnder saw early on that his start-up could not realize its full potential if he made himself solely responsible for its success (Heifetz *et al.* 2009) and that he needed to mobilize everyone to generate solutions. In 1978, he decided to transform the firm in which he was then the majority shareholder, chairman and CEO into an international partnership.[11] Still today, the firm is a 'society' in which every partner holds an equal share

of equity and has an equal say in all important decisions – decisions to open new offices, elect new partners and make appointments to the firm's few, but central, administrative functions.

In the late 1980s, a number of *"informal sector practice groups"* began serving as exchange platforms for industry-specific knowledge. Now sector specialists are organized into global practices. Each practice group within EZI brings together the firm's consultants and partners. Along with board consulting, executive search, management appraisal and venture engine, the full list of global practices now includes financial services, consumer, life sciences, technology and communications, industrial, services, insurance, private capital and sovereign wealth funds. EZI's differentiated model means that practice consultants can collaborate, without local limitations, and provide fast, high-impact solutions for EZI's clients – wherever they are based.

One of the major characteristics of EZI is the firm's long-established practice of putting the success of the team before the success of each individual. The partners share a pool of profits distributed according to a uniform formula. Everyone's compensation rises or falls with the firm's overall performance and the partners are "intertwined in substance and purpose".

From this equality in both earnings and power stems the all-for-one, one-for-all spirit. This stands in contrast to the industry as a whole, where "head hunters" live up to their nickname by operating a bounty system, with the recruiter receiving a proportion of the salary of the post filled. As one executive at another search firm put it to me: "I hoard my information and contacts, because I get compensated on the basis of my listings. I don't even know if I'll be working with the same company in another year – why should I give away my resources?"

At Zehnder International, people of 39 different nationalities and eight religions, in 48 offices spread across 39 countries, operate as a single unit. "The fundamental difference between our firm and others is that we find ourselves all on the same ship," says Loewenstein. "The more we collaborate, the more efficient we are."

The organization structure of EZ can be represented as shown in Figure 3.2.

The compensation model was a radical departure for the industry when Egon Zehnder instituted it. Also, the firm is owned equally and entirely by its partners (consultants typically are elevated to partnership level after about six years). Even Zehnder himself, who at one time owned the firm entirely, now holds just one share, like every other partner. "I understood that if I did that, I could retain the best partners," Zehnder says. "*It made us all entrepreneurs together.* How do we work so well together? Because we've decoupled individual performance from money."

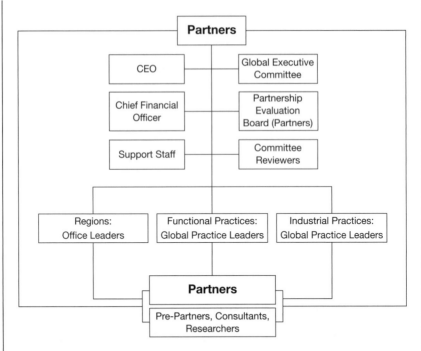

Figure 3.2 A representation of EZ structure

The firm is a partnership, wholly owned by the partners, each of whom holds an equal share. It is an arrangement designed to attract and retain top professionals who have already proven themselves in other sectors. New members of the firm, which continues to grow, are chosen carefully in line with rigorous standards. The aim is always to obtain a *"Lifelong Commitment"*. Because people join the firm to stay, there is a palpable sense of the company as a family. As one partner put it: "We know we will be working together for many years, and so we are prepared to invest time and effort into building relationships."

The success of the concept is reflected in very low fluctuation. Some critics think the concept idealistic or even outmoded. But through this approach Egon Zehnder blazed a trail for executive search in Europe, and today the organization he founded is one of the world's leading executive search firms.

Shortly after Egon Zehnder announced his retirement from the firm in June 2000, the EZI partners faced a crisis in the executive search market. The firm took a bottom-up approach to sketching out its future; the strategy review process involved each partner. Through the challenges of the downturn market, EZI tried to hold true to its core values. It eventually chose to preserve the social structure of the organization, crucial for long-term success and more important than short-term financial results. EZI remained a private partnership, they did not close any offices, and the firm opted to continue hiring and electing partners.

This form of a partnership of equals not only enabled EZI to retain the finest talent over the long term, but also proved a fine recipe for lasting personal relationships within the firm; friendships that go well beyond the customary bonds between colleagues. And so it was that the firm's distinctive entrepreneurial spirit was multiplied.

Sources: www.egonzehnder.com/.
www.egonzehnder.com/decades.
Egon Zehnder International (Harvard Business School,
N9-395-076, November 1994)
Heifetz, Grashow and Linsky (2009) "Leadership in a (Permanent) crisis"
Harvard Business Review, July–August, 62–69
Strategic Review at Egon Zehnder International
(A, B and C, Harvard Business School, N9-904-071,
May and August 2004)
Zehnder Egon (2001) "A simpler way to pay" *Harvard Business Review*,
April, 53–60

Core organizational principles able to govern new, innovative, human-capital intensive firms have in fact been indicated in the *"democratization" in decision structure and in the division of rent* (Miles *et al.* 1997; Rajan and Zingales 2000), which at the same time does not kill *"powerful incentives" to perform and innovate* (Zenger and Hesterley 1997) and takes adequate care of the *"specificity" of assets (in particular human assets)* to the firm (Blair 1996). Let us examine in detail the reasons for these prescriptions and some key organizational and human resource management practices through which they can be implemented. All the practices that we are going to present can be identified and discussed in the cases of this section, namely AX and EZ. These cases can then be analyzed in terms of more or less comprehensive applications of the following practice design principles.

"Democratic" decision structure – In general, decision rights should be allocated to actors holding the most relevant knowledge and having the most to gain from discretion. A consequence of this general principle, and more often an effective feature of the organization of new firms, is that relevant decision and control rights on activities are diffused, for both motivational and knowledge reasons. In fact, workers in new firms, even if they are employees rather than partners, are not likely to be "quasi-indifferent" to the nature of tasks, as should occur in classic authority-based employment relations. In fact, enquiries into the motivation driving people, both founders and non-founders, to join firms in the emerging and innovative sectors of the economy found that the content of work and the quality of other people – "task" and "love" – are prime motivators, i.e.

primary "modes of attachment" for a vast majority of participants. By contrast, extrinsic motivation and "money" is marginal as a prime motivator (e.g. Baron and Kreps 1999). In other words, participants and investors of human capital – and to some extent even investors of financial capital – put in their all mainly because they like the task or because they like the team, or both.

In addition to this motivational reason, the "democratization" and diffusion of decision and control rights has well-known information efficiency and knowledge governance reasons: the more tasks are complex, the more the relevant knowledge is likely to be distributed, rather than concentrated. Therefore, if decisions are to be made by the competent, the more they should be decentralized and based on teamwork (Burns and Stalker 1961; Grant 1996; Grandori 1999). In addition, even if competent, a single central decision maker would be "overloaded" by information and tall hierarchies would be very inefficient (March and Simon 1958; Galbraith 1974; Garicano 2000).

There are various ways though to achieve decentralized decision making and responsibility. A particularly significant dilemma in entrepreneurial firms is whether the diffusion of decision rights should be realized through an "*enlargement of partnership*" (as in the Egon Zehnder case) or through an "*enlargement of management*" (as in the AX case) (Colombo *et al.* 2010). In the end-chapter Minteos case the problem is practically illustrated by the engineer who initially co-opted in the entrepreneurial team as a partner and later preferred to shift to an employment contract. The most important variables to consider, according to what has been stated in the previous section and property right theory, are the *criticality of human capital investments* and the *riskiness of activities*. If a person provides mostly labor services (including directive work and expert decision making) but does not invest human capital (or money), she may prefer a risk-free reward for her services. The original entrepreneur, on his side, may not be interested in enlarging ownership in order to attract and lock in the human capital investment, or to retain the person's complementary know-how for necessarily very long periods. If the opposite situation occurs, then partnership is in order. Hence, a partnership relation should be more efficient and effective in activities when human capital investments are critical and the activities are moderately risky.

Fair rent division and moderate risk transfers – The most important set of organizational practices, complementary to decision practices, are reward policies. Incentives are a particularly delicate device when innovation is desired. This is a rather highly debated issue in fact. In the booming phase of the new economy, it was common to read and hear – from mass media and management consultants – that the new "recipe" emerging from new firms was close to "the higher the incidence of pay for performance, the better". This view though has not resisted conceptual and empirical scrutiny.

In principle, the optimal incidence of "pay performance" should vary as a function of at least four important factors (Milgrom and Roberts 1992):

- the extent to which performance is measurable;
- the agent's discretion, that is, possibility to affect results;

- the extent to which those results can be attributed to the performing agent, or rather, depend on factors beyond his control;
- the agent's degree of risk aversion (to a large extent depending, in turn, on the diversifiability of his investments).

It follows that the riskier an activity is, and the more results are influenced by exogenous variance, or are uncertain and measurable only in the long run, the less intense the optimal level of contingent reward, other things being equal. As these conditions are quite common in new firm activities the incidence of contingent rewards should not be excessively high. On the other side, in entrepreneurial firms, agent discretion should be high and thus they can substantially affect outcomes and should have a higher contingent component of reward.

In other words, in entrepreneurial firms, the prevailing factors affecting the optimal intensity of pay for performance are likely to have countervailing effects. This suggests that the optimal intensity should lie in some intermediate interval; that is, neither very high nor very low.

In addition, identification with the firm, the job, the profession, the social group is generally high in new firms. And it is well known that in conditions of high intrinsic motivation, the heavy use of monetary incentives is likely to generate undesirable reduction of intrinsic motivation. The phenomenon has been called "redundant justification" (Staw 1976) or "crowding out" (Frey 1997): instrumental motivation tends to kill, to substitute, to "crowd-out" intrinsic motivation; what was done out of passion, with monetary reward as a useful side effect, becomes something that would not be done if not in exchange for specific compensation.

Finally, firms, and new firms in particular, do not just generate normal profit; they generate *rent*, thanks to the combination of resources that are complementary, firm specific and not perfectly substitutable. If so, an issue of the fair division of rent among all the participants arises (Rajan and Zingales 2000).

If the new firm is organized as a team, or as a set of shifting teams, as it should be in highly innovative tasks, seizing and disentangling the contribution of each member or each team becomes quite difficult. This is called a "team production" situation. A somewhat egalitarian division of the firm rent is sensible in these conditions, rather than complicated or unfeasible calculations of individual performance (Blair and Stout 1999). In line with this argument, the most important component of "variable" compensation in new economy firms is not represented by individual or group or unit contingent pay schemes, but by stock options, or stock distribution or profit-sharing plans – in other words, by rights to share in the overall results of the firm.

Box 3.4 (as well as the Egon Zehnder case) illustrates how "moderate" individual pay for performance, diffused participation in firm rents, high autonomy and high incidence of teamwork can effectively characterize the human resources profile of new firms, even in different contexts.

Box 3.4 Human resource systems in new economy firms

Questionnaires were collected in Italy and in the Silicon Valley in firms listed on New Market and NASDAQ respectively, on organizational practices qualifying the degree of decentralization and team-like coordination, and the reward structure.

Reward structure – The incidence of share ownership, stock options and performance-contingent pay on the total compensation of top team members, as well as their eventual financial investments, were analysed.

Table 3.1 gives some descriptive statistics of the reward structure variables.

Table 3.1 Level and structure of compensation in the new economy (Italian NM and SV NASDAQ firms)

	Italian NM	*SV NASDAQ*
No. of respondents	163	20
Proportion of top team members investing own financial capital	41%	15%
Proportion of pay for performance compensation	23%	12%
Proportion of top team members with stock option plans	52%	60%

We also measured the variation of total compensation that accompanied entry in the first new ecomony (NE) firm with respect to the last job held in an old economy (OE) firm. Wherever top team members came from an established firm rather than another start-up (which occurred mostly in the Italian case, rather than in Silicon Valley), they experienced both increases in discretion and responsibilities and increases in total income (on average double) and in variable pay (from 14 percent to 23 percent) and especially in stock options or other property options (from 10 percent to 50 percent).

A substantial difference between Italy and California is the investment of own financial capital by the same people who also invest human capital. This difference can be ascribed to the limited development of adequate financial investors, such as financial angels and venture capitalists, whereby entrepreneurs have to invest not only their human capital but also their own financial capital.

Decision structure – The profile of the organization of work in the NE firms is pretty much aligned to a high-discretion, team-like organization, as described below.

New economy jobs are characterized by substantial levels of diffusion of decision rights. On average, in current NE jobs, people in directive positions declare that:

- the percentage of activities carried out without responding to anybody is between 30 and 40 percent;
- the time devoted to technical and professional problem-solving ranges from 50 percent (IT) to 30 percent (CA);
- the time devoted to teamwork ranges from 40 percent (IT) to 60 percent (CA).

With respect to previous jobs held in established, non-NE firms, for those who had work experience in traditional firms, all these indicators greatly increased, and the increase was almost unanimously declared as highly appreciated.

Source: data from Grandori (2002)

People mobility and firm tenure – An observable trend in new industries and new careers is a dramatic reduction in the average *firm tenure*: the period of time people stay with one firm. As testified by the "talent war" phenomenon, and by the growing concern about how to retain valuable people, the problem is created more by the propensity of people to move, rather than by firm policies. Actually, in the case of qualified work (quite unlike what usually happens in less qualified employment) there is evidence that firms prefer longer periods of stay while people would like to resell their experience, get superior positions and pay through external careers (Bagdadli *et al.* 2003; Grandori and Soda 2004). This tendency is also relevant, for various reasons, for human capital investors, that is, the entrepreneurs themselves, especially in innovative settings; for example, because they are interested in realizing economic returns on the investment or because to change company is a way of diversifying the investment over time, and because they may have a preference for starting new things and to work in informal small-sized organizations. On the other side, as previously mentioned when discussing the "entrepreneurial team" issue, firms may not realize that it is to some extent also in their interest to let people go and have a continuously renewed set of competences.

However, firm tenure should of course not be "too" short. For entrepreneurs, it cannot be shorter than the time span needed for testing the success of new projects and to actually fully contribute the required human capital. For hired managers, it cannot be shorter than the time needed to achieve some results and to increase their human capital through learning and experience so as to be able to access better positions.

The diffusion of retention devices, such as the "vesting of options" for human capital investors or "talent retention" programs for managers, seems to confirm that the preferences are not entirely aligned, and that people may prefer shorter tenure than the firms they work for. In fact, empirically it has emerged that on average (not in entrepreneurial firms) managers with relevant human capital (i.e. degrees and experience) evaluate that a firm tenure of four years is the best for them, while firms would prefer six to seven years for managerial positions (Grandori and Soda 2004). This situation is somewhat puzzling since the main reasons for firms preferring long stays are the following: (1) the rarity of talent, or (2) firm-specific competences. However, if human resources are firm specific and complementary to the firm's other assets, then all parties should prefer longer stays (Rajan and Zingales 2000). Nonetheless, both theory and empirical evidence on what human capital providers "really want" (Grandori and Soda 2004) indicates that there are a couple of conditions to be met if valuable "talent" is to be retained. They are willing to stay, provided that:

- the rents from the longer association are divided fairly;
- the firm contributes to the formation of competences, that is, invests *in* firm-specific human capital.

Part of the currently observed misalignment of preferences to firm tenure may be due to the undersized shares of rent distributed, and/or underinvestment in training and development of human resources – hypotheses that do not sound too wild.

Some firms do succeed, however, in creating long-term attachment. This may be particularly interesting where human resources are highly firm specific, are more important than technology (or embody the most relevant part of know-how), and the rate of external technical change is not very high – whereby the need to continuously change combinations of competences is not too high – a case well represented by the Egon Zehnder consultancy service firm as well as by the AX pharma firm.

The evolution of structure

In the "Stanford Project on Emerging Companies" (SPEC) (Baron and Hannan 1999; Baron and Kreps 1999), interview-based evidence was gathered on 170 high-tech firms in the Silicon Valley on the organizational model adopted, including the mode of attachment (reasons for people participation), the criteria for people selection, and the modes of coordination and control. New firms' organizational profiles were found to cluster around some key "models". Among these, an "engineering" model (based on task attachment), a "commitment" model (based on social attachment) and a "star" model (based on a leader vision and capacity) prevailed. Whatever the model, it was reported that it was hard to change: in 50 percent of cases, the interviewees could not identify any significant organizational change in those basic organizational traits after years. In other words, it seems that firms preserve some core traits they happen to be born with, as an "*imprinting*", for quite some time. This finding can be read as suggesting the need to pay a great deal of attention to the initial organization design since it is going to leave a mark. However, in half the cases, the organizational model did change, and where it did, the move was predominantly toward formal coordination and control and managerialization. In fact, if professional investors get involved, or the firm goes through an IPO, the presence of control roles and formal management systems will be required. Beyond investors, two often-related factors usually favor or even require this type of change, namely the eventual stepping out of the founder from the CEO role and the growth of the firm.

Statistical evidence indicates that, in innovative sectors, around a third of the CEO and entrepreneurial teams do leave the company they founded after some years, especially when the company goes public. This may be an indicator that, as should occur in an innovative economy, firm founders are more identified with entrepreneurship as a profession, rather than with a particular firm. But it may also indicate that founders are unwillingly losing the possibility of staying on because they are "kicked out" by new investors (Wasserman 2008). Second, although at times with some difficulty, a layer of managers is formed, and should be, as the firm grows in size, especially in uncertain sectors where intense information processing and decision making is required (Colombo and Grilli 2009).

The evolution in those organizational features is not necessarily bound to bring about convergence to a standard centralized and formalized corporation model. The Egon Zehnder case illustrates how a very successful professional firm, born as an individual entrepreneurial firm around the figure of its founder, managed to grow into a fully fledged democratic partnership, and to combine highly powerful incentives with high productivity and with continued participation throughout the firm's life.

Another possible evolutionary trajectory frequently followed by entrepreneurial firms, especially in innovative sectors, is bound to a strange fate: the more they are successful and grow, the more likely they are to "die" by *acquisition*. This is stated as an oxymoron since of course being acquired could be considered a change rather than a death. Nevertheless, if conglomerated in a corporation, the entrepreneurial firm ceases to exist as such, in spite of eventually preserving some of its organizational imprinting and some traits of entrepreneurial team-like governance "under the shadow of hierarchy". This fate is exemplified by The Body Shop case (Chapters 1 and 4), finally acquired by L'Oréal, although it is said (by its founder) to have "retained its unique identity and values" and to "continue to be run independently from its head office in Littlehampton" like a "Trojan horse in a big business".

Other cases indicate that still other routes and options are available. For example, the Virgin case (Chapter 2) highlights the possibility that the entrepreneurial firm becomes itself the "mother firm" of new entrepreneurial firms through spin-offs. In a sense, this is a way of growing without upsizing. This possibility is attractive from the point of view of sustaining the general incidence of entrepreneurial firms in the wider economic system (Baumol *et al.* 2007) and to promote economic growth not necessarily through the "internal growth" of single firms in size (which has a variety of drawbacks for entrepreneurship), but through the "external growth" through alliances and inter-firm networks.

The next two chapters are dedicated to these two problems and processes respectively: whether to grow internally or to grow externally through inter-firm networks (Chapter 4); and, if internal growth is in order, how to grow as a single firm without losing an entrepreneurial character (Chapter 5).

Key points

This chapter has defined and assessed some salient and distinctive governance and organizational configurations for entrepreneurial firms.

First, the *legal and governance structure* is considered. In connection with recent developments in the theory of the firm and of the entrepreneurial firm, a partition of forms of enterprise into the two classes of *people-based forms* and *asset-based forms* is proposed and discussed as particularly relevant for entrepreneurship – along with some hybrid forms among them. In entrepreneurial firms in fact, on one side the specific identity of people typically matters (whereby people-based forms would be appropriate); but on the other side, "capital" of both the human and the financial kind is invested and there is a need for "locking" it in (whereby asset-based forms should be better). In addition, the chapter discusses the possible attractiveness for entrepreneurship of forms enterprise – such as cooperatives and foundations – bounding the firm to a particular (non-profit) mission and to a particular (democratic) organization.

The second section examines the (surprisingly neglected) theme of the *internal organization of entrepreneurial firms*. Here too two classes are identified, with very different properties in terms of expected innovation: *"traditional" entrepreneurial firms* organized as *"simple hierarchies"* or *"simple communities"* (with lower innovation potential); and *"innovative" entrepreneurial firms* sustained by *"differentiated and integrated structures"* or by *"networked forms"*.

Analysis questions

On in-chapter cases

- How did the ownership and organizational structure of Egon Zehnder co-evolve? Which problems and eventual mismatches could be detected?
- In what respects do AX and EZ governance and organization forms differ? How can these differences be explained and assessed?

On end-chapter case

- How can the governance and organization structure of Minteos be characterized?
- How does it relate with the type of opportunities exploited (Chapter 1) and with the types of resources invested (Chapter 2)?
- Which further evolution of structure can be envisaged?

End-chapter case: Minteos

Anna Grandori and Milos Starovic, 2010

"Our vision is that of an 'Internet of Nature'. Trees and rivers that talk through the web. Imagine that nature can speak to you. Currently, the internet is just linking people and connecting machines; tomorrow it is going to work between industries. But nobody is thinking about nature" (M. Brini, CEO).

Groundbreaking in Italian and worldwide markets, with innovative solutions such as a wireless sensor network, nano-sensors and RFID[12] applications, the company focuses on environmental monitoring. Its core technology and product is in fact an environmental monitoring system: wireless-smart mini-sensors providing environmental information in real time; for example, wildfire detection, flood detection, landslides, pollution levels, industrial emission detection.

For example, FireLess is an automatic wildfire detection system based on innovative "in situ" monitoring. Many sensors are deployed in the forest, and in case of fire, they immediately send an alarm to the central server that sends a warning to firefighters by SMS or phone within a few seconds.

Many combined technologies are employed in the product: internet web, mobile technologies, chip radio frequencies, energy harvesting, sensor devices and geo-localization platforms.

Minteos was in fact founded by a team of entrepreneurs with experience in electronics, mobile computing, telecommunication and wireless markets. Minteos is focused on the machine-to-machine market. Machine-to-machine (M2M) refers to data communication between machines, the integrated use of telecommunications and informatics, especially by means of public wireless networks.

Opportunity identification and formulation of a project

Marco Brini, CEO of Minteos, has been working in the ICT sector since 1995. He received his math degree at the University of Turin. After completing several years of work experience in the IT sector, he decided to do an MBA program and advance his knowledge by coming into direct contact with the business environment. He was previously an R&D manager for a small company where he was unreservedly committed to the business development processes in the company, and as a result he usually used to work late into the evening.

"At one point I became aware that I worked too much and I asked myself: can I do any better than that? I had initial work experience in the field of computer and information systems. But I wished to be an entrepreneur. My father was. I did not like to spend my life in boring large organizations. It was a choice of profession, of a type of work. I liked philosophy and had a degree in math. To start with, I asked myself what I could do with my competences. I looked for a highly developing area in which my competences, eventually integrated with some others, could be fruitfully employed. During my university studies I worked on a project on the management of the IT network of the Polytechnic University of

Turin, specializing in IS safety. Hence, when I began to think of a start-up, I turned back to the researchers and technicians I knew at the university in order to share ideas and see whether somebody would like to join me with complementary technical competences. This process led to the identification of the wireless sensor networks field and to the formation of a tentative alliance with an electronic engineer as a potential partner in forming an initial entrepreneurial team.

"Systematic info gathering and discussions in the network of senior professionals within my previous contacts followed. We started out by analyzing the sector and the gaps in it: what products or services might be needed that were not offered. We assessed the attractiveness of various alternatives in terms of the possibility of occupying an advantageous position in the value chain and level of completion, since we were trying to identify an attractive but not overcrowded market. On the basis of these considerations, applications for the security and health sectors were rejected while environmental applications were selected. Environment seemed a good market at least for the following reasons: environment as an industry was under-populated, there were only a few big companies that were making serious investments; second, institutions on both political and economical levels were paying increasing attention to environmental issues.

"We had to travel all over the world. We went to Chicago, Boston, Northern Europe; we looked into the plentiful publications in the field of ICT and then sorted the best things that everybody links to the future. We then asked what the needs in the segment of environmental applications of sensor devices were. Risk prevention was identified as the area of highest demand. A lot of interviewing with environmental operators followed. We discovered that there were significant unspent budgets in public administrations allocated to fire protection. Therefore, we hypothesized that a device for fire protection could be the idea. We developed a prototype. You need to have an object, as soon as possible.

"This is especially useful in Italy and other EU countries where investors are not very used to putting money in something they cannot touch. In addition, some of the solutions offered by Minteos were not patentable, since they were mentioned in past publications of USA universities. So we put a lot of work into embodying knowledge into the solution; to make the prototype; to test the prototype; to make the prototype work.

"In addition, even if we had come up with two things to patent, we hadn't done so up to this point due to typical bureaucratic problems. If you want to register a good patent, you incur vast administrative costs. To be precise, we were going to solely patent products/technologies of great magnitude."

The Minteos founding team presented their prototype to technical, political and social experts and users. They gathered plenty of suggestions not only on fire detection, but also on many other possible functionalities and uses that their device might have (i.e. the detection of flood and landslides). The development of this and other similar applications is still flourishing and at a much lower and diminishing cost.

"We invested a lot in the planning process. The plan was the following: let's find a good sector and a good market. Let's form a good team in a good environment and then be patient and wait. Let's raise some money at the appropriate moment and then when the moment is right there is likely to be a boom in the machine-to-machine market and everybody would seriously start thinking of the environment."

Incubation and entrepreneurial team formation

Minteos brings together the expertise of business developers and engineers, working closely with several academic institutions.

"The firm was started in Turin within the new 'incubator' established in connection with the Turin's Polytechnic University. We worked intensively for a year to be admitted to the Innovative Enterprise Incubator of the Polytechnic University of Turin (*Incubatore Imprese Innovative Politecnico di Torino* – I3P)." I3P is a non-profit joint-stock consortium (Società Cosortile per Azioni) constituted by the Politecnico di Torino, the Province of Torino, the Chamber of Commerce of Torino, Finpiemonte, Torino Wireless Foundation, and the City of Torino. I3P was established to promote and support enterprise creation, building on the innovative potential developed in research institutions across the territory. The underlying goal of I3P is to promote the creation and growth of new knowledge-based enterprises that can benefit from the Incubator's close ties to the Politecnico di Torino, and its capacity to catalyze, stimulate and drive cutting-edge business initiatives. The objective is to encourage aspiring entrepreneurs who can benefit from the proximity of the university departments, to take on business challenges and to support them in the start-up of a new enterprise. To enter the incubation program, aspiring entrepreneurs need to develop an innovative or knowledge-based business idea into a suitable business plan, judged to be of interest to the market. There are approximately 120 ideas per year that compete to gain access to the incubator. I3P is an extremely selective institution. It was accredited with the best incubator in the world in 2004.

"We were two partners at the outset: myself and a researcher of PoliTO for the technical design activity. We started in a very pathetic way, that is, 50:50 percent property rights for the activity. After one year or so, it turned out that she would have preferred to be paid as a technician rather than as a partner. She felt her contribution was strictly technical and she could not withstand significant variations in the reward. I therefore searched for another technical partner through my professional network and the PoliTO incubator. Individuals with business degrees are pretty expensive. If I were to involve somebody with a business background we would have to pay this person in terms of shares, but there aren't shares for everybody. In the incubator, I found Lazarescu, a highly competent, motivated, enthusiastic engineering partner who co-invested his expertise and his time to get the project to take off. Our joint contributions were stated in advance with respect to defining a contract or knowing whether we would succeed. When we established this and really started we were three owner-entrepreneurs, me with 62 percent, Lazarescu holding 30 percent and my original partner with 8 percent. At the beginning, other collaborators played a limited role. The three of us were doing everything. We are now around ten people; we hired a professional junior resource data manager and are a more diversified team. It is important to understand what is within the technology. Personally, I cannot go to the core. But I can understand the substance. And that is what really matters. If you do not understand the limits or the opportunities of the technology, it is difficult to evaluate business ideas appropriately and as a result, never-ending exhausting meetings with technical guys will take place."

Product development

Potential customers for Minteos products are public institutions and companies that provide services for public institutions. Furthermore, private individuals who are owners of huge properties are enthusiastic about Minteos' solutions. For instance, private individuals owning large amounts of land in South Africa are keen on investing in solutions that can preserve their property from natural disasters.

It is very complicated to determine the market size in terms of potential industry earnings. "Suppose you ask the question: What is the potential market for Skype? Skype was born ten years ago when its founders were looking for venture capital funding. In order to define the potential market for Skype we have to count the number of people who use the internet every day. Besides, how many people will use the internet in the future? How many people will use Skype? Some people will use it for sure; but who really knows how many people are willing to pay to use Skype? Some questions have answers that are hard to quantify."

It could be said that the approach was about thinking and talking of the problems that can be solved with what products – actually problem size rather than market size.

"If a fire catches in one square meter you can solve this problem with a bucket of water; if it catches a one-hectare area you can still eliminate it. But, if the fire grabs hold in a three-hectares zone, there is going to be huge trouble. Taking into consideration changing weather conditions, wind, for example, it will take at least two days, working all day and night to defeat the fire and has the potential of becoming a natural disaster. This is the fundamental problem.

"People are trading carbon dioxide shares. There are currently several trading systems in place with the largest being the European Union's. The carbon market makes up the largest portion of these and is growing hugely in popularity. Many businesses have welcomed emissions trading as the best way to mitigate climate change. But if the forest is gone, there is no more carbon dioxide altogether.

"In addition, let's think about flooding. Yearly, there is between $1bn and $6bn of damage caused by flooding in the United States. This number is representative only of the US. Let's shift to the Italian example. Severe floods hit northern Italy during October of 2000. The hardest hit area was Piemonte (the Region of Tourin). There was no rail service between Milano and Turin for three days. If truth be told, nobody counted the damage this environmental disaster caused."

In connection with potential competitors, Mr. Brini judges that strong companies will not enter into the M2M sector very soon.

"If the powerful guys come into the sector when we are ready then this will be good news for us, because they are going to buy us. The good news is that we always pay attention to what occurs elsewhere in the world. And we are aware of the heavy investments made by Intel, Honeywell and Siemens in recent periods. Personally, I do not think we will have that many competitors. So far, our competitors have been mature companies. In each sector, you have some very experienced companies that have been present for 40 to 50 years in the sector and have well-established connections with public institutions. But those companies are not a threat to us because they are attached to traditional solutions and mature technologies. To the contrary, we are promoting modern technologies. We've made a choice to become cutting-edge; it is a risky business because when you use cutting-edge technologies, you have to demonstrate that it works effectively. We started with a basic sensor and are moving onto software and mobile. That would give us strength. We want to control the substance and once we control it, we will know exactly what we are doing and we'll be able to choose the best modules."

Financing the new venture

"The first source of finance we used was our own money. The second source of finance was our time, which is sometimes even more important than mere money!"

The founders of Minteos invested around €30,000 as initial capital: "There is no way to convince anybody at the very initial stage. You are forced to use personal funds or those of close personal relatives and contacts."

Acceptance in the I3P Incubator was also fundamental as a channel to gain access to sources of finance (in addition to technical contacts): "Usually barely one-eighth of ideas are accepted, but once you gain entry in I3P, you encompass a powerful brand. Acceptance by I3P is a convincing assurance for banks and opens the doors of the financial community in general."

The incubator allowed access to some funding received from public sources. The first professional investor was a financial angel: "I kept in touch with a few financial angels from my previous work experience, but it is like going against the stream. I have to admit that for the most part it was advantageous to belong to I3P. You need strong recommendations to be admitted to I3P, and to be recommended you need to be entirely devoted to the work. Moreover, supportive references were articles appearing in *Il Sole 24 Ore* and *La Stampa*,[13] which pointed out that Minteos was one of the most creative start-ups in the past several years."

In addition, in June 2007, Minteos was chosen to present its business for the first time at the IBAN Convention[14] in Milan. After the IBAN convention, the Italian financial angel network contacted them: "In the end, we have two financial angels: Maurizio and Filippo and they are part of our team, they risk and sweat with us. They talk a lot about us and present the company with pride."

Minteos considered other alternatives, such as industrial investors, private equity and venture capitalists but experienced various difficulties in those relations. The Minteos team found them very formal, cold and negotiation oriented. They got the impression that these formal financial communities did not understand the substance behind their product offering. On the other hand, business angels were less structured in their approach, more rapid and had more substantive commitment to the product. A two-page contract, a letter of intent oriented to defining the relationship sufficed. This informality, however, goes alongside the demand for geographical proximity to the business. For instance, in order to meet the investment criteria of London business angels, the start-up has to be located in the south-east of England. Although for Minteos it would be easier to collect funds in the UK or US, its team plans to stay in Turin due to the strong ties with a top-tier academic and research institution, the Polytechnic University of Turin and with I3P.

With reference to the monetary returns for financial angels, Mr. Brini was thinking of return on equity (ROE). ROE is a measure of a corporation's profitability that reveals how much profit a company generates with the money financial angels have invested: "Regarding monetary returns for financial angels, I hoped for around a 10 percent ROE, which is the prevailing percentage for financial angels."

As to ownership, financial angels entered with 15 percent initially and through a second round of financing are now at 23 percent. Correspondingly, the shares of the three entrepreneurs were respectively diluted to 52 percent, 26 percent and 7 percent in the first round and to 47 percent, 24 percent and 6 percent in the second round.

Organization

"All of us – entrepreneurs and financial investors – are on the board and very involved in managerial and technical decision making. As to organizational structure, we do not think of this in traditional vertical terms. Therefore, we choose to also represent it in a circular rather than pyramidal way. In addition, we included in the representation of 'our' organization important 'external' partners" [as can be seen in Figure 3.3].

Exit strategy

"Sooner or later there should be a way out," the CEO says. "The first alternative is an IPO[15] and I do not think I will still be here after it. I like to do new things. But if I were, my intention would be to go on starting up new projects within the firm. The second alternative is the sale of the company to a new investor – supposedly a multinational company such as Honeywell, Siemens or Google." Minteos' founders have expectations that their start-up could be evaluated in the range of €20–40 million: "If everything goes as planned, we shall get to this figure. Our technology is advanced, but we must still never forget to be in the right place at the right time."

Sources:
Starovic, M. (2007) "Financial angel networks"
Bachelor thesis in International Economics and Management, Bocconi
Grandori, A. (2007) Minteos – Interview with M. Brini
case study, Bocconi University

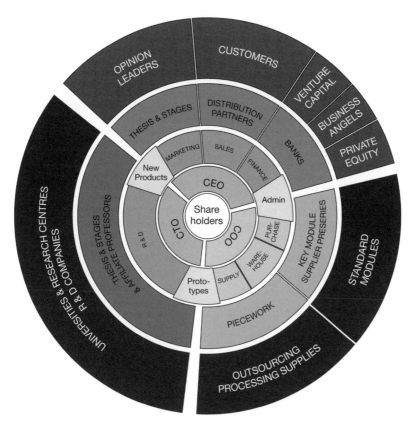

Figure 3.3 Minteos' representation of Minteos organization structure

Notes

1 In addition, there are forms of foundations in which neither the identities of partners nor objectives are specified and that therefore can also be used for commercial purposes. This is the case of the *Anstalt* (meaning "institute" in German), under which juridical personality is attributed to a patrimony or set of assets, for conducting any kind of activity. The form is present in the legislation of Liechtenstein and used by entrepreneurs of various European countries due to its flexibility and tax advantages.
2 Carl Schramm (2010) "All Entrepreneurship is social. Let's not overlook what traditional entrepreneurs contribute to the society" *Stanford Social Innovation Review* Spring: 21–22.
3 The real name of the company and its products have been changed as per the company's request.
4 Seventeen km east of Bydgoszcz.
5 We are in the year 2005.
6 AX's IT system is based on SQL language and CRM software for production planning and supervision. Statistical software is used to predict future sales. In future AX® may open an online store but this is not yet the case.

7 Commonly via the local newspaper, but of course the means depends on the need and skills required and thus particular decisions about where to communicate that AX® is recruiting is assessed on a case-by-case basis.

8 EZI website.

9 A pattern repeated in the early 1990s as new offices were opened in the capital cities of former Eastern Bloc states, including Budapest and Prague in 1992.

10 EZI website.

11 Step by Step – Internationalization (from "Decades of Leadership") 2004, www.egonzehnder.com/decades.

12 RFID – Radio Frequency Identification; automatic identification method, relying on storing and remotely retrieving data using devices called RFID tags or transponders.

13 Text available online: www.lastampa.it/_web/cmstp/tmplrubriche/tecnologia/grubrica.asp?ID_blog = 30&ID_articolo = 1848&ID_sezione = &sezione =.

14 Italian Business Angel Network (IBAN) convention, June 25, 2007 "Creation and growth of innovative companies: the International vs. the Italian experience".

15 IPO – Initial Public Offering. This is the first sale of a corporation's common shares to investors on a public stock exchange. The main purpose of an IPO is to raise capital for the corporation.

4 The internal and external growth of entrepreneurial firms

Anna Grandori and Laura Gaillard

Chapter 4 contents[*]

4.1 The boundaries of the entrepreneurial firm

4.2 Networked growth (and networked birth)

The problem of firm boundaries has a long, noble and Nobel-Prize tradition in organizational and economic studies, as it is connected with the problem of the nature of the firm (Williamson 1975, 1981). However, only recently that type of analysis has been applied to the specific problem of the nature and boundaries of the entrepreneurial firm (Alvarez and Barney 2007; Foss and Klein 2004). Actually, the "application" to the entrepreneurial firm has also enriched the theory, as it has integrated the traditional analysis of the problem based on the comparative *costs* of internal and external organization, with *knowledge* factors (Langlois 2007; Grandori 2010b).

It is worth highlighting that, building on those contributions, the assumption that start-ups are destined to grow – the growth is even a fundamental parameter for evaluating a firm success, widespread in the entrepreneurship literature and the world – is to be problematized. Whether and where to grow is a choice.

This chapter addresses that question and provides a basic model for a sound answer. Second, it addresses the related, ensuing question of what types of contracts and agreements with other firms may be used, should the choice be in favor of external organization of an activity rather than of internal expansion.

4.1 The boundaries of the entrepreneurial firm

From the very outset, a new firm faces some core questions affecting its boundaries and its external organization. Which activities should the firm conduct internally and which should it procure from others? If relying on other firms, how should coordination be achieved? Should the firm grow at all, and if

---

[*] Text by Anna Grandori, cases by the authors indicated in boxes.

so, how much and in what way? As a matter of fact, some firms grow to become vertically and horizontally integrated, while for others it seems efficient to remain small. Some firms externalize production, distribution, even R&D, while others do not. Some firms, or some activities in the same firm, grow by expanding their boundaries while others grow by forming alliances with other firms. Actually, those questions can even be applied to the very first set of activities constituting a firm: should the firm start out as an independent enterprise or in an affiliated mode?

What factors should be considered in these decisions?

Two basic factors – and a common "mistake" – can be appraised by considering the evolution of firm boundaries at AX (Box 4.1).

Box 4.1 The evolution of firm boundaries at AX

AX licenses its core product (P1) from Scandinavia.[1] The CEO constantly looks for new opportunities and provides ideas for the design of new products. The R&D manager elaborates the formulae. The final stage is selling the products to wholesalers.

The firm buys the materials (plastics, packaging, etc.) but internally produces all the liquids necessary for the final products. It also carries out the assembly process.

At the beginning and throughout almost all the year 2000, production was largely externalized, while sales were managed internally. It soon turned out that the internal sales force was a costly activity and so, in 2005, AX decided to outsource them. An agreement was signed with a promoter. "For the first year, it worked well", says the CEO, "but at some point, we realized that sales were no longer increasing and over time began decreasing for some products." Outsourcing sales was thereafter no longer judged a good choice, and by mid-2007, AX decided to internalize the sales force. Mr. ML hypothesized that four sales people would be needed to get it started plus an area manager.

Having observed the sales force market price and having made the appropriate calculations together with the accountant, Mr. ML concluded that AX would bear similar costs to the outsourced sales force. Straight away, practically as a team, the four sales people and the area manager[2] were employed. Over time the hypothesis was confirmed the salaries of the four sales people and area manager did not exceed the contributions previously paid to the promoter. Moreover, sales soon stabilized and by the end of 2008 had achieved a 20 percent growth rate.

With the internalization of the sales force though came an increase in administrative works: car-leasing, petrol refunding, etc. Mr. ML soon realized that the accountant could no longer be only part time and he was thus employed full time from 2008, although with flexible working hours. In 2008, the structure was as shown in Figure 4.1.

Figure 4.1 The organization structure of AX in 2008

Soon after these organizational changes took place, as the business was flourishing and new opportunities appeared (the Regional Entrepreneurship Incubator approved AX's application), part of the production was internalized. This investment proved to be successful and cost-effective. AX still needs to outsource the production of some products, as it does not own the appropriate technology yet, but is considering internalizing the production in the future, since its relationship with external suppliers is far from satisfactory.

"Even though I keep hearing from people that outsourcing is a cheaper solution, I now claim it is not always appropriate: not always cheaper nor beneficial" concludes Mr. ML.

Source: adapted excerpts from Leśniewska, A. (2010)
"The internal organization of an entrepreneurial firm"
Bachelor thesis in International Economics and Management,
Bocconi University

A common mistake – that AX ran into and tried to correct as a result of experience – is to decide on the basis of a simple comparison between the costs of internal production and the costs of external procurement as represented in prices.

Comparative production costs are of course important, but another category of costs is just as important. This second category of costs are *coordination costs* (also known as "*transaction costs*"). In fact, they include all the costs of transferring goods and services between economic actors and stages of activity: the costs of search for partners, of quality and performance evaluations, of negotiation of exchange terms and contractual provisions, of control of respecting established conditions (Williamson 1981). The cost of coordination rises with interdependence (Richardson 1972; Thompson 1967). Hence, the higher the interdependence, the more convenient it is to conduct the activities in the same unit/firm.

Interdependence is likely to be high if:

• exchanges are complicated by *uncertainty* and a lot of ad hoc adjustments are to be made to face variations in external conditions;

- activities, and the resources to conduct them, are *specific to the focal firm*, that is, higher value can be realized in conducting them by keeping these resources associated and a lot of ad hoc adjustments are made to meet the specific requirements.

New activities typically imply transactions that rank high in these criteria. In other words, high coordination costs with external partners on new activities favor internalization.

The second factor is *competence*. Which firm "knows more" and can realize better outputs? It is not just a matter of the cost of production of the "same" outputs, as the AX case indicates. Outputs can differ sharply in terms of quality, timeliness, reliability, assistance, etc. The level of development of possible competent suppliers "around" the new firm is therefore a fundamental factor in making outsourcing feasible. In the AX case, location in a medical district allowed it at least to find suppliers. If products and technologies are brand new, external providers of components may not exist at all. *The unavailability of suitable external competences limits externalization possibilities in new activities.*

By contrast, however, the case also illustrates the common new firm problem of not (yet) having the competences to perform all the relevant interdependent activities. *The unavailability of internal competences plays the opposite role: it forces searching for external partners.*

In sum, so far we have highlighted how *three fundamental factors are likely to affect new firm boundaries: the relative availability of technical capabilities (competence), the comparative production costs, and the comparative coordination costs.*

Still, this is not the whole story. Consider the factors that at the outset affected the decision to produce internally or outsource at Minteos, and the subsequent growth of the firm by expanding its product portfolio (Box 4.2).

Box 4.2 Minteos (II) The evolution of firm boundaries*
Anna Grandori 2010

Relations with partners and make-or-buy choices
"As to external partners, the problem, at the outset, is that it is difficult to predict all the possible functions of the product. This in turn tends to require flexible internal production. The lack of standards also contributes. Second, if you rely on external sources you may need to 'protect' yourself and to try to keep too many secrets, with the result of diminishing visibility and understanding of the potentiality of the product. It should be said, though, that our product did not have components that we could not realize ourselves." The "core" of Minteos was thus defined, and it was an engineering and production one.

"In order to develop though, we are going to sign a variety of big contract jobs in the area of risk prevention. But most important we define formal or informal partnerships with sector experts such as university professors, researchers or experienced consultants. We are going to use external producers of standardizable components more intensively. Although relatively standard, our components are extremely precise and delicate (e.g. chips), and even a very small imperfection would imply throwing away the entire lot. Hence, we are increasingly relying on external production but we use very strict, protective and elaborated contracts with a number of suppliers that we define as 'strategic suppliers'.

"On the client side, we increasingly rely on distribution companies rather than keeping track directly of all contacts with final users such as public administrations or industrial users. Our distributors are private companies who make a small technical and financial investment by specializing in our technical platform. In sum, we were born as an engineering and production firm, but we are growing into a design and commercialization firm."

From Minteos to Enveve: the expansion of the product portfolio

The range of products constantly expanded following the potential of new applications of the basic technological capabilities and the environmental mission. To accompany this evolution and expansion Minteos moved the HQ to Geneva in Switzerland, under the new name of Enveve.

Products

- *FireLess.* Real-time wildfire detection through temperature sensors fixed on trees. Phone call, SMS and email alerts in case of wildfire. Quick intervention, automatic risk reduction, no false alarms, low-cost. Risky forest areas (close to hospitals, chemical sites, etc.), interface areas (close to paths, houses, highways, etc.), shadow areas (where other systems cannot detect fire).
- *FireLess 2.* Wildfire dynamic risk monitoring through weather stations and soil moisture sensors. Allows the manager to better manage the intervention plan. Risky forest areas requiring local weather forecasts to plan and predict wildfire intervention.
- *FloodAlert.* Real-time flood warning through water-level monitoring installed in second rivers. Multichannel alerts in case of danger. Knowing the flooding risk in advance allows giving evacuation orders and to protect the valuable property earlier, saving both lives and money. Second rivers, groundwater, lakes; underpasses, tunnels, drains; tanks, dikes, silos.
- *Sewage Alert.* Real-time-level monitoring. Can activate pumps in overflow risk. Useful for sewage management. Sewerages, drains.
- *FireSens.* Fire detection for industrial warehouses through CO monitoring. Automatic, no false alarms, low-cost. Real-time alerts in case of danger. Warehouses, chemical sites, construction sites, buildings.

- *DamWatch*. Inclinometric variation monitoring through motion sensors for hydraulic structures.

Prototypes
- *SensAir*. Air quality control through wireless sensor network monitoring atmospheric gas concentrations (O3, CO, NO, NO2). Allows authorities to know the air quality in the urban area and to access the data in real time via internet. Uses: cities, chemical sites.
- *GasAlert*. Gas leak detection through spatially distributed gas sensors. Real-time alerts in case of leakage potentially saving lives in a workplace. Uses: chemical labs, industrial sites, ports, pipelines, tank trucks, etc.
- *Energy Efficiency*. CO, methane, temperature, humidity, light monitoring for energy building efficiency. Allows optimizing energy consumption in monitored conditions. Uses: buildings, factories, plants.
- *FOphID*. Optical fiber physical intrusion detection through light and motion sensors installed in the pipe. Real-time and geolocalized alerts when someone touches or drills a hole in the pipe. Uses: optical fiber cables.

Applications Users:
- *Watersense*. Water quality control through Ph, DO, dioxin, salt, hydrocarbon monitoring. Allows knowing through the internet the human impact on marine areas and avoid salt contamination to groundwater. Coastal areas, rivers, groundwater, etc.
- *Path Control*. Solution to count people on hiking paths. Can be converted to count cars on roads, highways. Provide land/traffic managers accessible data online. Paths, hiking paths, streets, roads, highways.
- *SmartTrash*. Sensors which provide a garbage can-level indicator. Useful for trash management optimization. Garbage cans.
- *Silo Control*. Silo monitoring through methane sensors and a level indicator. Allows farmers to avoid silo explosions and optimize stock management. Silos.
- *Food Monitor*. Food preservation monitoring through temperature and humidity (refrigeration), sulphur dioxide (oxidation), carbon dioxide (toxic inhibition) sensors. Allows agroalimentary companies to monitor food preservation conditions, optimizing their processes. Agroalimentary companies.
- *LandAlert*. Real-time landslide detection through motion sensors. Allows securing the moving areas before the landslide triggers. Second rivers, groundwater, lakes, underpasses, tunnels, drains, tanks, dikes, silos.

- *SnowAlert.* Real-time snow monitoring through motion, temperature, level sensors. Allows knowing the avalanche risk in real time and countermeasures to prevent the danger. Any risky mountain area.

Sources: Grandori, A. (2008) "Minteos, case study" Bocconi University; Enveve presentation, M. Brini, Bocconi University, March 2010
* Minteos (I) is the end-Chapter 3 case

The following features stand out as *additional, knowledge-related factors favoring the internal organization of activities*, which in fact have been stressed as central in the design of entrepreneurial and knowledge-intensive firm boundaries (Alvarez and Barney 2007; Acs 2005; Chesbrough *et al.* 2006; Grandori 2010b):

- the risk of *knowledge spill-overs*;
- the need to *discover the very design of new products by experimenting* in producing them;
- *the economies of scope* realizable by applying the firm's specific competences to new fields.

The factors examined thus far bring us to an apparently paradoxical conclusion: *the more innovative and therefore unique the activities of the new firms are, the more they should be internalized for both production and coordination cost and knowledge reasons; however, the less it is likely that the firm can master and own the competences to master all of them, then the more it needs external partners.*

Actually, the reality of new firms squares well with these firm boundary design propositions and shows that is possible to have *both an integrated "production core" and a variety of external agreements, especially to secure complementary competences.* The tools provided so far in this chapter should help in discriminating which activities should stay at the core and which should not. The factors analyzed hence allow understanding why and when the new firm is born with a very thin, rather than thick, production core. The AX case is actually representative of a "born disintegrated" pattern, Minteos of a "born integrated" pattern.

In this respect, it is worth noting that even if production is very specific and unique, whereby the new firm is born more integrated, a number of less unique, more standard activities are typically needed at least in administrative areas. In turn, these are areas where new firms typically lack consolidated competences as well as economies of scale. Hence, services such as accountancy, legal advice, financial analyses, personnel administration and purchasing are candidates for "out-sourcing" (as in AX). Alternatively, in order to avoid having to bear the entire coordination cost of outsourced services, these activities are candidates for "pooled-sourcing": the common provision of these services in association with other firms in the same sector or region. But in this case, the activities are not "outsourced" by way of market relations with other firms, but through the organized association of numerous entrepreneurs. This is the theme of the next section.

4.2 Networked growth (and networked birth)

In the light of the factors affecting effective firm boundaries, it should be observed that not all entrepreneurial firms should start-up small nor, if they do so, should they grow in the sense of expanding firm boundaries.

First, internal growth may not always respond to the relevant cost and knowledge factors affecting the effective boundaries highlighted in the former section. For example, knowledge mastering in science-based industries may require high specialization and enjoy few economies of scale; for instance, biotech firms tend to remain research-oriented, team-like firms, collaborating with large pharmaceutical corporations. Growth in an area rich in opportunities, in these cases, can be more effectively achieved through the founding of new firms rather than through the expansion of former start-ups. This process is often, however, linked to former entrepreneurial activities, as it "leverages" on these: new firms are founded in connection with formerly started entrepreneurial firms to perform complementary activities, often by former employees. This process of collective and "external" growth can be highly beneficial for the economic development of regions and industries (Grandori and Cacciatori 2010) as well as for the firms involved. In other words, *to grow or not to grow is a decision*, and growth is not a generalized must. The relevant factors that should inform this decision are the previously highlighted factors affecting efficient firm boundaries, considered dynamically over time. For example, as firm-specific competences become accumulated, further expansion can leverage on them through the development of new applications (Teece 1982). Alternatively, mergers and acquisitions may be justified to secure the coordinated provision of highly complementary competences or the coordinated conduct of highly interdependent activities. In other words, economies of scale and scope, together with interdependencies and specificities linking activities (actual or prospective), can not only tell *whether to grow* but also *in which direction* to grow (as illustrated in the Minteos case (Box 4.2)).

In addition, some specific internal coordination factors may limit firm size in entrepreneurial settings. Entrepreneurs may well assign a high negative weight to internal coordination cost increases due to increases in firm size: costs due to the need to write procedures and formal rules, to set up explicit control systems, to divide labor and assign stable jobs and responsibilities, etc.; in a word, to "bureaucratize" the organization. In addition, the loss of the team-like format and joint problem-solving atmosphere may reduce innovative decision quality, as examined in Chapter 1. In other words, the marginal costs of internal coordination, generated by the aggregation of further activities, may often be high for entrepreneurial firms. *Diseconomies of size are likely to be particularly important for entrepreneurial firms.* "External growth" can therefore be attractive. For example, the Virgin growth model ensued from a preference for keeping firm size small. Eventually growth was achieved by creating a group of firms through spin-offs, rather than by letting the original firm expand its own boundaries.

Second, entrepreneurial firms may be "*born large*" thanks to association strategies and to multi-partner societies. Although this option is particularly relevant nowadays, there are examples of this way of organizing entrepreneurship on a large scale even in ancient times, when the ventures involved risky exploration and an international dimension. An interesting example, not only considered one of the first forms of "enterprise" (Hansmann *et al.* 2006) but also rather similar to the modern entrepreneurial firm (Brouwer 2005), is the Middle Ages "commenda" used in the 1200s by merchants in Venice, Pisa and Genoa and later in various European countries to conduct large-scale uncertain explorative economic projects; for example, involving travel overseas for international trade. The commenda was set up as a large multi-partner equity-based, limited liability company, involving financial investors, the captain of a maritime venture and the ship providers, all sharing risk and profits.

Contemporary *"born global" firms* are typically started by entrepreneurs having constructed strong international business networks, so that they can pool inputs and/or sale outputs in multiple countries, benefitting "from extensive coordination among multiple organizational activities, the locations of which are geographically unlimited" (Oviatt and McDougall 1994). The international network of strong ties is transformed in a "proprietary network" by setting up an enterprise on that very social asset. Oviatt and McDougall (1995), for example, report that "One global start-up we studied identified its 'proprietary network' as its essential competitive advantage." Further studies by these authors (Oviatt and McDougall 2005) support the view that the main asset on which global start-ups are based is social capital transformed in a proprietary firm asset: "global start-ups internalize a minimal portion of their assets"; make greater use of less costly governance mechanisms (such as inter-firm networks and alliances); gain foreign location advantages from private knowledge that they possess or produce; and make them sustainable through both de facto and legal protection (imperfect imitability, patent, licensing).

One of the most vivid, and indeed ubiquitously present, contemporary examples of such an enterprise is Skype (Box 4.3).

Box 4.3 Skype: a contemporary "born global" enterprise
Laura Gaillard, 2010

Skype Technologies S.A. is the Luxembourg-based company that develops and operates the VoIP software Skype. Skype disrupted the telecommunications industry with free or low-cost calls routed over the internet. Skype also gets revenue from voice mail and other services, and offers a platform for business communications geared toward small and medium-sized firms. Skype has offices in the US, Europe and Asia, and 900 employees around the world, of which 300 are based in Tallinn (Estonia).

The company was co-founded in 2002 by Swedish-born entrepreneurs Niklas Zennstrom and Dane Janus Friis, who came together in London. They contracted much of their work to Estonia-based developers Ahti

Heinla, Priit Kasesalu and Jaan Tallinn, who had also originally developed the Kazaa media for music exchange over the internet. To this day, Skype's legal headquarters are in Luxembourg; its sales and marketing office is in London; and a third of Skype's global workforce is in the Estonian capital.

Skype was an early beneficiary of the European Commission's European Investment Fund (EIF) Start-up facility investment that placed start-up funds with the New Tech Venture Fund of Mangrove Capital Partners (Luxembourg). The EIF, in which the European Investment Bank is lead shareholder alongside the European Commission and a cluster of banks and financial institutions, does not lend money to SMEs directly, but specializes in venture capital financing and in guarantees for banks' SME activity.

Skype Technologies' founders had no product in 2003 when they pitched their business plan to Mangrove. Their idea was to attack the global telecom industry with an ad-based service that offered free phone calls over the internet – a plan that 20 venture capital groups had already rejected. Mangrove's partners cut a check for seed funding of $130,000. That move catapulted Mangrove into the ranks of the world's top-performing venture capital companies as Skype's service took off like a rocket when it launched in 2004. Eighteen months later, following several rounds of additional funding (including Bessemer Venture Partners, Draper Fisher Jurvetson, Index Ventures), eBay Inc. bought the company for $2.6bn, netting Mangrove $180 million on a total $1.9 million investment. Today Skype is owned by an investor group led by Silver Lake and which includes eBay Inc., Joltid Limited and Skype founders Zennström and Friis, the Canada Pension Plan Investment Board and Andreessen Horowitz.

In 2010 Skype expanded its operations in Silicon Valley, signing a lease with Stanford University for a 90,000 square foot office space in the Stanford Research Park in Palo Alto, CA. Silicon Valley adds to Skype's engineering team in Estonia, Prague and Stockholm, and will also become the home of regional marketing, business development and the Skype for Business team.

Skype has a very special relationship with Estonia, a tiny Baltic state, as this is where the product initially got started in 2003. Skype still accounts for around half the private sector research and development money spent in the country, and is also the first IT employer in Estonia.

For Linnar Viik, Associate Professor of intellectual capital theory at the Estonian IT College,[3] "There is no new technology in Skype, it is an example of how you put together bits and pieces of technology in a clever way. Estonians are very good at putting together bits and pieces." Estonia owes one thing to the Soviets; in the 1950s, the Baltic state was chosen as the site for several scientific institutes. Estonia wound up with the Institute of Cybernetics – basically a computer sciences center – that now houses Skype and many other firms.

"People here are kind of introverted and into technology," said Jaan Tallinn, who wrote the software code that is the basis of Kazaa and Skype. "We have long, cold winters when there isn't much to do, so it makes sense." Estonia is also the homeland of two other info-technological super-achievements: Hotmail and Kazaa.

Finally, entrepreneurial new firms may be *"born networked"*, in the sense they are not started as independent firms, but as *partners of existing firms* or affiliates of an *association of entrepreneurs*. In a sense, these situations are the other side of the coin of the "externalization" problem: the new firm may be the external supplier or the external distributor of another firm. Alternatively, many would-be entrepreneurs with thin competences and capabilities may be able to take off in an associated rather than independent form. These patterns of *"networked birth"* of entrepreneurial firms are indicated where new firms have the following, usually related, features: they are not founded on projects and competences strong enough to sustain independent life; competences are common rather than unique so that resource pooling is convenient; with similar competences diffused on a global scale, international reach can be more efficiently achieved by associating with similar firms around the world, rather than by growing international as a single firm.

All in all, *"external networked growth" (including that particular form of growth that is birth) is a particularly attractive option for entrepreneurial firms.* The rest of this section is devoted to providing some basic tools for designing and managing external networks. As in the case of internal organization, in fact, there are various "forms" from among which one should choose according to the type of activity to be regulated.

Forms of networked growth

Inter-firm agreements are defined as "networks" since they are characterized by: (1) juridically independent firms as "nodes"; and (2) coordination by organizational connections as "ties", rather than by market exchange or competition (Robertson and Langlois 1992; Thompson *et al.* 1991).

This section offers an overview of the forms of inter-firm networks that are more interesting for the expansion of entrepreneurial activities. They will be analyzed from the point of view of the possible positions of entrepreneurial firms in these activities. Box 4.4 introduces these various forms through the case history of the evolution of the inter-firm agreements network of a famous Italian fashion house: subcontracting relations and how they evolved from rather informal agreements with many suppliers to stronger contractual partnerships with fewer producers; franchised distribution and licensing and joint ventures for new products and services. The features of these forms (and of some others not present in the case) are discussed next, together with the conditions/situations to which they should be appropriate, and the main management problems that they entail for entrepreneurship. In order to provide such support to choice of type of agreement, a conceptual partition of network forms will be offered, based on theory and research on inter-firm agreements (for overviews oriented to network design cf. Mènard 2004; Arino and Reuer 2006; Hendrikse *et al.* 2007; Grandori and Soda 1995), as we did for internal governance and organization forms. In the case of inter-firm agreements and contracts, three dimensions will be used here, as they are particularly important for entrepreneurial firms: the *formalization of agreements*, the choice between *proprietary or non-proprietary agreements*, and, in the case of multiple partners, the choice between *multiple contracts with a single central contractor versus a parity-based association of all partners.*

Box 4.4 The evolution of Versace's network
Laura Gaillard, 2010

Showmanship drives the design house birth and growth in the 1970s– 1980s
In the same way as many Italian designers, Versace began his career as a freelancer, designing prêt-à-porter collections for different houses including Genny, Complice and Callaghan. Gianni Versace had his own label although he had not yet decided to start his own independent business. In 1974, the work for Complice, which he fully conceived himself, marked the first occasion where his own name was included in the brand name. Following the success of this line, Versace amassed the reputation and creative capital necessary to eventually start his own company. For many years, he continued in the role of external designer and consultant. Gianni Versace's hand was behind Genny for 19 years (until 1993). His collaboration with Callaghan was shorter (Versace left Callaghan in 1986) because the company wanted designs that were more avant-garde and in competition with Versace's own brand.[4]

Versace's first signature collection was presented in March 1978. His first menswear collection followed in September. He used the head of "Medusa" as his logo.

During the early 1970s, "Made in Italy" clothing was just beginning to surface. Versace's timing was superb. Milan was just starting to buzz as a fashion center, and success came quickly. Versace hit the fashion headlines with his suggestive, sexy, brightly colored outfits. His distinctive cuts, vibrant prints and unconventional materials united art and contemporary culture; he quickly earned international praise. Versace cultivated symbiotic relationships with the arts and artists, especially in the areas of theater, opera, popular music and dance. During the 1980s, he cemented his "love affair" with young, rich buyers by cultivating his image as couturier to rock stars. Versace understood the importance of marketing. He loved celebrities and knew that they not only attracted the attention of the press, but they also helped to set trends. With his newly earned wealth, Gianni began to invest in prestigious real estate (in New York City, Milan, Lake Como, and especially in Miami Beach) and live the decadent lifestyle that helped draw attention to the brand. Writing for *Business Week*, John Rossant commented, "No other major fashion house in the world is so closely identified with the lifestyle of its marquee-name designer." The designer also played a part in increasing the celebrity of "supermodels": "Before Versace, there were no supermodels, no celebrities at shows and in advertising, no screaming fans. Fashion was not entertainment, *it was merely clothes*."[5]

The evolution of Versace's networks
At the beginning, in 1978, the resources of the company – both financial and of competences – did not allow Versace to produce its collections internally. While creative and marketing operations were handled through the company, *manufacturing and retailing were performed by separate, totally autonomous units*. The *organization was simple and initially informal*, the stylist operated with a small team of designers, a personal secretary, two dressmakers and his brother Santo – who had a degree in business administration and was acknowledged as a very sharp business mind – had control over the finances; his younger sister Donatella and her husband, Paul Beck, also worked for the company. Participating in the work from the beginning were also photographer Richard Avedon and a small support team. Gianni and his designer team prepared the sketches; they also selected the threads and fabrics. *The production of the lines was sustained by a constellation of small external producers; they were relationships based on trust, and agreements based on handshakes.* They had known each other well for many years. Retailing through boutiques was handled directly for image purposes in Paris, London, New York, Madrid and Milan or through exclusive franchising and multi-label boutiques.

With the development of the brand, the small suppliers were no longer sufficiently reliable from various perspectives: they were no longer able to learn quickly enough, to follow technical change, to be as precise as required in realizing the models. Furthermore, there were risks of opportunistic behavior and of unauthorized use of the brand. Versace needed to rely on *a smaller number of connections with larger, more autonomous, more competent and prestigious producers*. Versace *licensed the production* of men's and women's apparel to the well-known Italian textile manufacturer Ermenegildo Zegna. In 1990, they also formed a joint venture to produce and distribute a new line of V2 men's sportswear. In 1991, they created Veze, a joint venture – 30 percent Versace, 70 percent Zegna – that still produces the Versace collection (a tailoring-based line targeted at professional men).

Versace became more structured: the group was split into three controlled firms: Versace Srl, GV Moda SpA and Istante. March 1985 saw the introduction of Versace's first Istante collection, a ready-to-wear line of "conservative-chic" clothing. Istante was organized not only as a separate brand, but also as a distinct subsidiary of the Versace group, Istante Vesa srl, to develop and commercialize all branded non-clothing products.[6] In 1989, Versace introduced Atelier Versace, a haute couture line. Also launched in 1989, the Versus line was Donatella's domain.

On the manufacturing side, the company increased controlling interest in its production facility. Control of manufacturing was necessary in order to monitor quality and image.

From designer to brand in the 1990s
In the 1990s, the challenge for Versace was making the leap from family-run fashion house revolving around a single designer to a global, professionally run brand. The family business stepped up the pace of growth through brand extension. Building on his success in women's ready-to-wear clothing, the designer started his diversification with fragrances. Accessories – mostly produced from Versace designs by licensees – ran from socks to umbrellas, sunglasses, jewelry and watches. Versace was also quick to make international forays, establishing *company-owned and franchised boutiques* in Europe and Asia. The growing group carefully carved out niches in the market. A line of Home Signature tableware, bath and bed linen, lamps, carpets and more, was launched in 1993. The company introduced Versace make-up in 1997. The rapid, but well-considered expansion was careful not to over-saturate and possibly diminish the brand's aura of exclusivity and cachet. The risk was losing control over licensing: markets can be flooded with mass-produced brand-name products, fatally damaging the brands' luxury image. Worldwide production, reasoned the Versaces, should be concentrated in just one place to ensure quality.

In 1996, Gianni Versace had a tightly organized head office team of 250 designers, photographers and public-relations spinners. *The bulk of revenues – a little over $1bn on a wholesale level, or $2bn at retail – came from the 15 percent to 20 percent royalties received from 32 manufacturing companies that used Versace designs to produce everything from sunglasses and umbrellas to watches, socks and suits.* Versace had taken the process one step further than most designers had. It actually had *majority stakes in ten manufacturing companies*, making it one of the few highly integrated groups in the business. Each company, though, was managed as an independent profit center.

High levels of integration can pose risks. Trying to be designer, manufacturer and retailer at the same time can create problems for a fashion group. But if the logistics are managed well, integration allows a group such as Versace to respond to increasingly short product life cycles. Owning stores in key cities such as New York, London and Paris allowed the Versace group to be in direct touch with customers without the filter of a franchisee. Versace could also capture more of the rich margins in each step of the game.

Gianni Versace was killed on the morning of July 15, 1997. At the time of his death, he was at his peak and had turned his clothing lines into a billion-dollar fashion empire. Just a few days previously, he had been planning to take Versace public so that it could finance further growth, and he declared he wanted to "give this group a life that is autonomous from that of its founders. A company that goes public is like a company that automatically acquires a second and third generation. It is a commitment to carry Versace beyond its founders."

Though many design houses have died along with their founders, fashion analysts cited several attributes that would help the Versace group outlive its namesake:

- with the well-known brand and Medusa-head logo, new product lines could continue to evolve;
- while Gianni Versace had been personally responsible for the creation of the signature lines, he had already assembled an international team of design assistants headed by his sister Donatella;
- Versace boasts highly skilled design teams that can respond quickly to changes;
- the company's ownership of a majority stake in ten of its manufacturing licensees enables it to swiftly turn the latest ideas off the street into ready-to-wear merchandise.

Santo Versace and sister Donatella could no longer take their time planning the transformation of Versace from designer to brand. Because of their brother's murder, this transformation had to be cruelly accelerated.

The missed challenges of the 2000s
Despite its global reach, Versace was always the archetype of Italian family entrepreneurism. Until his death, Gianni Versace held the position of director of his company. After the family tragedy, Versace left his half of the empire to his 11-year-old niece, Donatella's daughter Allegra, allowing his sister to take creative and business control. (Santo had 30 percent, Donatella 20 percent and Allegra 50 percent of the company's shares.)

Versace has experienced some "anni horribili" since its founder's death. The company incurred some loss in prestige and design influence. Not only Gianni's death and Donatella's problems, but also the global financial crisis that took a heavy toll, contributed to a sharp fall in revenue. Starting in

2003, after what Santo described as "seven years of woes", the Versaces acknowledged they could not run the company by themselves and hired a string of outside managers to straighten out the mess.[7]

In 2004, the first line of clothing still represented Versace's core business. The production was structured as follows: (1) Versace had a *major stake* in seven facilities for the production of the different lines (Alias, which produced the first line clothes; Diver for the production and distribution of leather accessories; Giver Profumi; Immagine for silk accessories such as ties; Verim for home decoration; Veze; and Versace SA, Precious items); and (2) *licensing agreements* with prestigious producers (Luxottica for eyewear, Ittierre for the youth lines, Zegna for Menswear, La Bonitas for beachwear and Rosenthal for the tabletops).

The retail distribution was restructured, increasing the *franchising* solutions. In 2004, Versace had a total of 277 stores worldwide including: 96 DOS (Direct Operating Stores), 85 Franchisees, 69 Duty Free Shops and 27 outlets.

A series of business managers stemmed some of the decline and tried to cut down on costs. In June 2009 Giancarlo di Risio, Versace's CEO for five years, left. The company hired management consultants and a new CEO, Gian Giacomo Ferraris. In 2009, revenues fell to €273 million from €336.3 million in 2008. In response to the crisis, Ferraris came up with a plan for 2009–14. Two major decisions concern the staff and production. It will cut about a quarter of its staff and rationalize production facilities. It is also expected to close unprofitable stores, and cut its capital investment and overheads. "There is no plan to sell the company or to sell a stake in the company," said Mr Ferraris. "The current restructuring plan in fact enables the company to remain independent because the cost-cutting measures are enough to guarantee stability and a return to profitability by 2011."

Using the Versace case, a range of inter-firm agreements and a framework for analyzing and choosing them can be illustrated.

A first important dimension and choice regards the *formalization of agreements*. The "informality" of inter-firm collaboration arrangements has been often celebrated as a sign of trust, and linked to contexts of long-standing, repeated transactions – as in the case of Versace's early production subcontractees network. Indeed, repeated exchanges may lower perceived potential conflict and increase reputation effects thereby reducing the need for formal contracts. However, this is not the whole story; and it should not be inferred that in the lack of a long history of exchanges, one is forced to resort to highly formalized and protected contracts; nor can the existence and persistence of informal agreements be due only to "nice" trust-based relations. In fact, objectives can be convergent also in lack of history; and unilateral power, rather than trust, may lie behind informal agreements.

An example of the first case – shifting but informal relations – is the sustainability of informal and relational contracts in creative industries (Meyerson *et al.* 1996). In that context, shifting teams and variety of collaborations are superior to long-lasting, repeated collaborations always among the same people or firms. However, the density of relationships in those industries, and the strong professional values, provide effective substitutes to highly formal and protective contracts, as reputation effects industry norms and professional codes. These elements constitute a peculiar form of industry-specific social capital, what Meyerson *et al.* have evocatively called "swift trust" (ready-for-use trustworthiness).

An example of the second case – informal but mostly power-based rather than trust-based relations – are the forms of long-lasting informal hierarchical sub-contracting around a powerful and poorly substitutable main contractor – as in the first phase of external production described in the Versace case, or in the relationships between automobile constructors and small components suppliers. In those cases, a more formal agreement may be justified as more fair (Grandori 1991).

In addition, there are other reasons for formalizing inter-firm agreements, beyond potential conflict of interests and fairness. In particular, a well-established organizational principle (and a widely observable regularity) states that larger and more complex systems should be more formal. In the case of inter-firm networks the *size of the network* (number of nodes) and *intensity of the ties* (range and complexity of services exchanged or of resources pooled) should make their formalization effective (Grandori 1997). The evolution of Versace's production and distribution growing network toward more formal contracts (e.g. franchised distribution and production on license) and even proprietary contracts (e.g the co-makership joint venture with Zegna) illustrate the point.

The case history on Versace's network also illustrates that an important choice in crafting inter-firm networks is between a set of bilateral contracts with a single central contractor and a parity-based association of cooperating partners. This choice greatly affects the *centralization of the network* and the distribution of power. Hence, as in the case of formalization, negotiation among partners with different interests is also likely over this dimension of inter-firm agreements. Bilateral contracts with a central contractor may expose the subcontractees or affiliated firms (which are more likely to be the entrepreneurial firms) to be "squeezed" by the firm in the central position (which is more likely to be a major firm). For example, complaints were common in the Italian fashion industry at the time of informal hub-and-spoke networks around fashion houses.

On the basis of this discussion, the presentation and assessment of some main forms of inter-firm networks in an entrepreneurial perspective is organized according to whether they are based on bilateral agreements (with a central contractor) or on parity-based associations; and the issue of formal versus informal agreements is discussed within each type along with some other specific management problems. These forms are also connected to the types of exchange or cooperation relations that they are able to regulate, according to existing studies on inter-firm networks. In particular, it is possible to connect the choice between bilateral and multilateral contracting with the type of interdependence among firms, as follows.

- Transactions (exchanges) of goods and services occur between two parties, eventually further linked sequentially with others in a value chain. This is called a situation of *"sequential" or "transactional" interdependence*. This type of interdependence is therefore regulated by *bilateral contracts*. If there are more than two phases or sub-activities to be coordinated, one firm in the chain or a third party can perform the role of central coordinator and common contractor in order to reduce coordination costs (in which case the arrangement is sometimes called *"trilateral contracting"*).
- *Multi-party associations*, rather than one-to-one bilateral or trilateral contracts, are effective in regulating the relation among firms cooperating in producing a common output, or using common pooled inputs (*pooled interdependence*). The reasons for all-to-all, parity-based association in those situations include the following basic factor: being interdependence all-to-all, it would be more costly to write and administer separate contracts rather than one for all. An additional important factor for setting up a partnership is that in pooled interdependence situations it may be difficult to disentangle and size up the contribution of each party: a circumstance called *"team production"* and in fact considered a reason for the constitution of stronger forms of partnership, involving partial or full property right sharing.

Networks based on bilateral contracts (and one central contractor)

Subcontracting can be used to expand the scale of production of a good or service through collaborations with *independent firms performing parts or phases of activity to be delivered to a contractor firm.*

Subcontracting was called, in more ancient times, *"putting out"*, and has been traditionally considered an "entrepreneurial" form of organizing production (Williamson 1980). In fact, it is a relevant option for developing entrepreneurial firms: in the position of contractor, since they may lack the competence to produce components or complements of their products; in the position of contractees, a stable flow of jobs and activities can be secured, thanks to the relation with a larger more established firm.

The subcontractees are not simple "suppliers": they work according to specific instructions from the main contractor, at times using materials supplied by it (such as in the textile sector), and normally under the supervision and assistance of the main contractor (who is responsible to the ultimate client). Typically, then, in a subcontracting system, there is a "central" firm, "managing" other firms through control, incentive, planning and supervision mechanisms. These features have led to defining subcontractees as "quasi-firms" (Eccles 1981).

Being in the position of a "quasi-firm" is not a problem-free condition. The relation is most often seen, in subcontractor literature, from the point of view of the outsourcing contractor firm. Entrepreneurial firms, however, are most often in the more problematic subcontractee position. A recurrent problem is that there is typically asymmetry in bargaining power and the subcontractees faces the risk of being "squeezed" (i.e. a large part of the rent created by the collaboration may easily be expropriated by the main contractor) and not "guaranteed" enough by formal and enforceable contractual provisions.

A case illustrating these problems is presented in Box 4.5. Rather than the usual automotive or textile case, the case illustrates an important form of subcontracting diffused in the agribusiness.

Box 4.5 Contract farming
Andrew Briganti, 2010

Contract farming is a codified inter-organizational partnership form in the agribusiness taking place between farmers and food processing and/or marketing firms for the production and supply of agricultural products under forward agreements, often at a predetermined price. In some cases, the arrangement involves the purchaser providing a degree of production support through, for example, the supply of inputs and the provision of technical advice.

The basis of such arrangements is a commitment by the farmer to provide a specific commodity in quantities and at quality standards determined by the purchaser, and a commitment by the company to support the farmer's production and to purchase the commodity.

With effective management, contract farming can be a means to develop markets and allow small-scale entrepreneurial farming to survive and grow through partnerships with large sponsoring companies, since it reduces risk and uncertainty for both parties compared to buying and selling crops on the open market.

The intensity of the contractual arrangement varies according to the depth and complexity of the provisions in each of the following three areas: market provision, resource provision and management specifications.

The contracts, which can take place either formally or informally, specify aspects including contract duration, quality standards, production quotas, cultivation practices, crop delivery, pricing arrangements and payment procedures.

Contract farming has significant benefits for both the farmers and the sponsors. However, with these advantages also come problems. The stronger position of sponsors with respect to that of growers can be seen as enabling them to transfer risks to growers, as illustrated next in a specific apri-business situation.

The Australian asparagus industry, concentrated in the Victorian region of Koo Wee Rup, involves a duopoly of vertically coordinated and centralized processors who buy from a number of farmers in the area and then market the asparagus domestically or export to Southeast Asia.

The contract farming system here is highly informal, which causes tension between the farmers and buyers. In fact, the only fixed agreements are that of a minimum quantity and quality standard of production, delivery timeliness, and the prohibition to supply to other firms.

The pricing system is flexible and determined according to two factors: first, fluctuations in international currency, because the largest part of production is exported; and second, the quality grade of the asparagus. Growers are paid at a higher rate for Grade A asparagus and at a lower rate for Grade B asparagus.

Growers often report that the firms manipulate quality assessment, which adversely affects their income. A percentage of the total price is then deducted from each delivery depending on the proportion of production deemed as waste. This is also a recurrent source of debate between the two parties, because growers are informed of the price at the end of every week by firm management, leaving little room for dispute or negotiation. As farmers are tied to exclusively deal with one firm, searching for fairer conditions with another firm voids their contract.

One of the critical problems of the Australian industry is the scarcity of labor; farmers complain that as the cost per kilogram paid to the cutters increases, the price paid by the firm remains constant, which further shrinks the profit margin from season to season.

Other issues are increasing demand risk due to the saturation of the Asian market, which is due to international competition and can mean that not all asparagus is purchased; and production risks caused by climatic conditions, pest epidemics or diseases to the crop, for which growers have no insurance cover.

In addition, the downstream firms do not provide any inputs or technical expertise. The growers would like communication and assistance regarding product development: how to tailor production to their specifications, how to minimize waste, and training of the labor force to optimize the quality of crop management, fertilization and cutting.

Franchising

Franchising is specifically suited to governing cooperation among firms based on *similar assets* and/or *between the producer firm and a distribution network*. Franchising allows similar firms to cooperate, through a nexus of bilateral contracts between one firm (the franchisor), having accumulated know-how and image in an activity, transferring it to other firms through processes of technical assistance, training, supervision and activity organization. These other firms (the franchisees) apply the technical and organizational know-how to the local business context, and pay royalties to the franchisor for the transfer of know-how and the use of the brand. This organization form is widely used in the large-scale commercialization of a product or service with a strong, highly firm-specific but standardizable identity. Examples include restaurants, the hospitality industry, retail distribution, clothing stores and medical laboratories.

Franchising has special relevance for entrepreneurial firms. On one side, it greatly facilitates the founding of new firms in an affiliated form, in a franchisee position. On the other side, it allows the growth of the entrepreneurial firm through external agreements, in a franchisor position. A case in point is the franchised take-off and early growth of The Body Shop (end-Chapter case).

The virtues of franchising are also the seeds of its problems though, rooted in the tension between autonomy and central coordination, and between the division of costs and rents between the franchisor and the franchisees. Box 4.6 describes the problems later encountered in the management of the franchise systems at The Body Shop; and Box 4.7 illustrates a different, less rigid approach to franchising adopted in an international delivery organization, where the balance between the franchisor and the franchisee is better dealt with.

Box 4.6 The Body Shop (II): the "franchisee rebellion"
Laura Gaillard, 2010

From its humble beginning as a modest niche retailer in the 1970s, The Body Shop (TBS) financed its growth through a network of franchises all over the world. Early on, Gordon Roddick realized that, with the young company's borrowing potential tapped out, the best way to expand was by shifting the cost to others through "self-financing" – franchising. By 1982, The Body Shop was expanding at the rate of two new shops a month including outlets in Iceland, Denmark, Finland, Holland and Eire. At this time, Anita Roddick and her husband Gordon began to charge a premium of £3,000 for a franchise and Anita kept strict control over the franchising process. When the company went public in 1984 and became "The Body Shop International plc" (public limited company), there were 45 stores in UK and 83 overseas. TBS had strong, specific advantages including their reputation and corporate social responsibility (CSR)-based policies; they were able to target a narrow group of environmentally conscious consumers across a wide number of countries. Young women who shared Anita's philosophy and values operated most of the franchises.

In 1988, TBS entered the US cosmetics market: they invested in a huge warehouse and production facility in New Jersey and opened 12 company-owned stores. When they began franchising in the US in 1990, there were 2,500 applications for a franchise, with demand for TBS products ever growing. By the end of the year, there were 37 stores but, due to the high cost of the initial infrastructure, the US operations still ran at a loss.

At the end of the 1980s, the process to become a TBS franchise took as long as three years; it involved a personality test, a home visit, and assessment of the candidate's attitude toward people and the environment. Roddick explained that they choose as franchisees "only people who are passionate about our products and our ideas".[8] Selected candidates had to undergo extensive training on product knowledge. Not only the franchisees but also employees and suppliers had to be active in the social and environmental agenda of TBS. The sales staff were specially trained to be friendly and knowledgable. By 1991, TBS had 580 stores, more than 400 overseas, and only 10 percent were company owned. The franchise contract involved an investment of £150,000 to £250,000, the start-up costs and a licensing fee. TBS chose the sites for the store location and maintained the lease. TBS was able to hold strict control over the sales and inventory. They offered a strong support system for the precise "packaging" of the stores; it was tested in the stores directly owned by the company and used as product and marketing laboratories. Through TBS Worldwide Limited the company led franchises overseas and appointed regional managers and head franchisees responsible for designated areas and for negotiating subcontracts.

Roddick was able to concentrate on the company's global vision, on the development of new product lines and on building ties with a number of key partners (Trade Communities, NGOs). She spent months every year traveling worldwide to learn from the skin and hair care practices of women all over the world. Initially product development was driven by samples brought back by Anita, and the creativity of Mark Constantine: "She was intuitive, she knew what customers wanted and she was right. At first, it was a small team of us – Anita, Gordon, Janis Raven, Deb McCormack and I. We would come up with ideas and, after spirited argument, Anita would decide what would and wouldn't get through."[9] Testing was carried out on staff volunteers, and risks were minimal because women had used the ingredients for centuries. In the 1990s, the company increased its in-house manufacturing, TBS had a large production and warehouse space in Wick, West Sussex, and they eventually established a formal research department.

"The Body Flop"[10]
The Body Shop's problems began in the early 1990s after an ambitious program of international expansion failed to pay off. "We just got everything wrong" Roddick admitted later.[11]

Environmental concerns had stepped from a marginal position in the culture and politics of the 1970s to a central position in debates. In the face of increasing consumer recognition and appreciation of environmental and ethical issues, the pioneering use of natural resources and the promotion of an alternative lifestyle no longer had the same significance for younger generations. In the 1990s, TBS was in danger of representing an older and outdated model of CSR. The competitive landscape had changed; TBS had to react to the hard competition of fresher products with better marketing and prices. Boots, for example, launched the Botanics and Natural Collection ranges in a head-to-head with TBS. Meanwhile, exotic and wacky new product ranges overshadowed TBS old favorites.

Trading problems with America also occurred. The company's penetration into the US market was particularly ill fated after it neglected to do enough market research and battled with local incumbents such as Bath & Body Works. TBS's franchise structure, which enabled it to grow very quickly in the early days, also introduced control problems. TBS owns UK, US, France and Singapore operations through subsidiaries. In other regions, they had partnerships; in some cases, the partners were larger than TBS (AEON in Japan, Newclicks Holding in South Africa). The over-development of some head franchises induced a form of saturation and TBS had to buy out some franchises.

In 1996, Roddick faced a "franchisee rebellion".[12] Each franchisee had to pay a start-up investment (from $300 to $700,000), was locked into undesirable positions as buyers of all the cosmetics and paid 5 percent on sales. For the idealistic young women that TBS had attracted, such costs were a daunting, sometimes insurmountable hurdle. Franchisees also questioned the rigidity of the contract, the right of TBS to terminate the franchise at any time and to take the assets, and the obsolete packaging of the products.

TBS had to face many costly problems including disputes with franchisees which ended up in court, TBS had to buy out franchises, 160 stores in the US,[13] and settle disputes; for instance, with the Norwegian head franchisee and with Anne Downer, who had franchise rights for eight countries in Asia. She collected $6.2 million (US) to settle a dispute that exploded when The Body Shop forced her to close her 12 Singapore stores. Furthermore, the media, which had been so instrumental in the success of TBS, was investigating and questioning the company's environmental claims,[14] a former employee dismissed it as "window dressing"; TBS had to defend itself. In 1996 TBS published its first Value Report, which acknowledged the importance of all stakeholders (employees, franchisees, customers, communities, supplies, shareholders and NGOs). Anita Roddick increased her activist engagements, and some franchisees expressed concern that the campaigns were becoming too political; all this had a dramatic effect on her business and led to it struggling financially. These pressures forced the company to undergo restructuring. The tension between the company entrepreneurial leadership, its strongly embedded organizational values and its commercial development, required change.

In 1998, Anita Roddick stepped down as CEO; she asked Patrick Gournay, who was then working for Danone France, to replace her. Anita stayed on the board of TBS as "guardian of the company's DNA"; she seemed to accept that she no longer possessed the "magic formula" for sales growth.

Yet the brand still had a good reputation and was voted the second most trusted brand in the UK (1999). In 1999 and 2000, TBS fully restructured its operations. The company created four new business units in the UK and Republic of Ireland, Americas, Europe and Middle East, and Asia Pacific, shifting operational and managerial structures to the regional headquarters. The communication became multidirectional between franchises, TBS and suppliers. The main focus was on cost reduction: TBS de-internalized its expensive manufacturing and wholesaling capabilities. They made clear contracts with a selected number of suppliers (15) with whom they already had long-term relationships. The Body Shop Supply Company Limited was dissolved. TBS International's Littlehampton manufacturing business was sold. The investment strategy focused on "new stores and store refurbishments, while continuing to invest in point of sale systems to improve operational efficiencies".[15] The new venture for TBS was the "at home business", where trained consultants "come to your home and demonstrate the products". It proved to offer great synergy with the store-based business and to be highly successful in the UK and was on trial in the US and in Mexico in 2000. In 2001, the company emerged with a new store format, a new logo, and for the first time in the company's history used an outside advertising agency.

But TBS values, management practices and beliefs had to also be conveyed into a more formal system although preserving the company's uniqueness. This was a difficult task that Anita and Gordon Roddick had to transfer to others. In 2002, they both quit the board of TBS International and chief executive Patrick Gournay also had to step down.

"Gordon and I are, and always have been entrepreneurs, idea junkies. We're not suited to formal corporate positions; myself, I can hardly sit still for a meal, let alone a board meeting. We are much better as advisors, mentors, and challengers. So we have both chosen to step down from our positions as co-chairs of the Board of Directors, but will stay on as non-executive board members."[16]

The departure of the Roddicks also followed a series of failed takeover talks with various suitors for The Body Shop (Grupo Omnilife, a Mexican retailer that distributes nutritional supplements, failed to borrow enough money to back its $500 million offer). At about the same time, The Body Shop also snubbed an offer from the cosmetics chain Lush (founder Mark Constantine).

The new chairman, Adrian Bellamy, was a Body Shop director who entered into a joint venture with The Body Shop in 1998, and Peter Saunders, chief executive of the company's North American operations, was appointed chief executive.

"When a company you've given birth to reaches the age of 26 – a good five years past its twenty-first birthday – it's probably about time you let it stand on its own two feet. Likewise, as I step down as co-chair of The Body Shop, I realize you could also make that joke the other way around. I'm probably old enough now to stand on my own two feet, too."[17]

Anita Roddick signed a two-year consultancy contract with the company, while she and her husband planned to stay on as non-executive directors. Anita continued to carry out PR functions and traveled the world for talks, in search of new products and campaigns. She said she needed "breathing space". She even started her own small activist communications center, Anita Roddick Publications. She liked to say they manufactured "weapons of mass instruction", experimenting with various forms and mediums to celebrate and advance the same things she always cared about: human rights, the environment and creative dissent.

Epilogue
In March 2006, L'Oréal purchased TBS for £652 million and de-listed it from the London Stock Exchange in July 2006.[18] This caused controversy, because L'Oréal is involved in animal testing, and because the company is part owned by Nestlé – criticized for its treatment of third world producers. Defending her choice Anita said: "I'm not an apologist for them, I'm just excited that I can be like a Trojan horse and go into that huge business and talk about how we can buy ingredients like cocoa butter from Ghana and sesame oil from Nicaraguan farmers and how we can do that in a kindly, joyful way and that is happening." In fact TBS retains its unique identity and values and the company will continue to be based in, and run independently from, its head office in Littlehampton. It operates independently within the L'Oréal Group and is led by the current management team of TBS reporting directly to the CEO of L'Oréal. Anita Roddick's life was sadly cut short in September 2007 by a brain hemorrhage.

Box 4.7 International Delivery (ID)

ID is an international company providing a door-to-door express delivery service in almost 200 countries. In order to serve its clientele by handling distribution of parcels and documents in almost every part of the world, the company created a network of locally owned branches, as well as indirect unit agents. It should be pointed out that as ID operates on an international level with a long-standing and consolidated image of reliability, and it imposes quality standards that are vitually identical throughout the world. One example of this is overnight delivery guaranteed practically anywhere in the world. To achieve its declared objectives of quality, ID requires substantial organizational integration with its suppliers (agencies, indirect units, cooperatives), considered as partners – to all effects, members of the ID network. None of these partners, however, work exclusively for ID and therefore part of their turnover is independent of their relationship with ID.

The current solution is a *commercial agreement* between ID and partners. The commercial agreement is drawn up by headquarters but some margin of negotiability is left to the district managers. In fact, the standards of quality required are uniform throughout the ID network, but within each district there are different problems, particular operating conditions that necessitate negotiation: the relationship is constantly negotiated through a task force named "fair costs". The team's goal is the analysis of the ID-partner exchange in terms of *fairness,* determining, area by area, the actual contribution of the partners and ID to the relationship and to the creation of the final value of the service, in terms of costs and investments, but also in terms of the quality of the service. Since the output is measurable (delivery in the required time at the level of the service requested) and the ratio existing between inputs and outputs of the parties can be determined, it is possible to apply a reward criterion proportional to contribution. As from 1994, ID compensates partners on the basis of the number of parcels handled by each employee (until then the co-ops were paid on the basis of the number of hours worked by each courier, regardless therefore of the number of parcels handled). ID asks its partners to make specific investments (managerial investments and physical assets) and to respond to its needs, but at the same time it has made a number of concessions: on the one hand, these are standardized contributions for the use of cellular phones, uniforms and logos on the vans (the advertising contract currently includes a fixed amount per day for each vehicle bearing the ID logo, for each courier who wears the uniform and equipped with a cellular phone); on the other hand, they are related to the particular necessities of the partners (special rates, material support, incentives). In addition, training (not only technical but also managerial) and management assistance are provided by ID.

In terms of procedural fairness, it should be noted that all the initiatives connected with the partnership are managed in collaboration with a considerable number of the partner companies, defined as "strategic", in respect therefore of the criteria of representativeness and voice. Until now, there has basically been no turnover among the partner companies.

As to the parties' utility, the ideal contract for ID is one with total variabilization of delivery costs. In this way, the partner would sustain the fixed costs completely. Related to this strategy is a tendency to become "brokers" of the transportation service rather than direct suppliers, and therefore to transfer the risks and costs of delivering to partners. ID's best alternative to a negotiated agreement can be considered to be the internalization of distribution with an estimated increase in administrative and transaction costs.

As to the partners' utility, the advantage that the partner companies derive from their relationship with ID is the possibility of synergizing their local distribution activity by means of their partnership with a major company known worldwide. However, the partners of ID aim to obtain a "platform" of fixed reward and contributions to specific investments, so as to reduce the risks borne and to appropriate a larger share of the surplus or rent created by the cooperation. The partners' best alternative can be considered as the possibility of entering into partnership with another delivery company. If the existing type of contract were not taken for granted, it would be possible to explore other feasible fair forms. The creation of a network of franchisees has recently been taken into consideration. It would appear to be a superior solution in terms of substantial and procedural fairness. In substantial terms, it could allow ID to complete the process of organizational integration with its partners and decentralize part of the activities that are now managed by the central organization (for example, invoicing) without increasing structural costs. At the same time, the franchisees could reduce the risks currently born by participating in the performance of the whole chain to which they are contributing rather than being entirely linked to local fluctuations in demand. In procedural terms, equal and formalized treatment for all partners could be appreciated. On the other hand, it may be noted that a formal franchising contract may entail some loss of utility for the franchisees if the system, as is usually the case, included an exclusivity clause.

The "niche" activities currently performed by couriers locally would be lost without any benefit for the franchisor. Indeed, ID always has difficulties in accepting local deliveries with particular characteristics (weight, size, number, value) and therefore it might prefer to let its partner make this margin rather than working almost at a loss, or "making a present" of the client to the competition.

Therefore, a fair contract that seems to be superior in this case, would be, so to speak, a non-mechanistic *"tempered franchising"*, in which greater organizational integration is associated with ad hoc contractual provisions tailored to the specific needs and preferences of local partners.

Source: case by Neri, M. (1999) in Grandori, A. (2001b)

Inside contracting

The arrangement called *"inside contracting"* is somehow borderline between a set of bilateral contracts and the constitution of an association, as the oxymoronic name also suggests. More precisely, it has both a bilateral contracting version and a partnership version.

In general, under inside contracting, one entrepreneur owns a set of fundamental tools and resources such as the buildings, central facilities, sales outlets and commercial brands. Other entrepreneurs, who provide their own labor and complementary assets such as technical instruments, software and know-how, carry out the transformation and the generation of products or services. In addition, they hire and manage their own co-workers.

The two variants derive from how separable the complementary inputs or their contributions into the final output are. If separable, the quasi-internal entrepreneurs may receive payment per unit of product according to an agreement negotiated in advance (Williamson 1980). This version of the system was common in entrepreneurial activities in agriculture (for example, the person skimming milk from cows and processing it was a different entrepreneur from the farmer). If not separable, parties can share in residual rewards according to some profit-sharing scheme. For example, in professional service firms we can find agreements of this type, as described in Box 4.8. The box also describes how different parties may propend toward one or the other version according to their position in the relation; with the professionals–entrepreneurs providing complementary assets and services being typically better off under a partnership rather than bilateral contracting agreement.

Box 4.8 Inside contracting in a business school

Peng Lee, a leading man in the electronics industry who believed that a top training school was vital for the economy of any country, founded the Osaka Business School in the early 1980s. The school owned a beautiful post-modern building facing a small artificial lake with ducks and lotus flowers and was equipped with the latest technology. Facilities included two auditoriums and 50 classrooms, each equipped with multiple sliding blackboards, video-beam, video camera and personal computers, an excellent snack bar-restaurant and a gym with a heated swimming pool. This entire infrastructure represented the "hardware" of the school. What the Taj School was lacking was faculty members and researchers. They were the actual "software" of the school, the people who held the scientific and technical knowledge to produce and deliver the service in question: training.

A large fraction of professors and professionals were then involved on the basis of contracts, and worked out of their own competences and certifications. All contracted activities were dedicated, specialized and compensated by output. The products that Taj offered on the market were courses, research studies and other projects that were planned with large (although not total) autonomy by the program/course coordinators who had the discretion to "hire" the best resources for the job.

Faculty members were compensated on the basis of specific categories. Teaching had a different rate of pay than other activities such as the

---

preparation of course material or research. A fixed portion of the budget of any initiative was destined to compensate the coordinator, who was thus paid based on his/her planning and management activity. Compensation based on the profit generated by an initiative could also be awarded. The remaining part of the profit was awarded to the unit running the project. The rules for this rent division had never been made very clear, though. A fixed share was destined to cover general and shared administrative expenses. As to the remaining part, there was an often emerging and unresolved issue of sizing the relative contribution of the school structure, name and contacts vis-à-vis those of the professional–entrepreneur. The school had a tendency to see the professionals as employees and to try to simply pay them at a fixed rate for their teaching, research and coordination work. The professionals–entrepreneurs tended to maintain that teaching and coordinating was not all they were putting in, as they were using their own contacts and social capital to gain participants, let alone the maintenance and use of their technical equipment.

Source: case by Silvia Bagdadli (2001),
expanded and revised by Anna Grandori, 2010

Multi-lateral parity-based partnerships

Let us consider three forms that are of special relevance to entrepreneurial firms (as we did for bilateral contract networks).

To constitute an *association* is the more general-purpose way of organizing pooled interdependence. There are different juridical forms of association – from trade associations, to consortia, to "groupment d'interest economique" (an EU legal form). In addition, they are not regulated in the same way in all legal systems – for example, in European countries the law has been historically more favorable to inter-firm associations; while in the US, especially in the past, the regulatory attitude has been more adverse, considering them as a possible vehicle of collusion, when not even a form of hidden enterpise, as the Best Western case in this section illustrates (Box 4.9).

Nevertheless, the formation of associations is widespread and important for activities ranging from the provision of common services (e.g. staff and administrative activities) to conducting joint production (whereby firms are specialized by phases or sub-activities or locations); from joint marketing (whereby trademarks are protected in distribution, e.g. Champagne, Parmigiano Reggiano) to joint research (whereby firms can pool competences for more effective development); to the realization of projects that require multiple competences (as in construction and engineering).

The common features of associations that are of special interest for entrepreneurs are: they can set *strict access rules*; they maintain the *independence of entrepreneurs* in all management respects and in their entitlement to profits; they are typically governed through *representative democracy*. The voting scheme in an association is traditionally paritarian (one member, one vote); however, if partners are not similar in size and amount of resources contributed, weighted voting and contribution schemes can be devised (Lammers 1993), as the Promatem (end-chapter case) illustrates. On the other hand, they require affiliation fees to sustain the common central structure; which in turn is entitled to regulate the division of labor among firms, to program activities, to evaluate timeliness and quality, and to sign contracts with third parties. Contracts of inter-firm association typically include penalties in case of unfulfilled commitments, and internal authorities with the functions of inspection, supervision and arbitration.

Associations are therefore valuable to entrepreneurial firms as a way to *jointly and more efficiently conduct common functions, while maintaining entrepreneurial independence*. A case where this double entrepreneurial advantage has always been the company flag is Best Western (Box 4.9), originally formed as a pooled service provider association that eventually grew to become a global player in the tourism industry, maintaining the form of an association among independent entrepreneurs.

Box 4.9 Best Western

Best Western International® is the world's largest hotel chain, providing marketing, reservations and operational support to 4,200 independently owned and operated member hotels in 80 countries and territories worldwide. Founded in 1946, this iconic brand is host to approximately 400,000 worldwide guests each night. A pioneer within the industry, dominating the three to four stars segment, Best Western is recognized for its distinctive member-owned business model and diverse hotel portfolio.

Table 4.1 Best Western Motel and Hotel history: 1946–present

1946	Best Western Motels was founded by M.K. Guertin, an hotelier with 23 years' experience in the business. The hotel chain began as an informal link between properties with each hotel recommending other lodging establishments to travelers. The "referral system" consisted of phone calls from one front desk operator to another.
1951	In a guest editorial published in *American Motel* magazine, Guertin spoke of the importance of advertising properties to the general traveling public. This was considered a very revolutionary approach in the industry.
1962	The Best Western Hotel Chain had the only hospitality reservations service covering the entire United States and Canada.
	Best Western began using the crown logo with a rope border to identify member properties.

1963   Best Western was the largest hotel motel chain in the industry with 699 member properties and 35,201 motel rooms.

1964   A group of motels east of the Mississippi River was affiliated as Best Eastern.

1966   The entire membership, Best Western and Best Eastern, joined under the Best Western name. A seven-person board of directors was elected by regional members to provide leadership and make policy decisions. Guertin retired.

The organization moved its headquarters from Long Beach, California, to Phoenix, Arizona. The board decided to relocate because of the savings involved in centralizing operations and the potential for further expanding membership services.

A major expansion of Best Western services was announced. Changes included: establishing a new hotel reservation center offering a toll-free service for business commuters, travel agents and vacationers through arrangements with American Express; expanding into Europe, the Caribbean and the Pacific; increasing membership standards; opening sales offices in Washington, DC, Montreal, Phoenix and Seattle; establishing tie-ins with airlines and representatives from other transportation industry members and investigating stronger infiltration of tour and business meeting markets.

1972   Properties were required to accept six major credit cards. Hotel reservations that were charged were considered "guaranteed" and a hotel room had to be held for the entire night. Properties had the right to bill for "no-show" clients.

1974   Best Western Hotels decided to drop its referral organization image, eliminated the word "motel" from its name and began competing directly with other full-service hotel chains.

1976   Best Western began its push for foreign expansion. Affiliation agreements were signed with 411 properties in Australia and New Zealand.

1977   To meet the demands of rapid growth, a multi-million-dollar Best Western International Headquarters complex was designed and built in northeast Phoenix.

1977   The phrase, "world's largest lodging chain" became a part of Best Western's identification and advertising theme.

1979   Best Western was accommodating 15 million guests and generating $1 billion in hotel room sales.

1980   Agreements were signed bringing 19 properties in Denmark, 120 properties in France, 19 properties in Finland, 23 properties in Spain, 19 properties in Sweden and 93 properties in Switzerland into the international hotel chain. By this time, Best Western's 903 international affiliates comprised 34 percent of the chain's total membership.

1980   Best Western membership rose to 2,654 hoteliers worldwide.

1981   In 1981, Homestead Motor Inns of Australia affiliated with Best Western. This move put "International" after the Best Western name. The company has been known as Best Western International ever since.

1984   Best Western, maintaining its status of association, was charged with actually being a franchising organization in some states. The most dramatic example of this was *Quist v. Best Western Int'l, Inc.*, 354 N.W.2d 656 (N.D. 1984) in which the North Dakota Supreme Court decided that Best Western was a franchisor and had to comply with the appropriate laws and regulations.

1988   The Gold Crown Club® International Program for frequent travelers was launched in September. Within a year, it would record more than 200,000 members and sales of over $40m.

1993   The brand identity study, now complete, recommended the adoption of a new Best Western logo and identity. On November 30, the members approved the adoption of a new logo and officially retired the Gold Crown logo.

1995   Best Western introduced its first hotel listings on the Internet at BestWestern.com. Full information on 150 member properties, including photographs, became instantly available via personal home computers.

2001   Best Western International established its Asia Head Office in Bangkok and became the pioneering Property Direct Relations office of BWI in the region with full support from the Best Western International headquarters in Phoenix, Arizona.

2002   Best Western introduced the Best Western Premier brand that was officially launched in Europe. Best Western Premier expanded into Asia a year later with its first hotel Best Western Premier Xiamen Central Hotel in Xiamen, China.

2002   Best Western members implemented BestRequests®, a uniform worldwide package of amenities and services.

2004   Best Western launched the hotel industry's largest High-Speed Internet Access (HSIA) initiative with the fastest implementation. In just eight months, the company established free wireless or hard-wired HSIA in some portion of the public areas and in at least 15 percent of hotel rooms in all its North American properties.

2004   Best Western became the first-ever Official Hotel of NASCAR®. The NASCAR® travel discount RaceFan®Rate was created.

2005   Best Western began averaging $1m in online hotel reservations per day through www.bestwestern.com.

2006   Best Western celebrated its sixtieth anniversary with the 1946 Room Rate Promotion, where lucky guests were provided with a special one-night charge of $5.40 – the approximate value of overnight accommodations six decades ago, when the company started.

In early 2007, Best Western Australasia took over the rights to operate Best Western properties in New Zealand from the previous company, the Motel Federation of New Zealand. This was a bold but beneficial move for the brand as it made way for better quality properties to be brought to the brand. Currently, Best Western Australasia has 205 properties in the group (11 in New Zealand and 194 in Australia).

2007   Best Western began using online surveys to keep track of customer satisfaction, one of the first steps in leading the industry in superior customer care.

2008   Best Western launched a new Atrea prototype. First Best Western Atrea opens.

2009   Best Western Premiers in Asia offer upgraded standards and services, enhanced amenities with international sense and style complemented by the refined essence of each hotel's cultural and geographical setting.

2009   Best Western celebrated the honor of being the "Best Mid-Range Hotel Brand" in Asia-Pacific for three consecutive years.

From Best Western's brochure to potential members

Best Western contractually offers its members:

- to use the global booking and distribution channels as Best Western
- to provide global and regional marketing programs in addition to individual products
- to increase a member hotel's average price and consequently the revenue per room.

By just adding the prefix "Best Western", members can make their regionally renowned hotel an internationally branded product while preserving its individual flair and uniqueness. "What distinguishes Best Western from all other hotel chains is that we DO NOT interfere in any way in the management issues of the member hotel."

Strict membership and admission criteria:

- minimum of 30 rooms
- the hotel does not belong to any other international hotel marketing organization or group
- it complies with the international three-star standards and with the international Best Western minimum standards

- the hotel switches its GDS connection to Best Western on commencement of membership.

Becoming a member implies following five steps exactly planned by Best Western including a three-day onsite training course (Best Western philosophy, systems, marketing programs as well as yield management, billing, Best Practice, etc.).

A global, democratic, regionally managed non-profit association of private hoteliers.

It is you owning Best Western – not vice versa!

- Best Western is a voluntary and democratic association of private hoteliers for the purpose of increasing hotel performance through joint marketing and sales and cross-selling.

On principle, all members of the democratically elected regional and international boards as well as the parent company's board must be hoteliers operating Best Western member hotels.

- Rights and obligations are the same for all members of one region and are defined by a joint cooperation agreement.

All Best Western hotels can individually manage their products through GDS, Pegasus and the Best Western booking engine "Lynx". In addition, recommendations between all 4,000 Best Western Hotels promote cross-selling.

- You will benefit from more than 30 affiliates' (regional) headquarters, two reservation call centers and hundreds of marketing and sales staff.

With detailed manuals, regular training, individual coaching and online help member support is available from our regional team at any time on application-related issues.

- Member meetings, newsletter, email and intranet inform all hoteliers about regional and global activities of Best Western, on best practices, statistics, tips, trends and developments in tourism.

Reasonable fees and transparent cost structure

- Best Western is unrivalled in cost-effectiveness because Best Western – as a non-profit organization – uses all members' fees only to their benefit. The cost structure is defined and approved annually by the Best Western Board. All cost items are transparent; monthly statistics show Best Western-originated revenues.
- The one-time admission fee (from €4,570 including administration, printed matter and an illuminated sign) depends on the number of hotel rooms. Membership fees are based solely on Best Western-originated revenues – and not on your hard-earned turnover.
- The annual membership fee is composed of a fixed amount (per hotel, per room) and variable, revenue-related payments. The reservation fees are charged for each reservation received. This ensures a fair spreading of costs (i.e. a small hotel has to pay less than a big one and a hotel receiving more Best Western bookings has to pay more than a hotel receiving fewer Best Western guests).

Sources: www.bestwestern.com/newsroom/history.asp
Best Western Promotion Brochure

Inter-firm cooperatives

A stronger form of partnership often used by associating entrepreneurs is the *inter-firm cooperative*. As the number of parties increases and the matters of cooperation expand/become more complex, *property right sharing* among contracting parties may become necessary. A form of association including common ownership and the set up of a new entity with the prerogatives of a firm, is a *cooperative whose members are entrepreneurial firms*. In fact, this option was considered as a possible solution to Promatem's problems (end-chapter case); actually, had the collaborating entrepreneurs been of more comparable contribution capacity, the co-op in all likelihood would have been formed.

Co-ops of entrepreneurs are a common, even a dominant, organization form in agribusiness (e.g. Hendrikse 2007). Box 4.10 illustrates the form through examples in other industries.

Box 4.10 Entrepreneurs' co-ops

Service Station Cooperative – Capricorn Society Ltd., Australia, New Zealand, South Africa

Capricorn Society Limited was formed as an unofficial buying group in the early 1970s by a group of Western Australian service station proprietors and established as a cooperative to assist automotive repair and service businesses in 1974. Today, auto electricians, paint and panel shops, mechanical workshops, auto transmission workshops and service stations, among others, use Capricorn to buy over three-quarters of a billion dollars in parts at competitive prices every year from more than 1,300 preferred suppliers in Australia and also in New Zealand and South Africa. In July 2003, Capricorn Mutual was established, as an initiative of Capricorn Society, to provide the members with an alternative to insurance. Capricorn Mutual provides business and personal risk protection to its members and was granted a license under the rigorous Australian Financial Services law.

Source: www.capricorn.com.au/ and
www.australia.coop/publish/article_35.php

Hairdressers' Co-operative

The Hairdressers' Co-operative Society (Hair Co-op) was founded in 1944. Today, more than 3,200 independent hairdressers in South Australia use their cooperative to purchase hair-care and beauty products as well as professional equipment for their hair salons. At the same time, they benefit from the frequent "cutting-edge" education courses and the support of qualified technical advisors. The high service level offered within the cooperative is reflected in its efforts to deliver ordered products on the same day and its strong orientation toward members' needs.

Source: www.haircoop.com.au/index.html

Taxi Owners' Cooperative – Assetamorwa, Rwanda

The Association de l'Esperance des Taxis Motor au Rwanda (Assetamorwa) is a cooperative of motorcycle taxi owners in Kigali, the capital of Rwanda, which counts over 2,500 members. Each of the motorcycle taxi owners is an individual trader, but together they support each other and can negotiate with authorities such as the traffic police. In turn, the cooperative helps the city authorities to organize and keep order in public traffic. Establishing the cooperative has also given the members a better chance of protecting themselves against crime on the dangerous streets of Kigali and to improve the security of passengers and of the drivers themselves. The members of Assetamorwa are conscious of the need to help young people. The cooperative has therefore established a training school where students can learn the motorcycle taxi driver business, as well as the Highway Code and basics in mechanics. To further support its members, the cooperative also runs a garage and spare parts depot. The members are encouraged to participate in savings and credit cooperatives (SACCOs) and this enables them to access long- and short-term loans. The cooperative has been able to buy 57 motorcycles for members to use. If this service were not available, beginners would have to rent their motorcycle from an owner charging premium rates. Assetamorwa is a perfect example of how organizing in a cooperative can help entrepreneurs in an informal economy improve their individual businesses through helping each other.

Source: Smith, S. and Ross, C. (2006) "How the SYNDICOOP approach has worked in East Africa – organizing out of poverty: stories from the grassroots movement", a joint publication of the ILO, ICA and ICFTU. Available from: www.ilo.org/dyn/empent/docs/F644557485/2006-SYNDICOOP-Case-Studies.pdf

As is apparent from the above cases, this form of proprietary partnership among entrepreneurs, taking the form of a cooperative firm, is common in moderate risk, known-technology activities (including complex ones, such as professional activities).

Joint ventures

Another proprietary partnership, which can govern cooperation in more risky and innovative activities, is the *joint venture*. The term "joint venture" (JV) indicates an agreement in which two or more firms contribute financial, technical and human capital for the constitution of a new jointly owned and jointly managed firm. Joint ventures give origin to new firms, born from two or more "mother firms", typically in the legal form of a corporation, allowing the division of ownership shares.

JVs have turned out to be a powerful vehicle for the realization of innovating activities that are difficult to conduct internally and to coordinate through market exchanges. In fact, the know-how that is relevant to the generation of innovation is often developed efficiently in different firms according to different paths of learning and specialization; there are many opportunities to combine these bodies of knowledge and technologies into new products; the combination of know-how often generates complex and intense interdependencies; and the potential for opportunism and reciprocal expropriation is often very high. Equity-based alliances can provide the adequate guarantees, information structures and incentives to regulate these complex webs of joint actions and exchanges.

JVs are in fact particularly widespread in high-technology sectors or highly innovative sectors. They resolve the difficulties in measuring the contribution of each party by assigning to each partner, in advance, residual reward rights according to the shares held in the new firm.

Based on this characterization, *JV relations are in many respects similar to capital venture relations.* The difference is that in JVs there is no clear qualitative difference between the type of capital invested (financial versus human); rather, the two (or more) investing parties maintaining their own identity in the new firm and bargaining over property rights are the co-investing (mother) firms. But the negotiated items and the recurrent solutions are the same; for example, shares are generally allocated in proportion to an estimate of the value of the resources invested, and to the relative criticality and substitutability of those resources, where they are measurable. In many cases, the perception of symmetric coalition power, of equally indispensable contributions and/or of contributions that are difficult to appraise, lead to the constitution of equal share joint ventures.

Box 4.11 illustrates the formation of a JV agreement for innovation between two high-tech firms, indicating elements of the negotiation process behind the division of property rights (shares and board positions), as well as the choice of a proprietary partnership over a possible alternative repeated bilateral exchange contract, in which the firm producing the component transfers it to the user firm.

Box 4.11 The formation of a JV for innovation

About AIV
One could easily guess AIV's activity when entering its headquarters located in the northern suburbs of Milan. Unpretentious offices, separated only by glass walls, huge files and, despite all this, a sense of chaos. No status symbols or the luxury that other companies like to show off. Moving around required the assistance of one of the company's technicians acting as a guide in what, at first sight, appeared to be a huge labyrinth. But, as expensive and very sophisticated equipment such as lasers, computers and electronic microscopes appeared everywhere, one soon realizes that this is a high-tech research laboratory.

AIV is indeed a high-tech company – number one in Italy and one of the best in the world – operating in two specific technological fields: special metallurgy (non-ferrous alloys) and vacuum technology. In 1986, this Italian joint-stock company – which shortly before had gone public – registered a $40 million turnover, 98 percent of which came from exports. The company's research efforts focused on the development of new products and applications, the innovation of the productive processes and the improvement of technical assistance to customers.

Almost 8 percent of the turnover was allocated to the research department where 50 of the company's 450 employees worked. Besides the head office in Milan, there were two production plants at Avezzano in central Italy, and subsidiaries in France, England, Germany, Japan and in the United States, where AIV had other production plants.

The company's main product was the "getter",[19] a special metal alloy that is placed in a vacuum tube to absorb residual gasses and is generally used in electron tubes, solar collectors, Dewar flasks,[20] lamps, particle accelerators, etc. AIV was the only Italian manufacturer of "evaporable getter", and retained a 70 percent share of the world market while, at the same time, it had almost total control of the "non-evaporable getter" market. The former accounted for nearly 50 percent of the company's turnover, the latter for 35 percent and the remaining came from other products, such as alkaline salt dispenser, mercury dispenser, getter ion-pump, etc.

The company's strategy had always been focused on a limited production of high value-added products, in order to exploit both the complex production technology it had developed to create special alloys and the acquired scientific expertise that had enabled it to deposit numerous patents over the years. The non-evaporable getter, therefore, seemed to be the most promising product in terms of market prospects and new applications in this field were being studied. However, research studies were carried out in areas very close to the traditional fields, to preserve strong synergies and exploit the available know-how. For instance, they were exploring the possibility of using the getter, not so much to create a vacuum in special equipment, but to purify gasses in order to obtain the one needed through the selective elimination of all the others contained in the mix. A few years beforehand, AIV had therefore started to manufacture small purifiers.

Tunyo's proposal

The initiative of a Japanese company, Tunyo, an AIV customer, gave a great and unexpected impetus to AIV's research efforts in this direction. Tunyo, a firm almost the same size as AIV, with nearly 800 employees, was a leading company in Japan in the pure gas and purifiers market. One of Tunyo's internal units, producing "Dewars", purchased AIV's newest getters because of their special features. This kind of getter had been used in the traditional way, namely to produce a vacuum, until the head of the Japanese technical department, perhaps after seeing AIV's purifying devices, thought of using the getter to purify inert gases such as argon.

The first results were extremely encouraging, but to progress along this path, Japanese technicians wanted to establish direct contact with AIV, since they were not allowed to produce the getters with the specific characteristics they required as AIV's international patents covered it. Moreover, they needed the cooperation of those who had the know-how for these complex applications. For this reason, Tunyo put forward the idea of establishing a form of cooperation with AIV.

First stage: technical cooperation

AIV welcomed Tunyo's proposal that offered them the opportunity to enter the field of "super-purifiers" (devices that can substantially improve gas purity levels) that could be used for interesting applications in the production of semi-conductors – a rapidly expanding sector – especially to obtain high information density (megabit). AIV initially considered the possibility of seizing this opportunity on its own, which was, however, discarded later on since AIV did not know the purifiers market sufficiently well. Moreover, from the production point of view, they did not have the necessary equipment to produce the other components of a purifying device, since the getter was just one of these used to improve the gas purity level. Tunyo controlled the purifier technology, knew the semi-conductor market very well and, above all, nurtured the same love for technology and research as AIV.

The Italian company decided to establish the first contact between the heads of the technical and research departments of the two firms, thus giving Tunyo the opportunity to better understand the technical features of getters and their potentials while, on the other hand, AIV could carefully assess future market opportunities for its products.

Technical cooperation started in late 1983 and was characterized by mutual opening, exchanges of visits to plants and laboratories, and joint research work that led to joint patents. Both companies learned a great deal from this experience and the head of the Japanese technical office clearly explained how the semiconductors market works, since this was the most interesting field for new applications of high-accuracy gas purifiers.

Second stage: the choice of a form of collaboration

It was evident that the sector was promising and that competences were complementary. The problem on the table was the form of cooperation the two companies would choose. They could work together to develop the new product and, at the same time, remain independent from each other, preserving the traditional relationship between supplier (AIV for the getter) and customer (Tunyo). To AIV this could mean wider room for maneuver since it remained free to sell the getter also to Tunyo's competitors. But, in so doing, they could not enter the purifiers market directly, especially the semi-conductors sector, which they were most interested in. This last consideration, together with the fact that the technical cooperation had reached such an advanced stage, and that the two companies had a number of joint patents, led to considering the possibility of setting up a third company, owned by both the Japanese and Italian firm. It would manufacture and market the super-purifiers by assembling the various components supplied by AIV and Tunyo.

The technical cooperation continued, since the decision had been taken to start a new pilot-plant, to test the effectiveness of the new product internally.

Meetings between the patent experts of the two firms were held, to be followed shortly afterwards (at the end of 1984) by the real and true negotiations that would lead to the creation of a joint venture.

Third stage: creation of a joint venture
The delegations of the two companies met in a relaxed and friendly atmosphere thanks to the pre-existing technical cooperation.

According to Tunyo's managers, cooperation between the two companies had to be as close as possible and geared to the long-term development of the new product and all its applications. Therefore, the new company should be entitled not only to the already existing patents – some of which had been jointly developed – but also to all those that were going to be developed in relation to the production and perfecting of the super-purifiers, including those relating to getters only.

AIV's managers had the unpleasant impression that Tunyo's offer was aimed at permanently taking away AIV's technical know-how– its most important and valuable resource. An accurate analysis of the future developments of getter applications in the field of purifiers led the Italian managers to the conclusion that the new company should not be entitled to all the patents that AIV was to develop in the future. This had to become a firm stand in the negotiations, since it was the only way to preserve a privileged position vis-à-vis the counterparty, which actually employed more common and easily replaceable technology. In addition, the decision was taken not to include AIV's limited production of purifiers in the agreement, thereby excluding it from the counterparty's and the new company's control. This was conceived as a strategic move, especially as far as small purifiers were concerned, since they had application fields besides microelectronics.

The counter-proposal that the Italian delegation submitted to the Japanese therefore included these two points:

- exclusion of future patents from the agreement;
- no limits to AIV's own production and distribution of purifiers.

Tunyo's managers asked to be allowed to reconsider the counter-proposal in private. The following draft agreement emerged from the Japanese counterparty meeting:

1   Patents: the conditions set by AIV were accepted.
2   Shares: because of the agreements undertaken with the Japanese government, it was essential for Tunyo to have a majority interest in the new company.

3   Management: it was in the interest of the new company to have a mostly Japanese management.
4   Exclusivity clauses on purifiers: only small purifiers and only those not used in microelectronics were excluded from the agreement. AIV should stop producing the remaining ones.

The Italian delegation accepted the conditions concerning exclusivity clause 4, but refused to sign the draft agreement, stating that the management of the new company had to be formed by an equal number of Japanese and Italian members.

Fifteen days later, a final agreement was reached and the new company was called "S&S Superpurifiers K.K.K.". Tunyo was to have a 51 percent share of the stock; at the same time, it accepted an equal number of Japanese and Italian members on the board of directors of the new company.

Source: adapted from Grandori, A. and Perrone, V. (1987)
The AIV-Tunyo Joint Venture, SDA Bocconi

Key points

For entrepreneurial firms "external organization" and "external growth" is more important than for other types of firms. This chapter addresses, first, a rather neglected topic in standard entrepreneurship literature: the design of efficient firm boundaries. It does so by enriching the important organizational economics models available on this issue, with criteria of particular importance in an entrepreneurial setting, that is, adding *knowledge factors* and *internal diseconomies of size* to the usual production and transaction costs. One of the conclusions to be highlighted is that the *growth* of entrepreneurial firms, if intended as expansion in size, should not be considered as universally positive, even an "outcome"; but *is a choice*. Not all entrepreneurial firms should grow (and some can be born large and "global").

The second section examines the organizational agreements and arrangements through which an entrepreneurial firm can grow in activities without growing in size. Two basic different configurations of interdependence and coordination are considered, and three forms of particular importance for entrepreneurship within each.

* *"sequential" or "transactional" interdependence*, regulated by *bilateral or trilateral contracts,* in particular: *subcontracting, franchising, and inside contracting*;
* *"multi-party associations"*, regulating the relation among firms cooperating in producing a common output, or using common pooled inputs (*pooled interdependence*): in particular, *associations of independent entrepreneurs, inter-firm cooperatives and joint ventures*.

Choosing among the two types of agreement is very important and subject to intensive negotiations in practice, especially in multi-party networks where entrepreneurial firms are not the central node. In fact, networks with a central coordinating firm may be more efficient and provide a way to start or develop new businesses while saving resources. On the other side, parity-based associational networks guarantee more decision rights to the participant entrepreneurs.

It is also shown that the degree of *innovation* that the various external forms of organizing entrepreneurship should be expected to generate and manage is *higher for association-based alliances*, especially if they involve *property right sharing*.

Analysis questions

On in-chapter cases

- Consider the growing and transforming agribusiness sector. Which problems should entrepreneurs address and solve in designing agreements among them, and along the value chain? What are some available solutions? What are the main advantages and disadvantages of bilateral contracts (e.g. contract farming) versus associations of producers (e.g. co-ops of farmers)?
- Which differences in approach to outsourcing decisions are there between AX and Minteos, and how can they be evaluated?
- Why was a joint venture formed between AIV-Tunyo for the production of new equipment? When should an entrepreneur demand property rights in inter-firm agreements for innovation? Which kind of PR is best? According to what criteria might property rights be shared among the parties?

On end-chapter case

- What is Promatem? A firm, an association, a cooperative of firms? What should it be, in the various stages of its development?
- How can the epilogue be explained? Which solutions to the problems that bring the experience to an end could have been available? What future entrepreneurial developments could be expected/advisable?

End-chapter case: Promatem

*Silvia Bagdadli, 1992, revised by Anna Grandori, 2010**

Note: *This case has been constructed and revised thanks to direct interviews in 1992, 2000 and 2010 with Gianni Dell'Orto, entrepreneur, co-founder and former President of Promatem.

Prologue

Ted Samuels' trip to Europe to search for someone to look after the interests of Wincomb on the continent had not come up with results. Wincomb was an American company with subsidiaries in the UK and Europe, specializing in executive search. Ted had met many people, but none of them seemed suitable to take over the job as vice-president for continental Europe. However, many of those he contacted appeared to have a great entrepreneurial attitude, and this gave him the idea of trying to find a way to get them together. When he returned to America, he got in touch with some of them again to fix a preliminary meeting in England. This was early in 1977.

In London, as well as Ted Samuels and Mike Jensen of Wincomb UK, there was Marco Colombo, an Italian who had been put forward by a friend for the vice-president position. Colombo did not seem suited to that job, but there was something about him that suggested he was maybe ready for a new international adventure. There was also a German, Chris Ulrich, and a Belgian at the meeting. Marco was working at Egon Zender, which Chris had just left. The enthusiasm of the participants and the immediate understanding this created made them decide to fix a second meeting soon afterwards. Once again there were five men taking part, but this time, Jacques Bernard, a lawyer who owned a French consultancy firm, took the Belgian's place. It had only taken a few hours to realize that the Belgian was unsuitable, as he was hungry for power and the wish to dominate the others. Ted summed him up as "a one-man band".

The idea, which had not yet developed, was to set up an international network of independent companies, capable of competing in the future with the multinationals operating in executive and top-level management search. The national companies were in fact limited in their expansion possibilities, when the client required a search to be made in more than one country.

The structure of this aggregate was still an unknown factor. What was clear, however, was that all the companies would have to maintain high-quality standards, that there would have to be absolute openness among the partners and that the new structure, whatever form it might take, should not weigh down the operations with useless bureaucratic procedures. In addition, and this was emphasized on a number of occasions, the companies had to remain independent and, in respect of the common principles, free to run their own business within national boundaries. The entrepreneurial spirit, common to all, made this a strict imperative. Jacques Bernard suggested opting for a French contract, the GIE (Groupement d'Intérèt Economique), whose briskness would enable the requirements of the aspiring partners to be satisfied.

After identifying the structure – the new company's skeleton – it was easy to proceed with the systematic analysis of the various problems. In a new meeting in June, the guidelines for the new aggregate were decided upon. A name was chosen – Promatem, containing a good omen for the future (pro maiora tempora?!), and it was decided to operate up until the end of the year on an informal basis, at which point the group would be announced at the panel meeting in Chicago, where the head office of Wincomb was located. The attitude of dynamic enthusiasm toward the new firm was strong and it never occurred to anybody to set fees for the work each member did for the others. In June, Marco said, "Let's not make our profits by billing each other." In other words, the clear message was: work for the others free of charge and exchange as much work as possible. The operations began, but the German, to whom a number of jobs had been given, was judged as not being up to the standards of the group, and the GIE was signed only by Ted Samuels, Marco Colombo, who in the meantime had left Egon Zender to set up his own company, Jacques Bernard, who had been working for some time with Legriver s.a., and Mike Jensen, of Wincomb UK Ltd.

It was February 1978.

Promatem International eventually became, in around ten years, one of the major players operating in the field of direct executive search. In the 1990s it was composed of 160 individual firms, operating in 45 offices in 25 countries. The annual cost of the structure was between $100K and 200K. With a turnover of $80 million, it was the fourth group in the world, and the first "Multidomestic". All this growth was achieved under the GIE contract.

The internal governance and organizational structure of the group was structured according to three heralded basic principles:

- democracy
  1 firm = 1 vote
  1 country = 1 independent firm

- entrepreneurship
  1 country = 1 independent firm
  each firm = self-sufficient
  managing power = general assembly

- multidomestic structure
  1 firm = 1 country
  no financial "central" liaison.

The history of Promatem's growth

1978–1983: learning and first development

The first years of the company's history were dedicated to learning. The partners had to get used to working together, and often the practice was more difficult than the simple principles laid down in the GIE. The group objective was "the development of specialist consultancy operations aimed at executive and senior management search, by means of the definition of common ethics, sharing experiences and exchanging information, and by means of the research into and study of new methods of operation in an international setting" (GIE statute). All the partners of the various companies were members of the general assembly. The assembly nominated the board, and each company had a vote. Originally, the four founding partners were the board members. The board elected the chairman with a yearly mandate. In the beginning, this was a purely formal appointment. The admission or removal of a member of the firm was by means of a unanimous vote by the board. The meetings of the partners were completely informal, with everyone free to speak at will. There was no precise agenda. Each partner operated in accordance with his personal style and culture. However, the founders were always honest, loyal and willing to push the projects ahead. Each country had an independent firm with the right to a vote. One exception to this was the UK, as the Americans owned 70 percent of the company there. The problem immediately arose as to whether or not it had a right to vote at board meetings. Generally speaking, the answer should have been no, as the company was not independent. However, the decision was taken to make an exception and grant it a vote. But not everyone was happy with this solution, and many alternatives were proposed, but Ted, as the creator of the firm, possessed strong charisma that had an effect on the others, and Mike, in spite of his minority share, had very high entrepreneurial capabilities. Promatem did not possess its own company capital and could not make profits. The expenses of the GIE, which were low, were divided among the members. A letterhead was created with the common name, and a brochure drawn up. Each company continued to operate under the name it was known by in its home market. There was still some uncertainty as to how the group should be presented to clients. Jacques cautiously suggested putting themselves forward as group members but at the same time independent. The entrepreneurial spirit typical of the partners tended to create the prevalence of the single companies over the new group. But they had to learn to take decisions on a joint basis. Jacques Bernard, in particular, had no partners in his company. Ted and Marco did, but with minority shares.

Right from the start, it was clear that the group had to set up bases in a large number of countries. This expansion took place by way of the entry of already operating firms, even though this differed from the method initially decided on. At the very beginning, the idea of capitalist expansion dominated. Each partner, in line with his possibilities, would open new companies in other countries. France would open a company in Spain and another in Belgium, Italy in Greece and America in Canada. In Holland, the idea was to set up a company in which each founder had a share. Bernard in particular, in spite of being one of the members with the greatest faith in the potential of the group, saw growth by means of companies already in operation and the consequent expansion of the board as a possible threat to the flexibility and speed of action of the group.

Also later, when it was decided to operate differently, Jacques did not want to let go of Spain, and he spent ten years trying to set up a firm in the Iberian Peninsula. It was immediately clear, however, that a capitalist development would be very slow and that it was very difficult to maintain the same quality standards in a large number of countries without investing considerable resources in expert consultants.

In the meantime, action was taken to replace the German company. Marco Colombo was given the task of going to Berlin to meet Chris Butner and his partners and to see if the firm was suitable to enter the GIE. The selection of a new company was critical for the success of the group. The quality of the search carried out and the company's image in the country, the entrepreneurial spirit of the partner or partners, and the ability to work alongside others without trying to dominate them were fundamental factors. The GIE was not a very strong aggregation tool and the shared values and ideas were the adhesive force that kept the structure together in spite of the often-intense pressure of personal independence. It was obvious that it was not possible to control the partners; they simply had to trust each other, and to do that they had to know each other well. Often, rather than preset criteria that went on to be formalized, the observations and feeling built up during the first meetings were more important. Butner & Partners, which, unlike all the other companies, was an equal partnership, entered Promatem between February and April 1978. The company, one of the biggest and most successful in Germany, was the motivational power behind expansion. As it was an equal partnership, it immediately put pressure on the other group companies to change their ownership structures. This factor also created certain problems within the board, since not all the equal partners accepted the decisions taken by the group. This was due, however, to the lack of undisputed leadership in Butner toward the other partners. Ted had partners too, though not with equal shares, but they willingly accepted the decisions he took in the board. At this time, on the suggestion of an Englishman who had worked in Belgium, it was decided to contact Josh Hartung, whom Colombo also knew. One Sunday in April, Marco Colombo phoned him to suggest his entry, and this took place shortly afterwards. Butner meanwhile, on holiday in Brazil, started looking for a company with a view to setting up a base in South America. After several years of searching, José Goncalves of Gombos entered the board.

1984–1989: consolidation and formalization

Under the pressure of the Germans, promoters of the "big is beautiful approach", opposed by the Latins and Americans, who preferred the concept of "boutique is beautiful", Promatem continued to take on new partners and expand its operations. The Americans granted their first territorial concession, with the entry of a Canadian company into the GIE. This operation had considerable importance for future developments. Australia was next to enter the group, but the company was represented on the board not by its owners, who were too old, but by a manager, Thomas van Dyck, the company's top consultant. An excellent relationship between the Australians and Germans developed almost immediately. The same applied to Hartung of Benelux, with a cultural approach very similar to that of the Germans and Swiss, who had been granted the first concession by the Germans. Jacques, on the other hand, was still obsessed with the idea of setting up a Spanish branch of Légrivèr, in spite of the emergence of a certain disgruntlement among the English-speaking partners, whose profit-oriented mentality had little patience with those who wanted to slow down the process of expansion. The America of Ted Samuels formed a kind of balance between the Latins and the English, but with the entry of Switzerland and South Africa the power balance moved decisively toward the latter, who were pressing for the rapid expansion of Promatem, along with greater regulation and formalization in the group. In addition, a number of very small companies entered the group, with positions very close to those of the Latins. Some of the more recent members had previously worked at Spencer Stuart. The new members were selected with the usual care, but now that the board contained more than seven members, things began to change and it was difficult to reach decisions, especially when unanimity was required. A number of procedures were introduced to simplify group operations and offer incentives in this regard, and for the reinforcement of the structural bodies. In 1981, under the chairmanship of Marco Colombo, this post became two-yearly and began to take on greater importance, even though the most significant change was to take place under the Australian chairmanship. The chairman was given the job of traveling to identify potential member companies and meet the partners of the firms already operating within the group. The decision was taken to appoint a vice-chairman to help him in his work and who would automatically become group chairman two years later. The management costs were divided equally among the members.

The role of the board was the definition of the general strategy and development guidelines of Promatem, and the implementation of these, where possible. The board studied the investment programs, prepared the group budget and decided on the admission of new members. In this light, it was decided in 1984 that a member could be admitted or removed with a 70 percent vote in favor of the motion. With more than ten countries represented on the board, the idea of unanimity was no longer democratic, and presented a serious obstacle to the decision-making process. In those years, the most important task of the board was the encouragement of the integration of its members, "serving the spirit of international partnership, that we all had good reasons to opt for and we all wished to belong to".[21] The value and role of the board was not based on the results achieved in each meeting, but on the fact that "the meetings continued to take place". Each country's representative took part in the meetings to promote continuing expansion, ensure acceptable standards, maintain contacts between people and companies, create business opportunities and work toward the stability necessary for growth. The board organized the meetings of the general assembly, which took place every 18 months and discussed the brochure.

In the meantime, the possibility of using a common name for the group began to be discussed. One of the suggestions, adopted in 1987, was that of adding the name of Promatem International to the names of the national companies – "Promatem International Wincomb Chicago S.A.", for example. The decision to do so was optional, but those who decided to use the name were obliged to strictly observe the quality standards.

> All the companies are expected to incorporate the Promatem name in their individual company names by 1992. The next step will be the use of Promatem alone, followed by the name of the base-country (such as Promatem France), but the group structure may change in the future.

The client communication standards were defined and incentives were introduced for the use of the group's headed paper, though this generally ended up simply piled on various desks, unused. The image of Promatem worldwide became the main objective, as its reinforcement meant the reinforcement of unity among members. The exchange of services among partners continued to take place free of charge.[22] Even expenses were unbilled. The indirect advertising that those who exchanged jobs received – provided these were done well – was considered sufficient reward. But this situation could not last forever, and the English began to suggest to the board that an internal fee of 30 percent be applied for the company that presented the client, as monetary equality seemed to them to be a necessary incentive for the exchanges, which had always been scant. In 1980, the Lead Castle Award was set up. This cup was awarded annually to the group company that exchanged the largest number of clients. From 1987, the inter-fee was applied, but in truth, the exchange of clients was a question of culture, which could not be changed by the offer of money, only by working together and following the examples of others. The Lead Castle Award, which still exists, went on to become a more and more desirable trophy, and for some operators the professional pride to be gained from winning the prize was a stronger stimulus than the commission earned.

The constantly growing number of countries and consultants involved made it essential to create something that helped the partners get to know each other better, to restore the team spirit typical of the founders. Greater emphasis was placed on the "two-yearly exercises", first set up in 1983, in which a partner went to visit a company in another country, and the common search for new firms to enter Promatem. This helped people get to know each other and the objectives shared helped bind the union. Marco suggested starting up a project for the identification of the tools that could encourage the integration of the partners, such as a common marketing plan. He was convinced that "there was enormous room for improvement between a completely integrated bureaucratic organization such as Egon Zender or Russel Reynolds and a broad-mesh federation such as Promatem". Toward the end of 1987, however, there was a drop in the quantity of business exchanged and, even worse, a strong reduction of the general enthusiasm in the group. The international image of the organization was important, but without client exchange there was no further justification for its existence. The Australians decided to give the partners the responsibility for this issue, and the criteria set in 1983, by which each member dealt with the jobs he received from the others in line with the quality standards, were confirmed and strengthened.

The smaller companies were highly unsatisfied, because the advantages of belonging to Promatem were beginning to be lower than the costs sustained for participation in the international meetings, among other factors.

In England in the meantime, things were going very badly since the professional level of the company was low. Even though the Americans promised a stronger presence in London and the merger with another company, everything seemed ready for a crisis.

1988–1989: the crisis

In 1985, Ted Samuels left Wincomb USA. In England, Mike Jensen had left in 1981 and his successor, Tolman, an equally capable consultant and manager, left in 1986. Thus, Promatem had lost two of its founders. Ted's successor, Nick Adams, regarded the GIE as being rather remote from his immediate interests. Like many Americans, he saw his own company as the priority. And in 1987, Jacques Bernard left the board. After the resignation of Tolman, the English company was managed by figures of questionable ability and the quality standards and results began to drop. The Americans were not very interested in taking over control, because their own situation was not what it ought to have been and the idea of strengthening the company by means of a merger had been shelved. The Germans and Australians started to protest and, unknown to the others, began looking for a new English partner. The crisis at Wincomb UK created tension, and the tension had a negative effect on the coherence of the group. The chairman, Hartung of the Benelux countries, did nothing to solve the problem. In fact, his solidarity with the Germans led him to hope for the replacement of the English. Pressure on the Americans to intervene intensified, but their chairman, in light of the lack of interest shown in the matter, walked out of the general partner and board meetings. The Germans, Australians and Dutch took cunning steps to set up a meeting between Wincomb USA and another successful American company, with a view to a merger that would partially solve the problems. But the agreement never took place. The tension increased and criticism became more intense. The Latins looked on, but they did not agree with the unclear methods of the Germans, which went against the general attitude of good faith among partners that had always existed. And they were unable to imagine Promatem without Wincomb USA, which had created the group. The trio of Germany, Benelux and Australia convinced the other American company to apply to enter Promatem. At this point, it was necessary to decide whether to keep Wincomb within the group or not. The Latins, especially the Italians and French, refused to budge – no one could be removed from the GIE unless the motives were truly serious. It was Wincomb itself that came up with the solution. Hartung had brought the question to the point where the Americans were so frustrated that they closed London and left Promatem. They were replaced by William Olson of Cunnigs Philadelphia. The English question was solved in 1991, when Colombo managed to involve a prestigious company after complex negotiations. This operation enhanced his standing in the group. But the problems did not end there because Cunnigs had a very profitable agreement with a Canadian company, the national leader, which the group was obviously unable to accept unless it could be incorporated into the existing situation. Once again, Promatem was divided into two factions. On the one hand, France, Italy, the Scandinavian countries and Brazil, for whom ethics were more important than profits, and on the other the English and Americans, who were more attached to following their own interests. Even though Marco and Jacques declared themselves ready to do battle for the Canadian company, even if this meant leaving the GIE, the company decided to pull out under pressure that would have led to a split in the group. Calm was restored, even though an existing agreement between the new English company and a South African firm created the threat of new conflicts.

These events had shaken the company badly. Loyalty, confidence and enthusiasm had fallen off. The growth of the group had made it more difficult for the various members to get to know each other and the integration tools at individual level were weakened. It was clear that, if the group was to continue in business, the structures had to be reinforced with greater formalization and the identification of new principles and objectives. Promatem had to become more of a company and less of an assembly of individuals.

1989–1992: decentralization and integration

In 1989, a new chairman was appointed. He was Thomas Van Dyck, the highly talented manager of the Australian firm, who seemed the right man for the renewal process. It was with Thomas that the role of chairman took on full power and dignity. He solved the common problems, integrated the various companies, and offered effective leadership with regard to the other executives and the running of the board, thanks to his sense of discipline and the introduction of, among other factors, the agenda.

Between 1989 and 1991, the group had grown considerably, from 14 to 22 companies (24 in 1992), 22 to 45 offices, with an increase in turnover from $28 million to $80 million. This rapid growth took place thanks to the operations of the three regions that had been set up – Europe and Africa, North and South America, and Pacific Asia. The search for new partners was delegated to these three blocks, which were able to act more rapidly in the identification of suitable companies. In this way, the group began to move toward the decentralization which its growth demanded.

The regional division was decided during the board meeting held in Sydney in 1990. The regions were to be responsible for the development of business and operating factors. All the partners in each region had to meet once a year to discuss marketing, development and efficiency, and to offer suggestions to the international board. In addition, each company was to appoint a representative to the regional board with the main task of dealing with growth strategies. Each region was to appoint its own chairman for the management of the meetings and the relationships between the various companies operating within his area. The structures of the regions were identical to those of the group as a whole.

At international level, the general assembly continued to meet every 18 months, before the meeting of the board, so that all the partners could suggest changes or initiatives to be considered at the meeting. The board met every six months to set objectives and strategies, decide on the acceptance of new partners and removal of existing ones and take all the decisions that altered the status quo. In operating matters the board had become inefficient, and for this reason it was decided to set up an executive committee made up of the three regional chairmen and the international executive and vice-chairman. This committee was a kind of executive branch of the board, which had the advantage of being able to carry out a five-man discussion of the questions that the board had already considered. Three sub-committees were also set up, each with a specific objective – quality, marketing and public relations, and development. These initiatives were handled in the regions by task forces.

The new regions worked very well during the first two years, and created great impetus for the group. But decentralization led to integration problems for the three geographical areas since the efforts geared to the communication of the decisions taken at the meetings were low. Sometimes, this poor level of communication was intentional, for example, when the English and Germans, without taking too much trouble to let the others know, suggested setting up a company in Poland. As they were unable to find a suitable partner, they had decided to give the locals 30 percent control and use the remaining 70 percent to form an equal partnership between them. The Americans and Canadians got to know about this initiative and decided to take part, even though they were clearly unhappy about the lack of publicity devoted to a common interest initiative. A partner took on the task of inter-regional communication to avoid separate operations. The fees for international search operations and the methods of dividing these up among partners were standardized.

The board approved a mission statement proposed by Thomas. Van Dyck had shown strong commitment to a common declaration of objectives and policies, for the sake of clarity and the reinforcement of Promatem's interests, and for the support of existing and new partners. Each company had to present a five- to ten-year development plan, which was not merely a general declaration of intentions but a true strategy to be followed with a view to the expansion and improvement of the firm's local competitive position.

The 1990s

Modified in this way, the structure made good progress, but it was too burdensome for the smaller companies. The possibility arose of delegating the votes for certain types of decisions to the bigger companies and the need emerged for greater decentralization toward the regions. Marco Colombo was convinced that the future of Promatem depended on the regions and the quality project, but the idea of what to leave in the center was still not clear. Before proceeding, the decisions to be taken by all the partners and those left up to a more restricted body had to be identified, as well as the basis on which the structures had to be modified. With this aim in mind, some partners were given the task of drawing up a proposal.

The proposal included the hypothesis of transforming the partnership into a cooperative firm. The idea of moving from the GIE to a limited liability cooperative emerged due mainly to questions of limitations in the GIE with regard to a number of important points. In the first place, the group was unable to protect its common name, "Promatem", which at the time was being used by a constantly growing number of partners and had become a point upon which future integration and the trading campaign had to be based. Those who left the group could keep the name

Promatem in the logos of their companies without the possibility of any legal action. In addition, the GIE did not allow common investments or the creation of profits. For these reasons, and others, a number of partners suggested transforming Promatem into a cooperative. Jacques had already left the board and, in his absence, it was easier to press for changes. The majority agreed, and there only remained the question of how much the operation would cost since the trade name had to be assessed by the French authorities. After receiving the preliminary opinion of a law firm, whose estimate was of a modest sum, other opinions were sought from companies based in France. The resulting estimate was a figure of as much as $6 million, which was impossible for the smaller companies to sustain.

In the end, it was decided to keep the GIE, but with all the modifications necessary to improve its operation, as identified by the studies carried out. The chairmanship of the group was transferred to Marco Colombo.

Epilogue

The idea of the cooperative had disappeared, but the problems it intended to solve remained under and often on the carpet throughout the 1990s. The two "parties" of the "small" versus "large" partners remained. Large partners were de facto contributing more resources and were asking for more representative and decision-making power. Small partners had difficulties in sustaining the expenses of a larger and larger common structure, and often even to live up to the standards implicit in the brand since the central structure was not equipped with any central staff able to provide services and know-how, or to control actual service standards.

In the 2000s, the announced "Diaspora" finally occurred. "Large" partners split away to follow their own individual trajectories: an IPO or a merger or acquisition by another large player in the industry. The "small" partners remained associated as a consortium, and merged with another association of consultancy firms of comparable size.

Notes

1 The P1 was invented in Denmark, and it came to Poland through a Swedish licensee with whom Mr ML made contact (see Box 3.2).
2 Also having custody over the other human resources.
3 http://estonia.eu/news/170-with-diversity-comes-innovation-interview-with-linnar-viik.html.
4 www.nytimes.com/1987/03/16/style/moonlighting-s-in-fashion-for-italy-s-top-designers.html?pagewanted = all.
5 Robin Givhan wrote of Versace in the *Washington Post* (1997).
6 From "An interview with Santo Versace", Anna Grandori (1986).
7 Dana, T. (2009) "Fashion disaster" *Newsweek*, November 16, 154(20): 52–56.
8 Anita Roddick (1991) *Body and Soul: Profits with Principles*. New York: Crown.
9 Mark Constantine (September 2007) Anita Roddick obituary.
10 Jon Entine (2002) "Body flop", *R.O.B. Report on Business Magazine*, www.jonentine.com/articles/bodyflop.htm.
11 "The end of Anita's heyday", *BBC News*, December 2, 2002.

12 Elaine Dewar (1995) *Cloak of Green: The Links between Key Environmental Groups, Government and Big Business*. Halifax, Canada: Lorimer.
13 Acquisition of TBS Inc. completed in 2001.
14 *Sunday Times*, 1996.
15 TBS Annual Report, 2001.
16 "Changes at The Body Shop", posted on February 12, 2002 by Anita (www.anitaroddick.com/readmore.php?sid = 32).
17 "Further thoughts on stepping down", posted on February 18, 2002 by Anita (www.anitaroddick.com/readmore.php?sid = 34).
18 http://ec.europa.eu/competition/mergers/cases/decisions/m4193_20060531_20310_en.pdf.
19 A getter is a reactive material used for removing traces of gas from vacuum systems, such as vacuum tubes.
20 Vacuum flask which provides thermal insulation (or Dewar flask, from its inventor, 1892).
21 Frankfurt, September 1983.
22 By the terms "exchanged business and billing", we mean the search carried out in another country by a local group member to whom the client had been referred.

5 Organizing entrepreneurship in established firms

5.1 Organizing for innovation in established firms: "corporate entrepreneurship", "corporate disaggregation" and other movements

The traditional domain of entrepreneurship is the initial identification of a potential opportunity followed by the acquisition of resources, and the set-up of a dedicated entity which serves as a vehicle for the exploitation of the opportunity, as examined in earlier chapters. Following the establishment of the venture, however, interest in entrepreneurship can tend to fade while interest in effective organization and management increases. The focus tends to move from the entrepreneurial problem to administrative and technical problems, and execution and implementation rather than innovation and entrepreneurship become the order of the day.

This process tends to go well beyond the necessary infusion of managerial competences. This bureaucratic "transformation" or "mutation" is unfortunate in modern contexts. In fact, organizational environments have become increasingly heterogeneous (more dimensions to be monitored and managed), dynamic (higher frequency and rate of change in different environmental sectors), hostile (more competitors for resources across the environments) and complex (increasing interactions among environmental factors leading to extreme unpredictability). Forces such as globalization, information technology, deregulation of many markets around the world, plus high rates of technological change have led to

---

* Text by Anna Grandori and James Hayton, cases by the authors indicated in boxes.

many organizations finding their traditional sources of advantages no longer sustainable. Organizations are therefore interested in continuing to identify and create new sources of value through new combinations of resources such as technology, knowledge, brands, human capital, production or marketing capabilities and so forth. In other words, established organizations may have to continuously address the entrepreneurial problem.

In light of this need to remain entrepreneurial, it is an unfortunate fact that as most organizations grow in size, develop routines and formalize operating procedures, create strong guiding cultures, and become embedded within networks of relationships with influential stakeholders, as all these developments tend to be sources of structural inertia. As they grow, established organizations thus often become less able to respond to changes, and particularly to radical transformations in their environments. Accordingly, many organizations can suffer from the "incumbent's curse" (Chandy and Tellis 2000) in which small firms and new market entrants are able to displace the established industry players (e.g. Christensen 1997). On the other hand, it is also apparent that some firms are able to overcome this incumbent's curse through the use of more flexible and dynamic organizational structures, frequent reliance on inter-organizational relationships and networks, the reduction of bureaucracy and enhancement of autonomy, i.e. though the creation of a supportive organizational context (e.g. McGrath and MacMillan 2000; Miller and Friesen 1983). In established organizations, the process of starting and organizing new ventures is always "complicated" by the embeddedness in an organized context. However, whether this helps or hinders the innovation process all depends on the nature of that context. If it is bureaucratic and predominantly efficiency oriented, it will mainly be a negative factor; if it is flexible and organized for innovation, it will be a positive factor, actually facilitating the establishment of new ventures with respect to starting an independent firm in a less friendly external environment.

Recognition of this challenge has led to an increased interest in how to maintain entrepreneurship in growing firms, or to infuse it in firms that were not born entrepreneurial but have always been something else; for example, classic firms based on financial and technical assets and coordinated by authority (as many large industrial firms are), or collective people-based firms, or public institutions, coordinated in communitarian and rule-based ways (as many large cooperatives or foundations such as universities are). Distinctive fields have developed in organization studies dedicated to this issue. The relations among them are not always recognized, and a contribution of this chapter is to integrate them, thereby reconstructing a wider set of useful organizational practices. These strands of studies include, first and foremost the *"corporate entrepreneurship"* field (Van de Ven and Engleman 2004; Block and MacMillan 1993; Burgelman and Sayles 1986; Kanter 1985; Morris 1998; Sathe 2003; Zahra *et al.* 2005); but also the *"corporate disaggregation"* perspective (Zenger and Hesterley 1997; Roberts 2004) and more specialized sub-fields as *"strategic human resources"* (Hayton 2005; Hayton and Kelley 2006) and *"new organization forms"* (Miles *et al.* 1997; Lewin and Volberda 1999; Pettigrew *et al.* 2000).

Before approaching the topic, it is worthwhile making a premise on the "corporate entrepreneurship" (CE) term. The term "corporate" has thus far been defined very loosely in corporate entrepreneurship studies, and for that matter also in corporate disaggregation studies. In particular, with the term "corporate" what is actually meant is not that the firm is, legally speaking, a corporation, but simply an established firm, typically organized along a traditional hierarchical model. Second, the term "entrepreneurship" in CE literature is not intended as a distinctive mode of organizing new businesses through dedicated entities, governed in a specific way (as specified here in earlier chapters) but as a generic capacity of starting new businesses and to innovate (something that can be done by managers as well). Third, although to a large extent it addresses organizational problems, CE literature has developed mostly in the strategy field, with limited efforts in connecting and integrating contributions in organization studies and organizational economics that, perhaps under different names, have addressed the same issues (this attitude having to a large extent been reciprocated in these fields).

Therefore, an approach to CE that is more precise and more integrated should be useful. This chapter contributes in developing this, building on the more organizationally and economically informed notion of entrepreneurship introduced in the early chapters of this book.

The approach is more precise because it does not equate CE with organizing for innovation in general, but it provides specific tools for organizing an established firm in an "entrepreneurial mode", that is, a mode based on establishing internal units that can be qualified as entrepreneurial project-based units, structured as internal entrepreneurial quasi-firms. The approach does not generically recommend that structures and systems are such to promote innovation, but specifies that organizational practices may be able to reproduce entrepreneurial governance "without the founding of new firms".

This definition is also more general since it integrates other relevant contributions that have been using different terms (e.g. "corporate disaggregation", "new organization forms") but analyzed the same problem. In addition, it is more general since if it is made clear that the problem is organizing an "established entity" (and not just a "corporation") in an entrepreneurial mode, we can see that the "entrepreneurial practices" recommended in this section are interesting not only for classic established industrial corporations, but also for any established entity wishing to become more innovative and entrepreneurial, including public companies and agencies imprisoned in bureaucratic red-tape functioning, or large-scale collective partnerships impaired by communitarian self-serving slack functioning, or entities plagued by both (as used to be the case for many universities).

Finally, the approach is also more practical as CE is defined by means of a set of "practices", that is, organizational actions and artifacts that can be clearly identified and also, if desired, applied. We shall examine what these practices are, both in the organization structure area and in the human resource system area, and what some of the crucial points in their proper design are.

5.2 Structural practices

As has been known since the early days of management and organization theory, "bureaucracy" is the main organizational enemy of innovation (Burns and Stalker 1961). The ingredients are also well known: high departmentalization, tall hierarchies, prevalent use of formal authority and procedures for coordination, weak performance incentives and heavy controls on behaviors.

Less uncontroversial are the remedies, that is, the organizational allies of innovation. For years, an almost exclusive emphasis has been put on what can be broadly called a "communitarian organization". The ingredients of this alternative to the bureaucratic model are identified in lateral open communication, decentralized decision making and flat hierarchies, team-based and community-based coordination, project-based organization, alignment of objectives through identification with the firm-community, and informal norms – from Burns and Stalker's "organic form" to the contemporary writings on the "new organization forms" for the management of innovation within large established firms (e.g. Whittington *et al.* 1999).

On the other side, as highlighted especially in contributions with economic background, another "alternative" to bureaucratic organization is possible in order to sustain innovation, and is different from the "communitarian" model. This is an organization driven by strong, "profit-like" incentives on results, individual or small group responsibilities, organizational units based on actual clusters of competences rather than on homogeneous pre-defined abstract criteria (e.g. specialization by function or product or geographic area). While the internal organization of the single units may well be team-like, the relations among units are thought of as simulating "market" relations (Zenger and Hesterley 1997). The communitarian and incentive-driven "alternatives" are often seen as mutually exclusive and the choice among them as puzzling – that is, both seem to work, but when? Are they equivalent or linked to different conditions (Roberts 2004; Foss 2007)?

This chapter contributes in solving the puzzle according to the following reasoning. These analyses have been produced by thinking of the "organization of innovation" within firms in general. This is an enormous problem and field. The problem and field considered here is only one part of it: the organization of innovation within firms in an entrepreneurial mode. If entrepreneurial governance is a distinct form of organizing, as argued in Chapter 3, and if it is conducive to innovation, then the internal organization of established or large firms can become more innovative by adopting entrepreneurial practices. This is how "corporate entrepreneurship" is defined in this book, and distinguished from a generic promotion of innovation in established firms. Posing the problem in terms of entrepreneurial organization "without new firms" (i.e. within non-entrepreneurial firms) contributes to observing that the two traditional structural alternatives of "communitarian" and "market-like" organization of innovation are in fact not mutually exclusive, and are not even the only alternatives. In fact, the "entrepreneurial way of organizing", as discussed, not only blends elements belonging to both models but also employs further and other elements; in particular, it blends "teamwork" and management by communities with "strong incentives", as well as elements of formal organizational democracy.

The core theme of this section, stated more precisely, is thus: how to sustain innovation by infusing entrepreneurial organizational practices within firms and entities that, as a whole, cannot be qualified as entrepreneurial? The reasons why established firms may be interested in such reforms are numerous: firms that were born capitalistic, or collective, or public now often wish to infuse stronger incentives and stronger capabilities for innovation; or born entrepreneurial firms that do not wish to lose this character, in spite of growth and the exit or dilution of the role of the founders as owners and directors.

Entrepreneurial organization without new firms: experiences analyzed

The discussion of the fundamental features of entrepreneurship as a governance and organization mode, discussed especially in Chapter 3, should help in reconstructing the core structural features of "corporate entrepreneurship" (CE). The current section proposes some celebrated cases and instances of organizations sustaining innovation through entrepreneurial practices (albeit not always celebrated under the CE label) and can therefore be used in identifying them. Those experiences and practices can be grouped in two classes, according to the main organizational function they perform: practices oriented to promote autonomy, experimentation and variety; and practices oriented to promote integration, knowledge sharing and complementarity of actions.

Promoting autonomy, experimentation and variety

Project organization. Oticon is one of the most famous and debated cases. In 1991, a radical reorganization, or rather de-organization, reform was implemented (Ravasi and Verona, 2001: 46, italics added):

> The *formal structures* regulating the task system were completely *dismantled.* Departments, positions, titles, and job descriptions were all abolished and a radical *project based organization* was introduced. ... *a multi-job system* replaced traditional job assignments – everyone being responsible for the development of a portfolio of jobs, corresponding to the activities performed in the different projects, according to their own inclinations, skills and personal aspirations.

Most headquarter activities were transferred to project teams, even though some financial and accounting activities were later reorganized as separate service units, given their repetitiveness and distance from the project members' interests.

Informal autonomous working groups. Projects do not come out of the blue. They flourish out of a web of *knowledge exchanges and more informal teamwork.* These mechanisms are deliberately established in innovative organizations. There is more than just teamwork in CE teamwork. Teams should be highly autonomous working groups whose primary objective is radical: breakthrough innovation explicitly intended to lead to the creation of new opportunities. This autonomy should allow organizational participants the freedom to explore and experiment with ideas without suffering the constraints that arise naturally from within the established structure, strategy, or customer expectations of the established venture. An interesting type of teamwork for CE is called "*skunk works*", after the Lockheed-Martin experience. In fact, the term was first used during World War II, when a "secret" team was working on the development of the P-80 Shooting Star. According to Ben Rich's memoir,[1] a member of the team, an engineer named Culver, was a fan of Al Capp's newspaper comic strip, "Li'l Abner", in which there was a running joke about a mysterious place deep in the forest called the "Skonk Works". There, a strong beverage was brewed from skunks, old shoes and other strange ingredients. One day, Culver's phone rang and he answered it by saying "Skonk Works, inside man Culver speaking." Fellow employees quickly adopted the name for their unconventional secret projects within the firm. "Skonk Works" became "Skunk Works", and the once informal nickname became a registered trademark of the company: Skunk Works®. Skunk Works is responsible for a number of famous aircraft designs, including the U-2 (spy-plane), the SR-71, the F-117 and the F-22.

Relations are informal in these experiences, both within the group and with customers, with whom the group is entitled to interact and even to contract. "Inside Skunk Works we were a small cohesive group … our forte was building a small number of very technologically advanced airplanes for highly secret missions," said ex-CEO Birch. Access by outsiders to the project and its personnel is still strictly controlled by appropriate security measures. "Only a few people will be used in engineering and most other areas" and indeed the number of people having any connection with the project "must be restricted in an almost vicious manner". "Customers like the CIA or the US Air Force would come to Skunk Works with a request and on a handshake the project would begin, no contracts in place, no official submittal process." This of course implied a high level of mutual trust between the military project organization and the contractor with very close cooperation and liaison on a day-to-day basis. This cut down misunderstanding and correspondence to an absolute minimum. A very simple drawing and release system with great flexibility for making changes must be provided.

The war ended, even the Cold War, but the features of Skunk Works, formed in conditions where secrecy and freedom were both necessary were maintained as a method of freeing research groups as far as possible from bureaucratic interlopers or the imperious will of overbearing organizational generals.

Individual autonomy and incentives. Individual-level autonomy provides the flexibility and freedom to pursue novel or interesting ideas, often for their own sake. Such individual experimentation and exploration is often the first step in the sequence leading from innovation to the establishment of new ventures. It is in recognition of the need for individual creative sparks that companies such as 3M, Hewlett-Packard and Google provide extensive "*free time*" as part of the working week, in which employees are encouraged to explore and develop their own innovative ideas.

It was in the 1950s when 3M first institutionalized the "15 percent rule" – technical people spend up to 15 percent of their time on projects of their own choosing or initiative in order to drive innovation. From this, masking tape and Post-It notes were born, both of which were the conceptual and developmental results of the labor of engineers who were engaged in innovation work without the benefit of formal budgets, planning or even management support.

The percentage was later raised to 20 for individual researchers, and also instituted for divisions as a "25 percent rule" – each division should produce 25 percent of annual sales from new products and services introduced in the previous five years (which later increased to 30 percent). Prizes, such as the "Golden Step" award, were given to those creating successful new business ventures originated within 3M.

This "Innovation Time Off" (ITO) practice – as it is called at Google, where it is also used – has an important intrinsic motivation function. It keeps employees challenged and engaged in ways that aid retention and keep staff learning and growing. Google is obsessed with talent. Its greatest assets walk out of the door every night, and the company desperately hopes that they will return the next morning! ITO ensures that at any time, every person is engaged in at least one project of his/her interest, which is effective in retaining the best talent in the organization.

"Bootleg" research projects have similar purposes (Burgleman and Sayles 1986). In these projects, researchers are informally allowed time, and sometimes limited resources, to pursue avenues that might be of future interest. In contrast to formal programs, bootleg research is condoned, but not formally sanctioned. It allows for higher risk exploratory research, which extends beyond an organization's existing knowledge base. Bootlegging in this way provides the opportunity for the creation of technological options, in the sense that if the exploration is a success, then the more formal pursuit of the technology can follow. On the other hand, if the experiments are unsuccessful, financial and career losses are kept to a minimum.

Championing. Ideas do not walk through an organization alone. They need someone championing and sponsoring them. A critical role for corporate entrepreneurship is that of *"idea champions"*. Champions identify with the project, and not only do they take responsibility for its success, but success is often dependent on champions (Burgelman 1983). Champions "inspire and enthuse others with their vision of the potential of an innovation ... show extraordinary confidence in themselves and their mission, and ... gain the commitment of others to support the innovation" (Howell and Higgins 1990: 320). Championing includes providing the underlying creative insight on an innovation's potential – effectively planting the seeds of an idea for which brokers seek and supply relevant knowledge and innovators work to discover solutions (Day 1994). On the other hand, there is often a distinction between the inventors or discoverers of opportunities, and those who recognize their value and take responsibility for moving it forward (Leifer *et al.* 2000). Champions represent a "catalyst for increased sponsorship or impetus" behind an innovation (Maidique 1980: 32). They create a vision around an opportunity and ensure continuance of the project, seeing it through to commercialization. Champions are frequently found among mid-level managers who have access to higher levels of the organization as well as direct links to the technical innovators who are more focused on technological specialties.

The specific behaviors needed for successful championing may be culturally bound (e.g. Shane 1995). Therefore, prescriptions of how champions should behave should also be context-specific. In the United States, there is a preference for organizational mavericks, renegades, and buffers who bypass organizational procedures in order to garner support. Particularly when innovation projects are high risk and costly, champions will use their power to get their projects supported. This is in contrast to collectivist cultures, where champions who appeal to group norms are preferred. When uncertainty avoidance dominates national cultures, adherence to organizational rules and procedures and a rational style are preferred. In all cases, regardless of the behaviors employed, the objective is the same: the champion attempts to ensure that there is support for the project. And in all contexts, competence in championing also requires an ability to negotiate a complex sociopolitical environment.

Sponsoring. In subsequent stages, ideas need *sponsors*. Sponsors help entrepreneurs gain access to the resources they need for their ventures. They ensure there is legitimacy and support for the project. They provide advice and guidance to the venture on how to best proceed. Higher-level sponsors use their power and control over resources to get the support necessary for the projects they value.

Sponsors differ from champions. Sponsors typically serve as a bridge linking the technical innovator and the firm's owner/founders. While a champion identifies and selects projects deserving support, a sponsor ensures that resources become available. The executive sponsor is the individual who has "direct or indirect influence over the resource allocation process and who uses this power to channel resources to a new technological innovation" (Maidique 1980: 64). The separation of the sponsoring and championing roles becomes increasingly likely as organizations grow and diversify. Sponsors are typically higher up in the organizational hierarchy, are likely to have access to a greater range of information about strategies, markets, competitors and opportunities, and can better locate specific resources. This is particularly important for ventures that are costly and represent new strategic directions.

Mentoring and coaching. Even in the absence of an authority regime, and actually, particularly in its absence, groups and teamwork need some coordination, and individuals may need help and support to learn and develop or be confronted with expert judgment. Useful roles, alternative to classic authority, are *mentor* roles: individuals who nurture and develop junior colleagues and so help an organization prepare its next generation of competencies. At Oticon, "mentors" were formally appointed, although not bound to follow a precise role model. They were assigned the responsibility for the growth of younger professionals, including contributing substantial input for performance evaluation and therefore career progress of the mentored. On their side, the mentored had a chance to choose/ change their mentors in a negotiated way.

A milder mechanism and role is that of *coaching*, an "evaluation-free" role focused on helping the person to assess him/herself and to find his/her own development path and strategies within an organized context, as appropriate to personal preferences and the characteristics of the specific context.

Specialist and expert roles. In addition to project leaders for group formation and coordination, and mentors for competence development, *specialist and expert roles* are also important. Innovating frequently demands a high degree of specialized knowledge, the specific nature of which depends on the particular business and industry. Individuals with higher levels of cognitive ability, education, training, and practical experience command more resources that are useful in problem identification, formulation, exploration and problem solving. The creativity needed to support innovation also demands broad skills and knowledge in a given technical area, as well as a high degree of intrinsic motivation. These tend to be coupled with individual skillfulness with respect to creativity-relevant processes such as goal setting and response to challenges. Some firms then institutionalize these expert roles in figures such as "technical innovators" or "technical coordinators" (e.g. 3M) or "professional managers" (e.g. Oticon). They are entrepreneurially responsible for developing professional areas and communities of knowledge (Cohendet *et al.* 2001) rather than projects. For example, at Oticon these professional areas were called "competence centers" and few of them corresponded to the old functional departments; they included audiology, integrated circuits, quality assurance, mechanical engineering and marketing. Their influence in the system was sustained by a responsibility in selecting, hiring and training new experts in their fields (Ravasi and Verona 2000).

Promoting integration, knowledge sharing and complementarity

A particular problem in entrepreneurship within established firms is that autonomy should be balanced with *integration*. Otherwise, there would be no advantage in belonging to the same organization. This means that Skunk Works, projects or other independent venturing units, should be interested in and able to maintain some connections among each other and with the parent organization. For example, when *Time* magazine was trying to develop a radically new product line tailored to the needs of the emerging cable television industry in the 1980s, a fiercely independent development group failed to take advantage of the resources available. Despite the fact that the parent corporation owning Home Box Office (HBO) had relevant expertise available, the new venture failed to take advantage of this resource due to an excessive drift toward independence and autonomy by the new venture group and the project never took off, producing only losses (Burgelman and Sayles 1986).

Knowledge exchange systems. Important mechanisms of integration, in an entrepreneurial and project formation perspective, cannot be only informal open communication and spontaneous knowledge exchanges. Elaborated and structured communication and knowledge-sharing mechanisms are often established – such as *"knowledge exchange systems", data banks, catalogs and maps of competences.* These practices and artifacts are intended to embody a large part of knowledge and know-how and to support its transfer from people and projects to common organizational knowledge. They are widely applied in knowledge-intensive firms, from consultancy to chemical firms (Davenport and Prusak 1998). A recurring problem in these systems, however, is that of incentives to contribute knowledge. This should not be seen as mere "resistance" as it involves a legitimate question about who owns the knowledge produced in a large company. Second, the information on who knows what, stored in the large databases of a large organization, is often too vast to be efficiently managed by employees and managers who typically work under time pressure. Hence, these information stocks and channels may present problems of underuse, unless they are accompanied by *brokerage* and *incentives* (see next points).

Brokerage. This is as important for internal entrepreneurship as it is for entrepreneurship in general (Chapter 1). Within established firms, broker roles can be and are explicitly recognized and formalized. The most important broker role, in an entrepreneurial perspective, is that of the "*knowledge broker*". For example, at Texas Instruments, "knowledge broker" roles have been formalized, with 50 per cent of their time devoted to mapping knowledge and facilitating encounters with high-utility potential, also on the basis of catalogs of best practices. The primary role of the broker is to access new sources of information and knowledge, transfer this knowledge and combine different sources, both existing and new. New opportunities often arise from this process of linking diverse perspectives and even contradictory ideas. Therefore, there is a close relationship between the role of the broker and the technical innovator: the broker role delivers new information to and from the technical innovator and to and from the broker's network. In fact, the broker and innovator may even be the same person.

Breakthrough ideas can arise from basic research exploring new science and technology. They can emerge from previous technology development and implementation efforts. They can also result from combinations of previously unrelated technologies. Innovation and new venture development requires the knowledge broker to access and combine diverse sources of knowledge, both existing and new, often with a high degree of unfamiliarity. Even though an organization may hire and develop people with diverse skills and the ability to innovate, it is unlikely an individual will possess all the knowledge needed for the complexities of this process. Transforming an idea into a viable business requires several skills that go beyond the expertise of one person. It is therefore essential to exchange knowledge and information among multiple contributors, who collectively provide a range of experiences and broad knowledge. In project-based work, teams typically reach outside the project and engage in a mix of communications with various individuals and groups within and outside the organization. This is particularly important for projects demanding a greater breadth of knowledge and involving highly complex tasks. Brokers identify the organizational members with the knowledge required and gain timely access to that knowledge.

Brokering can extend beyond organizational boundaries and have a "gate-keeping" and "structural holes bridging" role (Chapter 1). It involves bringing outside information in or integrating information from various internal sources.

"External" brokers acquire, translate and disseminate information. They keep abreast of external technical market demands, and link this information to those within the organization. Mechanisms and roles of this type include cross-boundary teams, scouting for problems and ideas with customers, or even expert personnel working full time for periods within client organizations.

Internal brokers act as facilitators for matching the relevant competences into new projects, or to coordinate the efforts of the project team and other units they may depend on. Since these communication networks are formed and cultivated over time, organizations should look to individuals who have chosen a brokering strategy within the organization (rather than, say, a specialist strategy), that is, people exploring diverse knowledge domains and linking knowledge from diverse domains to solve novel problems (Hargadon 1998; Hargadon and Sutton 2000).

Incentives to knowledge sharing. It is unlikely that knowledge is exchanged and shared without appropriate incentives and guarantees against plain expropriation. The issue is relevant at the individual level within an organization, and not only between an entrepreneurial firm with respect to other firms (Grandori 2001c). The case of 3M provides examples of the application within a firm of a particularly wide range of these incentive practices. An *internal patenting system* grants *property rights and royalties to internal inventors* and infuses transparency in the evaluation of "ideas" submitted, applicants for patent protection and exploitation. Systems such as internal "grants" that can be assigned to individual projects and ideas judged worthy by a scientific committee and independent from organizational units also help in financing "orphan projects" that no regular division or unit is willing to sponsor. Programs such as "Pathfinder" assign prizes to units that are able to use and recombine the patents and inventions of other units and divisions and succeed in launching business lines yielding more than a certain amount of revenue on this basis. "Pacing Paths" are programs for accelerating the innovation cycle (to bring the time to market of innovations to under three years) by guaranteeing a preferential high-speed development and production route to a selected group of product ideas (each business unit being entitled to propose one or two). Finally, the "Own business program" grants property rights to those who have provided the relevant knowledge on the business lines emerging from their human capital investments (Turati 1998). The philosophy behind all these mechanisms was, explicitly, to stimulate internal entrepreneurship by promoting "a small company within a big company feel" – by creating small autonomous business units and product divisions based on employees' new ideas and by providing the freedom, the means and the rewards necessary to share new ideas, cross-fertilize technology, stimulate innovation via customer problems, speed up product development and market introduction cycles. This is a view expressed with the following phrase by 3M leader McLellan: "We start from the assumption that it is not the firm that innovates, but people. The only thing a firm can do is to create and maintain an atmosphere in which people are willing to take risks and innovate."

Property rights. The "small companies within a bigger company" can be more than a "feeling". *Property right diffusion practices* can establish true firms or "islands" of entrepreneurial property within a larger firm. These practices are at the core of notions such as the "cellular organization" (Miles *et al.* 1997) and the "disaggregation of corporations" (Zenger and Hesterley 1997). Miles and colleagues have been clearer than others in pointing out that "networked" organization (all the horizontal communication, brokerage and project-based practices) is just not enough to promote innovation in knowledge-intensive settings. As per the authors' words, the *"cellular form"* goes beyond the "networkization" of organization and is further characterized by *"entrepreneurial responsibility"* (decision rights and residual rewards), *"self-organization"* (freedom of resource recombination) and *"member ownership"* (of inputs/assets, or outputs or both). These "property right diffusing practices" are core to an economically informed definition of entrepreneurship, such as that adopted in this book. The organization of firms such as Acer and TCG has been described as a "fully cellular form" since it presents all three features.

- *TCG* (Technical and Computer Graphics), develops IT products and services such as portable data terminals, computer graphic systems and electronic data interchange systems, and is formed by 13 entrepreneurial small firms. Some specialize in one or more product categories, some in hardware or software technologies. The overall structure functions on the basis of a formalized procedure for joint venture formation on projects. The procedure requires that the joint venture be formed by at least three partners: (1) one or more TCG firms, providing human and financial capital; (2) an external partner as expert in the technology and also providing equity; and (3) a principal customer providing large advance order contracts.
- *Acer* is also "a federation of self-managing firms held together by mutual interest rather than hierarchical control" (Miles *et al.* 1997: 14). This mutual interest can be seen as stemming from the complementarity of firms' assets (Rajan and Zingales 2000; Chapter 3, this volume) generated in this case by a client–server relation (while in the TCG case, complementarities were lying mostly among assets of different kinds co-applied to generate a new output). Some firms in the federation perform mainly marketing and post-sale service activities in certain regions; while others perform research, production and distributionactivities, and are "suppliers" of the former. Projects can originate anywhere in the federation and can involve external partners. "For example Acer America (a sales and marketing firm) wanted a stylish yet affordable PC for the North American market. It contracted with Frog, an outside industrial design firm. Manufacturing was undertaken by another Acer production firm, and the marketing campaign was jointly developed by Acer America and Acer International, another commercial regional unit based in Singapore" (Miles *et al.* 1997: 15). These alliances can take any appropriate contractual form, and can include internal and/or external partners. The Acer companies within the federation are jointly owned by their own management, a home-country investor, and the parent firm Acer Inc. (often in a minority position), and are free to stay or leave the group and to get listed on their local stock exchanges to raise capital for their own expansion.

The "simulation" of the processes and structures of entrepreneurial firm formation within a larger firm has gone so far to experiment the internal application of arrangements originally developed as inter-firm network forms; not only *internal joint ventures* – as described in the cases above – but also *internal corporate ventures* (simulating venture capital relations; cf. Chapter 2) and *corporate incubators* (simulating the multi-partner external incubators; cf. Chapter 6) – as described in the cases below.

Lucent New Ventures (LNV) was formed in 1997 to spin-out internal non-core technologies developed in its Bell Labs, and, later, to spin-in technologies complementing its own product line, LNV achieved extraordinary financial and strategic success.

Motorola Ventures was set up in 1998 with four core offices (Boston, San Francisco, Tel Aviv and Latin America) to invest in technologies that would strategically support its existing and emerging platforms and products. Siemens Technology Accelerator commercializes non-core technologies from Siemens' patent portfolio. The incubator is located at the central headquarters in Munich. It identifies unused patents and transfers their associated intellectual property rights to the newly founded start-up to prepare its later spin-off.

Ventures Organization grants managers the mobility to encourage a flow of information within the corporation. Employees from the business units can move into the incubator for a limited time to support their idea's realization before they return to their respective business units.

Nokia focuses on a close link between the technology venture and its business lines, as is reflected in the preferred exists of spin-ins to existing business units, or the forming of new Nokia business units. Cisco New Ventures defined resource flows to their technology ventures. For example, in one of their start-ups, Ardent Communication Ventures, the business idea for a traffic aggregation device for data and voice originally came from a Cisco employee who had already made plans to leave the corporation to start his own venture. Cisco first supported the start-up through investment and other resource flows before its later spin-in. A positive impact of the close connection with the parent was that Ardent Communication Ventures could define product specifications in line with Cisco's requirements. This enhanced the internal use of the device as well as leveraging Cisco's customers.

In sum all these experiences are based on the actual set-up of *new firms within (and around) the mother firm.* These organizational models can therefore be considered to realize "corporate entrepreneurship" in its fullest meaning – the establishment of entrepreneurial firms or quasi-firms "under the shadow of hierarchy".

Organizational democracy. Finally, the Semco model is worth mentioning here. Semco is another template case in fostering internal entrepreneurship, but the model is particular and highlights some additional practices with respect to those considered so far. In fact, Semco combines the "destructuring", "self-organizing" and "non-hierarchical" practices already highlighted in cases such as Oticon, 3M and Google, with micro-participation in the governance of the firm through formal *organizational democracy practices.* Semco was born as a traditional entrepreneurial firm: a single person owning and managing activities in the technical but not high-tech sector of industrial equipment manufacturing. The now famous son of the founding entrepreneur – Ricardo Semler – brought the firm to spectacular growth using an organizational model leveraging especially on *empowering practices* involving and promoting micro-entrepreneurial behaviors in all employees (Semler 2003): people were hired by the company and invited to find/negotiate a well-sculpted job for their competences and motivations; asking "why", critical mindset and dissent were strongly encouraged, actually required in the analysis of any new activity proposal. Work time controls were abolished, flexibility in where and when to work and job sharing were encouraged, and work groups and units were kept small so that people could monitor each other. Lamenting the weakness of trade unions with which to establish a negotiated industrial relation system, Semler implemented a representative governance system: employees in every group or location elected a trustee (117 in total); taking turns in a monthly 12-member board of trustees meeting and having two voting representatives in the board of directors. A radically open and transparent information and communication code was observed (including all administrative and financial information and documentation) not only to foster "knowledge sharing" and new project development, but also with the declared intention of preventing the accumulation of power based on privileged information.

"Our visitors want to understand how Semco has increased its annual revenue between 1994 and 2003 from 35 to 212 million dollars when I – the company's largest shareholder – rarely attend meetings and almost never make decisions" (2003: 7–8) and most "manuals, procedures and policies were abolished". Semler explains, and responds: "Instead of dictating Semco's identity, I let our employees shape it with their individual efforts, interests, and initiatives" (Semler 2003: 7–8), so that people are allowed to act as entrepreneurs.

An additional interesting and indeed particular trait of the Semco experience is that growth has been the result but is not used as an objective in decision making. Actually, when projects or action proposals in the end found no further justification than for the sake of growth, they were not undertaken. Semler stresses how none of the conventional "objectives" of the firm – growth, profit, even quality – are good guides for business innovative behavior. Anticipating a "stakeholder" approach, Semco refused to adopt any substantively predefined objectives for the firm, but adopted a *procedure for firm action improvement based on consultation* with stockholders, employees, customers, suppliers and the community in order to evaluate "success" from multiple points of view (Semler 2003: 98).

Entrepreneurial organization without new firms: a best practices profile

The experiences reported allow identifying a full range of "entrepreneurial" structural practices that are important for the achievement of high innovation performance in firms that are growing, or have become established and large. These practices are summarized in Table 5.1.

Table 5.1 Organizational practices for corporate entrepreneurship

---

Deregulation
- No predefined departmentalization
- Reduced predefined procedures and programs linking organizational units

Projectification
- Free definition of projects, project staffing and project organization within units
- Formal meritocratic transparent procedures for project selection and evaluation

Decentralization
- Reduced hierarchy to ideally two levels: a center and a constellation of units/projects
- Decision rights co-located with knowledge

Disaggregation
- Project-based, self-contained units operate autonomously; they are accountable for and entitled to results
- Incentives for innovation performance at both individual and unit/project level, linked to balanced performance indicators at individual, unit/project and firm level

Integration
- Open communication and linkages supported by knowledge sharing systems
- Formal and informal teamwork in all phases of project development
- Acknowledged communities of specialized practices, expertise and knowledge
- Formal integration roles: "knowledge brokers", "mentors" and "coaches", "project champions and sponsors", "project leaders"

Marketization
- The center functions as an internal competent financial investor of the capital venture type
- Internal patenting and knowledge markets
- Freedom of external alliances

Democratization
- Recognition of the people's human capital investments with property rights over outputs
- Representation of all investors (including human capital investors) on boards
- "Empowerment", competence-based self-designed jobs, and employee ownership provisions – if diffused, micro-entrepreneurship is sought

---

Let us now examine a couple of examples through these lenses. These are somewhat subtle cases in which the organization is innovation oriented and does actually introduce some of the CE "good practices" but apparently the experiment "does not work".

- The Oticon experience in internal deregulation and destructuring generated a lively but rather inefficient ensemble, deserving the nickname of a "spaghetti organization" (Foss 2003). Eventually a counter-wave of re-centralization occurred. These oscillations often occur in practice, according to the simplistic logic that if some action did not work it must have been wrong. However, the result is often to throw the baby away with the bath water

(Pongracic 2009). In fact, the destructuring and projectification reform does not appear to have been wrong, per se. The problem, according to the framework proposed here, is that it was not accompanied by some essential complementary mechanisms, in particular by a powerful incentives system, able to avoid the derailing of the system into mere anarchy. As Lindkvist (2004) observed, "projectification" is not only about infusing team-like communitarian elements, but also about infusing market-like competitive elements into firm organization.

• The currently popular reforms of universities (and of public administration) in the sense of tightening performance evaluation and pay for performance are intended to foster innovative productivity and to remedy the free riding of uncontrolled employees, and/or the rather self-serving "democratic" governance of restricted clans of "barons". It was conceived and implemented mostly by infusing powerful incentives and evaluations based on results (often accompanied by a centralization of decision making). Among the problems surfacing, along with some gains in productivity and innovation, were a loss of professional identification and intrinsic motivation, higher labor costs and the pursuit of rewards rather than relevant issues (which is particularly undesirable in professional fields, such as scientific research, health care, law, etc.). Again, it does not appear to have been wrong to provide incentives per se; however, the downsides were easy to predict using a sufficiently comprehensive framework such as that presented here. The problem resides in the unbalance: an exclusive or prevalent emphasis on incentives (usually monetary) on results (irrespective of how much they are measurable and subject to external uncertainty). Some essential complementary mechanisms were lost (or dismantled) along the way, such as: the participation of knowledgable employees in the definition of desired results, and their discretion over how to realize them; the control of the controllers; the availability of people for citizenship behavior and to help the community of colleagues, or even the clients/users – actually the availability to do anything unless the required behavior was explicitly rewarded. Hence, these reforms brought about a "marketization" but not an "entre-preneurialization" of the former bureaucratic systems.

The general point therefore is that the reforms described in both cases are too "one-sided". They apply only some of the "good practices" and only of one type – that is, all "communitarian" or all "market-like". These examples thus support the conclusion (also supported in wider quantitative analyses; e.g. Whittington *et al.* 1999; Grandori and Furnari 2008) that the *adoption of a wide range of complementary practices belonging to different categories does make innovation more likely*, while *the use of practices of just one type does not*. In particular, "projectifying", "disaggregating" and "deregulating" practices should be combined with "incentivizing" practices, and with both "integrating" and "communitarian" practices.

In conclusion, the overview of structural practices offered in Table 5.1 can also be used to detect the deficits of some kinds of practices in any specific setting and to improve the organization by the infusion of missing practices. The emerging fully fledged "model" of entrepreneurial organization within established and large firms uses all kinds of practices and is therefore rather mixed and combinative. It is not coincident to any classic organization model – for example, the functional, divisional matrix or even networked and organic form – and is not informed by a single principle or logic, not even by "decentralization", "informality" or "autonomy". It is both informal *and* formal, disaggregated *and* integrated, communitarian *and* competitive. This way of organizing has been called "*bi-modal*", and considered the main organizational "secret of the trade", in one of the few studies on the internal organization of Silicon Valley firms (Baharami 1996).

5.3 Human resources and industrial relations practices

Many of the organizational practices examined in the preceding section actually embody systems for governing relations with human resource providers, in all the key areas of human capital development and mobility, evaluation and reward. These themes are the specialized subject of the human resources field (HR) and the industrial relations field (IR). Let us therefore add some further organizing tools that can be drawn from those fields. This section should thus be read as an incremental addition to what has already been said about HR practices for entrepreneurship in the former section. In addition, it should also be read as an incremental addition to what has been said on HR systems for new entrepreneurial firms in Chapter 3. In fact, the profile of HR practices promoting innovation in new firms remains valid for the organization of entrepreneurship in established and large firms. The main point in CE is in fact to infuse similar practices in established organizations to keep or make them entrepreneurial. The specific main problems (in fact much stressed in CE literature) are the difficulties in doing so. Let us therefore summarize the indications that emerged in Chapter 3 into a "best practice profile" (Table 5.2) also applicable to established firms, and complementary to the organizational profile summarized in Table 5.1; and thereafter turn to the particularities and difficulties of using them in established firms, especially when large.

Hence, in human resource practices, as in structural practices, the basic principle is that practices that differ in kind are complementary in sustaining innovation, in particular those infusing powerful individual incentives co-applied with practices infusing team spirit and organizational identification (Laursen and Mahnke 2001). Introducing these practices in established firms, especially large firms, entails specific problems and difficulties that stem from at least the following three important differences between entrepreneurship in established and new firms:

Table 5.2 Best human resources practices for entrepreneurial organizations

- Co-investments in human capital by the firm and the individual, divided according to the specificity of competences of the firm (firms invest in specific components, people invest in transferable components).
- Investments in "specialized" knowledge should not be task-specific (since tasks are too variable and undefined) but specific to industries and professions (which tend to be the effective and real "boundaries" of "boundaryless careers").
- High internal labor market mobility, not only through people moving across positions through an open job market but also through "jobs moving and evolving with people" as they work on shifting job portfolios.
- Moderate speed/rate of mobility across boundaries, striking a balance between the need to allow specific competences and learning from experience to occur, and the need to renew the competence set.
- Moderate intermediate incidence of performance pay, striking a balance between high discretion (demanding higher contingent pay) and outcome uncertainty (decreasing the optimal level of result-based incentives).
- Combination of autonomous work and teamwork, and of individual and team incentives.
- Balanced performance evaluation systems, including a wide range of result and behavior parameters, over a sufficiently wide sample of records.
- "Flexible cultures", focused on high-level missions and critical mindsets, and including change and diversity values.

- In established firms, entrepreneurial organization may regard only parts and "islands" within a larger structure that also includes "managerial" parts and roles, and this may generate conflict and specific negotiation problems.
- In established firms, internal entrepreneurs bear more "career risk" than financial risk; and if career systems are not properly conceived and designed, distorted entrepreneurial behaviors (e.g. escalation of commitment and other biased investment patterns) may follow.
- In established organizations with a large number of employees, wider industrial relations issues can arise, in particular whether they should all be involved in widespread micro-entrepreneurship in the same way; and, if not, how to eventually govern different forms of employment in and around the same organization.

The following three paragraphs are dedicated to each of these problems respectively, and to their possible solutions.

Intra-organizational negotiated entrepreneurship

All entrepreneurs have to negotiate, but intra-organizational negotiations are somewhat different and somewhat more exhausting than negotiations among independent agents, and may make life difficult for internal entrepreneurs. A core underlying source of this greater exertion is that exiting from the relation, and the substitution of partners, is blocked or much more difficult. These problems cannot be eliminated, but they can be reduced. If one could substitute counterparties at will, one would be in a market and not in a firm. However, many entrepreneurially oriented firms do allow considerable freedom in finding *external partners* if negotiations with internal partners fail. This should not be seen as a loss of control, but as a necessary mechanism to prevent too many projects from dying before they are born.

Other solutions are based on the idea of creating *internal "free zones"* – "units" or "programs" for "free experimentation" – that are somewhat insulated from the wider structure. These "differentiation" and "ambidexterity" practices have a long history in the organization of R&D activities (Galbraith 1982; O'Reilly and Tushman 2004). As the Xerox PARC case illustrates (Box 5.1), they can, however, make integration all the more difficult.

Burgelman and Sayles (1986) described how a new idea is likely to have to pass through a series of "Caudine Forks" in its various development stages.

In the early *conceptualization* stage, the unit generating the idea must convince the other units and headquarters that it is worthwhile. For example, if the innovation is technology-pushed, the entrepreneur would typically be a technology-oriented specialist such as an R&D manager who identifies one or more technical inventions or innovations that may be combined in some way to produce a new product or process that *may* have market potential. In the case of market pull, the initial definition of a need, often from existing customers, leads to communications between customers facing employees such as marketing managers and managers in the R&D function to determine whether there are possible technologies that can contribute to satisfying this potential market opportunity. Convincing the internal counterparties or simply finding solutions on the basis of internal resources may be difficult.

At a later stage, the negotiation is typically between an enthusiastic group of entrepreneurs–promoters and business and accounting-oriented managers. The former are motivated by the challenge of problem solving and the generation of new knowledge. They often speak the specialized language of the scientific method. They are seeking "right" or "best" answers, and will resist pressure to find "good enough" answers. Meanwhile, professional managers are concerned with the challenges of obtaining and retaining customers, meeting their needs as quickly as possible, perhaps preventing competitors from stealing market share. The time orientation of the average manager is rather immediate. Problems need to be solved quickly, and "good enough" answers are more valued today than "right" answers next month. In addition, not only are managers unlikely to speak the professional language of the scientists, but they also have their own codes and jargon which mean little to the uninitiated. These significant differences between the groups create a substantial barrier to communication, sometimes creating a source of conflict and often becoming a significant potential stumbling block, as illustrated in Box 5.1.

Box 5.1 Xerox Palo Alto Research Center (PARC)
Laura Gaillard, 2010

Xerox Palo Alto Research Center (PARC) was founded in 1970 as a part of Xerox Research, and incorporated in 2002 as a wholly owned but independent research business. It not only conducts Xerox research but also partners with other companies to undertake independent research projects. PARC is located in the heart of the Silicon Valley, the intersection of major universities, research centers, global high-tech enterprises, start-ups and venture capital firms. PARC was responsible for such well-known and important developments as laser printing, the Ethernet, the modern personal computer graphical user interface (GUI), ubiquitous computing and advancing very-large-scale-integration (VLSI). Incorporated as a wholly owned subsidiary of Xerox in 2002, PARC currently conducts research into biomedical technologies, "clean technology", computing science, electronic materials and devices, hardware systems and intelligent systems.

John Warnock, a former researcher in Xerox PARC and later one of the two founders of Adobe Systems, remembers: "The atmosphere was electric – there was total intellectual freedom. There was no conventional wisdom; almost every idea was up for challenge and got challenged regularly." Larry Tessler, who later took part in developing the Macintosh and the Newton PDA at Apple, also enjoyed the liberties the PARC provided in the 1970s: "The management said go, create the new world. ... The problem, however, was that the company management on the East Coast of the USA did not care a straw for PARC's research results unless they were directly involved with photocopiers."

Steve Jobs' visit to PARC was a turning point in his life: the three technologies that the 24-year-old mathematician encountered were each revolutionary on their own: the first graphical user interface for computers, networked Alto computers and object-oriented programming. Even many years after this visit, Jobs can still remember exactly:

> they really showed me three things. But I was so blinded by the first one I didn't even really see the other two ... I was so blinded by the first thing they showed me, which was the graphical user interface. I thought it was the best thing I'd ever seen in my life. Now remember it was very flawed, what we saw was incomplete, they'd done a bunch of things wrong. But we didn't know that at the time but still thought the germ of the idea was there and they'd done it very well and within you know ten minutes it was obvious to me that all computers would work like this some day.

Steve claimed that "Xerox could have owned the entire computer industry today. Could have been, you know, a company ten times its size. Could have been IBM, could have been the IBM of the nineties. Could have been the Microsoft of the nineties."

"Could have." In fact, Xerox's failures in taking advantage of PARC's innovations have become famous. The GUI is the favorite example: "something like the first personal computer", although very significant in terms of its influence on future system design it was a commercial failure; and others followed. The first successful commercial GUI product was actually the Apple Macintosh, which was heavily inspired by PARC's work. After young Steve Jobs' visit to PARC in 1979, Xerox was given Apple stock in exchange for engineer visits and an understanding that Apple would create a GUI product.

It is also no secret that the basic characteristics of the Windows interface – graphical icons, pop-up menus, and the overlapping application windows that give the OS its name – did not originate at Microsoft. Ted Turner even made a TV movie about it – *Pirates of Silicon Valley* (USA 1999) – the origins of the Windows GUI predate Microsoft by many years.

Sources:
www.parc.com
www.xerox.com/downloads/usa/en/x/
Xerox_Fact_Sheet_Who_We_Are_Today.pdf
http://informbusinessnetwork.com/marketing/
historic-succession-xerox-550938a
Alexander, C. and. Smith, D.K. (1988)
Fumbling the Future: How Xerox Invented,
Then Ignored, the First Personal Computer.
New York: William Morrow, p. 274
Hiltzik, M. (2000) *Dealers of Lightning: Xerox PARC and*
the Dawn of the Computer Age.
London: Orion Publishing
Businessweek online, March 5, 2001

In sum, Xerox management failed to see the potential of many of PARC's inventions, or did not develop or secure appropriate complementary commercialization activities and assets (Teece 1986). Why?

First, Xerox executives often did not understand what PARC was doing; they did not take the time to do so and did not devote too much attention to it. After all, computing research was a relatively small part of PARC's operation, and PARC was a relatively small part of Xerox. Distance and poor communications contributed to many misunderstandings about the industry and Xerox technology, and about the great potential of PARC research for the computer industry. The central offices were enacting "directives" and "plans" and "strategies" about Xerox's positioning and industries that took little account of the trajectories followed by the research activities, and were more a cage than a support for their development. Xerox's management was often underconfident and disbelieved the economic potential of new technologies. After all, accounting and expected cost-benefit analyses were never exactly right to really justify the investments. Too many people were involved in any decision, for no particularly good reason. Procrastination and delays in turning breakthrough technologies into products were therefore common. In the end, PARC pioneered many technologies and produced important inventions, which had a great influence in the industry and supported highly successful products. But other firms exploited many of these inventions, and still other inventions and ideas were lost and unexploited.

Second, there are limits to the internal differentiation an organizational system can tolerate. In particular, a sharp divide between a "professional/research oriented/entrepreneurial" sub-system and an "administrative/bureaucratically oriented/managerial" sub-system is likely to be a major source of trouble. Actually, the problem has been recognized for some time in organizations that structurally have a "double line" of professionals and administrators, such as universities and hospitals, long before it was encountered by business firms trying to be research oriented and professional (Stinchcombe 1965). This closely resembles the duality between an entrepreneurial and a managerial component. To put it bluntly, if the two "lines" had equal weight, they would negotiate forever; and if the administrative structure prevails, innovation will suffer. If innovation and entrepreneurship is to take center stage, the solution, to put it succinctly, is for professionals/entrepreneurs to "hire" administrative services, rather than managers/bureaucrats "hiring" researchers/entrepreneurs. In flexible and innovative organizations, the administrative and staff structure (the HR function included) should be light and organized as a set of internal "service units", eventually competing with external providers of the same services; whereas the "clients" are the internal professional/knowledge-based/entrepreneurial units (Ulrich and Lake 1991).

Career risk and boundaryless careers

A crucial point of differentiation between corporate entrepreneurship and independent entrepreneurship is that the individuals who are formally or informally responsible for all the actions involved in creating an entrepreneurial organization are employees rather than owners of the venture. Although some property rights can and should be assigned to internal entrepreneurs, they can rarely be as extensive as those of an independent entrepreneur. On the other side, internal entrepreneurs are less exposed to financial risk as they rarely invest their own financial resources. However, they typically invest their own human capital and get exposed to *career risk*, where the success or failure of the ventures and innovation to which they contribute may reflect positively or negatively on their reputation, and influence access to future, more rewarding positions (Morris *et al.* 2008).

The lack of financial risk coupled with career risk is a particular source of problems. The risk of escalation of commitment is increased when the financial risks are not born personally by individuals, and further enhanced where individuals fear that project termination may reflect poorly on themselves (Staw 1980; Chapter 1 (this volume)).

The problem can be mitigated at the outset in various ways. First, people can be entitled to participate in the residual value that is created by their entrepreneurial contributions (thereby increasing financial risk along with incentives to take risk). Second, the link between result-based performance evaluations and careers can be loosened (thereby reducing career risk). In fact, these practices are sometimes observable in highly innovative organizations. They include: the already described bootleg projects and skunk works practices, which provide a sort of "evaluation-free" zone for trial and error; performance evaluation systems based on a wide range of parameters, including the quality of behaviors in addition to results; and relatively wide samples of performance measures (over time or across projects). As a result, in a CE organization, careers should not be conceived of as internal, vertical, and linked to a specified single type of activity, and single parameter results. They are "boundaryless" as they are chains of moves *across the boundaries of internal units as well as across the boundaries of firms, on a wide portfolio of projects/jobs.* After all, individuals also need to diversify risk in the face of uncertainty, as much as firms do.

Forms of employment between association and marketization

At the micro level of jobs and employment contracts, high discretion and loosely defined jobs help to avoid unnecessarily constraining the creative contributions of employees and encourage cross-unit communication. A tightly defined employment relationship, through contractual and internal job descriptions, may not only ossify behaviors but also have a negative influence on "atmosphere" and trust (e.g. Malhotra and Murnighan 2002). On the other side, autonomy alone may drift the system toward disintegration, rather than toward healthy disaggregation. This "autonomy versus control" dilemma is analogous to what has been described at the macro-structure level, for example, in the Oticon case.

Incentives help, as discussed, but, as also discussed, they can only be used to a limited extent in innovative tasks. Hence, a specific challenge as regards job specification and employment contracts in entrepreneurial settings is to be able to elicit desirable behaviors without unduly constraining individuals to predetermined patterns of action that would inhibit a creative contribution by reducing autonomy. In other words, the core question is: which job designs and employment contracts provide an effective alternative to classic dependent work and bureaucratically regulated jobs? The question is analogous to what the alternatives are to hierarchy and bureaucracy at the macro level. And again the common response, both in practice and in theory, has been somewhat polarized between a "communitarian" and "mercatistic" response.

Box 5.2 on Microsoft internal associated engineers and freelance "rented" engineering work illustrates the bifurcation, and some of the problems this entails.

Box 5.2 Microsoft, freelancers and stock options

Large corporations in the sector have increasingly adopted the practice of hiring temporary employees or independent contractors through temporary agencies specializing in information technology and electronics. Some of these firms offer very "flexible" contracts, by which the programmers can be "rented like cars: and they don't need to be filled up with petrol on return" (says the advertisement of one of those firms in Seattle).

This practice has led to a number of problems, legal and organizational.

For example, "freelancers", who work in the computer sector as independent entrepreneurs, were engaged as "independent contractors" through temporary employment agencies by Microsoft, when it needed to expand its workforce to meet the demands of new product schedules.

An issue broke out around a reward program Microsoft had for its permanently employed engineers. Every six months, the employees could exercise the option to be paid partly in shares at 85 percent of their current value. If a product is especially successful, the value of the share will rise and, at the same rate, so will the remuneration of the engineers and programmers who have elected to be paid in shares. Some of them have even become millionaires overnight.

This program led eight foreign collaborators, who worked for Microsoft in the United States between 1987 and 1990 as freelancers in the company's international division to file a suit. The reason was that, at the time, they had been told that owing to the limited duration of their residence permit they had no right to the stock options plan. Microsoft tried to take a tough line, but in vain. The court ruled in favor of the plaintiffs, stating that "*they are entitled to stock-option benefits under Microsoft's Employee Stock Purchase Plan (ESPP)*".

The feature of the contractual and organizational arrangement that the court judged to be illegitimate was to grant different rights in connection with the same activities and work services. In fact, an undesirable consequence of those arrangements is to create a first-class and a second-class employee. The problem is not minor, as for some time now many software houses have been letting programs be written in other countries. In numerical control programming, the offshore programming share may have already reached 85 percent. In addition, the use of such external collaborators has other organizational disadvantages: they are not available for the marathons that go on for several days and in which a team of programmers creates software under terrible time pressure in order to deliver to the client on the stipulated date. Projects of this kind require intense group work and strong incentives.

Sources: *Detief Borchers Die Zeit: Bulkware,* February 1998;
summary by Giuseppe Delrnestri
No. 94–35770. United States Court of Appeals, Ninth Circuit. Argued and Submitted Oct. 18, 1995. Decided Oct. 3, 1996; summary by Laura Gaillard

What could the solutions be?

There is little question about the need to offer protective, open-ended, associative and partnership-based contracts to the providers of work services stemming from highly qualified, relatively "rare" human resources, and/or from human capital that has been developed in firm-specific ways (Chapters 2 and 3). This is all the more valid for work services entailing some unrecoverable transfers of people's human capital in the firm, or vice versa, of firm's intangible assets in the hands of employees. Guarantees and protections against the breaking of those relationships are in the interests of all parties involved. These types of contracts respond to the autonomy versus control dilemma by basically transforming "agents" into "principals" of themselves. They do so by using the incentivizing power of property rights, rather than by using second-best solutions such as transferring risk through pay for performance, or looking for an optimal intermediate degree of task specification and delegation.

The more debatable and debated question is about workforce relations that are not firm specific and, more generally are easily substitutable (Lepak *et al.* 2002). A common response in practice (backed by some theories) has been to create a "dual" employment system: a "core" of "associated" and protected workers, surrounded by an outer ring of contracted-out or temporary work. This solution may have some entrepreneurial properties, since these "autonomous" workers are "self-entrepreneurs" of their services. In other words, external "market-like" contracts can sustain entrepreneurship through incentives on delivery (e.g. as in any putting-out system); while internal "partnership-like" contracts should sustain entrepreneurship by incentives based on shared property rights in the firm.

This solution also entails numerous problems especially concerning career and reward risk, and fair rent sharing. Continuity in the series of jobs held and related rewards may be jeopardized under those external and temporary contracts, particularly as they are supposed to concern relatively substitutable workers. In addition, these types of workers are likely to be more risk averse than wealthier workers, as they cannot absorb these discontinuities.

Fair rent division may also be undermined by highly asymmetric bargaining power. The situation is almost the opposite with respect to what happens with "critical" human capital. In this case, when human resources are poorly substitutable, the bargaining power is in favor of the workers and, in fact, firms struggle for their "retention", rather than the workers fighting for job continuity in the same firm. Indeed, these kinds of workers (entrepreneurial team members included) can count on (better and upgrading) job continuity across firms. The opposite tends to occur for more substitutable workers. This may end up in rent appropriation by the employer firm only (as in the Microsoft freelance case), as much as in any contracting-out relation with those features (see Chapter 4, this volume; Klein *et al.* 1978). In addition, as also described in the Microsoft case, the contracting out of work is likely to generate a series A–series B workforce problem, which often negatively and heavily affects the entrepreneurial motivation of external workers this is supposed to foster.

There are currently plenty of analyses of these problems since the "new forms of employment" have become a quite general and important social issue. We are interested here in the "entrepreneurial" solutions to this.[2]

A first solution is to unpack the "associational and communitarian" versus "transactional and marketized" alternatives, and to see that actually strongly "incentive-based", even "external" work, can be coupled with associational mechanisms. Microsoft freelancers being entitled to stock options is a case in point. Another interesting experience regarding lower qualification workers is Lincoln Electrics, coupling an extremely marketized reward system such as piece-rate compensation with employee ownership, in order to ensure against the well-known possible opportunistic use of that system by the management (Roberts 2004).

Other solutions point to outside the firm boundaries. Organizational networks are also extremely useful on this terrain and, in this case, they function as safety networks proper. Europe is particularly rich in these experiences (Regalia 2006), which tend to have a strong regional character (as the labor market they are intended to support has). These networks are typically associations involving one or all of at least the following partners: (1) associations of firms; (2) associations of workers; and (3) public regional institutions or agencies (Crora 2007). Examples include the following:

- Associations of firms for the collective and continuous hiring of workers under temporary contracts; in this way, firms achieve flexibility while workers achieve continuity of employment.
- Associated workers collectively offering work services on a contract basis to employer firms, while guaranteeing continuity of employment, as far as pension rights and minimum wages are concerned, on a mutual insurance principle basis. A typical form of this kind of association is a worker cooperative.
- Foundations and other institutionalized, public or private networks (some of them can be qualified as parts of regional systems of innovation and are more widely analyzed in Chapter 6) with a special focus on the formation and circulation of human resources, up to the support to the establishment of spin-off new entrepreneurial firms. A particularly fully fledged experience, which has managed to extend its reach internationally, is the Neue Grunderzeit Foundation in Berlin, an EU-nominated best practice in the field. This is a labor and technological transfer organization. Partners include adult education centers, employment offices, experts, consultants and banks. It has foreign partners in London, Rotterdam, Barcelona and Bologna. Sometimes these partnerships can take the form of superordinate firms. For example, the Greater Nottingham Partnership (GNP) is a limited liability company with 15 partners including firm associations, universities, public agencies and chambers of commerce, staff agencies, and voluntary organizations. Activities include technical and economic development initiatives, transportation and infrastructures, ICT, and investments in training and development.

All these solutions imply going beyond a single firm/single worker relation and to exploit firm embeddedness in larger sectoral and territorial systems of innovation – the topic of the next and final chapter.

Key points

How do you to reproduce entrepreneurial governance and organization "without the founding of new firms", within grown-up firms, or even within other entities which are not firms? This chapter integrates various contributions for responding to the question (including corporate governance, corporate disaggregation, new forms of organization, strategic human resources, new forms of employment). Through a variety of examples, case studies and research data the chapter contributes in specifying a set of key and complementary practices for infusing entrepreneurship in organizational structure and in HR systems. These practices are inspired to principles as *deregulation and disaggregation, coupled with "marketization" and "projectification", but also with integration, communitarianism and "democratization" through internal and external networks*. These mechanisms, albeit different, or precisely because of that, have been shown to be *complementary in sustaining innovation* and infusing entrepreneurship in established organizational entities, or in maintaining growing companies entrepreneurial in character.

Analysis questions

On in-chapter cases

- Gather information on the organization of an established firm with an innovative context and positioning and compare it with the best practices described in tables 5.1 and 5.2. In which aspects has such a firm maintained its profile of an entrepreneurial firm? In which aspect has it not? Which organizational practices may be usefully preserved, abandoned or introduced?

On end-chapter case

- The following case presents the full story of the growth of an entrepreneurial firm into a global corporation. The aspiration was to maintain an entrepreneurial mode of organizing while growing. To what extent and through which organizational practices was it realized? Areas of improvement? Challenges ahead?

End-chapter case: Permasteelisa[*]

Carmine Garzia, 2010

Permasteelisa is world leader in the design, production and installation of curtain walls and architectural façades for large buildings. Born in 1988 from the merger of the Italian ISA of Treviso with Australian Permasteel of Sidney, the company has been the protagonist of a growth path that has led it from a turnover of little more than €10 million in 1988 to around €1 billion in 2002 and from 10 to 4,300 employees. The company is present in 20 countries with a network of around 40 subsidiaries.

The growth of the company was accompanied by its gradual transformation into a public company. Massimo Colomban, founder of Permasteelisa, gradually transferred the majority of his shares to managers who have become partners of the company. In October 1997, Permasteelisa Pacific, the Asian subholding of the group, was listed on the Singapore stock exchange and in July 1999, the parent company Permasteelisa SpA was listed on the Milan stock exchange. In March 2002, Colomban definitively left the company to devote himself to the development of other entrepreneurial initiatives.

The strategic choices of Permasteelisa contributed to the birth of the global high-tech curtain wall sector, high-tech façades intended for monumental buildings. Over the years, Permasteelisa has participated in the projects of major international architects such as Norman Foster, Frank Gehry, Jean Nouvel, Renzo Piano, Richard Rogers, the SOM Studio and Kenzo Tange. Permasteelisa has realized the façades of some of the most important buildings in the last 40 years: the Sydney Opera House, the European Parliament in Brussels and Strasbourg, Channel Lloyds Register in London, the UOB towers in Singapore, the titan façade of the Guggenheim Museum Bilbao and the Walt Disney Concert Hall in Los Angeles.

The birth and development of ISA

Massimo Colomban, born in 1949 in Santa Lucia del Piave in Treviso, began working at age 15 at IALF, a company that produced windows and façades in aluminum and steel. After nine years of work, he decided to set up on his own and in October 1973 took over the window production activities of a small local engineering company. Some months later, in August 1974, he changed the name to ISA. ISA was born with ten employees, a small laboratory and some machinery for the production of doors and windows.

Colomban was convinced that aluminum windows were not adaptable to residential constructions. The aluminum façades had good market potential in constructions destined to service and commercial activities due to the aesthetic aspect, the contained maintenance costs and the technical performance. ISA production was focused on curtain walls and later also included internal partitions. The company mainly used internally designed aluminum systems and immediately turned toward the international market, mostly European, since in Italy the non-residential building sector was little developed. The ISA façades were comparable in terms of price and technology to those of major European competitors. However, Colomban aimed for a lean business organization from the start in order to have lower costs and greater flexibility in case of demand reduction. Toward the end of the 1980s, ISA implemented a differentiation strategy based on the customization of products according to the wishes of the designers and customers. In the space of a few years, ISA, thanks to the innovativeness of the products and the aggressiveness of its trade policies, asserted itself as one of the main European producers of curtain walls. Its activities in the European market gradually grew, bringing the turnover to over €8 million in 1982, achieved with the contribution of around 100 employees and with an export rate of approximately 60 percent.

The organizational approach to internal relations and growth

Massimo Colomban, during the years that he had worked as an employee of IALF, developed an organizational concept and institutional structure of the company that was in sharp contrast to the approach prevailing at the time: "As an employee of the company, where I worked for almost ten years, I witnessed the expansion of the company, which grew in terms of employees and turnover, but where the responsibilities and power were always in the hands of a few. The most valuable people did not tolerate this situation and either ended up leaving or, worse, losing identification with the company and its objectives.

"If you want someone to do the things the way you do them, who identifies with your objectives and has your same aspirations, you must place him in your same conditions; you cannot only reward with a system of incentives, but have to turn him into an entrepreneur who considers the company as his own."

Colomban decided to gradually distribute his capital shares to his closest collaborators, with the final objective of making ISA a firm wholly owned by its managers. To promote accountability on specific objectives, top managers were assigned a geographical zone of influence; some of them were placed at the head of commercial companies that operated in foreign countries. The lower levels of the organizational structure, such as the directors of the installation teams, were also involved in the association system.

Colomban established a simple and effective assessment criterion for the performance of managers based on the profits they generated for ISA and/or for the company they administered. If the results, measured over certain years, were positive, the manager received an option to buy ISA shares on favorable terms. The mechanism was able to combine the tension toward growth (increase in turnover) with the achievement of revenue objectives, without which the managers would not receive any extraordinary compensation. According to Colomban: "this mechanism stimulated the birth and the development of business skills: the ability to see further, to push sales without affecting financial exposure and planning investments while considering the potential economic return."

This incentives system would lead Colomban to the gradual loss of his majority shareholding for the benefit of managers who would become entrepreneur-partners of ISA's founder: "the best people would lead the firm toward expansion into new markets and growth. Already by 1974 I had the objective of bringing ISA to the world summits of its sector and create a company where responsibility and authority were widespread. The tension toward ambitious objectives could be maintained only by assigning maximum responsibility to the managers, turning them into entrepreneurs in a position to choose the natural leader from among themselves."

The organizational approach to technology

In order to obtain a high-quality and technologically advanced product able to compete on foreign markets, ISA had to develop the technology internally. The continuous improvement of the product was a priority objective. ISA designed, in just three years, six curtain wall systems. Product innovation was aimed at obtaining extremely flexible façade systems, able to satisfy the aesthetic demands of architects. ISA's competitors, especially the Germans, had a very low rate of product innovation because they were more vertically integrated in the production of aluminum systems and each modification entailed investments in extrusion tools and specific plant equipments.

ISA instead relied on external extruded aluminum system suppliers, and could thus alter its systems design without sustaining substantial investment in equipment. ISA could only count on a single assembly line for the curtain walls and when, due to the increase in turnover and orders, the company could no longer satisfy the orders, it turned to small external firms.

The logistics were organized to minimize fixed costs and be as flexible as possible. In door and window companies, transport and installation are critical activities: they together account for over 15 percent of the cost of the product. Incorrect installation of the curtain walls can jeopardize the success of a contract. The curtain wall producers paid particular attention to this phase. They were equipped with vehicles and teams of specialized assemblers. ISA, consistent with the idea of leanness that characterized the company, entrusted the installations to external agents. These were carried out by teams of independent assemblers, recruited in situ or brought in from the Veneto region. The external assemblers trained in the installation of the façades on prototypes in ISA's plants that the company produced and mounted there in order to carry out preliminary technical checks. In the following years ISA organized the work of the more expert assemblers, promoting the creation of a service company, which became its privileged installation service supplier.

The organizational approach to internationalization

The first international experiences of ISA were entirely sporadic. Contacts with foreign clients were via word of mouth or completely random. As Colomban recalled: "It was clear that for the type of product that we wanted to offer there was not a sufficient market in our country. We had to export. It was not yet clear where to go. At the start we went wherever there was work. Once, a Venetian emigrate who had made a fortune in Venezuela came to us and proposed realizing some of the work in his country. We thought about it a great deal and accepted."

In the 1970s, numerous Italian companies from the construction sector began to operate in the Middle East market. ISA's management believed that no conditions existed for the stable development of the Middle East market whose growth was related to exogenous factors, such as the price of oil. In addition, the company failed to locate a reliable industrial partner in that region.

Toward the end of the 1970s ISA started a systematic search to establish partnerships with qualified companies in the main European markets. To exploit the opportunities for expansion, offices were opened in Belgium, England and Germany.

According to Colomban: "The experience in the European market was an exceptional training ground for many of us. It was the opportunity to confront ourselves with very different business cultures to our own such as the rational and perfectionist German culture, which is among the most dynamic Anglo-Saxon. We understood a fundamental thing: we had to be prepared to face the foreign markets. Everyone could export, but few were able to build an international company. Since we were not exporting under the umbrella of large construction contractors, we understood that bank guarantees and customer trustworthiness were fundamental. We found that the process of constructing a building was governed by a logic similar to the production process of any industrial good. Suppliers were part of the assembly chain and had to scrupulously respect the specifications and timelines."

The birth and development of Permasteelisa

The birth of the global construction sector and the power of contractors, moving from one country to another to avoid cyclical crises impelled the managers of ISA to give additional impetus to the internationalization process.

The attention of ISA's management pointed toward Southeast Asia, Hong Kong and Singapore. In these two city-states the lack of space and the presence of large financial institutions and services companies stimulated demand for buildings destined for advanced services industries.

In 1982, Colomban was contacted by the management of Permasteel, an Australian company founded in 1949 that produced curtain walls, frames and metal structures with a turnover of around 7 million Australian dollars. From the early 1960s, the company grew thanks to the period of intense real-estate development of the main Australian cities financed by state funds. With the end of the public building plan, Permasteel found itself facing a severe reduction in demand. The reduction in orders brought the company to a situation of financial instability and the technological asset, accumulated in the construction of curtain walls, was likely to be lost. ISA signed a collaboration agreement with the Australian company, whose management was hired by Italian managers. The agreement foresaw the management in partnership of new orders in Australia and in the Pacific and an acquisition option of Permasteel by ISA. In the first half of the 1980s, Permasteel and ISA implemented numerous work orders in the Pacific, especially in Singapore, which was going through a period of extraordinary real-estate development.

In December 1986, ISA purchased a majority shareholding of the Australian ally. Thus, Permasteelisa was born, although the new company formally assumed this name only in 1988.

Permasteelisa implemented a development plan that included the construction of new production units, the strengthening of research facilities and the constitution of new commercial companies. The investments were sustained with the entry of private equity funds in the shareholding group. New plants were established with annexed research facilities in San Vendemiano and in Melbourne. The ISA plant was modernized, and to broaden the range of products offered, it was associated to the Steelbenetton group of Treviso – a company specialized in the production of steel and bronze high-end windows. At the end of the 1980s, the production capacity of the company tripled compared to 1985 and reached 300,000 m^2 of façades annually.

To effectively compete in the large curtain wall market required the coordination of production processes with those of major contractors, and therefore Permasteelisa, in parallel with investments in production plants, promoted a series of actions designed to obtain maximum operational excellence in all the activities of the value chain. The company acquired control of an engineering firm and a software house; all the plants of the group were connected telematically as were the three research laboratories in San Vendemiano, Singapore and Sydney. In this way, Permasteelisa could design and program the production of an order more quickly than competitors who were usually equipped with a single design center, making the research centers and the executive planning offices work simultaneously, 24 hours a day thanks to the time differences, and supported by the engineering center.

To be more effective in its commercial action, Permasteelisa promoted the development of direct relationships with designers. "The designer plays a decisive role in the choice of materials and in the direction of the work. High-tech architects are engaged in projects worth several hundred million dollars and are almost always financed by private individuals. The architect is not only an artist who creates the form, but a real and actual manager to interact with. Permasteelisa had to leverage on privileged relationships with the top designers," recalls Colomban. One of the first acts of the new company was to found, in 1988, IAITA – International Award for Innovative Technology in Architecture. This Association, through debates and publications, was to contribute to the spread of a new type of architecture based on curtain wall techniques. Permasteelisa, through this channel of communication, could understand the evolution of design before competitors and participate directly in the formation of new architectural "trends".

The evolution of technology: modularizing buildings

At the end of the 1980s, the company presented the Quarternario system, a system of façades, aerial floors,[3] indoor partitions and furnishings, for the construction of buildings for commercial use.

Buildings have three macro components: the skeleton, which has a very long duration (generally up to 100 years), the fixtures, which have a short duration (of about 25 years) and the façades, which have a duration of approximately 50 years. The Quarternario system had to protect the structure and allow the rapid and economic replacement of fixtures.

Colomban recalls: "There was no radical innovation in the Quarternario system, we just presented a series of integrated products. We didn't want to simply be producers of curtain walls, floors, tables and chairs for offices. We wanted to present ourselves to our customers as suppliers of a new construction technique by adding a high level of logistical service to a quality product."

The Quarternario façade was designed to be installed as a complete façade of the skeleton. The aerial floor, known as the Channel Floor, allowed the installation and replacement of pipes and cables without breaking the masonry. The perfect independence between the structure/façade/fixtures made the Quarternario system installation possible in a building in its construction phase. The façade modules could be mounted first, then the floor and finally the internal partitions. This drastically reduced the construction time of the building.

The Quarternario façade was composed of modules (cells) that were prefabricated in the factory with high levels of automation. A packaging system was designed for their transport and an installation system (from within the building, without the use of external scaffolding) with the related operational procedures to follow on the construction site.

The evolution of strategy: from metal works to architectural components

In Europe, the works of high-tech architects and the large initiatives for urban regeneration destined for the services industries sector were increasingly numerous, such as La Defense in Paris, Postdamer Platz in Berlin and Canary Wharf in London. Permasteelisa chose a penetration strategy based on their direct presence in foreign markets, through the association of the network of aluminum façade manufacturers in central and northern Europe.

In 1990, two new companies were set up and endowed with production plants and commercial structures: Permasteelisa Benelux SA and Permasteelisa UK Ltd. In 1995, Permasteelisa purchased the Dutch company Sheldebouw, founded in 1875 and among the first to realize aluminum façades in the 1930s. The Dutch company brought to the group a large plant with an advanced research and testing laboratory. In 1996, Belgo Metal was acquired, a window company for some time active in northern Europe. Commercial branches were opened in Spain and France, and in the second half of the 1990s in Poland and Hungary.

From 1992, Permasteelisa was awarded the foremost European orders for the implementation of curtain walls: the new European Parliament in Strasbourg, the Galeryes Lafayette in Berlin, La Tour du Midi, and the Tour Pleiad in Brussels, and finally the futuristic Guggenheim Museum in Bilbao designed by the American architect Frank Gehry and lined with titanium.

In the 1990s, the expansion continued also to Southeast Asia where, in 1990, Permasteelisa Pacific Pte Ltd in Singapore was constituted, in association with some local partners. New branches in China, Taiwan, Thailand and Hong Kong were also opened.

From 1990 until the end of 1996, the Permasteelisa group quadrupled its turnover, with over 1,000 employees and becoming a global enterprise present in Europe, Asia, Australia and North America and with a turnover of over 300 million. The tumultuous growth of the 1990s brought the company to the summit of the sector in terms of turnover, average amount of contracts, geographical coverage and technological level of productions. Consistently with its fundamental idea of a networked company and distributed ownership, Massimo Colomban over the years sold a large part of his shares to top managers who by the middle of the 1990s controlled a little less than 50 percent of the company, while the founder had a share of just over 20 percent. Colomban had every intention of giving further impetus to the shareholder spread and between 1996 and 1997 the partners reacquired the shares held by private equity funds in view of the possible stock exchange listing with the consequent transformation of Permasteelisa into a public company.

The evolution of structure

To increase production capacity and at the same time explore new markets, the managers of Permasteelisa decided to use the instrument of temporary association with local companies to create a network of manufacturers of façades.

Permasteelisa chose as partners small and medium-sized firms that were well embedded in the local market: they knew the logics, were able to assess the trustworthiness of customers and had a network of trusted suppliers. If the contract was acquired and run with success, Permasteelisa submitted to the ally a collaboration agreement that foresaw a systematic multi-annual commitment in search of new orders. The agreement could develop into the acquisition of a majority shareholding of the allied firm. The acquired company's management was left to the original entrepreneur who became a partner of Permasteelisa. The entrepreneur was motivated to manage the company to the best of his ability and at the same time was made responsible for the group's objectives with Permasteelisa share options. As Colomban recalled: "My company would have to be an extended but lean company. For this reason I immediately foresaw a network structure. The network of companies would allow ISA to grow while minimizing the use of its own means. The new entrepreneurs would confer their own firms to ISA and thus enter in new markets or strengthen its competitive position in the markets where they already operated.

"The idea of the network was in a sense complementary to that of the partnership with managers: associated entrepreneurs, on par with the manager-partner, would be evaluated on the basis of the results obtained and would retain (or not) the company's management."

During the years of growth, even under pressure from the representatives of the private equity funds, Permasteelisa started to provide itself with a management structure and control systems suitable for the size attained. In the years immediately following the entry of external members, a management control system was implemented and an administrative and financial management was created and headed by Enzo Pavan, a manager with significant experience in a multinational corporation.

Pavan was the company's first top manager with no technical training. Colomban recalls: "I was convinced that Pavan would know how to rationalize the control of our network, thanks to the experience accumulated in large companies. When we met to sign the contract, I proposed a relatively low fixed salary and a premium based on stock options. He reluctantly accepted and told me that the contract on stock options would be put in a drawer and that he did not believe in these systems. He changed his mind a few years later."

From 1995, the enterprise network structure was reorganized, based on three levels:

- level 1: global headquarters (in San Vendemiano);
- level 2: continental headquarters;
- level 3: peripheral network.

Permasteelisa SpA in Italy became the global headquarters (the group holding company). It also acted as regional headquarters in the Italian market. Three other regional headquarters (RH) – Permasteelisa Pacific in Singapore, Sheldebouw in the Netherlands and Permasteelisa USA – were assigned the coordination of activities of the network of companies in their respective markets. The peripheral companies (third level) were divided into three types: commercial, production and services (engineering, maintenance services and installation companies).

The holding company's stock was shared between Colomban and the partners. The middle of the 1990s saw the introduction of the intermediate figure of "Associate", namely managers who held shares in companies of the network or in one of the RHs, but not in the holding company. The associate level was preliminary to the achievement of partner status. The partners elected an executive committee, which acted as the network's board of directors. The committee, formed by ten partners, elected the president and chief executive. These two figures respectively had the tasks of the strategic and operational management of the relations between the firms of the network.

There were of two types of managers: those with technical tasks and those with administration tasks. Falling into the area of managers with technical tasks were:

- *Area managers* – managing directors of commercial companies, of regional headquarters and peripheral production firms, responsible for the commercial and production activities of a specific geographical area.
- *Project managers* – responsible for the management of orders. Their tasks were linked to the supervision of the design and implementation process of orders among the various network firms. They were employed by one of the RH companies.
- *Factory managers* – managers of the company's plants, responsible for the logistical and organizational aspects linked to production in the workshop.
- *Site managers* – construction site managers, managing the purchase of consumable materials and coordinating the activities of the assembly teams.

Managers with administrative responsibilities (administration managers) were distinguished in two levels:

- *Contracts financial managers* – responsible for budgeting, finance and the publication of internal and public financial statements, operating in the world headquarters and in the regional headquarters.
- *Accounting managers* – supporting the contracts financial manager, present in the regional headquarters, in the world headquarters and in the manufacturing companies of the peripheral network.

Both managers with technical responsibilities and those with administrative responsibilities could aim to become associates. The role of partner was instead reserved to *area, project and contracts financial managers*.

The intention of Colomban's system was to stimulate entrepreneurial-type management. The partners were accountable for the management of the company of the network of which they were shareholders and directors; furthermore, as shareholders of the holding company, they were discouraged from implementing opportunistic behavior on the level of companies in the network.

The possibility of becoming shareholders on a network company level or whole group level depended on the ability to demonstrate business skills through the management of the company (for the area managers), of orders (for the project managers) or of order support activities (for the factory managers, the site managers and the contracts financial managers).

The measure of entrepreneurship was based on the profitability of the activities conducted by the candidates, evaluated generally over a four-year period. The president and the chief executive officer had the task of proposing candidates for partners and associates to the executive committee.

The system ensured high commitment on the profitability of orders. The project managers were generally associates and partners, and their performance was evaluated on the ability to profitably manage the individual orders.

Decisions were unanimously taken within the executive committee. Colomban recalls: "During the dozens of meetings held between the partners during the

1990s I do not recall having voted once. Perhaps we debated for hours, closed in a room, but we always managed to make decisions unanimously. I was inspired by the Japanese. Even if it was a long process, in the end everyone was convinced and accountable for the decisions taken."

At the end of the 1990s the partners of Permasteelisa decided to invest to consolidate their presence in the USA and Europe, the markets with the best growth prospects. To support the development plan new financial resources were necessary that were found through 37 percent of the group's stock exchange listing in July 1999.[4] Financial resources raised with the IPO were invested in the development of new state-of-the-art production facility in Italy and in the support of growth.

In December 2000 Permasteelisa acquired control of the German company Gartner that, with 1,550 employees and a turnover of 460 million German Marks, was its biggest competitor. The integration process between the two companies was directly supervised by Massimo Colomban, who in March 2002 definitively left the company; Enzo Pavan succeeded him as president and CEO.

Table 5.3 Permasteelisa's production and commercial structure at IPO (1999)

Location	Activities performed in each location				
	Design	*R&D*	*Production*	*Installation*	*Project management*
Europe					
San Vendemiano (I)	X	X	X	X	X
Treviso (I)	X		X		
Corbanese (I)	X		X	X	X
Rome (I)	X		X	X	X
Middelburg (NL)	X	X	X	X	X
Paris (F)	X			X	X
Gavere (B)	X		X	X	X
Basel (CH)	X				
Lugano (CH)				X	X
London (UK)	X			X	X
Rijeka (HR)	X				
Warsaw (PL)*			X	X	X
Australia					
Sydney		X	X	X	X
Melbourne			X	X	X
Asia					
Singapore		X	X	X	X
Bangkok (TH)			X	X	X
Shanghai (RPC)*			X	X	X
Foshan*			X		
Hong Kong (SAR)				X	X
Kuala Lumpur			X	X	X
Bangalore (INDIA)*			X	X	X
Seoul (SK)*			X	X	X

* Third part production plant working on exclusive base for Permasteelisa.

Table 5.4 Management structure

Manager with technical tasks:	*Activities:*
Area managers	Area general management, marketing negotiation
Project manager	Executive design and order management
Factory managers	Production management, procurement, product realization and logistic
Site managers	Installation and quality control
Managers with administrative tasks:	
Contract financial managers	Budgeting, auditing, tax planning
Account managers	Auditing

Table 5.5 Historical evolution of turnover

	1988	*1989*	*1990*	*1991*	*1992*	*1993*	*1994*	*1995*	*1996*
Turnover (euros/000)	24,270	45,970	53,710	66,620	79,020	80,570	109,490	149,250	174,038

Table 5.6 Selected financial data (values in euros/000)

	1996		1997		1998		1999		2000		2001		2002	
Turnover	174,038	100%	256,340	100%	285,642	100%	305,724	100%	386,692	100%	791,388	100%	984,343	100%
EBITDA	12,822	7.4%	24,348	9.5%	29,281	10.3%	34,928	11.4%	42,851	11.1%	70,223	8.9%	93,359	9.48%
EBIT	9,208	5.3%	20,375	7.9%	29,568	10.4%	29,248	9.6%	36,338	9.4%	55,495	7.0%	76,933	7.82%
Net profit	4,545	2.6%	29,349	11.45%	11,625	4.1%	16,220	5.3%	19,011	4.9%	50,077	6.3%	55,537	5.64%

Table 5.7 Evolution of turnover by product class (values in euros/000)

	1996		1997		1998		1999		2000		2001		2002	
Curtain walls	90%	156,742	85%	218,632	89%	253,179	88%	269,744	86%	334,488	79%	622,081	82%	819,698
Internal partitions	9%	15,022	14%	35,098	10%	29,568	11%	33,017	12%	46,849	11%	89,073	11%	109,262
Industrial doors											1%	10,212	1%	9,067
Exxtrusion											8%	60,756	5%	46,316
Total operating revenues	99%	171,763	99%	253,730	99%	282,747	99%	302,761	99%	381,337	99%	782,122	99%	984,343
Other revenues	1%	2,275	1%	2,610	1%	2,895	1%	2,838	1%	4,001	1%	7,646	1%	7,232
Adjustments							0%	124	0%	1,354	0%	1,620	0%	3,451
Total	100%	174,038	100%	256,340	100%	285,642	100%	305,723	100%	386,692	100%	791,388	100%	995,026

Table 5.8 Evolution of curtain walls turnover by geographical area (values in euros/000)

	1996		1997		1998		1999		2000		2001		2002	
Europe	69,690	44%	76,233	35%	103,351	41%	143,417	53%	209,140	63%	378,344	61%	510,666	62%
Asia	68,893	44%	116,791	53%	126,544	50%	87,220	32%	80,372	24%	148,846	24%	140,008	17%
Australia	18,158	12%	24,436	11%	23,284	9%	35,237	13%	26,053	8%	16,656	3%	24,456	3%
USA			1,172	1%			3,870	1%	18,923	6%	78,235	13%	144,568	18%
Total	156,742	100%	218,632	100%	253,179	100%	269,744	100%	334,488	100%	622,081	100%	819,698	100%

Table 5.9 Staff evolution

Employees	1996	1997	1998	1999	2000	2001	2002
Europe	n.a	n.a	594	696	796	2,465	2,495
Asia	n.a	n.a	453	568	727	1,143	1,005
Australia	n.a	n.a	192	211	148	130	104
USA	n.a	n.a	22	39	110	407	700
Total	1,068	973	1,261	1,514	1,781	4,145	4,304

* Case constructed on the basis of publicly available documents and personal interviews by the author

Notes

1 Rich, Ben R. and Leo Janos (1995) *Skunk Works*. London: Sphere.
2 Therefore, we shall not touch on the commonly prospected, so-called "flexsecurity" solution to the problem, supported by state intervention.
3 Pre-drilled floors that allow the passage of pipes and cables.
4 Summary information on the group ownership structure, production structure, staff and economic indicators in the whole period examined is given in Tables 5.3–5.9.

6 Organizing environments for entrepreneurship

6.1 The spatial clustering of economic activity

The founding and growth of new firms for the creation of innovative products and services depends not only on the behavior of individual entrepreneurs, but also on the community and environment in which they live and work (Shoonhoven and Romanelli 2001). Not only do companies and innovation actors work and interact in informal and personal networks (professional, educational, gender, ethnic and other communities), but also in territorial networks (cities, regions, countries, and/ or geographical regions or associations). "What happens inside the companies is important, but clusters reveal that the immediate business environment outside the companies plays a vital role as well" (Porter 1998).

At the local level, regions have been shown to be key contributors to the creation of new ventures and to innovation. In fact, the wealth creation of countries is related to the development of geographically concentrated clusters of institutions and firms in a common field, and to the quality of the linkages between those institutions and firms (Porter 1998; Porter and Stern 2002). Regions are at the front line of the delivery of innovation support to enterprises. A large proportion of the total world output is produced in a limited number of highly concentrated core industrial regions – broadly identified as "districts" or "clusters": Hollywood for movies, Wall Street for finance, northeast Italy for shoes, California's Silicon Valley in the United States, Bangalore for software in India, and Cambridge for biotechnology in the United Kingdom are a few examples. The process of

---

* Text by Laura Gaillard Giordani and Anna Grandori, cases by Laura Gaillard Giordani.

geographic agglomeration tends to generate cumulative mechanisms that can perpetuate the advantages of a region over others. History and path-dependence play an especially important role in this context (Krugman 1991). There are also numerous and far less visible examples of clusters in early stages of industrialization in Latin America, Africa and Asia, which generate growth also through providing access to work and income for the poor and the unemployed.[1]

Aydalot (1986) highlighted the fundamental role played by local milieus as incubators of innovation. Among the reasons, he pointed out that "local environments ... act like a prism through which innovations are catalyzed and which give the area its particular complexion ... The history of an area, its organization, its collective behavior and its internal structure of unanimity are the principal components of innovation." Moreover, "behaviors inciting innovation are not found at the national level but are dependent on factors defined at the local or regional level". Seen from the "innovative milieu" perspective, the territory does not appear to be a set of juxtaposed elements that are given a priori, but a set of players and resources organized to create the specific sources of its *endogenous* development.

Recent research on innovation has shown that at the national level overall performance in technology-based and developing new products and processes depends not only on the amount of research undertaken by a country and its regions (R&D expenditure, number of researchers), or on the measurable outputs of that research (number of patents and so forth), but also to a great extent on the interactions between enterprises, institutions of higher education and public and private research (Etzkowitz 2008). Hence, the ways in which such interactions in proximate environments are organized matter for entrepreneurship.

The nature of knowledge behind innovation has an important influence on the relevance of proximity. The propensity to agglomerate locally increases when the industry depends on factors such as the exchange of tacit knowledge and external economies. While the new ICTs have facilitated the diffusion of codified knowledge, for the generation and diffusion of *tacit knowledge* some form of direct interaction is necessary, whereby proximity and geographical clustering helps. This idea has been present in economics since Alfred Marshall first raised it in 1890, but has recently reappeared as the dynamics of technology are receiving growing attention. This may seem paradoxical in the face of rapid growth in speed, availability and extent of the new information and communication technologies, but empirical research shows that clustering is still very important. Hence, *the presence of a cluster of related industries in a location will foster entrepreneurship by lowering the cost of starting a business, enhancing opportunities for innovation and enabling better access to a more diverse range of inputs and complementary assets* (Saxenian 1994; Porter 1998; Glaeser *et al.* 2010).

The current literature on regional agglomeration and entrepreneurship is part of a heterogeneous group of theoretical contributions. Researchers tend to focus on certain types of agglomerative factors or "forces": externalities (Marshall 1890), regional resources (Enright 1998), transaction cost economies (Scott and Kwok 1989), embeddedness (Piore and Sabel 1984), localized learning (Maskell and Malmberg 1999), and the exchange and growth of tacit knowledge (Audrestch and Feldman 1996; Kogut 2000). In fact, industrial activities can agglomerate for a variety of reasons. This variety has led to a proliferation of terms and many overlapping typologies to describe regional agglomeration:

- "Industrial districts" – Marshall's ideas were revisited in the 1970s, when Italian scholar Becattini (1979) explored the economic, social and cultural dynamics that gave birth to the industrial districts, through observations on the so-called "Third Italy".[2] These clusters, consisting of small firm networks, were able to establish strong positions in world markets in a number of traditional product categories. Industrial districts are fundamental for the economy of Italy and they are often assimilated to "Made in Italy". A variety of subtypes have been later defined (Markusen 1996), according to network shape (e.g. the "hub-and spokes" district with a central firm), and the nature of players (e.g. more or less supported by public players and subsidies).
- "Innovative milieus" – Scholars from the French group GREMI (Camagni and Maillat 2006) laid the ground for a regional endogenous development approach in the 1980s. They analyzed the firm not as an innovative unit itself, but as part of a "milieu" with a common innovative capacity.
- "Industrial clusters" – Michael Porter (1990) used the "cluster" concept in a geographical context as related to the "competitiveness" of industries and of nations. He further underlined (Porter 1998) that local competition creates incentives to import best practices and boosts pressures to innovate, while also connecting the strengths of competition with the virtues of selective co-operation. In Porter (1998), clusters are defined as a "geographically proximate group of interconnected companies and associated institutions in a particular field linked by commonalities and complementarities. Clusters encompass an array of linked industries and other entities important to competition … including governmental and other institutions – such as universities, standard-setting agencies, think tanks, vocational training providers and trade associations."
- "Regional clusters" – Enright (1998, 2000) describes the dimensions of regional clusters; he argues that clusters differ according to a series of factors (geographic scope, density, breadth, depth, activity base, geographic span of sales, etc.). Policy initiatives toward clusters play an important role. He makes a distinction between regional clusters (which involve a range of related industries) and industrial districts (which he defines as a subset of regional clusters, and that are often a single industry or even a single segment of industry).
- "Regional innovation systems and learning regions" (Cooke 1992) – Very similar to Porter's approach, the literature on regional innovation systems (RIS) and on the learning region emerged in the 1990s with the national innovation systems (NIS) literature (Freeman 1987; Lundvall 1992; Nelson 1993). Innovation is seen as an interactive process shaped by institutional routines and social conventions; knowledge is considered the most important resource.

- "Local and regional industrial systems" – Saxenian (1994) describes agglomeration of firms belonging to one or more correlated industries and localized in a region. The system is characterized by the density and intensity of relations between firms and firms and institutions. The description partly overlaps with Porter's concept of industrial clusters.
- "Geographical" and "industry" clusters have sometimes been intended as spatial agglomerations with little inter-firm linkages, little direct cooperation, and little dedication of local institutions. For example, Hardy *et al.* (1999) conclude their comparative study of the organization of opto-electronics in six regions saying that " proximity without intimacy or interaction seems to be the most common circumstance" (with some exceptions) and that "local ties appear more focused on sharing public infrastructure goods, such as a skilled labor force pool of human capital" and localized institutional resources such as universities.

Despite the increased focus on the subject in the last years, neither economists nor economic geographers have managed to produce a commonly agreed definition of districts and clusters. The theoretical fragmentation in the field has got to the point of even leading some researchers to question the very utility of the district concept (Martin and Sunley 2003).

A classification of these territorial networks according to the organizational concepts of type of specialization and modes of coordination (Grandori 1997) should be useful to reduce the proliferation of concepts in a perspective that can be used by entrepreneurial firms belonging to or wishing to enter those systems, and to public institutions interested in fostering or even designing them. A very general organizational principle, applicable to systems at different levels (firms, networks, industries) is in fact that the development and deployment of innovation potential is generally sustained by organizational arrangements allowing and sustaining high differentiation and high integration. Hence, as to specialization, an important dimension is the degree of *similarity* versus *differentiation* of competences and institutional entities populating the cluster. As to coordination, both its *intensity and shape (vertical or horizontal, partial or all-to-all)* is relevant. On that basis three salient ways of organizing environments for entrepreneurship are identified and discussed.

This classification is robust enough for being applicable to make sense of the array of local clusters that history has produced in an emergent and path-dependent way, as well as of the array of territorial systems that have been deliberately designed and implemented by private and public institutions (e.g. "poles", "parks", "incubators", "regional systems", etc.). This further distinction between "spontaneous and historically formed" local systems versus "designed and institutional" local systems is also useful in order to sustain entrepreneurship and innovation. In fact, in conditions where history does not help, intervention by public and private organizations to deliberately set up "innovative milieus" through institutionalized networks – such as industrial parks, technological poles and scientific parks – is a viable alternative to sustaining the creation of innovative new firms.

Section 6.2 is devoted to spontaneous/historically formed districts, while designed and institutional innovative milieus are illustrated in Section 6.3, according to the conceptual scheme represented in Table 6.1.

Table 6.1 Forms of organized environment for entrepreneurship

Resource pooling loosely connected networks	*Differentiated and integrated networks*	*Innovation communities*

Similar entrepreneurial firms Resources pooling Low direct inter-firm coordination Mono-industry		Differentiated entities (small and large firms, universities, financial investors, public agencies)
Examples:		Tight interconnections Reciprocal and intensive interdependences
EMERGENT: Industrial districts and filières	Differentiated entities (small and large firms, universities, public agencies)	*Examples:*
DESIGNED: Industrial parks and incubators	Coordination through integration roles Stable patterns of transactions and coordination	EMERGENT: Industrial communities (e.g. Silicon Valley)
	Examples:	DESIGNED: Innovative milieus and regional innovation systems (e.g. Sophia Antipolis)
	EMERGENT: Hub and spokes ID, constellations	
	DESIGNED: Science parks, technopoles	

○○ Local SMEs ○ Large firms ▢ Institutions (university, R&D, finance)

6.2 Variety and evolution of territorial entrepreneurial networks

History, organizationally classified, has produced at least the following three main configurations of local networks with special interest for entrepreneurship:

1 *The "Industrial District"* (Marshall 1890; Becattini 1979). The classic district is a *set of similar firms:* proximity and similarity allow such firms to constitute and use a common *pool* of resources concentrated in the area. *ID can vary in terms of intensity of direct communication/coordination*, but typically their longevity and internal homogeneity facilitates coordination by routinized know-how, accepted norms of behavior and shared values (Brusco 1982, 1999).
2 *The "Industrial Cluster"*. A *differentiated and integrated network of firms* (Lorenzoni and Ornati 1988; Markusen 1996; Lipparini and Lomi 1999; Grandori 1997) is connected *according to a stable division of labor*. Interdependence is complicated by information complexity and resource specificity, which necessitates dedicated coordination mechanisms, such as firms playing integration and liaison roles.
3 *The "Industrial Community"*. A *network of highly differentiated entities –* public and private, based on a variety of different resources (technical, financial, human, etc.) and missions – is *fully connected* (Saxenian 1990, 1994) by intense processes of information exchange in a flexible ad hoc fashion, according to projects.

Industrial districts

In 1890, Alfred Marshall, in a chapter entitled "The concentration of specialized industries in particular localities" of his *Principles of Economics*, offered the founding analysis of the reasons why similar firms might co-locate. Marshall exposed that the advantages of production on a large scale can also be attained by the aggregation of a large number of establishments in one district because: "In districts in which manufactures have long been domiciled, a habit of responsibility, of carefulness and promptitude in handling expensive machinery and material becomes the common property of all ... The mysteries of industry become no mysteries; but are as if were in the air, and children learn many of them unconsciously" (Marshall 1890).

Marshall emphasized three traits of an industrial district, also referred to as *Marshallian externalities*: (1) the presence of a local competent labor market, capable of loyalty and able to work in a flexible regime; (2) a local pool of production specialization, generally in one industry; and (3) knowledge spillovers, meaning transfers and exchanges of tacit and explicit knowledge. A district is therefore characterized by spontaneous emergence; it is composed of similar firms; and can perform with weak links of direct communication and coordination. The exchanges are based on tangible assets and transactions. It is a distributed network showing many links (everybody is connected to everybody) and no centrality.

According to Krugman (1991), important ideas were derived from the works of Marshall, and many of the existing theories of cluster innovative activities focus on externalities and agglomeration economies. Marshall saw the essential source of external economies in the "commons" – the pool of infrastructures, services and know-how that each individual firm in the district may draw from. Economies of labor pooling evolve with agglomeration as firms benefit from labor with particular knowledge and skills and local economies operate more efficiently because knowledge is shared among firms at a low cost through informal exchanges – with or without overt communication (as if "knowledge was in the air"). Literature defines a local external effect as "anything that raises the return of particular firms located in the region as a result of the location of other firms in the same region" (Bresnahan *et al.* 2001). In the last decades, such "pooled" infrastructures were considered an important part of the complex private and public arrangements that are said to be responsible for the vibrant economic growth of some regions.

Box 6.1 Apt, world capital of crystallized fruit

Preserving by means of crystallization appeared in Provence in the High Middle Ages. In those days the fruit was candied in honey, until sugar was introduced during the Crusades, permitting the technique to be improved. As long ago as 1365, the people of Apt made gifts of the crystallized fruit of Apt to Pope Urban V, who was on pilgrimage in their town. In the nineteenth century, an Englishman, Mathew Wood, discovered this Apt specialty and promoted it on the British market. The local specialty became an industry, and the great confectioners appeared: Jaumard, Rambaud, Marliagues, then Barrielle, Bardouin, Reboulin, Piton, Gay, Vial, Blanc, etc., a total of 12 SMEs. The orders for different types of crystallized fruit increased, all the families participated in the production, and the city became the "world capital" of crystallized fruit. The family-owned small firms used the local market for fresh fruit, they changed the production system from traditional to industrial, and sent thousands of tons of crystallized fruit all over the world. In the 1960s, the whole city of Apt was a giant "cauldron". As time went by, the SMEs felt old-fashioned in their old laboratories; they needed changes to face globalization and crises. Under the impetus of some of these firms and a local consultant company, they all merged into a big group of companies with a common brand "Aptunion" and one big production unit outside of the city with 1,000 employees. The family-owned SMEs usually cooperated – in their associations and through informal exchanges of information and orders – but they were not prepared to lose their autonomy. Disagreements grew as the group was managed as a small firm without improvements or real innovation. The industry received strong institutional support through programs to keep the development of the crystallized fruit industry on course in the Apt region. But in 1976, to avoid bankruptcy, Aptunion was sold to an international group that since then has used the premises to produce various food additives. The production of crystallized fruit now subsists in some very small local laboratories and the tools and objects of the old industry are shown in commemoration in the local industry city museum.

Source: adapted from Gaillard (1996)

The Apt case illustrates the characteristics of the "traditional industrial district" and some of its potential deficiencies as well. The emergence of this type of district is largely due to location-driven factors such as local resources, ancient artisanship tradition, access to transportation infrastructure, or proximity to an important customer base drawing companies to the location. The district is typically composed of small, locally owned firms. Low technological complexity and relatively stable product characteristics eliminate the need for high levels of cooperation between firms. Repeated social interactions that revolve around shared learning, and collaborative activities, create social capital that can enhance cooperation among economic actors and increase the performance of a region. Once a threshold number of firms accumulate in the region, the district growth becomes self-reinforcing, and continues until the emergence of agglomeration diseconomies.

Apt – representing an extremely cohesive cluster – was prone to problems of lock-in due to inadequate attention to external shifts and changes or threats from the market. There was an excess of redundant strong links. The district was specialized in traditional sectors and the exploitation of new technologies was rather weak.

The traditional ID is often cut off from external sources of technologies. There is limited knowledge of new global technical languages and new industrial organization. The entrepreneurial culture is significantly influenced by the importance given to independence. The initial strengths and characteristics of the ID of the past have sometimes turned into obstacles to innovate. The regional development became locked in by the very same social conditions that drove the economic success of these regions. Uzzi (1996) argues:

Organizational networks operate in an embedded logic of exchange that promotes economic performance through inter-firm resource pooling, cooperation, and coordinated adaptation but that can also derail performance by sealing off firms in the network from new information or opportunities that exist outside the network ... such that performance reaches a threshold as embeddedness in a network increases. After that point, the positive effect of embeddedness reverses itself.

These dynamics can produce a *"regional specialization trap"* (Grabher 1993), characterized by a highly developed and specialized infrastructure ("functional lock-in"), close inter-firm linkages and long-standing personal ties resulting in social processes such as group-think ("cognitive lock-in"), and strong institutional reinforcement either directly or through the physical infrastructure – such as the program to keep the development of the coal, iron and steel industry on course in the Ruhr region – thus blocking the settlement of new industries, even if the course was bound to be a dead-end ("political lock-in"). In the Ruhr example, these different forms of lock-in in the coal, iron and steel complex prevented an appropriate and timely reorganization of the region in the 1970s and paralyzed political innovation. However, Grabher's lock-in concept is important as an explanatory concept not only for classic old industrial areas, such as the Ruhr area, but also for the decline of a large variety of differently structured industrial areas.

Akron, Ohio was once the "rubber tire capital of the world". This case is often referred to by the Nobel laureate Paul Krugman, whose father used to work in the rubber plants (Krugman 2008). During its heyday, Akron included many of the world's leading tire companies such as Goodyear and Firestone. In the 1970s and 1980s, the Akron rubber industry experienced a major decline. Today, Akron is the proud home of the World of Rubber Museum.

In the 1970s, northeast and central Italy (Third Italy) demonstrated rapid growth that attracted the attention of social scientists. In a number of sectors where small firms predominated, groups of firms, clustered together in specific regions, seemed to be able to grow rapidly, develop niches in export markets and offer new employment opportunities. In traditional industries, such as shoes, leather accessories, knitwear, furniture, tiles, musical instruments and food, clusters of SMEs were able to expand production and exports in the 1970s and 1980s at a time when large enterprises in Europe were in decline. The apparent vitality of SME clusters in Italy led to considerable interest in the bases of their success. The concept of "industrial districts" was used to capture the success of agglomerations of small firms: scholars started out with a Marshallian legacy, but then enriched it by observing that *the industrial district is a socio-cultural as well as an economic entity* (Brusco 1982; Lorenz 1992). The main attributes of industrial districts that emerged from research were first of all the geographical proximity of SMEs, sectoral specialization, and the predominance of small and medium-sized firms. IDs were characterized by loose inter-firm collaboration, inter-firm competition based on innovation, active self-help organizations, and supportive regional and municipal governments. The key feature was a socio-cultural identity that facilitated trust and interactions. Becattini defined IDs as "a socio-territorial entity that is characterized by the interactive presence of a community of people and a population of firms in a both historically and naturally bounded area" (Becattini 1990).

A further enrichment of the notion of industrial districts came from the observation that they are *not necessarily composed of identical firms*, even when they are mono-industry clusters. They can be composed of *different firms in a value chain*. An example is the case of Prato, emblematic of the subtype of industrial districts also called "*filiére*" (Johnston and Lawrence 1991; Perrier-Cornet and Sylvander 2000).

Box 6.2 Prato

From the minutes of the trial of Lapo Piccini, textile entrepreneur of Prato, sued for disturbing the peace on Christmas day because textiles needed to be shipped to America by the end of the year.

H. Judge: Please tell us your version of the story.

Piccini: Since I was 15 I have worked in the textile industry. My father was a textile worker and at 13, I already knew everything about textiles. I started working on a loom when I was 15, as an apprentice. I worked hard and I could double my monthly pay by working overtime. This is the only way to start a business on your own: no holidays, 12 hours of work a day, and close relationships with others (workers, clients, owners of other factories who subcontract work to you and lend you machinery).

Time went by and the use of the word "fashion" meant that we needed to change everything every three to four months. We were in the 1970s and the whole city of Prato was like a giant loom: the only way to keep up with orders was to contract them out, even to families who had looms in their living rooms or cellars. Finally, if you were good enough you could go out on your own. I was pretty good: at 35 I already had two looms in my house and I was working them with my wife. At age 40 I built my own small factory based on all the experience I had gained over the years and confident that my old boss, happy that I had left to set up a business on my own, would send along extra work. From that point on, I started to hire some workers – all of whom I knew personally, so that I could work with them the same way my boss used to work with me: to plan the product together, reset machines together, produce by working as hard as possible, and trying to acquire more orders than the competition.

It's almost as if we gave up part of the salary today in order to have it tomorrow – increased and in the form of profits. And independence. You know, all of us from Prato have always had this dream about independence.

Source: Angelo Fanelli, Bocconi University 1995 (translation)

The Italian textile industry is known worldwide for its high fragmentation, its organization in industrial districts, and the prevalence of small and medium firms, vertically specialized in one or a few phases of a supply chain. For example, in Prato, and in other districts such as Como (silk district), the "impannatori", in a tradition inherited from the Middle Ages, where brokers liaised with the final market and coordinated subcontracting activities (they designed the products, bought the raw materials, and distributed various phases of the production process among small, specialized producers) – and rag-collectors (stracciaroli), spinners, warpers, weavers, dyers, finishers, etc. Moreover, they also coordinated all logistics and dealt with customers, both national and international (Lorenzoni 1990).

The analysis of the Italian experience indicates that the development of a cluster of SMEs is a long-term process. The division of the production between many subcontractors and component suppliers allows firms to be highly specialized in complementary phases of production. The presence of many final firms helps avoid excessive concentration and hierarchy. SME clusters are, however, also characterized by dynamic competitiveness, linked to the accumulation of technical know-how.

In the past, Italian textile firms have prospered in these "protected", semi-closed environments (Camuffo *et al.* 2009). Social embeddedness and geographical proximity facilitated the development of relational self-enforced contracts among them, fostering knowledge diffusion and mutual learning among buyers, suppliers and even competitors. Due to globalization and digital technologies, these characteristics have tended to turn into structural weaknesses.

In other old industrial areas, however, political initiatives and institutional renewal have led to the successful promotion of new industrial activities and thus to restructuring (Cooke 1996). Hassink (2005) argues that regional economic path-dependency can be unlocked by applying some principles qualified as "learning region strategies": carefully identifying resources in the region that could impede economic development (lock-ins); responding positively to changes from outside, particularly where this involves "unlearning'; developing coordination mechanisms across both departmental and governance (regional, national, supra-national) responsibilities; encouraging openness to external impetuses; and fostering redundancy and variety (Hassink 2005).

Industrial clusters

The crisis that touched many industrial districts in the 1980s has led to a new stage of reflection. Traditional districts had to overcome the fierce competition between subcontractors specializing in the same products or phases of production. This has favored, in successful experiences, a growth in the differentiation among local firms.

Some districts, in addition, have always been different from the traditional Marshallian model, due to a more complex nature of activities. Industries such as furniture, wine-making, or textiles are characterized by relatively simple technologies where individual firms may possess most or all the knowledge and capabilities needed in production, and thus have little need for inter-firm coordination. By contrast, industries based on more complex technologies – for example, the bio-medical or optic fiber – typically induce firms to specialize and coordinate more. In such industries, the product system is often broken down into more manageable components, permitting firms to specialize in a narrower range of activities. As a result, in some districts firms are not "clones" but hold differentiated competences and/or master different stages of a production process. This in turn requires more systematic inter-firm coordination.

Let us illustrate the two cases of the emergence of more complex, differentiated and integrated districts: due to the change and opening up of traditional districts; and due to more complex technologies.

In contrast to the traditional view of clusters as self-contained systems and the almost exclusive focus on local interactive learning, a new strand of literature links local cluster theories with global value chain theories (Loebis and Schmitz 2005). The connections of local help with external sources of knowledge – especially transnational corporations (TNCs) – explaining the better access to global markets of certain clusters (Archibugi and Pietrobelli 2003; Giuliani and Bell 2005; Humphrey and Schmitz 2002; Pietrobelli and Rabellotti 2004). In order for small regional systems to have access to (extra-cluster) knowledge, they needed to create the conditions for the existence of intermediate agents (*technological gatekeepers,* Gambardella 1993), which connected extra-cluster knowledge and knowledge accumulated by local firms. Technological gatekeepers are conceived of as firms or agents that channel extra-cluster knowledge into the local, intra-cluster knowledge system. Alternatively, it may be that the final stage firm is in a gatekeeper position: in this case, the last stage *boundary-spanning entrepreneur* links the production filière to the markets; as in the traditional textile districts, or in the modern and international versions described in Box 6.3, where the gatekeeper and assembler is an international enterprise and (one of) the "districts" it connects to markets is "off-shored" in Indonesia.

Box 6.3 The Jepara furniture cluster (Java, Indonesia)

The industrial district of Jepara, Indonesia is specialized in furniture production. The Jepara cluster emerged in the sixteenth century, grew in the mid-1980s, reached a maturity stage in 1999 to 2000, but tended to decline afterward. The ancient carving industry attracted many related economic activities linked to furniture making. This concentration of industrial activity stimulated a substantial economic boom in Jepara and the surrounding areas and attracted local political support. In addition to serving the huge domestic market in Indonesia, Jepara is well connected to foreign markets and thereby acts as a bridge between local people, forests and global markets. The production organization is characterized by (1) a prevalence of small and very small units in various steps of the production. A total of 15,271 production units have been identified, employing approximately 170,000 workers in Jepara (there are at least 14,091 small and very small units, run by a single extended family; 871 medium units; and 309 large units). Small firms participate in networks that share workers, equipment and market channels. (2) Multi-layer subcontracting among highly specialized production units. These networks of SMEs are usually linked to a large firm or trader that acts as a broker between the group of SMEs and large international buyers. Work is not only outsourced by LMEs, but also by SEs. Enterprises that receive a job contract typically re-subcontract to another enterprise.

Traditionally SMEs in the cluster have focused on the domestic market, where quality standards were low and requirements in terms of design often did not suit the tastes of the international customer. The situation changed in the mid-1980s, when the government sponsored the participation of Java furniture producers in an international fair in Bali that evoked the interest of international buyers in the local production. Since then, the cluster has been dominated by large international buyers (IKEA is one of these).

Many firms in the cluster do not have direct access to customers. Large firms in the cluster benefit from information and knowledge received from the international buyers, with whom they relate directly. SMEs, on the other hand, do not usually have direct access to the international buyer but through traders and brokers that connect many small firms with international buyers. The brokers became the main customers of the small-scale producers and took more than 50 percent of their product. Brokers can easily shift from one producer to another.

Source: Roda *et al.* (2007); Andadari (2008); Berry *et al.* (2002)

In general, vertical interdependence typically gives some firms greater centrality in the network (Brusoni 2001), and that in turn favors the formation of a hierarchical organization.

The asymmetries among clustered enterprises were noticed early on, in both mature and emerging industries (Lorenzoni and Ornati 1988; Shepherd 1991). These works emphasized the frequent presence of "leading firms" – defined as those firms occupying strategically central positions in the ID thanks to the great number of relationships they have with both customers and suppliers – and the "constellation" surrounding them. The "constellation" can thus be seen as a particular type of network, characterized by the presence of a "central star" able to coordinate a series of entrepreneurs who work together with it. Lorenzoni and Ornati show that what they call the "external-growth model" and the reliance upon external organizations was the condition of survival and growth of small firms in districts such as Prato. These "stars" or "hubs" are often relatively large leading firms that establish a form of hierarchy (Lorenzoni and Baden-Fuller 1995). In these cases, following Marshall, the districts can still be seen as an "equivalent" of a large firm made up of a cluster of independent entrepreneurs, but scale is not achieved by simply multiplying units. The units typically perform different tasks and are deliberately coordinated by one or more central firms, giving rise to a *"hub and spoke" configuration* (Markusen 1996).

In industries with more complex technologies, hubs are likely to be multiple. For example, Lipparini and Lomi (1999) describe how in the Modena bio-medical "valley" different firms coordinate different types of transactions; for example, for materials and supply, for research, for distribution. Those "hubs" are likely to be embedded in long-distance relationships with branch plants, suppliers, customers, as well as competitors outside of the region, as described in the case of the "Etna Valley" in micro-electronics (Box 6.4).

Box 6.4 The Etna Valley

The seed for the development of Etna Valley was laid down in 1997 when ST Microelectronics, a multinational microchip producer, decided to start an advanced research center in collaboration with Catania University. The company had been present in the area since 1962 and had a long-standing collaboration with the University of Catania. Pasquale Pistorio, Sicilian by birth, after a long experience in the USA, took over as manager of ST Microelectronics. He was very tenacious in his desire to give a new opportunity to his land, Sicily.

ST Microelectronics has over 4,600 employees working in Catania. The main site extends over 140,000m^2 and houses "M5", one of the world's most advanced production centers for Memory products. What has influenced the development of STM in Sicily is the presence of a highly qualified workforce and strong cost advantages in hiring highly specialized workers (a Sicilian engineer costs around 40 percent of a similar specialist in the USA). The region offers a wide availability of trained workers: around 18,000 students and 1,700 university graduates in Sicily every year in ICT related subjects, almost half of these in the Catania area. Furthermore, as a European Union Objective 1 area, Sicily has maximum access to EU financial backing.

There are 200 national SMEs, 23 multinational R&D companies (Nokia, Canon, IBM, Alcatel, Vodafone, Selenia Communication) and 1,000 local micro firms now concentrated in the region of Catania, just down the slopes from the Etna Volcano, which has given the agglomeration the name of Etna Valley. The hi-tech activities developed around those giants are producers of chips and semi-conductors, micro- and nano-technologies, robotic, automation, advanced technological material, wireless communication devices.

Source: www.etnavalley.com

In sum, the organizational configuration of industrial clusters is characterized by the agglomeration in a territory or region of a large number of small firms, highly specialized, in evolution (new firms and actors continuously enter the cluster); production is divided along suppliers–customers "filières" or producers of complementary products, and the various agents are typically aggregated and coordinated by some key firms or "hubs". Sometimes the "hubs" are not local, and the local production system is "off-shore" (Ernst 2008; Ravi and Singh 2005) with respect to the coordinating/gatekeeper firms.

This model is complex, but it has still been demonstrated that it faces limitations in the kind and intensity of innovation it can produce and regulate. This observation and argument has been, for example, substantiated by the comparison between Route 128 and Silicon Valley. The development of electronics-related companies on the 65-mile highway surrounding Boston and Cambridge was influenced by academia, industry and government. The Massachusetts Institute of Technology is engaged in world-class scientific research and has produced some of the best engineers in the country. Organizations ranging from the National Science Foundation (NSF) to the National Aeronautics and Space Administration (NASA) to the Department of Energy (DoE) provided universities and firms with millions of dollars for research. Whole new industries have sprung up from these efforts: computer, biotechnology and artificial intelligence among others. By 1990, the state contained over 3,000 high-technology firms. Some companies stand as the pillars of the "Route 128" community: Digital Equipment Corporation, Raytheon and Lotus Development. The core technologies and industries in Route 128 and Silicon Valley are the same (computer and semiconductors) but have very different development paths and network structures. In her book *Regional Advantage: Culture and Competition in Silicon Valley and Route 128*, Saxenian (1994) proposes a hypothesis to explain why California's Silicon Valley was able to keep up with the fast pace of technological progress during the 1980s, while Route 128 fell behind. In Route 128, structures are hierarchical with a few large firms dominating smaller companies. As a consequence, engineers identify with internal labor markets; technology that enjoys economies of scale tends to generate large firms. To the contrary, in Silicon Valley the network is decentralized and flat. Identification proceeds along professional competences in projects and there is very high labor mobility. Saxenian emphasizes that the key was Silicon Valley's decentralized organizational form, non-proprietary standards, and tradition of cooperative exchange (sharing information and outsourcing for component parts), in opposition to the hierarchical and independent industrial systems on the East Coast. The following section is dedicated to that "communitarian" version of territorially concentrated (but no longer "local") clusters of entities (and not only firms).

Industrial communities

Agglomeration per se is not enough to ensure growth capability to local production systems: the industrial district evolutionary processes clearly show that the hidden mechanisms of district growth are not rooted in the "neutral aggregative forces or positive externalities related to the co-localization of firms specialized in the same activity" (Gargiulo and Benassi 2000). Industrial cluster growth entails a level of dynamism and amount and quality of linkages between cluster actors, and external linkages to international markets that evolve through innovations that can lead the system as a whole to regenerate itself.

The emergence of new technologies has had implications in all regions. While these technologies contribute to a large extent to disorganizing the existing territorial production systems, they also act as levers for reconstituting and transforming them (Cooke 1996). An innovative cluster is therefore characterized by its capability to generate and develop breakthrough innovations that create new industrial domains and to *radically redesign* its industrial value chain. The competitive advantage of an innovative cluster is based on its capability to nurture the founding of start-ups developing breakthrough technologies that underpin new industrial sectors rather than incremental innovations that improve established competitiveness in a specific industrial sector (Ferrary and Granovetter 2009). Innovative clusters are local agglomerations but they are not characterized by one specific industry, or by one type of player (firms), or by "local" and only internal relationships.

Saxenian (1999) completes the definition and speaks of "informal self-reinforcing coordination through dense networks of social and professional relationships". In her studies of the Silicon Valley and Boston Route 118, she emphasizes the key characteristics of an innovative cluster: a high level of research capability and abundance of highly qualified manpower are fundamental. Infrastructures and the proverbial "open-mindedness" of California is important too. But other players also provide fundamental inputs: research institutes, universities, enterprises in a wide range of related industries, financial capital providers of the proper kind (venture capital and financial angels).

The fully differentiated and fully integrated network structure of Silicon Valley is generally considered to lie at the heart of the superior innovation capacity of this region. Silicon Valley represents a good example of a cluster where firms, operating on the technological frontier, have strong knowledge bases. The local knowledge system is dense but firms tend to have *a high degree of external openness*. In this respect, since Silicon Valley is a place where knowledge is primarily created, extra-cluster knowledge linkages are more likely to flow outward than inward: "expanding in distant locations, Silicon Valley firms simultaneously enhanced the capabilities of these independent, but linked, regional economies" (Saxenian 1994). Silicon Valley is therefore a good example of a high-performing cluster with high "absorptive capacity"; that is, high ability to recognize the value of new, external information, assimilate it, and apply it to commercial ends (Cohen and Levinthal 1990). Box 6.5 provides a further illustration of this international benchmark of innovative clusters.

Box 6.5 Silicon Valley

The beginnings
Silicon Valley, an area located on the San Francisco peninsula, radiated outward from Stanford University. "Putting this university here in the middle of nowhere was itself an enormous entrepreneurial act by a gentleman, Leland Stanford, who made his money in railroads and was himself an entrepreneur," says Paul Saffo, a Stanford graduate, now a professor at the university (BBC News, 2010). In the 1930s, Professor

Frederick Terman was recruited by Stanford University and started a lifelong promotion of the benefits of the Valley. Later, Terman became known as the father of Silicon Valley. In 1937, encouraged by Terman, William Hewlett and David Packard started a company to produce their audio-oscillator. After World War II, Fred Terman, then Dean of the University, rented out part of the university land to deal with financial problems. In 1951, the Stanford Industrial Park was established as a "center of high technology close to a cooperative university". Varian Associates, General Electric and Eastman Kodak quickly signed leases. It was a stroke of genius, and Terman, calling it "our secret weapon", quickly suggested that leases be limited to high-technology companies that might be beneficial to Stanford. In 1957, Fairchild developed the semiconductor. And in 1971, Intel produced the first microprocessor 4004 chip. The 1970s were years of rapid growth, technological vitality and entrepreneurial culture. Many semiconductor companies, computer firms using their devices and programming and service companies serving both, grew in the Valley. The term "Silicon Valley" was coined in 1971 by Don C. Hoefler (journalist), as a "congerie of electronic firms mushrooming in Santa Clara county". The industrial space was plentiful, and at that time housing was still inexpensive. Growth was fueled by the emergence of the venture capital industry – notably, Kleiner, Perkins & Byers created by Kleiner, ex-Fairchild Semiconductor, in 1972. In 1976 the first personal computer, Apple 1, was introduced by Apple Computer.

Silicon Valley resurgence(s)
The 1980s witnessed the overcapacity and declining profits of leading semiconductor producers, also due to Japanese competition. "Despite this battering, more than 85 semiconductor firms were started in the 80s" (Saxenian 1990). Firms in computer systems and related businesses were also flourishing. In 1980, Apple went public. The Apple IPO was followed by an explosion of venture capital availability. The semiconductor start-ups were small firms created by engineers who quit their jobs in the big semiconductor firms to create their own businesses, pioneering a new approach to production, flexible manufacturing, mini-fab, etc. The newcomers focused on high-performance, high-value-added components, product design, quality and service, and not only on low cost. This is an example of the ability to restructure when conditions change through rapid and frequent reshuffling of organizational and institutional boundaries. This occurred in SV thanks to an exceptionally high rate of inter-firm mobility, and the capacity of building on informal networks. Venture capitalists are central to these networks (coming from successful local networks). After the computer revolution in the 1980s, the internet revolution in the 1990s and the tech bursts, a common response to "How is the Valley?" in 2000

was "In a nuclear winter". The dotcom crisis had incinerated an entire generation of start-ups. But some of the most innovative ideas for the Web emerged from the Bay Area right in the middle of the crisis. For example, in February 1999 Marc Benioff founded Saleforce.com to move business applications to the internet, pioneering "cloud" computing. Except for a few headline stories, the new Silicon Valley start-up was very different from the exuberant start-ups of the 1990s. The term "ramen profitable" was coined by venture capitalist Paul Graham to refer to a start-up that makes enough money to pay the bills. Economic crises have always been good for conceiving completely new business sectors in Silicon Valley: in the 2000s an emerging theme was energy and recently cleantech.

In 2007, 175,100 tech workers were employed in computer design and related services, telecommunications companies, internet service providers and Web-search portals, data processing, hosting and related services, and computer and electronic product manufacturing. Total jobs in the Valley: 1,184,061 (The Silicon Valley Index).

Source: Hancock and Carson (2010); Castilla *et al.* (2000); Longhi (1999)

It has been said that "Silicon Valley is the only place on Earth not trying to figure how to become Silicon Valley" (Robert Metcalfe).[3] However, Silicon Valley is not immune to crisis and problems. Actually, industrial fragmentation – the very source of Silicon Valley's flexibility and dynamism – is also its greatest vulnerability. Venture capitalists, consulting firms, business organizations and universities are largely private and narrowly specialized. The local public sector is focused exclusively on providing the physical infrastructure for development. There are no vehicles for developing a regional response to shared challenges – shortage of engineers, external technological shifts. Entrepreneurs describe their successes in terms of individualism and entrepreneurship, and the traditional attitude toward public intervention is certainly not positive.

However, some "lack of coordination" started to be perceived and associations of various kinds have been developed in response (e.g. Semiconductors Industry Association, Sematech) as well as the role of government and of federal investments starting to be reconsidered, as illustrated in Box 6.6.

Box 6.6 Silicon Valley in 2010: the limits of spontaneous coordination

"2009 was a rough year. We learned the hard way that Silicon Valley is not immune to the larger forces at work in the global economic recession. Like other regions, we have lost tens of thousands of jobs, absorbed thousands of home foreclosures, and seen our incomes decline. Despite our many strengths – from talented people to world-class technology – we could not insulate ourselves from the larger economic downturn.

Silicon Valley's economic and innovation engine has cooled off (decline of the number of patents, total venture capital is down by 35.2 percent). We are no longer able to draw on the same level of foreign talent (critically – 60 percent of engineers coming from outside the US). Our traditional way of funding innovation – through locally raised venture capital and public offerings – can no longer be taken as a given. Major structural shifts are underway in the funding community, while at the same time the federal government has re-emerged as the major investor in innovation and basic research. But Silicon Valley is not attracting significant shares of federal funding, and has not for some time. California's budget crisis and the political dysfunction in Sacramento have direct and debilitating effects on our ability to prepare our workforce, provide crucial infrastructures."

Numbers 2010: Area: 1,854 square miles. Population: 2.9 million. Jobs: 1,322,634 (–5,8 percent), job losses are spanning the economy. At the moment the joke in Silicon Valley is: "What's the new status symbol in Silicon Valley?" Answer: "A job" (Paul Saffo, Technology forecaster, *BBC News*, August 2010).

Source: Hancock and Carson (2010); Castilla *et al.* (2000); Longhi (1999)

The Silicon Valley index reported in 2010 that there are indeed clear warning signs suggesting Silicon Valley has entered a new phase of uncertainty, and that its competitive standing is at risk: Silicon Valley, which relied on diversity and talent flow for many decades, no longer appears to be able to draw on the same level of foreign talent. The actions of the USA in the wake of 9/11, and the rise of other global regions, have made Silicon Valley less accessible and less attractive than it once was. Furthermore, since the fall of 2008, the region has been hit hard by employment losses. Major structural shifts are underway in the funding community, while at the same time the federal government has re-emerged as the major investor in innovation and basic research. The traditional way of funding innovation – through locally raised venture capital and public offerings – can no longer be taken as a given and Silicon Valley is not attracting significant shares of federal funding, and has not done so for some time. Silicon Valley experienced a substantial drop in venture capital investment in 2009, clearly vulnerable to global financial turbulence.

Historically, the federal government has played an important role in the emergence of Silicon Valley as a high-technology region, and throughout its development. Its most vital role has been to invest in research and development (R&D), and in the procurement of high-tech products and services. In addition to direct weapons procurement during the Cold War, Silicon Valley attracted funding through the Advanced Research Projects Agency (ARPA), resulting in the creation of the internet among other things. Current DARPA (Department of Defense) spending is investing in game-changing technologies that will support the needs of US troops such as compact fuel cells and mobile renewable energy systems. In 2007, ARPA-E was created to support the rapid development of clean energy technology. Not only is Silicon Valley not a major player in federal R&D funding – Silicon Valley receives just over 1 percent of federal procurement, well behind Washington DC (13 percent) – but they have also been losing ground to other regions since the early 1990s: the average annual growth rate for federal procurement is over 3.5 percent; regions such as Washington DC (7.2 percent) and Huntsville (4.5 percent) have attracted increasing levels of funding, while Silicon Valley's levels have declined.

Nevertheless, Silicon Valley continues to invent, invest and transform – laying the foundation for the next "rebound". Silicon Valley has continued to generate new companies and to attract existing companies. Between January 2007 and 2008, the region witnessed a net gain of approximately 9,500 establishments.

Silicon Valley is increasingly investing venture capital in international markets. This activity builds strong interpersonal connections among global regions, and facilitates an exchange of technical know-how and also of business practices. While total venture capital investments from Silicon Valley increased by almost 15 percent ($57 billion to $65.4 billion), over the past ten years foreign investments by Silicon Valley venture capital firms have more than tripled (4 percent to more than 12 percent of total venture capital from Silicon Valley) over that same period. Since 2000, China has been the preferred foreign market for Silicon Valley venture capital. Between 2006 and 2008, Chinese companies received more than $2.2 billion in venture capital from Silicon Valley investors.

But the question is: can venture creation be sparked to create other Silicon Valleys?

6.3 Institutional and designed innovative milieus

It's October 2009 and Johan P. Bång has just finished addressing 400 delegates at China's largest annual geographical information conference. He has just marketed the Swedish cluster Future Position X, and in doing so has brought a number of Swedish SMEs to the attention of a market which in principle they would never be able to enter as individual companies. "Being a cluster, we are able to present ourselves as one unit" says Johan P. Bång, who is the FPX Manager (and was awarded the title of Cluster Manager of the Year 2010). "As a company with 75 employees, you're a nobody in this context. As a cluster, we can state that we have 26,000 members and net sales of SEK 44 billion. Then we start to become interesting."

(Europa InterCluster 2010)

Motives of public support for innovative SMEs and "innovative milieu"

The cases analyzed so far (in Section 6.2) represent emerging, spontaneous, path-driven industrial networks that evolved through endogenous dynamics. They developed through agglomeration, growth and diversification in sectors, without any "designer" or "planner". Legal and political conditions supporting entrepreneurial behavior have played a role, but not to the point of designing and realizing a cluster. However, that is possible, and indeed "cluster policies" have become an increasingly popular governmental intervention. In the 1980s and 1990s, analyses of successful regions and nations drew attention to the fact that these success stories were home to networks of collaborative firms, from the same sector of activity, that created a "competitive advantage" through the construction of mixed complementary and competitive relations (Porter 1990). One element of these networks was that they built connections between firms and technological suppliers, and integrated technology transfer (TT) into innovation (Piore and Sabel 1984; Saxenian 1994). It was later observed that less successful regions could improve their economic performance with an institutional/policy solution borrowed from a more successful region (Hassink 1993; Lundvall and Johnson 1994). This has led to unprecedented efforts by policy makers.

Since 1990 and Porter's definition of a (business) "cluster" as a geographically proximate group of interconnected companies and associated *institutions* in a particular field, linked by commonalities and complementarities, this is the definition of a cluster generally used in the policies and strategies of public authorities – for example, "Cluster policies are pursued by public actors for the purpose of increasing socioeconomic benefits through the creation or further development of clusters" (Andersson *et al.* 2004). Types and contents of cluster policy vary considerably from country to country. "Cluster initiatives" are organized efforts to increase the growth and competitiveness of clusters within a region, involving cluster firms, government and/or the research community (Sölvell *et al.* 2003). And a "cluster organization" includes the office, the cluster manager, the services, etc. of a cluster initiative.

Decades later, clusters are not only a reality of economies across the world, but increasingly they are also an important policy lever on different geographic levels.

At the national level, the Europe INNOVA Cluster Mapping Project in the European Union identified and analyzed the cluster policies, institutions and programs of 31 European countries and found that all the countries surveyed have cluster policies on a national and/or regional level and have established institutions to implement these (Europe INNOVA 2008). Ireland has for a long time used the cluster approach to structure its economic policy initiatives; for example, in the area of foreign direct investments (FDI) attraction. Sweden has created specific institutions such as Vinnova that are charged with employing the cluster approach to regional growth policy. Clusters are also considered relevant for developing countries (Nadvi 1999), motivating significant policy initiatives within industrial development strategies (UNIDO 2000, 2001), or even to establish an enabling environment in post-conflict societies (Rwanda, Balkan, Columbia). Cluster-based policies are set up to assist firms in developing countries to move up in the value or commodity chain, as opposed to maintaining a position as dependent subcontractors (Pietrobelli and Rabelotti 2004). At the regional level, different types of cluster initiatives have been launched by local or regional government agencies trying to engage industry associations and individual companies in collective efforts (ceramic tiles in Catalonia, automotives in Styria, or textiles in Emilia-Romagna). Clusters are indeed considered a new paradigm for defining a new industrial policy based on the knowledge economy; and research also increasingly explores whether and how clustering can be intentionally supported (Fromhold-Eisebith and Eisebith 2005).

"Support" or "direction'? Approaches to cluster policies

Cluster policies acknowledge that firms are "embedded"/included in socio-economic contexts (Powell *et al.* 2005), that the economic sphere "is then not separable from other social spheres" (Johannisson and Mønsted 1997) and that, therefore, the target of policy measures for innovation should not be limited to the individual firms (Johannisson *et al.* 2002).

Cluster policies, however, face the dilemma of how to intervene without constraining, how to support and coordinate without putting firms "in a straightjacket, or in a nutshell" (Europa InterCluster 2010). It is commonly acknowledged that "entrepreneurship being a quirky thing, it can be foolish to make top-down or directive efforts" and that "clusters of innovative activity do not respond well to being directed, organized or jump-started", while nevertheless "accommodative government policies can be an important part of cluster development" (Breshahan *et al.* 2001).

Hence, even if "top-down" approaches are ruled out, there is still a lot of latitude, in particular between two intervention approaches, that have been called "support" and "direction".

"Support". Institutional support can be indirect: framework conditions can hinder innovation activities and better regulation is needed to spur innovation and economic growth. Intellectual property laws facilitate and encourage the pursuit of innovation and the disclosure of knowledge into the public domain for the common good. A good educational system and in particular higher education, is crucial for the supply of highly skilled workers, professionals and researchers. Extra-firm institutional supports play a critical role in strengthening and sustaining inter-firm dynamics within the cluster, community building and the integration of various instruments and interests. The joint actions of associations and institutions have an especially significant influence on the compliance of clusters with global standards. Evidence on cluster-wide institutional joint action was observed, for example, by Nadvi (1999), in the context of the Sialkot surgical instrument cluster in Pakistan. Compliance with global quality assurance standards, a necessary requirement of the Sialkot cluster to export to leading global markets, came through the catalytic role of the local trade association in channeling new know-how on quality management practices to the cluster. Through this process, Nadvi

found that the vast majority of SMEs in the cluster could comply with international standards over a relatively short period of time. Had the association not taken on this function, most small firms would have shut down given that the United States and the European Union accounted for over 90 percent of the cluster's sales.

Government support of innovation activities can also take the form of direct support: financial support for individual firms and innovation projects; tax reductions for R&D and innovation expenditures; subsidies for buildings/ infrastructure for innovation activities; and subsidies for acquiring machinery, equipment and software. It can also improve the visibility of the firms in the cluster – participating in trade fairs or trade missions; and provide information on market needs, conditions, new regulations, etc.

"*Direction*". As noted by Porter (1998), "the mere co-location of companies, suppliers, and institutions creates the potential for economic value; it does not necessarily ensure its realization". The actual creation or development of a designed cluster requires planning and monitoring the conditions that will make the emergence of the cluster possible, and "joint action is the cornerstone of any successful cluster" (Reid *et al.* 2007). Material infrastructure (transport, housing, community facilities, etc.) and cooperation tools (business incubators, innovation platforms, shared laboratories, etc.) are useful but not sufficient. In fact, the development and management of clusters initiatives typically involve the creation of a dedicated organizational structure: a project team or Cluster Steering Committee (CSC), a cluster advisory board, or Cluster Strategy Team (CST), and later defining the Cluster Organization (cluster manager, project-manager, etc.). The CSC is the key institution for coordination and cooperation between the government, the private sector and other stakeholders for the formulation and monitoring of strategies, policies and programs to promote and support the development of competitive and innovative industrial clusters. The CSC may be a formally designated ad hoc committee. The CST is the advisory and visioning group that is responsible for overseeing the cluster. Ideally, the CST should comprise representatives from industry, academia and the community (CLOE 2006).

There are key steps in forming a cluster, starting from the diagnostic phase (defining the core industry and the potential cluster region, inventory of the potential cluster members) and ending with concrete collaboration projects. The set-up process of a cluster initiative varies substantially according to the purpose it is to fulfill and the circumstances under which the companies involved are supposed to cooperate. For example, in early cluster life-cycle stages, or in earlier stages of economic development of a country, or during economic crises, the intensity of effective and called-for public "coordination" and "direction" (as opposed to mere "support') is typically higher.

The proliferation of institutional forms

The variety of possible types and levels of intervention, and the complexity of designing them according to all these relevant factors, have generated a problem of proliferation of interventions and entities. As it has been recently denounced, this may hinder rather than help entrepreneurship by creating a very confused organization of the environment. In fact, the large number of schemes means that businesses may be unclear about what is available to best meet their needs. In the UK a "Business Support Simplification Programme" (see Box 6.7) was actually set up to reduce the number of support schemes from 3,000 to 30!

Box 6.7 "Solution for Business": Business Support Simplification Programme (BSSP/UK)

In 2006, there were over 3,000 business support schemes available in England. Support was provided by many organizations including central government departments and their agencies, regional development agencies and local authorities. The large number of schemes meant that businesses could be unclear about what is available to best meet their needs. The Annual Small Business Survey carried out for the Department of Trade and Industry's (DTI) Small Business Service in 2005 showed that over half the businesses surveyed wanted government support but struggled to find out what was available.

In the 2006 budget, the chancellor of the exchequer challenged the entire public sector to simplify business support by reducing the number of schemes available. The aim was to make it easier for businesses to access support, use public money more efficiently by reducing the amount spent on administration, and ensure value for money by measuring the effect of business support on the economy and on public policy goals.

In response to this challenge the DTI Department for Business announced that the design and roll-out of "Solutions for Business" – its streamlined portfolio of business support products – had been completed *with over 3,000 schemes reduced to 30*. For the first time, all government help for business now shared an identifiable banner and could be accessed through Business Link. The aim of the "Business Support Simplification Programme" is in line with the multiple European Programs and Initiatives that contribute to the overall modernization of SMEs and cluster support services in Europe. It is to ensure that, wherever it is carried out, publicly funded business support is simple for businesses to access, and has a real impact on economic or public policy goals.

Sources: Department of Trade and Industry (2007) *Simplifying Business Support, An Introductory Document*, www.dti.gov.uk; PACEC (2005) *Mapping of Government Services for Small Business*; The Grants & Support Directory www.businesslink.gov.uk

When the European Cluster Observatory refers to 2,000 clusters currently existing in Europe, it should be clear that these clusters are not all "cast in the same mold". European cluster profiles are highly diversified, as their names are: they can be technopoles, business areas, science parks, education and research parks, incubators, platforms, etc.

The organizational dimensions used to clarify and assess the innovation potential of emerging industrial local systems of innovation are also useful to analyze the more formalized, institutional and designed local systems of innovation. In fact:

1   *Industrial parks and incubators* are designed to support the birth and growth of new firms in a given technology/industry; hence firms are based on similar competences and are loosely connected among them – they share premises and infrastructures, and are connected with (and tutored by) common institutions.
2   *Scientific parks and technological poles* are designed to support integration among differentiated players contributing to innovation (especially universities/research institutions and business players), formally connected according to a stable roles system and/or by common projects.
3   *Regional innovative systems and innovative milieus* can be characterized as highly differentiated and fully connected communities, free and enabled to employ all kinds of formal and informal mechanisms for flexible coordination and new firm/projects formation.

Industrial parks and incubators

An industrial park (IP), broadly defined, is a zoned area planned for the purpose of industrial development, more precisely: "a large tract of land, sub-divided, and developed for the use of several firms simultaneously, distinguished by its shareable infrastructure and close proximity of firms" (Peddle 1993). The common types and synonyms of IPs include industrial estate, industrial zone, export processing zone, business park, industrial estate and office park, and satellite platforms (among others). Organizationally speaking, then, they are "designed districts" oriented mainly to creating positive externalities and resource pooling economies, and ready-to-use social capital.

What is considered the first industrial park, Trafford Park, was established by a company called Shipcanal and Docks near Manchester in 1896. Industrial parks were established later in Germany, where the first industrial park was set up in 1963 (Euro-Industriepark München). A greater number of industrial parks and parks for small and medium-sized industrial companies emerged in the second half of the 1980s that were basically public investor initiatives. In fact, most formal IP development efforts are led by public agencies, non-governmental organizations and university teams rather than by businesses.

An example is given in Box 6.8. China's rapid economic growth has attracted the attention of foreign investors from all over the world and the flow of foreign investment into China has had much to do with the country's establishment of development zones.

Box 6.8 Industrial parks in China

Industrial parks were developed in China to avoid land waste and create industry clustering; these industrial parks have become major vehicles for attracting foreign direct investment (FDI) in China's manufacturing sector. These industrial parks promise a developed infrastructure, relatively efficient administration and, above all, attractive business terms.

However, the sheer size of China and the wide developmental gaps between different regions makes it a daunting task for prospective investors to decide where to go. Many foreign investors, before starting their initial research, are confused by the different types of industrial parks such as Special Economic Zones (SEZ), Economic and Technological Development Zones (ETDZ), High-tech Industrial Development Zones (HIDZ), Free Trade Zones (FTZ) and Export Processing Zones (EPZ).

The five Special Economic Zones (including Shenzhen and Zhuhai) were the first areas opened to foreign investors. The establishment of Economic and Technological Development Zones was inspired by the success of the SEZ. ETDZs have general functions. Currently, there are 54 state-level ETDZs – 29 in the Eastern Region and 25 in inland China under the supervision of the Ministry of Commerce. High-tech Industrial Development Zones are another major type of industrial park. In the late 1980s, the Ministry of Science and Technology initiated the "Torch Program". The main objective of this nation-wide innovation program was to utilize the technological capacity and resources of research institutes, universities, and large and medium-sized enterprises to develop new high-technology products, and accelerate the commercialization of innovations.

Source: www.export.gov/china/exporting_to_china/
developmentzones.pdf

As already apparent from Box 6.8, there are many, and variously named, variants of IP. Let us specify two salient and diffused forms, one more centered on a "support" logic and loose coupling, the other involving more "direction" and tighter coupling: satellite platforms and incubators.

Satellite platforms (SPs)

SPs usually indicate a territorial cluster created by the policies of national/local governments to attract foreign investment, and therefore typically made up of "a congregation of branch facilities of externally based multi-plant firms" (Markusen

1996). Key investment decisions are made outside of the district/park, and tenants of the SP must be able to more or less "stand alone", namely, to be spatially independent from upstream or downstream operations as well as from the agglomeration of other competitors and suppliers in the same area. There tends to be minimal collaboration among platform firms, often engaged in different activities and industries. SPs are characterized by a high rate of skilled labor in-migration, and the incidence of spin-off activities (entrepreneurship and suppliers) is relatively small. Firms in SPs enjoy moderate to high levels of economies of scale and have almost no linkages within the area.

The category covers very different territorial situations, from traditional to high-tech locations. Since the decision centers are external to the local system, rendering the situation unstable, SPs often represent a stage in the development of a cluster. With the right support and initiatives, local industrial capabilities and local innovation processes can be induced; local systems are sometimes able to move from their satellite platform configuration toward a high-technological cluster. This was the case, for example, in Sophia Antipolis (see Box 6.13 below). Sophia Antipolis started from a satellite platform built on very different activities, and moved toward a technopole (Longhi 1999). The Sophia Antipolis project took off based predominantly on the on-site location of external organizations that were attracted by the quality of the infrastructures made available to them.

Incubators

An even more important and characteristic form of designed organizational environments for entrepreneurship is the *incubator*. This form is still targeted to similar firms, specialized in a defined field/technology, but is much more elaborated in terms of coordination. A business incubator typically offers a shared office space, a facility that seeks to provide its "incubatees" (i.e. "portfolio-" or "client-" or "tenant-companies") with a strategic, value-adding monitoring and business assistance intervention system (i.e. business incubation). This system controls and links resources with the objective of facilitating the successful new venture development of the "incubatees", while simultaneously containing the cost of their potential failure (Hackett and Dilts 2004). An incubator, in addition to a shared-space office facility and infrastructure, also offers the benefits of a network of individuals and organizations including the incubator manager and staff, incubator advisory board, local universities and university community members, industry contacts and professional services providers such as lawyers, accountants, consultants, marketing specialists, venture capitalists, angel investors and volunteers.

It is generally accepted that the first incubator established was the Batavia Industrial Center in 1959 in Batavia, New York. In the 1960s and 1970s incubation programs diffused slowly and typically as government-sponsored responses to the need for urban/Midwestern economic revitalization. Up to now most incubators were publicly funded, and many private initiatives foundered after the 2000 technology burst.

Business incubation evolved in the last 30 years from the experiences of earlier industrial estates and small enterprise service centers. The "first generation" incubators in the 1980s essentially offered affordable space and shared facilities to carefully selected entrepreneurial groups. This led to the "second generation" incubators, more connected and innovation oriented.

A common feature is the provision of physical space and intangible support to new firms engaged in the development and commercialization of new products and services. In most cases there is a link with public or private research laboratories or research universities (OCDE 1997).

Incubators vary widely in their sponsors (state, economic development group, university, business, venture capital), objectives (from empowerment to technology commercialization), location (urban, suburban, rural and international), sectoral focus (technology and mixed) and business model (not-for-profit or for-profit). Thus a very colored terminology exists: from "pépinière d'entreprises" (green house nursery – France), to "ruche" (hive), "couveuse" (brooder – Belgium), "grappes", and "vivier" or nursery, etc. Incubators are also useful in serving remote locations in poor countries. Recent examples of incubation focused on small-town and rural environments are the agri-based Ruhuna Business Incubator in Matara in Sri Lanka and the tourism-based Luxor Incubator in Egypt. In Nepal, Lotus Holdings provides design, export marketing and other in-situ support to entrepreneurs producing carpets, handmade paper and pashmina products. In Mongolia, the New Path Incubation Center is a joint initiative resulting from the relationship between InfoCon, the Mongolia Development Gateway, and the Mongolian Academy of Sciences.

The late 1990s saw the appearance of new forms of incubator organizations to nurture and grow technology companies; they are referred to as "technology incubators" – networked incubators encourage collaborations and partnerships among members. In the new generation of incubators, the "accelerator" or post-start-up incubator appeared, designed to help young high-tech firms achieve high rates of growth.

Box 6.9 The National Alliance of Clean Energy Business Incubators, a National Renewable Energy Laboratory (NREL) Initiative

NREL is the US Department of Energy's (DOE) premier laboratory for the commercialization of renewable energy efficiency and distributed energy technologies. The National Alliance of Clean Energy Business Incubators is a NREL initiative to help emerging clean energy companies take more effective advantage of opportunities stimulated by the restructuring of the utility markets, sustainability concerns, and more stringent environmental regulations. Among the DOE National Labs, the NREL mission is uniquely focused on developing and facilitating deployment of renewable energy efficiency and other clean energy technologies; and this mission has remained essentially the same for the entire 22 years of NREL's existence.

NREL catalyzes strategic alliances among selected business incubators across the country to provide an array of business and financial services to start clean energy companies. Key features of the incubator alliance include: national scope and reach, leveraging existing investments (relationships and funding) in established incubators, access to a wide range of expertise/ advisors, and improved linkages to regional market development opportunities. The framework for the Alliance necessarily differs by region, reflecting differences in players and stakeholders, methods of operation and preferred working relationships, and opportunities for clean energy and economic development.

In Texas, where there is growing public-sector support for clean energy technologies and a world-class technology incubator, NREL and ATI – the Austin Technology Incubator – have formed a strategic alliance to assist Texas-based energy companies in making the difficult transition from a technology-focused start-up company to a successful market-based enterprise. Since 1989, ATI has graduated more than 50 companies, five of which have gone public. Cumulatively, these businesses have created nearly 2,000 jobs with revenues approaching $800 million.

Source: Lawrence M. Murphy, Julie Brokaw, Jane Pulaski,
Katie McCormack, Enterprise Development Programs,
August 2000 – NREL/BK-720-28724

Science parks and technological poles

These types of institutional clusters typically involve more established entities specialized in different phases of the innovation process: discovery and new knowledge production, application and industrialization, and marketing. Hence, those entities have identifiable and stable roles in the cluster, whose purpose is primarily to foster the relations among those different entities. While the definition of this cluster is rather clear, the terminology is heterogeneous: in the United States, "technology park", "research park" or "research and technology park" are frequently used, "science park" is popular in Britain and Europe and "technopole" is widely used in France to represent hierarchical governance systems. Numerous terms are often used interchangeably – in literature and by policy makers – with "science park" and "technology park": business park, cyber park, hi-tech park, industrial park, innovation center, R&D park, research park, research and technology park, science and technology park, science city, science park, technology incubator, technology park, technopark, technopole, and technopolis. Although they are very similar, two salient forms, one more centered on a "support" logic and loosely coupled, the other involving more "direction" and tighter coupling can be described: (1) science parks and (2) technological poles.

Science parks

Science parks are generally land-based, campus-like developments designed to accommodate technology-based firms, research institutes and appropriate support services. They are expected to provide an environment that is favorable to the "cross-fertilization" of technical and business ideas and supportive of the commercialization process. The environment is designed for research and development organizations, high-tech firms and support service providers, and is often linked with a university. In a scientific park there is more interdependence between the member organizations: knowledge and technology flows from universities and R&D institutions to companies and eventually to markets link entities in webs of sequential and reciprocal interdependence.

The first formal science park was established in the US at Stanford University (1951), but science park creation really took off in the 1980s. The objective was to support economic development and job creation, and to encourage the growth of knowledge-based industries in different sectors.

Science parks promote the economic development and competitiveness of regions and cities by creating new business opportunities and adding value to mature companies; they foster entrepreneurship, incubate new innovative companies and generate knowledge-based jobs. Their role is also to build attractive spaces for the emerging knowledge workers and to enhance the synergy between universities and companies. Public ownership, governments and public administrations at different levels (national, regional, local) are still the main engine behind science parks. In fact, 40 percent of science parks are owned exclusively by such public bodies (IASP, Statistics 2007).

A formal definition for science parks has been framed by the International Association of Science Parks (IASP):

> A Science Park is an organization managed by specialized professionals, whose main aim is to increase the wealth of its community by promoting the culture of innovation and the competitiveness of its associated businesses and knowledge-based institutions. To enable these goals to be met, a Science Park stimulates and manages the flow of knowledge and technology amongst universities, R&D institutions, companies and markets; it facilitates the creation and growth of innovation-based companies through incubation and spin-off processes; and provides other value-added services together with high quality space and facilities.
>
> (Official definition, IASP International Board, February 6, 2002)

The IASP is a worldwide network. Its definition embraces the different models that exist all over the world. An effort has been made to identify the main common denominators of the different models, as well as to set the minimum standards and requirements that any project must have in order to be acknowledged as a "Science Park". The University Research Park is a property-based venture that has a contractual and/or formal ownership or operational relationship with one or more universities or other higher education institutions, science research, and a role in promoting research and development by the university in partnership with industry (AURP, Association of University Research Parks, 2010).

Box 6.10 The Research Triangle Park

The Research Triangle Park was founded in January 1959 by a committee of government, university and business leaders as a model for research, innovation, and economic development. By establishing a place where educators, researchers and business come together as collaborative partners, the founders of the Park hoped to change the economic composition of the region and the state, thereby increasing the opportunities of North Carolina's citizens.

The "Triangle" after which RTP was named is formed by the geographic location of the region's three highly regarded educational, medical and research universities – the University of North Carolina at Chapel Hill, Duke University, and North Carolina State University. In addition, RTP draws on the intellectual capacity of a host of other community colleges and higher education institutes. Together, these institutes create knowledge assets and provide a steady supply of trained scientists, engineers, managers, and technicians to the region's workforce.

The vision was to provide a ready physical infrastructure that would attract research-oriented companies. The advantage of locating to RTP would be that companies could employ the highly educated local work force and be close to the research being conducted by the state's research universities.

Since it was established, the Park has witnessed a steady and stable increase in the number of companies and employees. Currently, there are more than 170 research and development-related organizations in RTP.

Source: The Research Triangle Park, http://www.rtp.org

Technological poles

Technological poles (or technopoles) are regionally based networks involving both public and private actors that focus on the development of technologies and industrial activities in one specific sector of high value-added industrial activity. Technological poles aim at redefining the businesses in which they compete (see, for example, the Torino Wireless Pole in Box 6.11), incorporating leading technological innovation and adding advanced services: technological, economic and juridical monitoring necessary for research, development, innovation and the collective expertise for research and development projects, as well as competitiveness reinforcement initiatives. Intensive interdependence on common activities is thereby generated. The pole should facilitate the coordination among the relevant private and public entities to the purpose.

Founded in 2002, the Torino Wireless Pole is an example of regional and national policy for innovation to grow new firms in existing networks and to foster integration among research, business and finance in one specific industry.

Box 6.11 Torino Wireless Pole

The Torino Wireless Foundation is the governance body of the Piedmont district (Italy) where both private and public players decided to co-invest in a shared and coordinated project for the knowledge-based development of the Piedmont Region. This has enabled Torino Wireless to act as a multiplier of the public investments and, with an endowment of €27 million from the government for the first five years, to attract an additional €117 million from both public and private investments.

From 2003 to 2008, the Torino Wireless Foundation helped 390 companies in their technological, managerial and commercial activities to grow and succeed in the market. All the services provided by the Foundation were activated together with public and private partners, which not only represent funding institutions but are also concretely involved in the promotion and development of the cluster.

The Torino Wireless Pole offers different services to companies: steering of the district's R&D priorities and actions; stimulating applied research to increase district competences, also supporting the mobility of highly skilled resources from R&D institutes to district companies and funding joint projects between businesses and R&D centers; coaching entrepreneurs to start new enterprises and supporting existing ones; organizing innovative financial instruments to support the development of enterprises in size and strength; setting vertical and horizontal networks among SMEs; generating new opportunities at international level with education, research and the attraction of talented people. These activities are carried out directly or in close cooperation with a number of partners in the region with specialized roles.

Source: http://www.torinowireless.it

Other poles are more focused on regional competitiveness in a given market, rather than on technology. A "pole of competitiveness" is, in a given field, the association of business companies, research centers and training institutes engaged in a collective approach (common development strategy) aimed at establishing synergies around innovation projects jointly undertaken in the direction of a given market. The "poles de compétitivité" (regional competitiveness clusters) initiative was launched in France in 2005 to raise the international profile of French industries and to promote *growth and job creation in high value-added industries,* anchoring these industries to a *regional context*. The French government accompanies cluster development at both local and national levels with the allocation of financial support for the best R&D and innovation platform initiatives via calls for projects; providing financial support for theme-based collective actions via the various Regional Directorates for Industry, Research and the Environment (DRIRE); by carrying out and publishing studies; by involving various partners, such as the Caisse des Dépôts, or the French National Research Agency (ANR) and OSEO, both of which finance R&D projects led by cluster stakeholders; by bringing new means from public research centers; and, finally, by seeking assistance from local authorities who can also provide financial support for cluster projects (R&D, innovation platforms) (http://competitivite.gouv.fr).

Regional innovation systems (RIS) and innovative milieus (IM)

"We need to be both innovative and resilient to succeed in a future where uncertainty will be the new normal. Without investment in our talent and technology base and supportive state and federal policies, we will not be able to take advantage of the strengths of our global connections. Above all, we need a shift in our mindset from one of complacency to one that recognizes the challenges that we face and mobilize to address them as a regional *community*."

This is the conclusion of the Silicon Valley Index report for 2010 (Hancock and Carson 2010). Even the representatives of the most acclaimed "Valley of entrepreneurship" recognize, at a certain point of their evolution, that they do need "supportive state and federal policies". "Ironically," writes Daniel J. Isemberg, "even Silicon Valley could not become itself today if it tried" (Isemberg 2010). Silicon Valley's "eco-system" evolved under a unique set of circumstances that defies the determination of cause and effect. Are there formulae or road maps for "creating" such "entrepreneurial regions" by design?

The experiences and concepts of regional innovation systems (RIS) and of innovation mileus provide a positive answer to the question. In fact, these are two variants of "designed communities": (1) in RIS, the public coordination role is emphasized, through formal regional innovation strategies and schemes; (2) in the IM, the mix of formal and informal coordination roles, mechanisms and networks (associations, ONG, clubs and cultural activities) is wider, and simulates more closely the historical forms of innovative industrial community.

Regional innovation systems

The notion of RIS has emerged as a territorially focused perspective of analysis derived from the broader concept of National Innovation Systems (NIS) (Freeman 1987; Lundvall 1992; Nelson 1993). The innovation systems approach later shifted from a solely national perspective to one including and emphasizing regional and local systems. A RIS may thus be defined as follows: "A regional innovation system consists of interacting knowledge generation and exploitation sub-systems linked to global, national and other regional systems for commercializing new knowledge" (Cooke 2004). The core idea is that the economic performance of a region depends on the way in which localized networks of actors and institutions, in the public and private sectors, interact to generate, import, modify and diffuse new technologies within and outside the region. Together these organizations constitute an infrastructure, which functions as a "system of innovation". A RIS can be considered a regional cluster of firms surrounded by a regional "supporting" institutional infrastructure. The firms and organizations are embedded in a specific region and characterized by localized, interactive learning. However, policy interventions lend these systems a more planned character through the *intentional* strengthening of the region's institutional infrastructure – for example, through a stronger, more developed role for regionally based R&D institutes, vocational training organizations, and other local organizations involved in firm innovation processes. The system model assumes that the knowledge generation inherent in innovation takes place in many more places than just the R&D laboratory. Further, the many different knowledge generation and use activities are linked to each other in a dense network of connections between activities, institutions and agents.

The concept of regional innovation systems emphasizes that innovations result from effective linkages between the knowledge generating, the knowledge transferring and the knowledge exploiting components of these systems (Braczyk *et al.* 1998; Cooke 2002; Etzkowitz and Klofsten 2005), as well as from virtuous interactions between political, industrial and academic institutions. Regional networks and localized knowledge spillovers may explain why knowledge diffusion is concentrated close to the locus of knowledge generation but also why innovation activity is found to be clustering in space (Feldman 1994; Audretsch and Feldman 1996; Oerlemans *et al.* 2001; Malmberg and Maskell 2002).[4]

The comparative analyses of different RIS has led to identify variants in which state intervention plays a more or less pronounced role.

An example of RIS stimulated by active regional innovation policy by the Japanese government is given in Box 6.12.

Box 6.12 RISs in Japan

In terms of the roles of industrial policy and science and technology policies in the context of regional development, the development of RISs in Japan has seen three separate phases: (1) "Catch-up" after World War II to 1980; (2) the mid-1990s; and (3) "Science-based local innovation" from 1995 to the present day, including local cluster initiatives. The Regional Industrial Policy of the central government, led mainly by the Ministry of Economy, Trade and Industry (METI), from the 1960s until the early 1990s was to promote regional development through the relocation of factories to non-urban regions from larger metropolitan areas. Since the late 1990s, the emphasis has shifted to revitalizing the industry in order to overcome the "hollowing out" of the manufacturing base caused by the shift of production from domestic sites to overseas nations, located primarily in China and other Asian countries. Policies inducing regional industrial agglomeration to raise industrial competitiveness (e.g. cluster strategies) have emerged in this political economy. The main legal institutional framework promoting industry–science relationships in Japan is the Science and Technology Basic Plan drawn up based on the Science and Technology Basic Law every five years. There are two steps to drawing up the basic plan. First, the Council for Science and Technology Policy (CSTP) deliberates the basic science and technology policy. Second, based on this, the government formulates and decides a basic plan. The current basic plan is the third plan, which began in April, 2006.

Source: Bureau of Science and Technology Policy, Government of Japan
www8.cao.go.jp/cstp/english/basic/index.html

Innovative milieus

The argument of the particular role of the local territory/the region is developed further with the concept of "milieu" as a synergy space and a cooperation space of networking and innovation.

> To the extent that innovation presupposes a command of new scientific knowledge, it can no longer be the preserve of companies. It also depends on the territorial scientific system, that is, on the relations that are forged between research institutions, the training system and the production system. The interactions between these different elements give rise to forms of co-operation that enrich the milieu.
>
> (Maillat 1998)

A central definition of the European Research Group into Innovative Milieus (GREMI)[5] describes the innovative milieu as a complex network of relationships on a limited geographical area, "often determining a specific external 'image' and a specific internal 'representation' and sense of belonging, which enhance the local innovative capability through synergetic and collective learning processes" (Camagni 1991). Three main sets of elements mark creative/innovative milieus: effective actor relationships within a regional framework; social contacts that enhance learning processes; image and sense of belonging. Proximity in such settings is developed including geographical, organizational, social, institutional and cognitive proximity. The GREMI approach stresses the dynamic nature of clusters and their capacity to generate change.

With globalization the dynamism of territorial production systems springs from a link between the local (territorial) level and the global level, between endogenous and exogenous growth. The innovative milieu is not only a set of resources, actors, firms or local institutions, but also "a complex system made up of economic and technological interdependencies ... a coherent whole in which a territorial production system, a technical culture, and protagonists are linked" (Maillat 1991).

In economic and geographic regions, networks of institutions cooperate to create a positive "milieu" for innovation. Knowledge capabilities are embedded in regional institutional settings: the heavily networked structures of technology driven industries, the heterogeneity of the actors and the complex relationships within those networks. The innovative milieu is a techno-economic network – a coordinated set of heterogeneous actors (Callon 1992) organized within an innovation-based region.

The innovative milieu can be defined as a set of relationships bound in a geographical area that unites a production system, a set of actors, a system of representation and an industrial culture, which generates a localized dynamic process of collective learning and acts as an operator for the reduction of uncertainty in the innovative processes (Camagni 1995).

The key elements of the infrastructure include three distinct sectors: the business sector; knowledge sector and public sector; and innovation process enablers (Corona *et al.* 2005) or institutions for collaboration, in a favorable regional context. Regional development, innovation and entrepreneurship are sustained by an articulated set of various enablers: incubators, science, technology, or research parks; proximity capital in the form of seed and venture capital, government grants and funding programs; a champion entity, such as committed individuals or organizations providing leadership roles; large organizations or early tenants that provide operational stability ("anchor organizations"). It also requires the presence of significant university–industry or research laboratory–industry technology transfer (TT) activity and support services (technical, engineering, legal). The "glue" that enhances learning processes and the emergence of a "sense of belonging" among the local stakeholders is nurtured by clubs, associations, forum of exchange, cooperation and technology transfer programs. As a result, a web of informal relationships, quite similar to those found in spontaneous industrial communities is also formed.

Hence, *IM involves all the players in the innovation game so far analyzed: a mix of large firms organized for innovation and small innovative entrepreneurial firms – as well as of institutional "clusters" ranging from industrial parks and incubators, to science parks and competitive clusters.*

The evolution of Sophia Antipolis from a green land to an innovative milieu is illustrated in Box 6.13.

Box 6.13 Sophia Antipolis
Laura Gaillard, 2010

Introduction
Sophia Antipolis is located in the Côte d'Azur between the Mediterranean Sea and the Alps. The Sophia Antipolis (SA) "scientific park" was created in 1972. It is a joint development by the PACA[6] region council, chamber of commerce and cities, with the support of the French government. The region was a vacant space with no research, university or industry tradition but it was, and still is, one of France's leading tourist destinations. Today Sophia Antipolis is a multicultural, multidisciplinary community focused on innovation. SA extends to an area of 2,400 hectares (quarter of Paris). The park is a concentration of international expertise with 1,400 companies, 31,000 jobs, 14,000 engineers and technicians, 4,500 researchers, 53 percent high-qualified jobs, over 5,000 students and 170 companies with foreign capital, 70 nationalities, and 40 percent of companies involved in R&D activities.

The "Sophipolitan" model, which celebrates its fortieth anniversary in 2012, was based on the development of an ecosystem based on knowledge requiring that the different spheres interlink, and that the boundaries between the different actors (public decision makers, finance contractors, knowledge institutions, innovative companies) should disappear to encourage rallying points for projects. The Sophia Antipolis Foundation fulfills a fundamental task on the SA site: the scientific and cultural organization of the park. Assistance is provided by the foundation team, in which the honorary Senator Pierre Laffitte still has a role, and leads a large number of projects aimed at encouraging transnational cooperation, the promotion of excellence of cluster organizations and improving the integration of innovative SMEs in the clusters. The park includes eight "competitiveness clusters" and attracts a range of skills that is unique in Europe, alongside major public research organizations, such as INRIA and INSERM.

Sophia Antipolis is Europe's leading science park, the catalyst of developing the Alpes-Maritime region into a "global innovation hub". Sophia Antipolis is a policy-driven regional development instrument, fostering the transition to a more knowledge-based economy.

The development of Sophia Antipolis
The start-up period
Much of the development of the project is attributed to one person: Pierre Laffitte. He played a pivotal role as initiator, facilitator and organizer of the development of SA. As early as 1960, Laffitte – member of the board of the "Ecole Nationale Supérieure des Mines de Paris" – wrote an article in *Le*

Monde – "The Latin Quarter in the Fields" – in which he raised the idea of decentralizing R&D and engineering activities to green places outside Paris, arguing that Parisian life was not conducive to research and "cross-fertilization" between scientists working in different fields. Today he is a senator and still actively involved in the park.

The area has a number of significant assets, including an international airport, a pleasant climate, infrastructures linked to the tourism industry and a cosmopolitan tradition. Tourism has been the key factor of the region's development in the last centuries. The attractiveness of SA offers corporations a comparative advantage over alternative locations. The attraction of the French Riviera was the basis for IBM's decision to relocate a research center to the region (in La Gaude) in 1962, shortly followed by Texas Instruments, which established its European center in the area (Villeneuve-Loubet). The presence of these companies signaled and demonstrated the opportunities related to high-technology development and to the assets of the region.

In 1964, a plan was launched to industrialize the Alpes Maritimes by allocating 120 hectares of land for an industrial park. Five years later, in 1969, Laffitte presented his vision of creating a city of 20,000 researchers; he gave the city the name Sophia Antipolis[7] and created the "Sophia Antipolis Association". The SA park was formed and commercialized in 1970 by Savalor; a GIE[8] formed with a non-profitable aim composed of different actors including the Alpes Maritimes department. The project was extended thanks to the state, the PACA region and the five initial communes (Biot, Valbonne, Mougins, Vallauris and Antibes).

The first buildings rose in 1972. The French Interministerial Committee for Territory Development approved the creation of a 2,300ha "high-level scientific, industrial and service sector park with international scope" to be developed on the Plateau of Valbonne. Sophia Antipolis was made official in April 1972. In 1974, SYMIVAL, a joint development syndicate, delegated SA's operational workload to the French Riviera Chamber of Commerce. Franlab, a subsidiary of the Institut Français du Pétrole (French Oil Institute), and the French Company of Geophysics were the first companies to set up onsite. In the beginning, it was Laffitte and his team's persistent promotion of the area that convinced large numbers of companies and people from many parts of the world to establish in the new "science park". Expansion came about through international and national companies and institutions setting up their divisions or departments in the area where they implanted their own resources.

The park is located in a very attractive region with a good climate and living conditions, and the road system as well as the buildings fit in nicely with the landscape.

Construction in SA has always observed a golden rule: "two-thirds nature, one-third business premises". These principles were stipulated in a charter by the Ministry for the Environment in 1976, just four years after the official creation of the park. The Science Park Charter still represents a moral commitment by all those involved in terms of site development and preservation of the environment. This charter imposes preserving a ratio of green land as well as making sure that the design and architecture of any construction harmoniously fits with the surroundings.

In addition to the attractive living conditions and physical infrastructures it was offering, the park benefited from two phenomena: (1) the explicit decentralization policy the French government exerted during the 1970s; and (2) the active advertising strategy of the local authorities to promote SA as a high-tech business park, especially in the United States. An example of decentralization is Air France's World Reservation Centre, which moved away from Paris in 1977. As to the second point, SA activities were compared to a "Trojan horse": the first phase of the business park's development consisted mainly of the entry of extra-European firms that wanted to open an R&D facility in which they could adapt their products to the specific requirements of the European market. By 1982, 125 companies were settled in the park and represented 3,700 jobs. The park brought together a broad spectrum of expertise in two major areas: information technologies (telecommunications, networks, microelectronics, optics, software engineering, multimedia, audiovisual, imaging, robotics, telecoms operators, etc.) and life science and fine chemistry (pharmaceuticals, biotech, medical imaging, etc.). Nearly a quarter of the companies were not French, most came from the United States and northern Europe. They included some of the world's foremost names (Amadeus, AT&T, Cisco, Hitachi, HP, Siemens, and many others for IT; Allergan, Bayer, Dow, Elaiapharm, etc. for life science). They were mostly the R&D centers of international groups and national public research institutes.

The dynamics at the local level were based on resources and actors from outside the region. Due to their international background, the companies had a wide array of international relations beyond SA's boundaries, whereas local interactions were almost completely absent. The park looked like a co-location of high-tech firms, completely lacking a local interaction structure. Highly qualified personnel, employed by small and medium-sized firms established in the park, were absorbed into larger firms. In the 1980s, the park was characterized by a centralized system dominated by independent self-sufficient corporations and mainly bottom-down initiatives. There were a small number of investors; activities were mostly financed by government contracts and public capital; and growth was driven by public and local institution willingness to inject funds into the park.

Intermediate crisis and new growth

At the end of the 1980s and the beginning of the 1990s, the growth process in terms of number of firms and employment started to slow down, particularly in SA's main information technology sector. The SA business park started to suffer from a number of shortcomings. First, it lost competitiveness in relation to other regions concerning the attraction and retention of international companies, since those companies changed and expanded their set of location requirements and obtained better knowledge of the alternatives. Ireland and Scotland, for instance, could provide cheaper qualified labor in comparison with SA, while central cities such as Paris and London offered closer proximity to customers and/or financial and administrative services. As a consequence of this shift in location preferences, the growth of the number of companies in SA stagnated and some of the established companies even decided to relocate to other areas. Second, following the recession in Europe and in the US, in 1992, multinationals stopped establishing subsidiaries in SA and many companies were forced to downsize their activities.

After the crisis in the early 1990s, the information technology and life sciences industry in SA showed a strongly divergent development pattern. In the information technology industry the shrinking presence of multinationals triggered important *endogenous* developments. The relocating international companies left a pool of highly qualified labor that to a large extent did not move along with the company and wanted to stay in the Côte d'Azur region. Many of these people started their own companies. Spin-off activities from larger firms resulted in the emergence of a number of technologically advanced SMEs. This was an important stimulus to local development: typically, the number of locally developed start-ups was around 40 during the second half of the 1990s, but by the end of the decade start-ups reached a level of over 80 per year. During the same period there were also exits, but the entire period saw a net growth of jobs. As a result of the shift in IT from growth led by foreign multinationals to growth mainly based on local spin-offs and high-tech start-ups, for this industry the crisis turned out to be only a relatively short interruption between the initial emergence of the cluster and the subsequent follow-up phase of extensive growth. The period of transition from externally driven to locally based growth took off from the first half of the 1990s onward and still continues today.

This transformation from externally driven to locally based growth in the IT industry was further reinforced by the arrival of public and private education and research institutes in SA. Most of these institutes, such as the University of Nice Sophia (in 1986), INRIA (National Research Institute on Informatics and Automation) and CNRS (National Centre of Scientific Research), were not present onsite in the early development stages of the park, but were established there only at a later stage. The research institutes were attracted in the late 1980s on the basis of an explicit strategy of the national and regional authorities to promote synergies between science and industry. These synergies consisted largely of building a highly qualified local labor market, and PhD students undertaking traineeships or projects in firms. The same applied to the European Telecom Standardization Institute (ETSI) that located to SA in 1989. These new developments mainly concerned the Information Technology industry in SA. The life sciences sector did not follow the same development pattern. The concentration of life sciences firms was not strongly affected by the crisis, but at the same time it did not show an increase in the second half of the 1990s in the same way as the information technology sector. In fact, the growth of the number of firms in the life sciences sector has always proceeded at a slower rate than in the IT sector. The increase of the number of life sciences firms came to a standstill in the 1990s. Today, information technology firms constitute around 75 percent of SA high-tech companies, whereas life sciences firms are around 13 percent. Consequently, from the middle of the 1990s onwards, SA progressively specialized toward information technologies at the relative expense of life sciences companies and energy and earth sciences.

The increasingly locally based growth in information technology made this sector diversify in terms of size. Whereas the park was strongly dominated by large firms in the early stages, the changing nature of the growth in the information technologies industry resulted in an increasing share of small and medium-sized enterprises.

The current situation: actors and links in Sophia Antipolis
Sophia Antipolis has been a "slow-burning" project and it took Laffitte many years to realize his vision of a research, academia and industry tri-polarity.

Activities to nurture the local industries are intense – it is indeed the premise of the technopark. About 10 percent of the tech firms, and about 20 percent of their employees located in SA are foreign, providing a natural basis for international networking. This cluster strategy has yielded some very encouraging results. While the number of patents stays average, the impressive number of mobile and technology start-ups per 100,000 inhabitants is unrivalled. There is strong interaction between science, business and government. The clear evidence is that combined intentions, strategies and projects among universities, industries and governmental agencies foster the development of innovations.

Today, SA is living its founding concept: to enhance innovation through "cross-fertilization" between small and large companies and research teams. The concept of SA was developed as if the entire park were a big incubator where entrepreneurial spirit should be at home. The cross-fertilization between research centers, higher education with special courses devoted to entrepreneurship, engineering schools, research centers with technology transfer departments, start-ups, is helping this incubation process.

Major institutional contributors

There are essentially two governing bodies that oversee the technopole's activities. The SYMISA (Mixed Syndicate of Sophia Antipolis) has 44 members who are responsible for general management, financial policy, promotion and services to corporations. One of the major functions of the SYMISA is to decide whether to approve an application for technopole residency. In making this decision, the SYMISA considers the following factors: (1) the technological nature of the activity; (2) the absence of pollution or other nuisance factors; (3) the type and number of jobs created. A second body, SAEM Sophia Antipolis Côte d'Azur, is responsible for the development and commercial mission of the Sophia Antipolis Science Park, acting as the authorized agent for SYMISA. Functions of the SAEM include negotiating the initial land sale or lease contract and assisting a company in obtaining government permits.

The Sophia Antipolis Foundation fosters cultural and scientific exchange within SA and prospective members under the supervision of its historic founder, Senator Pierre Laffitte.

The other institutions contributing to the regional development are Team Côte d'Azur, the regional economic development agency of the Alpes-Maritimes region, responsible for the external communications and marketing of Sophia Antipolis. The Sophia Antipolis Urban Authority, comprising the 16 communes, is involved in the science park general development policy, and sits on SYMISA alongside the Alpes-Maritimes General Council, the French Riviera Chamber of Commerce, and the city of Mougins.

Also to be mentioned are the Prefecture Des Alpes-Maritimes (the administrative body of the department), DATAR and its Interministerial Co-Ordination Group for Sophia Antipolis, the Alpes-Maritimes General Council, and, last but not least, the French Riviera Chamber of Commerce.

Private firms

Most companies establishing in SA now choose to locate their R&D departments in Sophia. One of the reasons is the possibility of collaborating with other companies.

It is in the area of research that Sophia Antipolis excels today: 40 percent of SA-based firms pursue intense R&D activities with 4,000 researchers working in the fields of IT, life sciences and environmental sciences in pure and applied research.

Information technology was fundamental to the expansion of Sophia Antipolis: in 2010 IT accounted for almost 50 percent of all jobs and 25 percent of companies. It occupies 29 percent of the premises. For several years now, SA has witnessed the emergence of a content industry centered on image processing for motion pictures, internet applications, mobile telephony, location-based systems as well as video games and special effects.

Partly due to the presence of the ETSI (European Telecom Standardization Institute) for the establishment of telecommunications standards – and of the World Wide Web Consortium (W3C) (main international standards organization for the World Wide Web) – most of the information technology firms work in segments of the same value chain. Today, Sophia Antipolis' IT sector consists of three main building blocks: infrastructure (equipment, networks and hardware), platforms (interfaces and software) and applications (including services). These three building blocks are more or less equally present in SA and are strongly related to each other. The interrelatedness of the products and services they develop positively affects opportunities for collaboration and collective learning.

In the electronic sector, many diverse technologies have been developed: components for telecommunications, medical or military applications. Thomson Marconi Sonar is the second largest employer of SA.

The Côte d'Azur ICT cluster owes its appeal to the long-standing presence of big names in key sectors, including mobile telecommunications (with companies such as Alcatel Lucent, Cisco, Nortel Networks and Orange Labs), intelligent embedded systems and microelectronics. Sophia Antipolis is the only place in the world, other than Silicon Valley, where the global leaders in semiconductor design – Cadence Design Systems, Mentor Graphics and Synopsys – are all represented. Major international groups such as Accenture, Amadeus (the company that has seen the fastest, highest growth in the technology park's history), IBM and SAP are also based in the region and provide support services, notably in the development of advanced IT applications for communications, space, automotive technologies, health and biotechnologies, finance and corporate management. Services now account for 50 percent of the total number of companies providing 26 percent of jobs and occupying 32 percent of the premises.

Other notable tenants are: France Telecom, Honeywell, Motorola, Nortel Networks, Oracle France, Qualcomm, Altran Praxis, ARM, ASK, Autodesk, DailyMotion, Dassault Systèmes, Fortinet, Hitachi, HP, Icera, Infineon Technologies, Lagardere Active, Mentor Graphics, Oracle, ST-Ericsson, Sunplus mMobile, Symantec, the creator of Norton AntiVirus (setting up its new European R&D coordination center in Sophia Antipolis), Texas Instruments, UDCast, Thales Alenia Space, Thales Underwater Systems, and Wall Street Systems.

Life sciences only account for 4 percent of firms, 8 percent of jobs and occupy 12 percent of the premises. Health-care science, fine chemicals and biotechnology have 60 companies that employ 2,000 people, mainly in research.

Local finance

Institutional capital, regional (public) capital, and national research funding. Sophia Antipolis offers a variety of financial incentives to attract businesses, including European, French and regional subsidies and loans, whose amounts vary depending on the amount invested and the number of jobs created and the level of technology transfer involved. Also, up to a 50 percent reduction in corporate taxes is available for a period of five years.

SA has recently developed a series of supports and financing initiatives: incubators, venture capitalists and business angels.

Incubators (linked to universities, pre-start-up): INRIA-Transfert was established in 1998 with support from the French Research Ministry; it is a subsidiary of the national research institute INRIA. Institute Eurécom, one of the leading European centers in advanced communications and networking research, also works as an incubator; incubator CERAM was set up in 2000 as part of the high-tech entrepreneurship chair; PACA Est was set up in 2001, and there is also an Incubator CICOM (Centre for International Communication).

Business angels play an increasingly important role in SA. When Candace Johnson arrived in SA (she is an international telecommunications expert and entrepreneur, and one of the 50 most powerful businesswomen in Europe), all her investors at Johnson Paradigm Ventures came with her, and she became a co-founder with Caisse des Dépôts, AXA, and Bavarian State Bank of Sophia EuroLab, a ten-year fund. Prior to this, SA did not have a venture capital fund or industry. Then in 2002, C. Johnson was a founding member – with Senator Lafitte – of the Sophia Business Angels (SBA): 50 serial entrepreneurs, of 18 nationalities, grouped together into a not-for-profit organization, to privately invest in high-tech companies in Sophia Antipolis, France and the world. SBA is at the origin of a model of teaching and mentoring entrepreneurs through venture academies, informal network sessions/boot-camps, competitions and cross-border investment. The SBA members make investments and mentor companies not only in ICT, but also cleantech, medtech/health, and B2B. SBA is among the major European groups that have helped build the concentrations of high-tech businesses. SBA was the winner of the 2010 EBAN (European Trade Association for Business Angels) Award. SBA works hand-in-hand with government-financed research, institutes, incubators, etc. to provide links to business, other angels, companies and venture capitalists.

Venture capital in SA is represented by regional funds and national funds. Regional funds: Sophia Euro Lab, started in 2000, is a mix between an incubator and seed-money fund; I-Source Gestion, started in 1999, whose main owner is INRIA-Transfert; FCPR Sud Capital No 1, started in 2000. National funds: CDC PME, owned by Caisse des Dépots et Consignations (CDC); and Sofinnova Partners, created in 1972, the oldest in France.

Competitiveness clusters
There are eight "pôles de compétitivité" in SA. The purpose of these competitiveness poles or clusters is to set up multinational R&D teams to work on projects selected by industrial or high-tech firms. The companies participating in an R&D project within the clusters benefit from certain tax exemptions, reduced charges for employees and contributions to R&D budgets in the form of subsidies. In 2006, Sophia Antipolis was ranked France's number one Competitiveness Cluster and received the "global cluster" seal of approval for Secured Communicating Solutions (SCS), signifying worldwide scope and influence. The other Competitiveness Clusters designated by the French government as national range clusters and present in SA are: marine sciences and technologies (Pole Mer), photonics and optoelectronics (Optitec), risk management and land vulnerability (Pôle Risque), non-green-house-gas-emitting energies (Capenergie), health and biotechnologies (Eurobiomed), the PASS pole (for Perfumes, Aromas, Smells and Flavors), and Pegase for aeronautic and space. The park also hosts "The Sophia Antipolis Clusters Project", initiated by the European Union to foster growth, development and collaboration on a pan-European level in the field of mobile technologies; and the CIM PACA (Center for Microelectronics Provence-Alps-Riviera), created by ARCSIS[9] in 2005, is built around three interconnected R&D platforms – Characterization, Design and Micro-PackS – to create better regional industry competitiveness on a national and international level.

Major professional associations
Many informal and formal, non-profit and business-driven associations and networks play a significant role in knowledge production, distribution and use within and between firms. A number of international business start-up competitions are designed to promote the development of novel projects, such as the European Satellite Navigation Competition-Galileo Masters, now entering its seventh year. To stimulate the role of venture capital, the first International Venture Capital Summit was organized in Sophia Antipolis in 1997 by the regional authorities and the chamber of commerce. Since then the event has been organized annually.

Another aspect of the policy is to develop network mechanisms and support professional organizations also through shared technology resources. An important private initiative in this respect is the Telecom Valley Association. Telecom Valley was established in 1991, as a non-profit organization to map the competences of agents in the park and promote the emergence of clubs and associations that attempt to link small firms, large firms and research institutes in the field of information technology. With around 80 members, this organization aims at developing a unique pool of competencies based on members' expertise.

SA has developed a network of shared technology platforms that allows start-ups and SMEs to test their applications using resources that are generally available only to large businesses. These include: CIM PACA (Integrated Center for Microelectronics), with three platforms to test microelectronic solutions; and the PACA Mobile Center, a test bench for new-generation mobile phone applications.

Other associations are also active and, to promote the development of the area, different governmental support institutions have been organized. Sophia presents itself as a network community with many clubs and associations; the proliferation of many organizations has sometimes led to "congestion" and visibility problems. There are, for instance: the Association Junior Enterprise – DESSI – for software engineering; CARMA, support for technological development in the field of materials; the CLUB des Dirigeants de Sophia Antipolis, managers participating in the action to ensure the cultural and economical impact of Sophia Antipolis; the Club High-Tech – to create synergy between R&D and higher education; INTECH'SOPHIA is a scientific and technical club devoted to computing, scientific calculation and automation; J3E – Junior Electrical Electronical Engineering – studies and realization of contracts in the fields of electronics, computing, signal processing, telecoms, monitoring, measuring and controls; PERSAN coordinates public research and education institutes in the Alpes-Maritimes and promotes their scientific R&D group; SAME is an association for the valorization, promotion and development of excellence in the microelectronics sector covering the design of advanced integrated circuits in the region.

Most important research institutions

The park hosts 50 public and private establishments. Public research centers include the CNRS – national scientific research center, providing administrative services for the laboratories on the site and for the Alpes-Maritimes department. There are many laboratories such as: CNRS–UNSA–I3S – Sophia Antipolis computer science, signals and systems laboratory, providing fundamental and applied research in computing, control, robotics, and signal and image treatment; the CNRS–UNSA–LEAT – electronics, antennae and telecommunications laboratory, providing fundamental and applied research in microwaves, antennas, imaging radar and mobile communications, higher education. And the laboratories of some major French institutions such as: INRIA – France's largest IT and informatics institute, and a member of the pan-European ERCIM organization of research centers in IT, National Institute for Research in Computer Science and Control; INRA – National Institute for Agronomic Research; INSERM – National Institute for Health and Medical Research. And also France Télécom R&D – European telecommunications R&D

center; ADEME – French agency for environment and energy management; AFSSA – French agency of research on food safety; CEP – Centre for Energy and Processes, providing research and training on technological innovations in energy and environmental sectors; CERMICS – research in computer science and applied mathematics; and CMA – Applied Mathematics Centre, providing research activities ranging from computer science to systems theory.

Higher education institutions
Higher education, training and research represent 12 percent of jobs and 5 percent of companies. Some 14,000 engineers and technicians are employed by SA companies and 53 percent of total jobs are defined as highly skilled. These specific skills are now backed by various higher education institutions. The park benefits from the proximity of: the SKEMA Group (previously CERAM Sophia Antipolis) – graduate studies in management, finance and high-tech entrepreneurship, now the largest business school in France in terms of student numbers; the UNSA – University of Nice Sophia Antipolis; ESINSA – School of Engineering of Nice Sophia Antipolis; ESSI – School of Computer Engineering; ENSMP – The National School of Mines; Eurécom Institute – higher studies in communication systems (corporate/ multimedia/ mobile communication); and the Theseus Institute – management studies.

The first stone of the ICT campus (Graduate School of Information and Communication Sciences) was laid in Sophia Antipolis in December 2009, marking the start of a massive construction program. The new ICT campus will be home to students and researchers from the University of Nice-Sophia Antipolis, CNRS and Eurecom. At the beginning of the 2012 academic year, the campus will welcome its first 1,500 students and then gradually build up to its full complement of 7,000 students and 3,000 researchers.

The future
In addition to Sophia Antipolis, activities are expanding on the outskirts of Nice. The *French Riviera Eco Valley* is being developed as part of the first National Interest Project (Opération d'Intérêt National) focused on sustainable development challenges. This far-reaching ecological sustainable development is part of a policy to promote best practices in sustainable governance and to set a global example for regional planning by responding to the challenges of sustainable development for future generations in an area that spans over 25,000 acres, from the Mediterranean coast to the Alpine foothills.

Sources: Bernasconi *et al.* (2006); Bernasconi (1993); Longhi (1999); www.sophia-antipolis.org/

Key points

Entrepreneurship can be organized in important respects by "organizing environments" rather than only firms. "Milieus" organized for innovation are extremely important for the formation and development of entrepreneurial firms. This point has been established by studying the various forms of "district" and "cluster" that have emerged in history and have supported the development of entrepreneurship in many regions around the world. On that basis, a range of possible designed institutional interventions, aimed at recreating those conditions, have been elaborated and became diffused (industrial and scientific parks and poles, incubators, regional systems of innovation).

These (extremely varied) forms have been classified and analyzed here in terms of their organizational properties, with the aim of understanding what they are, which advantages they provide, and what relations they have with innovation. Three types of organized environments have been thus identified, having both an emergent/spontaneous version, and a designed/institutional version, and an increasing potential in fostering and coordinating innovation:

- *Resource pooling clusters*, supporting the birth and growth of similar firms, with limited direct interaction and coordination among them – including the historical forms of industrial districts, and the institutional forms of industrial parks.
- *Differentiated and integrated clusters*, coordinating webs of sequential and reciprocal interdependencies among specified entities in specified processes of production and exchange or products/services of knowledge – including the spontaneously established industrial cluster, and the institutional forms of science and technology parks and poles.
- *Fully connected communities* of highly differentiated players enabling them to self-organized into new projects/firms – the historical forms of industrial communities, and the institutionalized forms of regional innovation systems and innovation milieus.

This scheme and assessment should be useful for firm decisions of territorial location of activities and on which cluster to join; and for devising public policies appropriate to the type of innovation and development sought.

Analysis questions

On in-chapter cases

- The features of Silicon Valley and Sophia Antipolis can usefully be analyzed in a comparative case study approach. What are the differences in supporting innovation and new firm formation? What are the respective strengths and weaknesses?

On end-chapter case

- How can the rise of the Bangalore region be interpreted?
- Which configurations did it assume in its development?
- What possible future trajectories can be conceived for further entrepreneurial development in the zone?

End-chapter case: Bangalore

Laura Gaillard, 2010

Bangalore houses several high-tech clusters (defense, aeronautics and IT) and is considered the scientific and engineering center of India in terms of research, training and manufacturing. India's best research university – the Indian Institute of Science – is based in Bangalore.

The development of this particular city-region was largely shaped by the industrial development in the US rather than local cluster-effects and regional government body policies. In fact, easy access to qualified and relatively cheap technical human capital attracted a number of transnational corporations (TNC) during the 1990s. Large firms such as IBM, Motorola, Hewlett-Packard, Siemens, 3M, Texas, Honeywell (India Software Operations), etc. located in the area. These companies were also attracted by the fact that none of the firms' workforces had to be unionized, software exports were not taxed in India, benefits were a relatively minor cost, and the profit potential was enormous. Though it should be stressed that Bangalore's growth until the late 1980s (when the software export boom began) relied on local (largely public sector) investments, Bangalore was already the center for advanced science and military research and had a number of good educational institutions, mainly paid for by the central authorities. Even the government located the public telephone company as well as other large state enterprises in high-tech sectors to Bangalore.

The IT cluster in Bangalore is dominated by the large transnational corporations located there. Two types of SMEs can also be found: those tied to a TNC through a subcontracting agreement, and a limited number of independent SMEs. Frequently, SMEs undertake task-specific job-work for the large client firm which settles the parameters of the production and final outcome and tightly controls the performance of the SME. Innovation is mostly determined by large firms.

During the first phase, US-firms mainly outsourced to India routine IT services such as the maintenance of existing codes or re-engineering codes from one programming language to another. The human capital base in Bangalore was mainly characterized by well-educated engineers who were perfectly capable of undertaking these activities; Indians undertaking these activities were in fact most often over-qualified.

In recent years, Indian firms have to some extent been able to move up the global value chain. On the one hand, TNCs adopted a deliberate strategy to modularize and standardize some of their IT processes. This provided the background for the distance work which in turn allowed the Indian firms to maintain a broader knowledge base at home.

Collaboration between SMEs based on social networks is limited in the IT cluster, but it does exist: interpersonal networks are based on common schooling and alumni links built around the many technical schools located in the region, as well as on previous working relationships. However, consortia of SMEs have often been prone to failure due to the competitive tendencies among group members. Social capital transcends the regional boundaries in this cluster. The social capital of the Indian transnational community played a crucial role in establishing the IT industry and in shaping outsourcing decisions in the US firms.

Recently, a significant growth in interaction between Bangalore firms and US and European firms has taken place, as well as a diversification of the profiles of firms investing in Bangalore. The Bangalore firms have developed a certain degree of autonomy from the lead firms in the US and Europe. This has allowed them to move up the global value chain. Part of this process was facilitated by increased cluster-effects and spin-offs from the different universities located in Bangalore. However, the Indian firms engage in interactive learning only to a limited extent compared to more bustling IT clusters such as Silicon Valley.

Nevertheless, Bangalore is now called the "Silicon Valley of India" and the government has plans to develop an information technology corridor linking the Whitefield Park (in the northeastern outskirts) and Electronics City (in the southern outskirts). Over 200 information technology corporations have facilities in Bangalore including Infosys and Wipro, India's second and third largest software companies. Infosys Technologies Ltd., founded in 1981, offered its clients an offshore model whereby the company could replicate the systems and infrastructure of its international clients in India.

Sources: Chaminade and Vang (2006);
www.thisismyindia.com/about_bangalore/bangalore-economy.html

Notes

1   For example, employment-generating vehicle repair and metalworking clusters. Dawson's (1992) study of the Kumasi, Ghana auto-parts and vehicle repair clusters reported over 5,000 workshops employing some 40,000 persons engaged in metalworking, the manufacture of auto-parts and in vehicle repair.

2   The prosperous firm structures of the northeast and center of Italy were confronted with the stagnating situation in the poor south ("second Italy") and the recession in the traditionally rich and early industrialized northwest ("first Italy"). The term was first coined by Italian sociologist Arnaldo Bagnasco in the mid-1970s, and popularized in English-speaking countries in the 1980s by two MIT social scientists, Michael J. Piore and Charles Sabel (1984).

3   Video interview of Robert Metcalfe on March 10, 2009 at the Computer History Museum. Robert Metcalfe was a member of the research staff for Xerox, at their Palo Alto Research Center (PARC) and one of the two inventors of Ethernet. "Ethernet: Distributed Packet-Switching For Local Computer Networks" (Metcalfe and Boggs 1975).

4   See also: P. Cooke, *Knowledge Economies: Clusters, Learning and Cooperative Advantage* (London: Routledge, 2002); P. Cooke, M. Heidenreich, and H. Braczyk, eds, *Regional Innovation Systems: The Role of Governance in a Globalized World* (London: Routledge); J.H. Dunning, ed., *Regions, Globalization, and the Knowledge-Based Economy* (New York: Oxford University Press, 2004).
5   For a complete presentation of the innovative milieu concept see Crevoisier (2004): "GREMI I (Aydalot 1986) and GREMI II (Maillat and Perrin 1992) revealed what companies found in the region or beyond it during innovation processes. GREMI III (Maillat, Quévit, and Senn 1993) explored innovative networks and showed their spatial, local, and extralocal functionings; this survey made it possible to define the principal concepts. GREMI IV (Ratti, Bramanti, and Gordon 1997) was centred on comparing the trajectories of regions that are active in identical sectors." The GREMI V (Crevoisier and Camagni 2000) was dedicated to urban milieus and the GREMI VI (Camagni, Maillat, and Matteaccioli 2004) focused on natural and cultural resources."
6   Provence Alpes Cote d'Azur.
7   The name Sophia Antipolis derives from the Greek words for "thoughtful" and "anti-city".
8   Groupement d'Intérêt Economique.
9   ARCSIS associates five large groups – Atmel, Gemplus, Philips, STMicroelectronics, Texas Instruments – dozens of SMEs, 15 schools, research laboratories and universities in the region.

References

Acs, Z.J. (ed.) (2009) *The Knowledge Spillover Theory of Entrepreneurship*. Cheltenham, UK: Edward Elgar.

Adler, P., and Kwon, S. (2002) "Social capital: prospects for a new concept" *Academy of Management Review* 27(1): 17–40.

Aldrich, H.E., and Sasaki, T. (1995) "R&D consortia in the US and Japan" *Research Policy* 24(2): 301–16.

Altshuller, G. (1973) *Innovation Algorithm*. Worcester, MA: Technical Innovation Center.

——(1984) *Creativity as an Exact Science*. New York: Gordon & Breach.

Alvarez, S.A., and Barney, J. (eds) (2007) "The entrepreneurial theory of the firm" *Journal of Management Studies,* Special Issue 44(7).

Andadari, R.K. (2008) *Local Clusters in Global Value Chains. A Case Study of Wood Furniture Clusters in Central Java (Indonesia)*. The Tinbergen Institute Research Series no. 421, Tinbergen Institute & Vrije Universiteit, Amsterdam

Andersson, T., Schwaag Serger, S., Sörvik, J., and Wise Hansson, E. (2004) *The Cluster Policy White Book*. Malmö: IKDE.

Andretsch, D.B., and Litan, R. (eds) (2009) *Entrepreneurship and Openness*. Cheltenham, UK: Edward Elgar.

Aoki, M. (2004) "Comparative institutional analysis of corporate governance" in A. Grandori (ed.) *Corporate Governance and Firm Organization*. Oxford: Oxford University Press.

Archibugi, D., and Pietrobell, C. (2003) "The globalisation of technology and its implications for developing countries. Windows of opportunity or further burden?" *Technological Forecasting and Social Change* 70: 861–83.

Arino, A., and Reuer, J. (eds) (2006) *Strategic Alliances: Governance and Contracts*. London: Palgrave.

Audretsch, D.B., and Feldman, M.P. (1996) "R&D spillovers and the geography of innovation and production" *American Economic Review* 86(3): 630–40.

AURP (Association of University Research Parks) (2010) www.aurp.net.

Aydalot, P. (1986) *Milieux Innovateurs en Europe*. Paris: GREMI Groupe De Recherche Européen Sur Les Milieux Innovateurs.

Baden-Fuller, C.W., and Stopford, J. (1994) "Creating corporate entrepreneurship" *Strategic Management Journal* 15: 521–36.

Bagdadli, S., Solari, L., Usai, A., and Grandori, A. (2003) "The emergence of career boundaries in unbounded industries" *International Journal of Human Resource Management* 14: 788–808.

Baharami, H. (1996) "The emerging flexible organization: perspectives from the Silicon Valley" in P.S .Myers (ed.) *Knowledge Management and Organization Design*. Boston, MA: Heinemann.

Bandura, A. (1986) *Social Foundations of Thought and Action*. Englewood Cliffs: Prentice-Hall.

Baron, J.N., and Kreps, D.M. (1999) "HRM in emerging companies" in J.N. Baron and D.M. Kreps (eds) *Strategic Human Resources*. New York: Wiley.

Baron, R.A. (1998) "Cognitive mechanisms in entrepreneurship: why and when entrepreneurs think differently than other people" *Journal of Business Venturing* 13: 275–94.

——(2004) "The cognitive perspective: a valuable tool for answering entrepreneurship's basic 'why' questions" *Journal of Business Venturing* 19(2): 221–39.

Baron, R.A., and Shane, S.A. (2005) *Entrepreneurship. A Process Perspective*. Mason, OH: Thompson South-Western.

Bartlett, C., and Ghoshal, S. (1989) *Managing Across Borders: The Transnational Solution*. Cambridge, MA: Harvard Business School Press.

Baumol, W.J., Litan, R.E., and Schramm, C.J. (2007) *Good Capitalism, Bad Capitalism, and the Economics of Growth and Prosperity*. New Haven, CT: Yale University Press.

Bazerman, M.H. (1986) *Judgment in Managerial Decision Making*. New York: John Wiley and Sons.

Bazerman, M.H., and Lewicki, R.J. (eds) (1983) *Negotiating in Organizations*. Beverly Hills, CA: Sage.

Becattini, G. (1979) "Del settore industriale al distretto industriale" *Rivista di Economica e Politica Industriale* 7(1): 7–21.

——(1990) "The Marshallian Industrial District as a socio-economic notion" in F. Pyke, G. Beccatini, and W. Sengenberger (eds) *Industrial Districts and Inter-Firm Co-operation in Italy*. Geneva: International Institute for Labour Studies.

Becker, G.S. (1964) *Human Capital*. Chicago, IL: University of Chicago Press.

——(2002) "Human capital theory" in *The Concise Encyclopedia of Economics*. New York: Columbia University Press.

Bernasconi, M. (1993) "Creating an entrepreneurship culture: high-tech start-up and spin-off creation in Sophia Antipolis", working paper Ceram, Sophia Antipolis.

Bernasconi, M., Dibiaggio, L., and Ferrary, M. (2006) "High-tech clusters: network richness in Sophia Antipolis and Silicon Valley" in, M. Bernasconi, S. Harris and M. Mønsted (eds) *High-Tech Entrepreneurship: Managing Innovation, Variety and Uncertainty*. London and New York: Routledge.

Berry, A., Rodriguez, E., and Sandee, H. (2002) "Firm and group dynamics in the small and medium enterprise sector in Indonesia" *Small Business Economics* 18: 141–61.

Bjerke, B. (2007) *Understanding Entrepreneurship*. Cheltenham, UK: Edward Elgar.

Blair, M. (1996) *Wealth Creation and Wealth Sharing: A Colloquium on Corporate Governance and Investments in Human Capital*. Washington, DC: Brookings Institute.

——(2004) "The neglected benefits of the corporate form: entity status and the separation of asset ownership from control" in A. Grandori (ed.) *Corporate Governance and Firm Organization: Microfoundations and Structural Forms*. New York: Oxford University Press.

Blair, M.M., and Stout L.A. (1999) "Team production in business organizations: an introduction", Georgetown University Law Center, Business, Economics, and Regulatory Law Working Paper No. 180991.

Block, Z., and MacMillan, I. (1993) *Corporate Venturing*. Cambridge, MA: Harvard Business School Press.

Braczyk, H.-J., Cooke, P., Heidenreich, M., and Krauss, G. (eds) (1998) *Regional Innovation Systems. The Role of Governance in a Globalized World*. London: Routledge.

Bresnahan, T., Gambardella, A., and Saxenian, A. (2001) "'Old economy' inputs for 'new economy' outcomes: cluster formation in the New Silicon Valleys" *Industrial and Corporate Change* 10(4): 835–60.

Brouwer, M. (2005) "Managing uncertainty through profit sharing contracts from medieval Italy to Silicon Valley" *Journal of Management and Governance* 9(3–4): 237–55.

Brusco, S. (1982) "The Emilian Model: productive decentralization and social integration" *Cambridge Journal of Economics* 6(2): 167–84.

——(1999) "The rules of the game in industrial districts" in A. Grandori (ed.) *Interfirm Networks*. London: Routledge.

Brusoni, S. (2001) "Managing knowledge in loosely coupled networks: exploring the links between product and knowledge dynamics" *Journal of Management Studies* 38(7): 1019–35.

Burgelman, R.A. (1983) "A process model of internal corporate venturing in the diversified major firm" *Administrative Science Quarterly* 28(2): 223–45.

Burgelman, R.A. (1984) "Designs for corporate entrepreneurship" *California Management Review* 26(2): 154–66.

Burgelman, R.A., and Sayles, L.R. (1986) *Inside Corporate Innovation*. New York: Free Press.

Burns, T., and Stalker, G.M. (1961) *The Management of Innovation*. London and New York: Tavistock Publications.

Burt, R.S. (1992) *Structural Holes*. Cambridge, MA: Harvard University Press.

——(2002) *Brokerage and Closure. An Introduction to Social Capital*. Oxford: Oxford University Press.

Callon, M. (1992) "Variety and irreversibility in networks of technique conception and adoption" in D. Foray and C. Freeman (eds) *Technology and the Wealth of Nations*. London: Frances Pinter, 275–324.

Camagni, R. (1991) "Local 'milieu', uncertainty and innovation networks: towards a new dynamic theory of economic space" in R. Camagni (ed.) *Innovation in Networks: Spatial Perspectives*. London: Belhaven.

——(1995) "The concept of innovative *milieu* and its relevance for public policies in European lagging regions" *Regional Science* 74: 317–40.

Camagni, R., and Maillat, D. (2006) *Milieux Innovateur: Théories et politiques*. Paris: Economica.

Camagni, R., Maillat, D., and Matteaccioli, A. (eds) (2004) "*Ressources naturelles et culturelles, milieux et développement local*" [Natural and cultural resources, milieus and local development]. Neuchâtel, Switzerland: EDES-IRER.

Camerer, C., and Lovallo, D. (1999) "Overconfidence and excess entry: an experimental approach" *The American Economic Review* 89(1): 306–18.

Campbell, D.T. (1960) "Blind variation and selective retention in creative thought as in other knowledge processes" *Psychological Review* 67: 380–400.

Camuffo, A., Vinelli, A., Pozzana, R., and Benedetti, L. (2009) "How to compete and thrive: small firms' business models in the italian textile industry", Working Paper Series 09–005 CROMA – Center For Research in Organization and Management, Bocconi University, Milan.

Casson, M. (2003) *The Entrepreneur. An Economic Theory*, 2nd edition. Cheltenham, UK: Edward Elgar.

——(2005) "Entrepreneurship and the theory of the firm" *Journal of Economic Behavior and Organization* 58: 327–48.

Castilla, E.J. (2003) 'Networks of venture capital firms in Silicon Valley" *International Journal of Technology Management* 25(1–2): 113–35.

Castilla, E., Hwang, H., Granovetter, M., and Granovetter, E. (2000) "Social networks in Silicon Valley" in Chong-Moon Lee, W.F. Miller, M. Gong Hancock and H.S. Rowen (eds) *The Silicon Valley Edge: A Habitat for Innovation and Entrepreneurship*. Stanford, CA: Stanford University Press.

Cavusgil, S.T., and Knight, G. (2004) "Innovation, organizational capabilities and the born-global firm" *Journal of International Business Studies* 35(2): 124–41.

Chaminade, C., and Vang, J. (2006) "Innovation policy for Asian SMEs: exploring cluster differences", WP 2006/03, Circle, Lund University.

Chandy, R., and Tellis, G.J. (2000) "The incumbent's curse? Incumbency, size and radical product innovation" *Journal of Marketing* 64 (3): 1–17.

Chesbrough, H.W., and Vanhaverbeke, W. (2006) *Open Innovation: Researching a New Paradigm*. Oxford: Oxford University Press.

Chesbrough, H., Birkinshaw, J., and Teubal, M. (eds) (2006) Special Issue for the 20th Anniversary of Teece's "Profiting from innovation" *Research Policy* 35(8).

Christensen, C.M. (1997) "Making strategy: learning by doing" *Harvard Business Review* (November–December): 141–46, 148–56.

Clarysse, B., Roure, J., and Schamp, T. (eds) (2007) *Entrepreneurship and the Financial Community*. Cheltenham, UK: Edward Elgar.

CLOE: Clusters Linked Over Europe (2006) *Cluster Management Guide – Guidelines for the Development and Management of Cluster Initiatives*. www.clusterforum.org.

Cohen, W., and Levinthal, D. (1990) "Absorptive capacity: a new perspective on learning and innovation" *Administrative Science Quarterly* 35: 128–52.

Cohendet, P., Creplet, F., and Dupouet, O. (2001). "Organisational innovation, communities of practice and epistemic communities: the case of Linux" in A. Kirman and J.B. Zimmermann (eds) *Economics with Heterogeneous Interacting Agents*. Berlin: Springer Verlag.

Cohendet, P., Creplet, F., Diani, M., Dupouët, O., and Schenk, E. (2004) "Matching communities and hierarchies within firms" *Journal of Management and Governance* 8(1): 27–48.

Colombo, M.G., and Grilli, L. (2005) "Founders' human capital and the growth of new technology-based firms: a competence-based view" *Research Policy* 34(6): 795–816.

——(2009) "The managerial professionalization of high-tech entrepreneurial ventures: the determinants of the creation of a middle-management layer" DRUID Summer Conference, Copenhagen, Denmark.

Colombo, M.G., Grilli, L., and Piva, E. (2006) "In search of complementary assets: the determinants of alliance formation of high-tech start-ups" *Research Policy* 35(8): 1166–99.

Colombo, M.G., Grilli, L., Piva, E., and Rossi Lamastra, C. (2010) "The enlargement of the managerial ranks of entrepreneurial ventures", Working Paper Politecnico of Milan.

Cooke, P. (1992) "Regional innovation systems: competitive regulation in the new Europe" *Geoforum* 23: 365–82.

——(1996) "The new wave of regional innovation networks: analysis, characteristics and strategy" *Small Business Economics* 8: 1–13.

——(2002) *Knowledge Economies: Clusters, Learning and Cooperative Advantage.* London and New Routledge: York.

——(2004) *Knowledge Economics.* London: Routledge.

——(2008) "Regional innovation systems: origin of the species" *International Journal of Technological Learning, Innovation and Development* 1(3): 393–409.

Corona, L., Doutriaux, J., and Mian, S.A. (2005) *Building Knowledge Regions in North America: Emerging Technology Innovation Poles.* Cheltenham, UK: Edward Elgar.

Côté, R.P., and Hall, J. (1995) "Industrial parks as ecosystems" *Journal of Cleaner Production* 3(1–2): 41–46.

Crevoisier, O. (2004) "The innovative milieus approach: toward a territorialized understanding of the economy?" *Economic Geography* 80(4): 367–79.

Crevoisier, O., and Camagni, R. (eds) (2000) *Les milieux urbains: innovation, systèmes de production, et ancrage.* Neuchâtel, Switzerland: EDES.

CRORA (2007) "Relazioni industriali come relazioni interorganizzative: strutture e meccanismi della concertazione locale" *Rapporto di Ricerca CRORA Bocconii.*

Cyert, R.M., and March, J.J. (1963) *A Behavioral Theory of the Firm.* London: Prentice-Hall.

Davenport, T.H., and Prusak, L. (1998) *Working Knowledge: How Organizations Manage What They Know.* Cambridge, MA: Harvard University Press.

David, P. (2005) "Some new standards for the economics of standardization in the information age" in P. Dasgupta and P. Stoneman (eds) *Economic Policy and Technological Performance.* Cambridge: Cambridge University Press.

Davidsson, P., and Honig, B. (2003) "The role of social and human capital among nascent entrepreneurs" *Journal of Business Venturing* 18(3): 301–31.

Dawson, J. (1992) "The relevance of the flexible specialisation paradigm for small-scale industrial restructuring in Ghana" *Institute of Development Studies Bulletin* 23(3): 34–38.

Day, D.L. (1994) "Raising radicals" *Organization Science* 5(2): 148–72.

De Laat, P. (1999) "Protection of intellectual property in software: towards property right or property left?" EGOS Colloquium, Warwick, UK.

De Man A-P. (ed.) (2008) *Knowledge Management and Innovation in Networks.* Cheltenham, UK: Edward Elgar.

Drucker, P.F. (1985) "The discipline of innovation" *Harvard Business Review* 63(3): 67–72.

Dubini, P., and Aldrich, H. (1991) "Personal and extended networks are central to the entrepreneurial process" *Journal of Business Venturing* 6(5): 305–13.

Eccles, R.J. (1981) "The quasi firm in the construction industry" *Journal of Economic Behaviour and Organizations* 2: 335–57.

Elster, J. (1985) *Sour Grapes. Studies in the Subversion of Rationality.* Cambridge: Cambridge University Press.

Enright, M.J. (1998) "Regional clusters and firm strategy" in Alfred Chandler, Orjan Solvell and Peter Hagstrom (eds) *The Dynamic Firm.* Oxford: Oxford University Press.

——(2000) "The globalization of competition and the localization of competition: policies toward regional clustering" in N. Hood and S. Young (eds) *The Globalization of Multinational Enterprise Activity and Economic Development.* London: Macmillan.

Ernst, D. (2008) "Innovation off-shoring and Asia's upgrading through innovation strategies", Honoloulou East-West Center Working Papers, Economic Series, n.95.

Etzkowitz, H. (2008) *The Triple Helix: University-Industry-Government Innovation in Action.* London and New York: Routledge.

Etzkowitz, H., and Klofsten, M. (2005) "The innovating region: toward a theory of knowledge-based regional development" *R&D Management* 35(3): 243–55.

Europa InterCluster (2010) www.intercluster.eu.

Europe INNOVA (2008) *Promoting European Innovation Through Clusters: An Agenda for Policy Action*. The High Level Advisory Group on Clusters.

Feldman, M.P. (1994) *The Geography of Innovation*. Dordrecht: Kluwer Academic.

Feldman, M., Feller, I., Bercovitz, J., and Burton R. (2002) "Equity and the technology transfer strategies of American research universities" *Management Science* 49(1): 105–21.

Felin, T., and Zenger, T. (2009) "Entrepreneurs as theorists: on the origins of collective beliefs and novel strategies" *Strategic Entrepreneurship Journal* 3(2): 127–46.

Ferrary, M., and Granovetter, M. (2009) "The role of venture capital firms in Silicon Valley's complex innovation network" *Economy and Society* 38(2): 326–59.

Fiet, J.O. (2002) *The Systematic Search for Entrepreneurial Discoveries*. Westport, CT: Quorum Books.

Fisher, R. (1983) "Negotiating power" *American Behavioral Scientist* 27(2): 149–66.

Foss, N.J. (2003) "Selective intervention and internal hybrids: interpreting and learning from the rise and decline of the Oticon spaghetti organization" *Organization Science* 14: 331–49.

——(2007) "The Emerging Knowledge Governance Approach: Challenges and Characteristics" *Organization* 14(1): 29–52.

Foss, N.J., and Klein, P.G. (2004) "Entrepreneurship and the economic theory of the firm: any gains from trade?" in R. Argwal, S.A. Alvarez, and O. Sorenson (eds) *Handbook of Entrepreneurship: Disciplinary Perspectives*. Dordrecth: Kluwer.

Foss, N.J., and Michailova, S. (2009) *Knowledge Governance*. Oxford: Oxford University Press.

Foss, K., Foss N., and Vàzquez, X.A. (2006) "Tying the manager's hands: constraining opportunistic managerial intervention" *Cambridge Journal of Economics* 30: 797–818.

Frank, E., and Jungwirth, C. (2003) "Reconciling rent-seekers with donators: the governance structure of open source" *Journal of Management and Governance* 7(4): 401–21.

Freeman, C. (1987) *Technology Policy and Economic Performance: Lessons from Japan*. London and New York: Pinter.

Frey, B.S. (1997) "On the relationship between intrinsic and extrinsic work motivation" *International Journal of Industrial Organisation* 15: 427–39.

Fromhold-Eisebith, M., and Eisebith, G. (2005) "How to institutionalize innovative clusters? Comparing explicit top-down and implicit bottom-up approaches" *Research Policy* 34(8): 1250–68.

Gaillard, E.M. (1996) *Les fruits confits d'Apt: Histoire et Technique*. Avignon: Barthelemy.

Galbraith, J.R. (1974) "Organization design: An information processing view" *Interfaces* 4: 28–36.

——(1982) "Designing the innovating organization" *Organizational Dynamics* 10(3): 5–25.

Galgano, F. (1974) *L'imprenditore*. Bologna: Zanichelli.

Gambardella, A. (1993) "Innovazioni tecnologiche e accumulazione delle conoscenze: quale modello per le piccole e medie imprese negli anni '90'" *Piccola Impresa/Small Business* 2: 73–89.

Gargiulo, M., and Benassi, M. (2000) "Trapped in your own net? Network cohesion, structural holes, and the adaptation of social capital" *Organization Science* 11(2): 183–96.

Garicano, L. (2000) "Hierarchies and the organization of knowledge in production" *Journal of Political Economy* 108: 874–904.

Gartner, W.B. (1989) "Who is an entrepreneur? Is the wrong question" *Entrepreneurship Theory and Practice* summer: 47–68.

Gavetti, G., and Levinthal, D.A. (2005) "Strategy making in novel and complex worlds: the power of analogy" *Strategic Management Journal* 26: 691–712.

Gilsing, V. (2005) *The Dynamics of Innovation and Interfirm Networks.* Cheltenham, UK: Edward Elgar.

Gimeno, J., Folta, T.B., Cooper, A.C., and Woo, C.Y. (1997) "Survival of the fittest? Entrepreneurial human capital and the persistence of underperforming firms" *Administrative Science Quarterly* 42(4): 750–83.

Gimmon, E., and Levie, J. (2010) "Founder's human capital, external investment, and the survival of new high-technology ventures" *Research Policy* 39(9): 1214–26.

Giuliani, E., and Bell, M. (2005) "The micro-determinants of meso-level learning and innovation: evidence from a Chilean wine cluster" *Research Policy* 34(1): 47–68.

Giuliani, E., Pietrobelli, C., and Rabellotti, R. (2005) "Upgrading in global value chains: lessons from Latin American clusters" *World Development* 33(4): 549–73.

Glaeser, E.L., Kerr, W.R., and Ponzetto, G.A.M. (2010) "Clusters of entrepreneurship" *Journal of Urban Economics* 67: 150–68.

Grabher, G. (1993) "The weakness of strong ties: the lock-in of regional development in the Ruhr area" in G. Grabher (ed.) *The Embedded Firm: On the Socioeconomics of Industrial networks.* New York: Routledge.

——(ed.) (1993) *The Embedded Firm.* London and New York: Routledge.

——(2002) "Cool projects, boring institutions: temporary collaboration in social context" *Regional Studies* 36(3): 205–14.

Graf, H. (2006) *Networks in the Innovation Process.* Cheltenham, UK: Edward Elgar.

Grandori, A. (1984) "A prescriptive contingency view of organizational decision making" *Administrative Science Quarterly* 29: 192–209.

——(1991) "Negotiating efficient organization forms" *Journal of Economic Behavior and Organization* 16: 319–40.

——(1997) "An organizational assessment of interfirm coordination modes" *Organization Studies* 18(6): 897–925.

——(ed.) (1999) *Interfirm Networks: Organization and Industrial Competitiveness.* London: Routledge.

——(2001a) *Organizzazione e governance del capitale umano nella nuova economia.* Milan: EGEA.

——(2001b) *Organization and Economic Behaviour.* London and New York: Routledge.

——(2001c) "Neither hierarchy nor identity: knowledge governance mechanisms and the theory of the firm" *Journal of Management and Governance* 5: 381–99.

——(ed.) (2004) *Corporate Governance and Firm Organization.* Oxford: Oxford University Press.

——(2009) "Poliarchic governance and the growth of knowledge" in N.J. Foss and S. Michailova (eds) *Knowledge Governance.* Oxford: Oxford University Press.

——(2010a) "A rational heuristic model of economic decision making" *Rationality and Society* 22(4): 1–28.

——(2010b) "Asset commitment, constitutional governance and the nature of the firm" *Journal of Institutional Economics* 6(3): 351–75.

Grandori, A., and Cacciatori, E. (2010) "Networked resource access and networked growth: a double network hypothesis on the innovative entrepreneurial firm" in M. Tuunanen,

G. Cliquet, G. Hendrikse, and J. Windsperger (eds) *New Developments in the Theory of Networks: Franchising, Cooperatives and Alliances*. Berlin: Springer Verlag.

Grandori, A., and Furlotti, M. (2006) "The bearable lightness of alliances: associational and procedural contracts" in A. Arino and J. Reuer   (eds) *Strategic Alliances: Governance and Contracts*. London: Palgrave.

Grandori, A., and Furnari, S. (2008) "A chemistry of organization: combinatory analysis and design" *Organization Studies* 29(03): 459–85.

Grandori, A., and Soda, G. (1995) "Inter-firm networks: antecedents, mechanisms and forms" *Organization Studies* 16(2): 183–214.

——(2004) "Governing with multiple principals: an empirically-based analysis of capital providers, preferences and superior governance structures" in A. Grandori (ed.) *Corporate Governance and Firm Organization*. Oxford: Oxford University Press.

Granovetter, M. (1983) "The strength of weak ties" *American Journal of Sociology* 87(1): 1360–80.

——(1985) "Economic action and social structure: the problem of embeddedness" *American Journal of Sociology* XIC: 481–510.

Grant, R.M. (1996) "Toward a knowledge-based theory of the firm" *Strategic Management Journal* 17 (Winter Special Issue): 109–22.

Greenwood, R., Hinings, C.R., and Brown, J. (1990) "'P2-form' strategic management: corporate practices in professional partnerships" *Academy of Management Journal* 33(4): 725–55.

Groen, A.J. (2005) "Knowledge-intensive entrepreneurship in networks, a multilevel/ multidimentional approach" *Journal of Entreprising Culture* 13(1): 69–88.

Gustaffsson, V. (2006) *Entrepreneurial Decision Making*. Cheltenham, UK: Edward Elgar.

Hackett, S., and Dilts, D.M. (2004) "A systematic review of business incubation research" *Journal of Technology Transfer* 29(1): 55–82.

Hancock, R., and Carson, E. (2010) *The Silicon Valley Index 2010*. R. Hancock, Joint Venture: Silicon Valley Network and E. Carson, Silicon Valley Community Foundation.

Hansman, H. (1996) *The Ownership of Enterprise*. Cambridge, MA: Harvard University Press.

Hansmann, H., Kraakman, R., and Squire, R. (2006) "Law and the rise of the firm" *Harvard Law Review* 119(5): 1333–403.

Hardy, C., Brown, J., Defillippi, R., and Hassink, R. (1999) "Industry cluster as commercial, knowledge and institutional networks: opto-electronics in six regions in the UK, USA and Germany" in A.Grandori (ed.) *Interfirm Networks*. London: Routledge.

Hargadon, A.B. (1998) "Firms as knowledge brokers: lessons in pursuing continuous innovation" *California Management Review* 40(3): 209–27.

Hargadon, A., and Sutton, R.I. (2000) "Building an innovation factory" *Harvard Business Review* 78(3): 157–66.

Harrysson, S. (2006) *The Know-how Based Entrepreneurship. From Knowledge Creation to Business Implementation*. Cheltenham, UK: Edward Elgar.

Hart, O., and Moore, J. (1990) "Property rights and the nature of the firm" *Journal of Political Economy* 8(6):1119–58.

——(1994) "A theory of debt based on the inalienability of human capital" *Quarterly Journal of Economics* 109(4): 841–79.

Hassink, R. (1993) "Regional innovation policies compared" *Urban Studies* 30(6): 1009–24.

——(2005)" How to unlock regional economies from path dependency? From learning region to learning cluster" *European Planning Studies* 13(4): 521–35.

Hassink, R., and Lagendijk, A. (2001) "The dilemmas of interregional institutional learning" *Environment and Planning C: Government and Policy* 19(1): 65–84.

Hayton, J. (2005) "Promoting corporate entrepreneurship through human resource management practices: a review of empirical research" *Human Resource Management Review* 15: 21–41.

Hayton, J.C., and Kelley, D. (2006) "A competency-based framework for promoting corporate entrepreneurship" *Human Resource Management* 45(3): 407–27.

Heifetz, R.A., Grashow, A., and Linsky, M. (2009) "Leadership in a (permanent) crisis" *Harvard Business Review* July/August, 87(7/8): 62–69.

Hendrikse, G. (2007) "Screening, competition and the choice of the cooperative as an organisational form" *Journal of Agricultural Economics* 49(2): 202–17.

Hendrikse, G., Tuunanen, M., and Windsperger, J. (eds) (2007) *Economics and Management of Networks*. Heidelberg: Physica-Verlag, Springer.

Howell, J.M., and Higgins, C.A. (1990). "The champions of technological innovation" *Administrative Science Quarterly* 35: 317–41.

Hsu, D.H. (2007) "Experienced entrepreneurial founders, organizational capital, and venture capital funding" *Research Policy* 36(5): 722–41.

Humphrey, J., and Schmitz, H. (2002) "How does insertion in global value chains affect upgrading in industrial clusters?" *Regional Studies* 36(9): 1017–27.

IASP, Statistics (2007) www.iasp.ws/publico/index.jsp?enl=2.

Isemberg, D.J. (2010) "How to start an entrepreneurial revolution" *Harvard Business Review* June: 40–50.

Jensen, M.C., and Meckling, W.H. (1976) "Theory of the firm: managerial behavior, agency costs and ownership structure" *Journal of Financial Economics* III: 305–60.

Jensen, R., and Thursby, M. (2001) "Proofs and prototypes for sale: The licensing of university inventions" *American Economic Review* 91(1): 240–59.

Johannisson, B., and Mønsted, M. (1997) "Contextualizing entrepreneurial networking" *International Studies of Management and Organization* 27(3): 109–36.

Johannisson, B., Ramirez-Pasillas, M., and Karlsson, G. (2002) "Institutional embeddedness of inter-firm networks: a leverage for business creation" *Entrepreneurship and Regional Development* 14(4): 297–315.

Johnston, R., and Lawrence, P. (1991) "Beyond vertical integration: the rise of the value adding partnership" in F.J. Thompson, J. Frances, R. Levacic and J. Mitchell (eds) *Markets, Hierarchy and Networks*. London: Sage.

Jones, C., Hesterly, W.S., and Borgatti, S.P. (1997) "A general theory of network governance: exchange conditions and social mechanisms" *Academy of Management Review* 22(4): 911–45.

Jones, G., and Wadhwani, R.D. (2007) *Entrepreneurship and Global Capitalism*. Cheltenham, UK: Edward Elgar.

Kahneman, D., Slovic, P., and Tversky, A. (eds) (1982) *Judgment Under Uncertainty: Heuristics and Biases*. Cambridge: Cambridge University Press.

Kanter, R.M. (1985) "Supporting innovation and venture development in established companies" *Journal of Business Venturing* 1: 47–61.

Kaplan, S.N., and Strömberg, P. (2003) "Financial contracting theory meets the real world: an empirical analysis of venture capital contracts" *Review of Economic Studies* 70: 1–35.

——(2004) "Characteristics, contracts and actions: evidence from venture capitalist analyses" *Journal of Finance* 59(5): 2177–210.

Kaplan, S.N., Sensoy, B.A., and Strömberg, P. (2009) "Should investors bet on the jockey or on the horse? Evolution of firms from early business plans to public companies" *Journal of Finance* 64(1): 75–115.

Karpik, L. (1989) "L'économie de la qualité" *Review Française de Sociologie* 30(2): 187–210.

Katznbach, J.R., and Smith, D.K. (1993) *The Wisdom of Teams*. Cambridge, MA: Harvard Business School Press.

Kirzner, I.M. (1973) *Competition and Entrepreneurship*. Chicago, IL: Chicago University Press.

——(1979) *Perception, Opportunity, and Profit: Studies in the Theory of Entrepreneurship*. Chicago, IL: University of Chicago Press.

Kitagawa, F. (2005) "Regionalization of innovation policies: the case of Japan" *European Planning Studies* 13(4): 601–18.

Klein, B., Crawford, R., and Alchian, A. (1978) "Vertical integration, appropriable rents and the competitive contracting process" *Journal of Law and Economics* 21: 297–326.

Knight, F.H. (1921) *Risk, Uncertainty and Profit*. New York: Houghton Mifflin.

Kogut, B. (2000) "The network as knowledge: generative rules and the emergence of structure" *Strategic Management Journal* 21: 405–25.

Kogut, B., and Kulatilaka, N. (2001) "Capabilities as real options" *Organization Science* 12(6): 744–58.

Kogut, B., and Metiu, A. (2001) "Open-source software development and distributed innovation" *Oxford Review of Economic Policy* 17(2): 248–64.

Krugman, P. (1991) *Geography and Trade*. Cambridge, MA: MIT Press.

——(2008) "The increasing returns revolution in trade and geography", Nobel Prize Lecture, December 8.

Lalkaka, R. (2001) "'Best practices' in business incubation: lessons (yet to be) learned", European Union – Belgian Presidency International Conference on Business Centers: Actors for Economic & Social Development Brussels, November 14–15, www.businessgrowthinitiative.org.

Lammers, C. (1993) "Interorganizational democracy" in S. Lindenberg and H. Schreuder (eds) *Interdisciplinary Perspectives on Organization Studies*. Oxford: Pergamon Press.

Langlois, R.N. (2007) "The entrepreneurial theory of the firm and the theory of the entrepreneurial firm" *Journal of Management Studies* 44(7): 1107–24.

Laursen, K., and Mahnke, V. (2001) "Knowledge strategies, firm types and complementarity in human resource practices" *Journal of Management and Governance* 5(1): 1–22.

Lawrence, P., and Lorsch, J. (1967) *Organization and Environment*. Cambridge, MA: Harvard Business School.

Leibenstein, H. (1968) "Entrepreneurship and development" *American Economic Review* 58: 72–83.

——(1978) *General X-efficiency Theory and Economic Development*. Oxford: Oxford University Press.

Leifer, R., McDermott, C., O'Connor, G., Peters, L., Rice, M., and Veryzer, R. (2000) *Radical Innovation: How Mature Companies can Outsmart Upstarts*. Boston, MA: Harvard Business School Press.

Lepak, D.P., Scott, A., and Snell, S.A. (1999) "The human resource architecture: toward a theory of human capital allocation and development" *The Academy of Management Review* 24(1): 31–48.

——(2002) "Examining the human resource architecture: the relationships among human capital, employment, and human resource configurations" *Journal of Management* 28: 517–43.

Lewin, A.Y., and Volberda, H.W. (1999) "Prolegomena on co-evolution: a framework for research on strategy and new organization forms" *Organization Science* 10(5): 519–34.

Lindkvist, L. (2004) "Governing project based firms: promoting market-like processes within hierarchies" *Journal of Management and Governance* 8(1): 3–25.

——(2005) "Knowledge communities and knowledge collectivities: a typology of knowledge work in groups" *Journal of Management Studies* 42(6): 1189–210.

Link, A.N. (2006) *Entrepreneurship and Technology Policy*. Cheltenham, UK: Edward Elgar.

Lipparini, A., and Lomi, A. (1999) "Interorganizational relations in the Modena biomedical industry" in A. Grandori (ed.) *Interfirm Networks*. London: Routledge.

Loebis, L.,and Schmitz, H. (2005) "Java furniture makers: globalisation winners or losers?" *Development in Practice* 15(3–4): 514–21.

Longhi, C. (1999) "Networks, collective learning and technology development in innovative high technology regions: the case of Sophia-Antipolis" *Regional Studies* 33(4): 333–42.

Lorenz, E.H. (1992) "Trust, community and cooperation. Towards a theory of industrial districts" in M. Storper and A.J. Scott (eds) *Pathways to Industrialization and Regional Development*. London: Routledge.

Lorenzoni, G. (1990) *L'architettura di sviluppo delle imprese minori. Costellazioni e piccoli gruppi*. Bologna: Il Mulino.

Lorenzoni, G., and Baden-Fuller, C. (1995) "Creating a strategic center to manage a web of alliances" *California Management Review* 37 (spring): 146–63.

Lorenzoni, G., and Ornati, O. (1988) "Constellations of firms and new ventures" *Journal of Business Venturing* 3(1): 41–57.

Lozano, S., and Arenas, A. (2007) "A model to test how diversity affects resilience in regional innovation networks" *Journal of Artificial Societies and Social Simulation* 10(4): 8.

Lundvall, B.-Å. (1992) *National Systems of Innovation: Towards a Theory of Innovation and Interactive Learning*. London: Pinter.

Lundvall, B.-Å., and Johnson, B. (1994) "The learning economy" *Journal of Industry Studies* 1(2): 23–42.

Magnani, L., Nersessian, N.J., and Thagard, P. (eds) (1999) *Model-based Reasoning in Scientific Discovery*. Dordrecht: Kluwer Academic.

Maidique, M.A. (1980) "Entrepreneurs, champions, and technological innovation" *Sloan Management Review* 21(2): 59–76.

Maillat, D. (1991) "The innovation process and the role of Milieu" in E. Bergman, G. Maier and F. Todtling (eds) *Regions Reconsidered: Economic Networks, Innovation and Local Development in Industrialised Countries*. London: Mansell.

——(1998) "Innovative milieus and new generations of regional policies" *Entrepreneurship & Regional Development* 10: 1–16.

Malhotra, D., and Murnighan, J.K. (2002) "The effects of contracts on interpersonal trust" *Administrative Science Quarterly* 47: 534–59.

Malmberg, A., and Maskell, P. (2002) "The elusive concept of localization economies: towards a knowledge-based theory of spatial clustering" *Environment and Planning A* 34(3): 429–49.

March, J.G. (1991) "Exploration and exploitation in organizational learning" *Organization Science* 2(1): 71–87.

March, J.G., and Simon, H.A. (1958) *Organizations*. New York: Wiley.

Markusen, A. (1996) "Sticky spaces in slippery space: a typology of industrial districts" *Economic Geography* 72(3): 293–313.

——(2008) "Human versus physical capital: government's role in regional development" in J. Martinez-Vazquez and J. Vaillancourt (eds) *Public Policy for Regional Development.* Oxford: Routledge.

Marshall, A. (1890) *Principles of Economics.* London: Macmillan.

Martin, R., and Sunley, P. (2003) "Deconstructing clusters: chaotic concept or policy panacea?" *Journal of Economic Geography* 3(1): 5–35.

Maskell, P., and Malmberg, A. (1999) "Localised learning and industrial competitiveness" *Cambridge Journal of Economics* 23(2): 167–85.

McGrath, R.G. (1999) "Falling forward: real option reasoning and entrepreneurial failure" *Academy of Management Review* 24(1): 13–30.

McGrath, R.G., and MacMillan, I.C. (2000) *The Entrepreneurial Mindset: Strategies for Continuously Creating Opportunity in an Age of Uncertainty.* Boston, MA: Harvard Business School Press.

Mènard, C. (2004) "The economics of hybrid organizations" *Journal of Institutional and Theoretical Economics* 160(3): 345–76.

Metcalfe, R.M., and Boggs, D.R. (1975) *Ethernet: Distributed Packet-Switching For Local Computer Networks*, CSL·75·7 May, Xerox, Palo Alto Research Center.

Meyerson, D., Weick, K.E., and Kramer R.M. (1996) "Swift trust and temporary groups" in R.M. Kramer and T.R. Tyler (eds) *Trust in Organizations: Frontiers of Theory and Research.* Thousand Oaks, CA: Sage.

Miles, R.E. *et al.* (1997) "Organizing in the knowledge age: anticipating the cellular form" *Academy of Management Executive* 11(4): 7–21.

Milgrom, P., and Roberts, J. (1992) *Economics Organization and Management.* Englewood Cliffs, NJ: Prentice-Hall.

Miller, D., and Friesen, P.H. (1983) "Strategy-making and environment: the third link" *Strategic Management Journal* 4: 221–35.

Morris, M.H. (1998) *Entrepreneurial Intensity.* Westport, CT: Quorum Books.

Morris, M.H., Kuratko, D.F., and Covin, J.G. (2008) *Corporate Entrepreneurship and Innovation.* London: Thomson Learning.

Murphy, L.M., Brokaw, J., Pulaski, J., and McCormack, K. (2000) *The National Alliance of Clean Energy Business Incubators: An NREL Initiative, Status and Progress to Date.* NREL/BK-720-28724. Golden, CO: National Renewable Energy Laboratory, Enterprise Development Programs.

Nadvi, K. (1999) "Shifting ties: social networks in the surgical instrument cluster of Sialkot, Pakistan" *Development and Change* 30(1): 141–75.

Nadvi, K., and Barrientos, S. (2004) *Industrial Clusters and Poverty Reduction.* Vienna: United Nations Industrial Development Organization (UNIDO).

Nahapiet, J., and Ghoshal, S. (1998) "Social capital, intellectual capital, and the organizational advantage" *Academy of Management Review* 23(2): 242–66.

Nelson, R.R. (1993) *National Innovation Systems: A Comparative Analysis.* New York: Oxford University Press.

Nisbett, R., and Ross, L., (1980) *Human Inferences: Strategies and Shortcomings of Social Judgment*, Englewood Cliffs, NJ: Prentice-Hall.

Nooteboom, B. (1999) *Inter-firm Alliances: Analysis and Design.* London: Routledge.

O'Reilly, C.A., and Tushman, M. (2004) "The ambidextrous organization" *Harvard Business Review* 82: 74–82.

ODCE (1997) *Technology Incubators: Nurturing Small Firms*, OCDE/GD(97)202 60358. Paris: Organisation For Economic Co-Operation and Development.

Oerlemans, L., Meeus, M., and Boekema, F. (2001) "Firm clustering and innovation: determinants and effects" *Papers in Regional Science* 80: 337–56.

Ouchi, W.G., and Bolton, M.K. (1988) "The logic of joint research and development" *California Management Review* 30(3): 9–33.

Oviatt, B.M., and McDougall, P.P. (1994) "Toward a theory of international new ventures" *Journal of International Business Studies* 25(1):45–64.

——(1995) "Global start-ups: entrepreneurs on a worldwide stage" *Academy of Management Executive* 9(2): 30–43.

——(2005) "Defining international entrepreneurship and modeling the speed of internationalization" *Entrepreneurship: Theory and Practice* 29(5): 537–54.

——(eds) (2007) *International Entrepreneurship*. Cheltenham, UK: Edward Elgar.

Padgett, J.F., and Ansell, C.K. (1993) "Robust action and the rise of the Medici, 1400–1434" *American Journal of Sociology* 98(6): 1259–319.

Padgett, J.F., and McLean, P. (2006) "Organizational invention and elite transformation: the birth of partnership systems in Renaissance Florence" *American Journal of Sociology* 111: 1463–68.

Peddle, M.T. (1993) "Planned industrial and commercial developments in the United States: a review of the history, literature, and empirical evidence regarding industrial parks and research parks" *Economic Development Quarterly* 7(1): 107–24.

Pencavel, J. (2001) *Worker Participation*. New York: Russel Sage Foundation.

Penrose, E. (1959) *The Theory of the Growth of the Firm*. New York: Wiley.

Perrier-Cornet, P., and Sylvander, B. (2000) "Firmes, coordinations et territorialité: Une lecture économique de la diversité des filières d'appellation d'origine" *Économie rurale* 258: 79–89.

Pettigrew, A.M., Whittington, R., Melin, L., Sanchez-Runde, C., Van den Bosch, F.A.J., Ruigrok, W., and Numagami, T. (eds) (2003) *Innovative Forms of Organizing*. London: Sage.

Petty, R., and Guthrie, J. (2000) "Intellectual capital literature review" *Journal of Intellectual Capital* 1(2):155–76.

Pietrobelli, C., and Rabellotti, R. (2004) *Upgrading in Clusters and Value Chains in Latin America: The Role of Policies*, Sustainable Department Best Practices Series. New York: Inter-American Development Bank, 97.

Piore, M., and Sabel, C. (1984) *The Second Industrial Divide: Possibilities for Prosperity*. New York: Basic Books.

Podolny, J. M., Stuart T. E., and Hannan, M.T. (1996) "Networks, knowledge, and niches: competition in the worldwide semiconductor industry, 1984–91" *American Journal of Sociology* 102(3): 659–89.

Pongracic, I., Jr. (2009) *Employees and Entrepreneurship*. Cheltenham, UK: Edward Elgar.

Popper, K.R. (1989) "The critical approach versus the mystique of leadership' *Human Systems Management* 8: 259–65.

Porter, M.E. (1990) *The Competitive Advantage of Nations*. New York: Free Press.

——(1998) "Clusters and the new economics of competition" *Harvard Business Review* 76(6): 77–90.

——(2003) "The economic performance of regions" *Regional Studies* 37(6,7): 549–78.

Porter, M., and Stern, S. (2002) "National innovative capacity" in *World Economic Forum, The Global Competitiveness Report* 2001–2. New York: Oxford University Press.

Powell, W.W. (1990) "Neither market nor hierarchy: network forms of organization" *Research in Organizational Behavior* 12: 295–336.

Powell, W. (2001) "Practicing polygamy with good taste: the evolution of inter-organizational collaboration in the life sciences" *Shorenstein APARC, SPRIE Seminar Series*, February 2.

Powell, W.W., Koput, K., and Smith-Doerr, L. (1996) "Inter-organization collaboration and the locus of innovation: networks of learning in biotechnology" *Administrative Science Quarterly* 41: 116–45.

Powell, W. *et al.* (2005) "The institutional embeddedness of high-tech regions" in K. Porter, K. Bunker, and W.W. Powell (eds) *Clusters, Networks, and Innovation*. Oxford: Oxford University Press.

Raiffa, H. (1982) *The Art and Science of Negotiation*. Cambridge: Cambridge University Press.

Rajan, R.G., and Zingales, L. (2000) "The governance of the new enterprise" in X. Vives (ed.) *Corporate Governance*. Cambridge: Cambridge University Press.

Ravasi, D., and Verona, G. (2000) "Organizing the process of knowledge integration: the benefits of structural ambiguity" *Scandinavian Journal of Management* 17: 41–66.

Ravi, A., and Singh, J.V. (2005) "Getting offshoring right" *Harvard Business Review* February: 135–42.

Regalia, I. (ed.) (2006) *Regulating New Forms of Employment*. London and New York: Routledge.

Reid, N., Michael, C.C., and Smith, B.W. (2007) "Critical steps in the cluster building process" *Economic Development Journal* 6(4): 43–52.

Richardson, G.B. (1972) "The organization of industry" *Economic Journal* September: 883–96.

Robert, E.B. (1991) "High stakes for high tech entrepreneurs: understanding venture capital decision making" *Sloan Management Review* 32(2): 9–21.

Roberts, B.H. (2004) "The application of industrial ecology principles and planning guidelines for the development of eco-industrial parks: an Australian case study" *Journal of Cleaner Production* 12(8–10): 997–1010.

Roberts, J. (2004) *The Modern Firm. Organizational Design for Performance and Growth*. Oxford: Oxford University Press.

Robertson, P., and Langlois, R. (1995) "Innovation, networks and vertical integration" *Research Policy* 24(4): 543–62.

Roda, J.M., Cadène, P., Guizol, P., Santoso, L., and Uzair Fauzan, A. (2007) *Atlas of Wooden Furniture Industry in Jepara, Indonesia*. Montpellier, France: French Agricultural Research Centre for International Development (CIRAD); and Bogor, Indonesia: Center for International Forestry Research (CIFOR).

Rohlfs, J. (2001) *Bandwagon Effects in High-Technology Industries*. Cambridge, MA: MIT Press.

Rosenfeld, S. (2002) *Just Clusters: Economic Development Strategies that Reach More People and Places*. Carrboro, NC: Regional Technology Strategies, Inc.

Santangelo, G.D. (2004) *Transnational Corporations, FDI and Local Capabilities in Peripheral Regions: The Etna Valley Case*, UNCTAD/ITE/IIT/2004/3, The United Nations 13(1).

Sapienza, H.J., and Gupta, A.K. (1986) "Impact of agency risk and task uncertainty on venture capitalist/CEO interaction" *Academy of Management Journal* 37(6): 1618–32.

Saravasthy, S. (2001) "Causation and effectuation: towards a theoretical shift from economic inevitability to entrepreneurial contingency" *Academy of Management Review* 26(2): 243–63.

Sarasvasthy, S., Dew, N., Velamuri, S.R., and Venkatraman, S. (2003) "Three views of entrepreneurial opportunity" in *Handbook of Entrepreneurship Research* Dordrecht: Kluwer Academic.

Sathe, V. (2003) *Corporate Entrepreneurship: Top Managers and New Business Creation.* Cambridge: Cambridge University Press.

Saxenian, A. (1990) "Regional networks and the resurgence of Silicon Valley" *California Management Review* 33(1): 89–111.

——(1994) *Regional Advantage: Culture and Competition in Silicon Valley and Route 128.* Cambridge, MA: Harvard University Press.

——(1999) *Silicon Valley's New Immigrant Entrepreneurs.* San Francisco: Public Policy Institute of California.

Schmitz, H., and Nadvi, K. (1999) "Clustering and industrialisation: introduction" *World Development* 27(9): 1503–14.

Schoonhoven, C.B., and Romanelli, E. (2001) "Emergent themes and the next wave of entrepreneurship research" in C.B. Schoonhoven and E. Romanelli (eds) *The Entrepreneurship Dynamic.* Stanford, CA: Stanford University Press.

Schumpeter, J. (1934) *The Theory of Economic Development.* Cambridge, MA: Harvard University Press.

Scott, A.J., and Kwok, E. (1989) "Inter-firm subcontracting and locational agglomeration: a case study of the printed circuits industry in southern California" *Regional Studies* 23(5): 405–16.

Semler, R. (2003) *The Seven-day Weekend.* New York: Penguin.

Shackle, G.L. (1979) *Imagination and the Nature of Choice.* Edinburgh: Edinburgh University Press.

Shane, S. (1995) "Uncertainty avoidance and the preference for innovation championing roles" *Journal of International Business Studies* 26(1): 47–67.

——(2003) *A General Theory of Entrepreneurship.* Cheltenham, UK: Edward Elgar.

Shane, S., and Stuart, T. (2002) "Organizational endowments and the performance of university start-ups" *Management Science* 48(1): 154–70.

Shepherd, J. (1991) "Entrepreneurial growth through constellations" *Journal of Business Venturing* 6(5): 363–73.

Siegel, D.S. (2006) *Technological Entrepreneurship.* Cheltenham, UK: Edward Elgar.

Simon, H.A. (1955) "A behavioral model of rational choice" *Quarterly Journal of Economics* 69: 99–118.

——(1969) "The architecture of complexity" in H.A. Simon (ed.) *The Sciences of the Artificial.* Cambridge, MA: MIT Press.

——(1977) *Models of Discovery and Other Topics in the Method of Science.* Dordrecht and Boston: Reidel.

——(1987) "Making management decisions: the role of intuition and emotion" *The Academy of Management Executive* 1(1): 57–64.

Singh, J., and Robert, P. (2000) *Entrepreneurial Opportunity Recognition Through Social Networks.* London: Routledge.

Slavensky Dahl, M. (2003) "Knowledge diffusion and regional clusters. Lessons from the Danish ICT Industry", PhD thesis, Aalborg University.

Sölvell, O. (2009) "Clusters – balancing evolutionary and constructive forces". www.cluster-research.org/redbook.htm.

Sölvell, O., Lindqvist, G., and Ketels, C. (2003) *The Cluster Initiative Greenbook.* www.europe-innova.eu/c/document{_}library/.

Starovic, M. (2007) "Financial angel networks" Bachelor thesis in International Economics and Management, Bocconi University.

Staw, B.M. (1976) *Intrinsic and Extrinsic Motivation*. Morristown, NJ: General Learning Press.

——(1980) "Rationality and justification in organizational life", in B.M. Staw and L.L. Cummings (eds) *Research in Organizational Behavior*, vol. 2. Greenwich, CN: JAI Press.

Steier, L., and Greenwood, R. (2000) "Entrepreneurship and the evolution of angel financial networks" *Organization Studies* 21(1): 163–92.

Stinchcombe, A.L. (1965) "Social structure and organizations" in J.G. March (ed.) *Handbook of Organizations*. Chicago, IL: Rand McNally.

Stuart, T., and Sorenson, O. (2007) "Strategic networks and entrepreneurial ventures" *Strategic Entrepreneurship Journal* 1(3–4): 211–27.

Teece, D.J. (1982) "Toward an economic theory of the multiproduct firm" *Journal of Economic Behavior and Organization* 3: 39–63.

——(1986) "Profitting from technological innovation: implication for integration, collaboration, licensing and public policy" *Research Policy* 15(6): 286–305.

——(1989) "Inter-organizational requirements of the innovation process" *Managerial and Decision Economics* 10: 35–42.

Thompson, F.J., Frances, J., Levacic, R., and Mitchell, J. (eds) (1991) *Markets, Hierarchy and Networks: The Coordination of Social Life*. London: Sage.

Thompson, J.D. (1967) *Organization in Action*. New York: McGraw-Hill.

Thompson, L.L. (2008) *The Mind and Heart of the Negotiator*, 4th edition. Upper Saddle River, NJ: Prentice-Hall.

Turati, C. (1998) "Minnesota mining and manufacturing", case study, SDA Bocconi.

Tversky, A., and Kahneman, D. (1974) "Judgment under uncertainty: heuristics and biases" *Science* 185: 1124–31.

Ulrich, D., and Lake, D. (1991) "Organizational capability: creating competitive advantage" *The Academy of Management Executive* 5(1): 77–92.

UNIDO (2000) "Cluster development and promotion of business development services (BDS): UNIDO's experience in India" *PSD Technical Working Papers 6*. Vienna: UNIDO.

——(2001) *Development of Clusters and Networks of SMEs: The UNIDO Programme*. Vienna: UNIDO.

Uzzi, B. (1996) "The sources and consequences of embeddedness for the economic performance of organizations: the network effect" *American Sociological Review* 61(4): 674–98.

Vaghely, I., and Julien, P.A. (2010) "Are opportunities recognized or constructed? An information perspective on entrepreneurial identification" *Journal of Business Venturing* 25(1): 73–86.

Van de Ven, A.H., and Engleman, R. (2004), "Event- and outcome-driven explanations of entrepreneurship" *Journal of Business Venturing* 19: 343–58.

Varian, H.R. (1990) "Monitoring agents with other agents" *Journal of Institutional and Theoretical Economics* 146(I): 153–74.

Verganti, R. (2006) "Innovating by design" *Harvard Business Review* December: 1–8.

Vermeulen, P.A.M., and Curşeu, P.L. (2010) *Entrepreneurial Strategic Decision-making: A Cognitive Perspective*. Cheltenham, UK: Edward Elgar.

Villani, M., Bonacini, S., Ferrari, D., Serra, R., and Lane, D. (2008) "An agent-based model of exaptive processes" *European Management Review* 4(3): 141–52.

Wason, P.C. (1960) "Reason about a rule" *Quarterly Journal of Experimental Psychology* 20: 273–83.

Wasserman, N. (2008) "The founder's dilemma" *Harvard Business Review* February: 1–8.

Whittington, R., Pettigrew, A., Peck, S., Fenton, E., and Conyon, M. (1999) "Change and complementarities in the new competitive landscape: a European panel study, 1992–96" *Organization Science* 10(5): 583–600.

Wilkins, A.L., and Ouchi, W.G. (1983) "Efficient cultures: exploring the relationship between culture and organizational performance" *Administrative Science Quarterly* 28(3): 468–81.

Williamson, O.E. (1975) *Markets and Hierarchies: Analysis and Antitrust Implications.* New York: Free Press.

——(1980) "The organization of work. A comparative institutional assessment" *Journal of Economics Behavior and Organization* 1: 5–38.

——(1981) "The economics of organization: the transaction cost approach" *American Journal of Sociology* 87: 548–77.

Zahra, S. (2003) "A theory of international new ventures" *Journal of International Business Study* 36(1): 20–28.

Zahra, S., Korri, J.S., and Yu, J.F. (2005) "Cognition and international entrepreneurship implication for research on international opportunity recognition and exploitation" *International Business Review* 14(2): 129–46.

Zenger, T.R., and Hesterley, W.S. (1997) "The disaggregation of corporations: selective intervention, high powered incentives and molecular units" *Organization Science* 8(3): 209–22.

Index

Note: Pages numbers in *italics* are for tables.

Abbott, T. 68
Acer 200
acquisitions and mergers 125, 142
Adams, N. 184
adaptation 36–7, 38
adhesive technology 25
administrative structure 210
Advanced Research Projects Agency
    (ARPA), US 248–9
aesthetic exaptation events 37–8
agency costs 14
agency theory 2
agglomeration 236, 243, 244, 250;
    regional 231–3
agri-business 153–4
AIV 172–6
Akron, Ohio 238
Albunia, A. 71, 72
Alcatel-Lucent 99, 272
Alexander, R.C. 209
ALFA microelectronics 36
alliances 75–7, 125–6
Amadeus 268, 272
ambidexterity practices 207
American Mobile Satellite Corporation
    (AMSC) 93, 95, 96
analogical reasoning 34
Andadari, R.K. 242
Andersson, T. 250
Anterior Technology 92
antidilution clauses 89
AOL 97
Apple 246
Apt 236–7
ARCSIS 274
Ardent Communication Ventures 201

asset-based forms of enterprise 103, 104,
    105–8, 126
associated workers 107, 214
Association de l'Esperance des Taxis
    Motor Rwanda (Assetamorwa) 170–1
associations 59–60; of entrepreneurial firms
    163–9, 177, 214; professional 60, 274–5
asymmetric information 57, 58, 90
AT&T 98, 268
Austin Technology Incubator 258
autonomy 193–7; individual-level 194–5;
    versus control dilemma 211, 213; of
    working groups 193–4
availability heuristic 43
AX 110–14, 119, 124, 136–7, 141
Aydalot, P. 231

Bagdadli, S. 163, 177
Balsillie, J. 93, 94, 98, 99, 100
Bangalore 278–9
banks 78; investment 81; *see also*
    Grameen Bank
Baron, R.A. 27
Batavia Industrial Center 256
Becattini, G. 232, 238
Becker, G.S. 54
Bellamy, A. 158
BellSouth Wireless Data 93, 94, 95, 96
Benioff, M. 247
Bernard, J. 178, 179, 180, 184
Bernasconi, M. 276
Berry, A. 242
Berry, K. 66
Best Western 164–9
'betting on the jockey or the horse'
    dilemma 57, 58, 91